SOCIAL WORK *and Social Problems* ▶

SOCIAL WORK
▶ ▶ *and* ▶ ▶
Social Problems

NATHAN E. COHEN, *Editor*

NATIONAL ASSOCIATION OF SOCIAL WORKERS, INC.
2 Park Avenue, New York, N.Y. 10016

3

Foreword ▶

The activities which resulted in the publication of this volume were instituted by a group of NASW members who were searching for a way in which there could be some productive thinking about the "multi-problem" family, a subject that had been receiving a great deal of social work attention in the late 1950's and early 1960's. These members envisioned a conference which would examine whether the approaches then in use added up to a new approach to social problems. These approaches might briefly be described as (1) reaching out to unaffiliated antisocial groups; (2) work with families who did not want help but whose behavior defined them as symptomatic of social problems, and (3) civic action by indigenous populations of ill-favored neighborhoods.

With support made available by the Ford Foundation, Dr. Nathan E. Cohen became project director. As a first step, a group of persons expert in the three approaches were brought together and given an opportunity to consider whether the subject was worth examining. Out of a two-day meeting came something quite different than had been expected. It was, in fact, the model for viewing social problems from a social work viewpoint which Dr. Cohen presents in his introduction to this volume. As Dr. Cohen explains, the model was then tested in respect to specific problems and this resulted in the current volume.

Because it was neither possible nor desirable to rush into print following the production of the papers included herein, some of the data presented is already outdated and some recent developments are not included. However, this does not detract from our purpose, which is to examine the problems induced and the potentials discovered by a social work approach to social problems.

As Dr. Cohen would be the first to agree, this is by no means the last word. The Ford Foundation has provided an additional grant so that exploration can continue. In the course of that exploration we may solve some of the problems we have defined. Even more important, however, we will involve thousands of social workers and persons concerned about social work in a process of considering the ramifications of a social problems approach. Out of such considerations will come changes in social structure, social work practice, and social work education that can only be beneficial.

BERTRAM M. BECK, ACSW

Associate Executive Director
National Association of Social Workers
New York, N.Y.
April 17, 1964

Contents ▶

Introduction ▶

The purpose of this special project of the National Association of Social Workers on social problems, financed by the Ford Foundation, was to define more clearly the contribution of social work to the solution of social problems. Interest in the project emerged from the growing recognition that social work should raise its sights from amelioration of problems to their prevention. Among other aims, the project involved taking stock of the position social work occupies as a profession and as a field in the important areas of knowledge, attitude, and skill and exploring the possible patterns of intervention in social problems.

The first step in the project was to convene a task force of leaders in the field for a two-day conference at the School of Applied Social Sciences, Western Reserve University, on February 24 and 25, 1961. The meeting was concerned primarily with development of a model for use in analyzing social problems. Various social problems to which the model might be applied were identified.

The model emphasized the following major considerations:

1. Definition and etiology of the problem.
2. The societal norms and values and the assumed social work norms and values affecting the problem.
3. The current programs (actual), both social work and non-social work, dealing with the problem and the consequence of continuing these programs.
4. The ideal or the social change objective.
5. The relationship between the actual and the ideal: identification of the gap between them, sources of resistance to and support of closing this gap, action priorities for social work, and theory and research needs for attaining necessary knowledge and programs.

In the development of the model the following were avoided:

1. The usual tendency to utilize treatment and program instruments as a diagnostic tool for social problems. Since treatment tools are

primarily geared to the individual and to his psychological self, use of this instrument could lead to a fragmentation of the social problem.

2. Fragmentation on the level of social institutions as well as on the individual level.

3. Utilization of the classification "official disorder," since it tends to limit full analysis of the social problem because of its basis in the institutionalized services provided to deal with it.

In brief, the model is value-oriented and emphasizes the gaps between the ideal objectives and the actual operations. As such, it provides for full analysis of the social problem and also points toward an emphasis on social change theory.

A second task-force conference was held on September 22 and 23, 1961. Its purpose was to assemble the individuals who would undertake the task of developing papers on suggested social problems, using the model as the general framework. Contributors were selected on the basis of their competence in specific social problem areas.

This conference was utilized to explain the model further and to provide an opportunity for each contributor to present ideas and to raise questions. Questions tended to center around the lack of consensus about values within the profession, differences between intervention, problem management and control, and sources for deriving theory for social change which could be made operational for use in social work.

Ten social problems were selected for testing the model. However, seven of the ten papers submitted followed the model more consistently than the others and consequently proved to be more useful for the purpose of this project. It was on this basis that the following social problems were selected for consideration in this volume (authors are listed next to their respective subjects):

Poverty (by Norman Lourie), marital incompatibility (by Werner A. Lutz), child neglect (by Elizabeth G. Meier), deterioration of the inner city (by Lawrence K. Northwood), unmarried mothers (by Helen Harris Perlman), the broken family (by Otto Pollak), and racial discrimination (by Whitney M. Young, Jr.).

It was evident from the discussion that many common problems would emerge for each author. These include the following:

1. *Definition of the problem.* Is it societal or individual? Is it dependent on the group that formulates it?

2. *Magnitude and complexity of the problem.* Are some of the social problems selected too global for analysis through this type of model? Can such problems be broken down into programmatic areas for analysis?

3. *Social condition versus social problem.* Is there a difference between a social condition and a social problem? Is one of the differentiat-

ing factors that a social problem has a recognizable behavioral sequence and a recognizable process? For example, is the "inner city" a social condition or a social problem? Is the social problem perhaps the alienation of the people in the inner city from the services and resources of the community?

4. *The scope of social work.* Are these larger, more complex problems, such as "deterioration of the inner city," "displacement of individuals from their cultural milieus," and "poverty," within the purview of social work in its present stage of development?

5. *Uniqueness of contribution as a criterion.* Many of the social problems may also be the provinces of other professions. Does social work give priority only to those problems with which it has a unique competence?

6. *Resources for solution as a determinant of selection of social problems.* If the solution of a social problem is not within the power of social work, does it relinquish responsibility for solving the problem? For example, has social work the responsibility for social problems that involve changing societal norms?

Out of the meetings emerged the realization that a primary purpose was to test the model in an attempt to find a way of looking at social problems and a structure for analyzing them. It was not expected that the assignments would lead to direct solutions of these social problems but that making the problems more explicit would in itself represent a contribution. Furthermore, in exploring the gap between the "ideal" and the "actual," helpful suggestions might develop in regard to the appropriateness of existing methods and structures in social work and of the sponsorship of such services, adequacy and inadequacy of planning goals, and leads for social work education. Also important would be helping social work to examine, in the light of available theory, its own attitudes as well as those of society toward social problems.

Following the second conference, Herman Stein of the Columbia University School of Social Work and Irving Sarnoff of New York University, who had developed the model, were asked to refine it for use by the various authors. This is the model as it was revised:

I. *The Problem*

  A. Definition of the problem
    1. Definition of the terms
    2. Who "suffers" from the problem—and with what consequences?
    3. Who defines it as a problem? Why?
    4. Who does not define it as a problem? Why?

  B. Etiology of the problem (in terms as defined in A-1)—sources
    1. Inherent in social structure

2. Inherent in individual personality
3. In existing organizations designed to cope with the problem
4. In transitory social phenomena
5. Other

II. *Values*

A. Societal norms and values
   1. Supporting existence of the problem
   2. Opposing existence of problem
   3. Neutral to the problem

B. Assumed social work norms and values—in the profession and in its organizational framework
   1. Supporting existence of the problem
   2. Opposing existence of the problem
   3. Neutral to the problem

III. *Current Operations—"The Actual"*

A. Social work operations related to the problem
   1. Implicit definitions of the problem
   2. Implicit value perspectives
   3. Congruence with societal norms
   4. Congruence with posited social work values

B. Non-social work operations related to the problem
   1. Implicit definitions of the problem
   2. Implicit value perspectives
   3. Congruence with societal norms
   4. Congruence with social work norms

C. Consequences of continuation of present program
   1. For the extension or diminution of the social problem
   2. For social work programs related to it
   3. For non-social work programs related to it

IV. *Objectives—"The Ideal"*

A. The value position for social work advanced—the social change objective

B. Implications
   1. Relationship to existing societal norms
   2. Implications for change of societal norms
   3. Relationship to existing norms of the social work profession and organizational framework
   4. Implications for change of social work norms

C. Total view of program approaches consonant with analysis of etiology and value position advanced

D. The sector appropriate to social work
   1. Existing definition of scope and function
   2. Revised definition of scope and function

E. The sector appropriate to non-social work operations
   1. Identify non-social work groups in relation to program objectives
   2. Relationship of social work to each of these

V. *Relationship between the Actual and the Ideal*
   A. Specification of the gap between the actual and the ideal
   B. Sources of resistance to closing the gap
      1. In social work
      2. Outside social work
   C. Sources of support for closing the gap
      1. In social work
      2. Outside social work
   D. Action priorities for social work
      1. In direct operations
      2. Intra-social work change in norms and organizational framework
      3. In relation to non-social work groups and forces
   E. The needs in theory and research
      1. For specifying etiology
      2. For testing program

The papers written contain excellent content that will be helpful to the field. The major focus, in evaluating the effectiveness of the model, however, may be around a series of questions:

1. Does the model provide not only a fuller diagnosis of the social problem but, even more important, a more meaningful one?

2. Does it provide leads for further study of basic issues facing social work?

   a. Integration and use of new knowledge from various theoretical systems.
   b. The scope of social work.
   c. The relationship of concern and responsibility for the individual and public policy.
   d. Priorities in community planning.

3. Does it provide clues for new patterns of intervention?
4. Does it provide clues for new directions in social work education?

In the last chapter (page 362) I have presented my conclusions drawn from the study of the papers submitted. I have reviewed those papers, not as independent statements concerning social problems, but as examples of the strength and limitations of the particular model when viewed as a vehicle for social work analysis of community problems.

All of the authors found that they had to make certain adaptations of the model in order to present relevant materials. There was, however, great variation in the degree to which the model was utilized. It seems likely that both the nature of the problem and the viewpoint of the author influenced the degree to which the outline was utilized in the composition of this paper. For my purposes of testing the model I could take advantage only of those papers that made the fullest use of the model. The reader will find, therefore, that most of the quotations employed are drawn from five of the papers.

I have arranged my conclusions in a sequence that more or less follows the outline of the model itself. Under each heading I have dealt with the problems that seemed to be inherent in the use of the model as well as with the general conclusions or ideas that can be derived from a reading of the paper in reference to the particular topic.

My general conclusion at the completion of this first phase of the project is that, although the model itself has certain grave weaknesses and social work is posed with some vexing dilemmas as it attempts to grapple more successfully with social problems, we have made a promising beginning and with continued effort will find ways to make an ever increasing contribution to the solution of some of society's problems. For this I am deeply grateful to those who attended our two conferences and to the authors of the papers.

NATHAN E. COHEN

Poverty ▶

NORMAN V. LOURIE

THE PROBLEM

Poverty as a condition is relative rather than absolute. As a negative term, it has been used to denote absence of material wealth—destitution. To be more accurate, it must be described in terms of insufficiency either in possession of wealth or flow of income.

Galbraith believes that there is no firm definition of poverty and that, save as a tactic for countering the intellectual obstructionist, no precise definition is needed. In part, it is a physical matter. People are poverty-stricken when their income, even if adequate for survival, falls markedly behind that of the community. They cannot have what the larger community regards as the minimum necessary for decency, and they cannot wholly escape; therefore the judgment of the larger community that they are indecent. They are degraded, for in the literal sense they live outside the grades or categories regarded by the community as acceptable.[1]

Economist Boulding makes a distinction between poverty that is the result of some peculiar accident or venture and chronic poverty. He contends that chronic poverty is always in some meaningful sense a condition of a society or of a subculture within a society and that within wide limits poverty is a state of mind more than a state of income.[2] Hollander points out that in ordinary usage poverty is applied to three distinct conditions: economic inequality, economic dependence, and economic insufficiency.[3] In commenting on Hollander's "acceptance of insufficient flow of income as the essential aspect of poverty," Rubinow

---

[1] J. K. Galbraith, *The Affluent Society* (Cambridge: Riverside Press, 1958).

[2] Kenneth E. Boulding, "Reflections on Poverty," National Conference on Social Welfare, *Social Welfare Forum*, 1961 (New York: Columbia University Press, 1961).

[3] J. H. Hollander, *The Abolition of Poverty* (Boston: Houghton Mifflin Co. 1914).

1

points out that this "merely shifts the difficulties of definition, since this concept predicates the assumption of standards, physiologic, psychologic or social."[4]

For this paper poverty is defined as long-term inaccessibility to material resources that are adequate to provide a minimum standard of living consistent with the productive capacity and social requirements of the community. Interpretation of insufficiency and determination of a state of poverty must be based on distinctions between legitimate and excessive needs and desires and on appraisal of deviations from a prevailing level of economic well-being. These, in turn, depend on underlying values and norms regarding the purpose of human existence and the historic destiny of a society. Consequently, at different times in history, among different peoples and between groups among the same people, the definition of and attitude toward poverty vary.

Until comparatively recent times scarcity and poverty in its starkest sense was man's normal lot. It has now been reduced from a problem of the majority to that of a minority.

Rubinow says:

> Modern social science treats poverty as an aspect of social pathology. Since the term pathological is used to describe an abnormal condition of deviation from the average or the prevailing type . . . such a concept obviously arises within a society whose economic development has succeeded in forcing nature to yield in sufficient quantity the products necessary for its well being.
>
> . . . as one passes from the consideration of the poverty of an entire community to that of individuals, families, groups or classes within the community, the problem becomes more complex. In addition to the discrepancy between existing needs and available resources as a whole one must take into account such factors as the influence of prevailing social standards, the inevitable if sometimes semi-conscious comparison of differences of standards within the community and its resultant stimulation of desires.[5]

The first broad-gauged attempts to measure the extent of poverty were made in England. (Studies by Arthur Young and Sir Frederick Eden were forerunners of the monumental survey by Charles Booth, beginning in the 1880's. Booth discovered that on the basis of a minimum weekly income the population of London included more than 30 percent who were poor.[6]

---

[4] I. M. Rubinow, "Poverty," *Encyclopedia of the Social Sciences*, Vol. 12 (New York: Macmillan Co., 1934), pp. 284–292.

[5] *Ibid.*

[6] Charles Booth, *Life and Labor of the People of London* (London: Macmillan & Company, 1892–1903).

Efforts to estimate the extent of poverty in the United States (as elsewhere) have been blurred by the use of varying, usually unsatisfactory indices. These indices have included such measures as family income, per capita income, numbers receiving relief, number (or rate) of unemployed, and number living in substandard housing. Classification systems exist in large numbers. Typical nomenclature includes insufficiency, minimum subsistence, health and decency, comfort, and luxury. Measurement of the extent of poverty is hampered by the difficulties of delineating and devising objective measurements of these levels. What was a luxury becomes a comfort and comforts become necessities. The changes occur more frequently as economic growth and productivity of a society or a nation increases its pace. Compared with past and many contemporary civilizations, modern Western nations, including the United States, possess undreamed-of luxuries. Attempts to measure degrees of poverty have usually been on the basis of income distribution. These have been in terms of costs of living, family budgets, and establishment of minimum standards of health and decency. The standard is based on the assumption that all families whose income is lower than the standard are in the "poverty" group. In comparatively recent times there evolved in industrial societies a concept of poverty based on scales and standards of living. The concept of standard of living has yet to be worked into definitive form, but it has been elaborated in modern economics as a parallel to discussions of standards of value, especially the value of money. Monetary values change quickly and standards also vary, making consistent measurement difficult.

Governmental bodies, labor groups, individual economists, and other professionals have developed methods of arriving at standards. Several classic standards are kept current and are utilized for many economic measurement purposes. Recognizing the difficulties of adequately defining a satisfactory income level, the Federal Bureau of Labor Statistics in 1957 established, for purposes of investigation, an arbitrary cut-off ranging from $1157 for a single-person family to $3750 for a family of seven or more as criteria of relative need. Based on this stringent definition, 32.2 million Americans (19 percent of the total) fell into the "low-income" brackets in that relatively prosperous year. President John F. Kennedy, in his January 22, 1962, economic message to the Congress, used $2000 as a base for poverty, saying that seven million Americans had incomes below that point (individuals and families).

The U. S. Department of Labor estimates that a city worker's family of four at 1958 prices would require an income of about $4800 to maintain a "modest but adequate standard of living." Family income studies of the Bureau of the Census for 1958 reveal that one third of the American families of four had incomes below this level. In 1958 36 million

Americans were living in households of *at least* two persons on incomes of *under* $3000 (less than $58 weekly *before* taxes). Another 5.5 million single-person families (not living with relatives or in institutions) were subsisting on incomes *under* $1500 (less than $30 a week before taxes).

According to the 1960 Statistical Abstract, eight million families in the United States had incomes less than $2500 per year in 1960; seven million had incomes between $2500 and $4000. In 1958 14.3 percent of the families and unattached individuals in the United States had incomes of $2000 a year or less; 10 percent, between $2000 and $3000 a year; 12 percent, between $3000 and $4000. The inescapable conclusion, even allowing for progress since 1958, is that at least 20 percent of all Americans today live close to the poverty line—or below it.

Different groups of conscientious investigators, working with different sets of data, produced different calculations. The various analyses confirm Allen's 1952 observation:

> There are still islands of deep poverty in the United States, and there are families and individuals by the millions who through illness, age, adversity, or marginal ability, live on the ragged edge of want.[7]

Allen reviewed midcentury data regarding the income groups that comprise the lowest third of the nation. He points out that—with the partial exception of the Negroes—they are not "the masses" but rather "a great number of people very widely scattered, who are in very different sorts of trouble, economic and otherwise." The lowest group (10.6 percent of the families and individuals with incomes of less than $1000) include private businessmen and farmers who may have had a poor year, a great number of rural poor, old people, victims of broken families or disability, and chronic "ne'er-do-wells." The next lowest rank (with incomes between $1000 and $2000) comprise more businessmen, marginal farmers, old people, divorced or deserted wives, and marginal laborers, plus an additional group whose wages even in a time and land of plenty are so low that they are kept in a constant struggle with poverty. In most of these groups there is an unduly large representation of Negroes.[8] During the next decade the composition of the lowest income group shifted only to include a higher proportion of the aged and of the unemployed or underemployed urban workers. Statistical analysis of available data shows the incidence of poverty to be disproportionately high for the aged, for nonwhites, for family units headed by women, and for persons with less than eight years of schooling. Among 32.2 million low-income persons in 1957, 8 million were sixty-five or over, 6.4 million were nonwhite, 8 million were in family units headed by women;

---

[7] Frederick Lewis Allen, *The Big Change* (New York: Harper & Brothers, 1952).
[8] *Ibid.*

and 21 million were in units headed by persons who had not gone beyond the eighth grade.

That involuntary poverty is pernicious to the individuals involved and to the society in which they live is almost axiomatic in this century. Nonagreements exist primarily in definitions of poverty, its causes, its effects, and the possibility and means of its eradication. Specific effects of poverty, per se, have not been clearly demonstrated. Syndromes among various social pathologies, including poverty, recur in countless studies. Efforts to isolate dependent and independent variables, to distinguish causes and effects of varying types and manifestations of poverty have been slender or nonexistent.

At least during the last hundred years relationships have been observed or assumed between poverty and high morbidity and mortality rates, poor housing, broken families, low education, and high incidence of crime.

Rubinow writes of the detrimental influence of poverty on mental health and happiness:

> A sudden reduction in the levels of economic well-being creates fear, depression, despondency and suicides. Persistent chronic poverty results in apathy, inertia, indifference and loss of initiative. Mass poverty has been responsible for most revolutions. Comparative poverty causes envy, bitterness, self depreciation of the ego. . . .[9]

Burnham, as well as others, has discussed the effects of adverse circumstances and emotional stress on mental development.[10] Charlotte Towle trenchantly points out that "within our society money has been the symbol of adequacy, even of worth. It wins respect for the individual."[11] Studies and observations confirm Merton's thesis that internalization of cultural goals of success coupled with recognition of limited realistic opportunities invite deviant behavior.[12] On the other hand, findings by Kornhauser, Hyman, Centers, Cantril, and others demonstrate that motivations and expectations are reduced in members of the "lower class." Hollingshead and others, studying stratification, reveal class differences in various aspects of conduct. These and studies of delinquency by Ohlin, among others, confirm the importance of the reference

---

[9] Rubinow, op. cit.

[10] W. H. Burnham, The Normal Mind (New York: D. Appleton-Century Co., 1924), chap. 18.

[11] Charlotte Towle, Common Human Needs (rev. ed.; New York: National Association of Social Workers, 1957).

[12] R. K. Merton, "Social Structure and Anomie," in R. K. Merton, ed., Social Theory and Social Structure (Glencoe, Ill.: Free Press, 1949).

groups with which an individual identifies as a factor in his outlook and behavior.[13]

Despite lack of conclusive evidence, it seems not unreasonable to hypothesize a relationship of poverty to a negative self-image, to hostility or to anomie, to disturbed role identifications, or to limited achievement. Poverty and its affects or constellation of related pathologies have an impact not only on the individuals and families but also on those with whom they come in contact and on society as a whole. Poverty is obviously objectionable, not only on the humanitarian premise of alleviating distress, but also on the practical premise that as long as poverty is permitted to exist it is possible that someday anyone may be in want. The continued existence of poverty leads to insecurity and fear, even on the part of those not directly affected. Elimination of poverty thus adds to the security of all. The ignorance, illness, slums, and crime bred by poverty also have a direct and far-reaching effect which none can escape. Poverty often represents underutilization of labor and other resources that should be tapped in the national interest. At the same time, the existence of poverty indicates that potential buying power not now effective promises a new frontier for further economic development.

There is no school of thought that accepts poverty as a desirable condition. There are differences of opinion on how to measure poverty: what to define as a poverty-stricken person; whether poverty-stricken persons do enough to relieve their condition; measures that will relieve poverty; etc. Except for the ascribed virtues in voluntary poverty as practical throughout history, mostly on religious grounds, the literature reveals no defenders of poverty as a value. Many question whether we are ready to eliminate poverty, whether we are socially and mentally able to do what is necessary to accomplish the goal.

Etiology

Throughout history and in most parts of the world masses of people have suffered from scarcity. The poverty that exists in present-day industrial Western culture is different in degree, kind, and etiology.

In the United States the face of poverty has been radically altered since colonial times. Most of this transformation is attributable to changes in the social structure and its functioning, which include the shift from an agricultural to an industrial economy, urbanization, population growth, importation and freeing of slaves, burgeoning and subse-

---

[13] Herman D. Stein and Richard A. Cloward, *Social Perspectives on Behavior* (Glencoe, Ill.: Free Press, 1958) ; August B. Hollingshead and Fredrick C. Redlich, *Social Class and Mental Illness: A Community Study* (New York: John Wiley and Sons, 1958).

quent halting of immigration, closing of the frontier, geographic mobility of the population, spectacular increase in wealth and the gross national product, advances in technology, including medicine, organization of public and voluntary health and welfare services, and introduction of social insurance programs of various types. In 1905 Seligman pointed out that poverty is tied to the facts of complex economic life. Concentrating on one factor as cause has proved useless. Redundant population was blamed by Malthusians; private property by communists; property in means of production by socialists; property in land by single taxers; competition by cooperators; government by anarchists; speculation by antioptimists; metallic money by the currency reformers; and alcohol by prohibitionists. Certainty that genetic and heredity factors were the cause of poverty prompted action programs such as sterilization and isolation.[14] Throughout history widespread poverty existed in the face of absence of these causes. Each has been absent at different stages of history, yet society had poverty. Each phase had poverty. The causes are apparently as complex as the base of civilization and the growth of wealth.

In a wealthy, highly industrial economy, rich in resources, the bulk of the problem of poverty must be attributed to the structure or functioning of the system and the extent to which it fails to make available to all the cost of goods and services that provide a decent, healthy, and satisfying existence. Crop failures, natural disasters, and personal inadequacies still account for some poverty.

Some sources of poverty are: (1) A low proportion of the population in the labor force. (2) Low productivity of labor. (3) Unfavorable terms of trade (the price for which labor or products can be sold) for a segment of the labor force.

Imbalance in the relationship between available resources and the need for expenditure may be described in terms of those factors contributing to smallness of resources and those contributing to largeness of need. Factors contributing to smallness of resources may be summarized as lack or inadequacy of earnings, income from other sources, or reserves. Industrialization, urbanization, and geographic mobility have promoted isolation of nuclear family units or individuals totally dependent on a limited and monetary income. Inflation shrinks the value of reserves. Factors contributing to largeness of need include large families, costs related to illness, unusual expenses (legal, moving, payment of debts, etc.), inefficient household management, and addiction to alcoholic beverages or narcotics. Advances in medicine have reduced

---

[14] Amos G. Warner, *American Charities* (New York: Thomas Y. Crowell & Co., 1908).

rates of mortality at all ages. Increased communication, geographic mobility, rural-urban-suburban migration, pressures to maintain a high level of productivity and of consumption, and unstable family patterns have operated to create new demands.

The source of most urban and much of the agricultural income in a money economy such as ours is earnings from employment. Unemployment, underemployment, inability to work, and low wages create low-income situations. In order to explain the continuing existence of poverty in the midst of plenty, labor force status and level of earnings of those responsible for their own maintenance or for the support of others must be taken into account.

Operating factors are economic, social, and/or personal. Economic factors include economic recessions, technological changes in production processes, variations in increase of productivity within an occupation, market variations, irregular or seasonal demand for labor, and migration of industry from particular communities. Among social causes for low income are loss of earnings of the head of the family because of death, absence from the family group, or other responsibilities, discrimination in employment because of race, color, sex, religious belief, age, physical handicap, or record of mental illness or imprisonment, and geographic or occupational immobility.

Personal factors contributing to restrictions on employability and earning power encompass physical and mental disabilities, including temporary incapacity and handicaps owing to age, limitations in required work skills because of inadequate education and training, including lack of acculturation, and limited innate ability and other individual inadequacies such as unreliability. Lack of education and training is a fundamental cause of low income in that it prevents achievement of full potential. This problem is compounded because it is self-perpetuating. Children from low-income families are most likely to drop out of school for various reasons. As Boulding points out, low income may also result from the "rejection of the psychological cost of getting rich and a rejection of the whole middle-class way of life. . . ." [15] To maintain its population and meet other conditions for societal survival, provision must be made for those who cannot or do not produce.

The system of capitalism, industrialization, and urbanization introduced many hazards which cannot be overcome by the individual and the family alone. Programs to prevent economic need based on lack of earnings have been developed. They now include a system of direct care, public assistance, and varied social insurances. Insofar as these

---

[15] Boulding, *op. cit.*

resources fail to provide "material resources which are adequate to provide a minimum standard of living consistent with the productive capacity and social requirements of the community," they can exacerbate the personal factors contributing to low income.[16] The extent to which they fall short of meeting needs is itself a source of or a factor in perpetuating poverty.

In April 1961 unemployment reached 6.8 percent of the labor force, one of every fifteen workers. In that month 2.1 million persons had been out of work fifteen weeks or longer. According to the United States Department of Labor, in the summer of 1961 the rate of unemployment was even higher, with unemployed totaling 5.5 million, despite a record high of 65.5 million employed. Five vulnerable groups are most often noted: youth, especially those who have dropped out of school, unskilled workers, Negroes, older workers (now forty-five years of age or older), and workers in "depressed" areas. Twenty-six million young people will enter the job market by 1970.

More than 16 million Americans are sixty-five years of age or older, and it is estimated that there will be more than 20 million in 1970. In President Kennedy's message on housing to the Congress, March 9, 1961, he said, "most of these elderly people have very limited financial means. More than half of the families headed by a person over sixty-five have annual incomes below $3000 and four fifths of all people of this age living alone must subsist on less than $2000 per year."

According to the January 1962 *Social Security Bulletin*, in June 1961 about three-fourths of a million of the aged on the old-age, survivors and disability insurance rolls were receiving public assistance to supplement benefits that did not meet their needs under the assistance standards of their states of residence. They constituted 6.5 percent of all beneficiaries aged sixty-five and over and 30 percent of the 2.4 million recipients of old-age assistance, medical aid for the aged, and aid to the blind or disabled.

In most states the public assistance grant is below the standard established by local studies of a minimum health and decency level. Thus for many people even the insurance-assistance combination does not get them over the "poverty line."

> It is not till it is discovered that high individual incomes will not purchase the mass of mankind immunity from cholera, typhus, and ignorance, still less secure them the positive advantages of educational opportunity and economic security, that slowly and reluctantly, amid prophecies of moral degeneration and economic disaster, society

---

[16] Helen Harris Perlman, "Are We Creating Dependency?" Minnesota State Welfare Conference, May 9, 1951. Reprinted in *Public Aid in Illinois* (Springfield, Ill.: Illinois Public Aid Commission).

begins to make collective provision for needs which no ordinary individual, even if he works overtime all his life, can provide for himself.[17]

In these terms of R. H. Tawney, Galbraith, who exemplifies a contemporary group of social-welfare-minded economists, discussed the theory of poverty related to social balance.[18] He describes an implacable tendency to provide an opulent supply of some things and a niggardly yield of others. This becomes a cause of "social discomfort and social unhealth." The line that divides our area of wealth under this theory from our area of poverty is roughly that which divides privately produced and marketed goods and services from publicly rendered services. The country's wealth in relation to the privately produced is great compared to that of public care. And the wealth in privately produced goods is a major cause of the crisis in the supply of public services. In this theory alleviation of poverty becomes a matter of achieving and maintaining a balance between the two.

The theory of social balance has been attacked by those opposed to expanding public services. The cost of these services was held to be a threat to individual liberties. These fears have somewhat abated since it was realized that social imbalance produced disorders that had to be met. The arguments against development of public services continue by those who do not understand the need for balance between private and public services, although they do not actually take vigorous steps to curtail public assistance. This is evidenced by the facts of public service growth under some conservative political regimes on both the federal and state levels.

VALUES

Societal Values and Norms

As Wilensky and Lebeaux point out, necessary conditions for societal survival include, first of all, population. Society must provide its members with food, protect them against injury, and ensure the reproduction of new organisms. The second condition is some system of specialization and stratification. To get essential work done, society assigns different activities to different individuals. In doing so all societies develop an economic role system to cope with the distribution of the available supply of goods and services.[19]

Values determine the choices men make, their norms and goals. Within a society prevailing value systems can be identified which are

[17] Richard H. Tawney, *Equality* (4th ed.; London, England: Allen and Unwin, 1952), as quoted in Galbraith, *op. cit.*, pp. 134–135.

[18] Galbraith, *op. cit.*

[19] Harold L. Wilensky and Charles N. Lebeaux, *Industrial Society and Social Welfare* (New York: Russell Sage Foundation, 1958).

neither always consistent nor universal. A diversified social structure is likely to encompass numerous value conflicts.

Throughout history recognition has been given to the need of caring for the poor. Biblical references are many. As De Schweinitz points out:

> In Greece, in Palestine, in Rome, there were extensive measures for the care of the poor; and in the cultural background from which we approach any discussion of poverty is the influence of Aristotle, St. Paul, St. Francis of Assisi, and many other classical and medieval thinkers. . . . Under feudalism there could, at least in theory, be no un-cared-for distress.[20]

With the shift from feudalism to capitalism wages came largely into use as a means of emancipation of the laborer from serfdom, but the advance toward freedom was accompanied by loss of economic security.

This loss of economic security produced new forms of poverty. The concomitant rise of capitalism and of the "Protestant ethic" has had a continuing effect on the value-orientations and norms in American (as well as other) societies.

No one advocates poverty as a value for society to cherish. Until recently almost no one has seriously advocated and worked toward the total abolition of poverty. Some social values operate more toward its alleviation; others tend to perpetuate it. Among the value-orientations in American society identified by Williams, several would tend to oppose or to support the continued existence of poverty, depending on the interpretation of individuals or groups of the best achievement of a goal.[21]

American value orientations opposing the existence or mitigating the effects of poverty include the humanitarian mores, equality (at least of opportunity), democracy, and progress.

Values that, in combination and as frequently interpreted, tend to support the continuation of poverty include those of achievement and success, activity and work, material comfort, freedom (primarily from restrictions), individual personality, and racism or group superiority.

Value orientations that might operate in either direction include efficiency and practicality, moral orientation, external conformity, science and secular rationality, and nationalism-patriotism.

As Williams warns:

> It must be always kept in mind that these themes, values, and systems

---

[20] Karl De Schweinitz, *England's Road to Social Security* (Philadelphia: University of Pennsylvania Press, 1943).

[21] Robin M. Williams, "Value Orientations in American Society," in Stein and Cloward, *Social Perspectives of Behavior, op. cit.*

of belief do not operate as single and separate units but are in continually shifting and recombining configuration marked by very complex interpenetration, conflict, and reformulation and that, moreover, they are not separately functioning, disembodied elements.[22]

To date, obviously, the attitudes and values that permit the continued existence of poverty have prevailed. The statement, "The poor always ye have with you," (John 12, 8) is still utilized. With the commercial and Protestant revolutions, however, poverty rather than being meritorious or a misfortune to be pitied and relieved was seen as evidence of a moral failing to be condemned. Prudence, diligence, moderation, sobriety, and thrift were not only Christian virtues but proved also to be the very qualities most conducive to commercial success. Practical success was at once the sign and the reward of ethical superiority. The greatest of evils was idleness; the poor were victims, not of circumstances, but of their own "idle, irregular and wicked courses," of what the Poor Law Commissioners of 1834 called "individual improvidence and vice."

Status was replaced by contract. Tawney quotes a characteristic sentiment: "The law of God saith, 'He that will not work, let him not eat.' This would be a sore scourge and smart whip for idle persons if . . . none should be suffered to eat till they had wrought for it." [23]

The concept of individualism and ideology of laissez-faire have operated against efforts to wipe out poverty. The main economic dogma of the mercantilist had an undesigned affinity with the main ethical dogma of the Puritan. Production, not consumption, was the pivot of the economic system. Economic progress became an end to be consciously sought. A minister could write, "It is an undeniable maxim that everyone by the light of nature and reason will do that which makes for his greatest advantage . . . . The advancement of private persons will be the advantage of the public."

The social character of wealth, which had been the essence of the medieval doctrine, was supplanted by the theory expressed by Locke when he described property as a right anterior to the existence of the state and argued that "the supreme power cannot take from any man any part of his property without his own consent."

These attitudes, peppered with selected interpretations of nineteenth-century liberalism, the materialistic concepts explicated by Marx, Malthusian doctrine, and Social Darwinism, appear in modern guise. What is good for one corporation will benefit all of society. General economic expansion will inevitably benefit everyone. All increases in taxation

---

[22] *Ibid.*
[23] Tawney, *op. cit.*

are to be resisted. Each individual should pursue his self-interest with minimal interference. Unemployment and bankruptcy are necessary and useful consequences of competition. Social legislation should be delayed and kept as limited as possible. The accent is on individual responsibility and the importance of activity, work, and status to be achieved through accomplishment. It is unwise or dangerous to pamper those who fail.[24]

Many of these attitudes, including the theory of "less eligibility" of the 1834 English Reform laws, are reflected in recent proposals, including the much-publicized Newburgh "welfare code" which resulted from the controversy over public assistance in Newburgh, New York, in the summer of 1960. The code purported to reduce "excessive" relief costs, eliminate "chiselers" from the welfare load, and relieve the community of some costs by denying relief to those who did not meet certain "moral" standards. The fact that the code could be promulgated and praised by many indicates some continued acceptance of punitive, restrictive attitudes.

On the other hand, the more general negative reaction to the Newburgh proposals exemplifies the widespread, explicit stress on the values of security, equality, and humanitarianism which support a more constructive approach toward elimination of the problems of poverty. A trend toward dominance of these values is apparent in many other programs and official pronouncements which are not necessarily focused on economic need, per se.

President Kennedy, on February 1, 1962, issued to the Congress the first "welfare" message by any President of the United States. It followed the traditional State of the Union message, messages on trade, agriculture, and others, all of which stressed, apart from the program and budget details, a national desire to eliminate poverty.

In the February 1 message the late President, in emphasizing rehabilitative programs, declared that responding to the ills of the needy "with scorn and suspicion is inconsistent with their nearly universal preference to be independent."

Without mentioning Newburgh, New York, he said:

> Communities which have . . . for whatever motives . . . attempted to save money through ruthless cutbacks in their welfare rolls have found their efforts to little avail. The root problems remained. . . .

The President's program attempts to strike at the causes of poverty represent a set of values consistent with those of social work. The national value set in this message by the nation's leader is an attempt to

---

[24] Stein and Cloward, *op. cit.*; Warner, *op. cit.*

strike, in part, at the causes of the existence of poverty in the midst of abundance.

In his first economic report delivered to the Congress on January 22, 1962, which embodied the report of his statutory Council of Economic Advisers, President Kennedy said in talking about the need to eliminate poverty and of our goals of economic policy:

> But prosperity has not wiped out poverty. . . . In 1960 seven million individuals and families had personal incomes lower than $2000. In part our failure to overcome poverty is a consequence of our failure to operate the economy at potential!

These two desires: to operate the economy at its full potential and to provide adequately for those who are either the victims of the economy's maladjustments or are unable to make their way for other reasons represent practical expression of current social values relating to poverty which contradict the mainly materialistic values within which poverty has flourished.

Assumed Values and Norms of Social Work

The assumed values and norms of social work, like those of other social institutions, are rooted in those of the society of which it is an instrument. Frequently, however, varying emphasis on selected values and norms gives the impression of incongruence. At the present time, although the dominant societal norms and values allow for toleration (or nonrecognition) of the phenomenon of poverty, social work stresses values directed toward its amelioration or eradication. Within the field and its organizational framework the difference is less clear-cut. Like other institutions, social work perpetuates earlier identifications in active, modified, or vestigial form,[25] which emphasize values that oppose the existence of poverty or which support the possibility of rescuing the "deserving poor."

Origins of welfare activities lie in early colonial times, with succor to the unfortunate reflecting humanitarian mores and protection of the community. The stress on deterrence and restrictiveness, although never demonstrably effective, has persisted in the organizational structure of most public and some private welfare agencies.[26] Modern social work traces its beginnings to movements of the nineteenth century. These mirrored differing values. One source of inspiration was Thomas

---

[25] Bronislaw Malinowski, *The Dynamics of Culture Change* (New Haven: Yale University Press, 1945).

[26] Frank Greving and Norman Lourie, "Restructuring Community Services for Orthopsychiatric Practice," paper presented at American Orthopsychiatric Association, New York, March 23, 1961.

Chalmers who opposed any poor law and attacked "the principle that each man, simply because he exists, holds a right on other men or on society for existence." Efforts were concentrated on rescuing the worthy—and the young—from unfavorable conditions, on discouraging abuse, and promoting effectiveness of almsgiving.

High evaluation of humanitarian mores was coupled with regard for achievement and success, activity and work, individualism, secular rationality, and practical efficiency. Only for a period of approximately three decades preceding World War I was there a concentrated effort to abolish undesirable conditions—including poverty. These efforts stemmed in part from a commitment to Christian socialism, pragmatism, a stress on humanitarian mores, equality, democracy, progress, science, and secular rationality.

The selection and terminology of Friedlander is more familiar to and accepted by social workers than is this paper's use of value-orientations delineated by Williams.

> The feelings, attitudes, orientation, and practices of social workers in the American culture are inspired by the following democratic values:
>
> 1. Conviction of the inherent worth, the integrity, and the dignity of the individual.
> 2. Conviction that the individual who is in economic, personal, or social need has the right to determine himself what his needs are and how they should be met (right of self-determination).
> 3. Firm belief in equal opportunity for all, limited only by the individual's innate capacities.
> 4. Conviction that man's individual rights to self-respect, dignity, self-determination, and equal opportunities are connected with his social responsibilities toward himself, his family, and his society.[27]

For decades after World War I social work stressed a drive toward professionalism and improvement of techniques in helping individuals adjust to or improve their personal difficulties or circumstances. Dominant values of individualism coupled with efficiency and practicality did little to focus the attention of social work as a profession on efforts to abolish poverty. Widespread control by non-social workers of policies and funds probably furthered these trends in some areas and fostered emphasis on values predominant in the business world. Certainly in the voluntary field the nature of the sponsorship guided the values of social agency policy.

During the depression of the thirties social workers were represented among those who recognized the need of a new approach. Schlesinger

---

[27] Walter A. Friedlander, ed., *Concepts and Methods of Social Work* (Englewood Cliffs, N. J.: Prentice-Hall, 1958).

calls attention to the influence on the broad-gauged New Deal social program of the thinking and values of social workers identified with the reform movements earlier in the century.[28] Since that period there has been a trend toward stress on the values of humanitarianism, equality, progress, and security represented in what Wilensky and Lebeaux term the "institutional" approach of welfare services as a positive "first line" normal function of modern industrial society. This conception is in contrast to the "residual" approach which, representing emphasis on the values of individualism and freedom, envisages social welfare institutions as coming into play only when normal structures break down. Basic principles of American social work are rooted in our religious tradition and our economic institutions. They are formulated in the axiom that the nation's people are its most important resource. Its values stem from American developments of Western Christian religion which emphasize a normative set of values culminating in supreme good. Based on progressive and pragmatic philosophy, reformist in spirit, American social work goal norms are complementary to and supportive of a free-enterprise economy.[29]

The conviction that society must provide for those who cannot care for themselves has corollaries:

1. Dependent and maladjusted persons should be helped to help themselves.

2. Remedial steps should be taken to eradicate the basic causes of distress.

3. Efforts with individuals should promote the more effective approaches of the free-enterprise economy.

Modern social work's disassociation from the doctrine that to be in need is to be inferior is in conflict with long-cherished beliefs. The convictions that dependency is encouraged not by giving but by withholding and a nonjudgmental view in treatment of deviant behavior are also in conflict with prevailing norms.[30]

CURRENT OPERATIONS: "THE ACTUAL."

Social Work Operations Related to Poverty

Consideration of current social work operations related to the problem of poverty is hampered by unresolved conflicts or ambiguities, the first of which is the delineation of the term social work.

---

[28] Arthur M. Schlesinger, Jr., *The Crisis of the Old Order* (Boston: Houghton Mifflin Co., 1956), esp. p. 25.

[29] Arthur P. Miles, *American Social Work Theory* (New York: Harper & Brothers, 1954).

[30] Stein and Cloward, *op. cit.*

A United Nations document makes these points:

> In no country have the frontiers of social welfare or social service or social work been established beyond cavil. In no country has terminology been so standardized as to make possible the assignment of precise meaning to such terms as "social welfare," "social service," "social work," and "welfare work." [31]

In the *Social Work Year Book, 1960,* Kidneigh draws a distinction:

> The term social welfare is currently used to denote man's humanitarian desire to help his fellow man . . . the term social work has come to be used to denote particular sectors of social welfare activities.[32]

The introductory article, "The Development of Social Welfare Programs in the United States," in the 1960 *Social Work Year Book* concludes with a discussion of social welfare programs and social work, noting that programs today operate under varied auspices. Although another introductory article, "Social Work Status and Trends," stresses the responsibility of social work and social workers for social action, the section devoted to that subject more or less eschews the term social work in discussing "that aspect of social welfare activities which is directed toward shaping or modifying the social institutions and policies that constitute the social environment in which we live." [33]

Side-stepping, as inappropriate for this paper, the problem of semantics (although it is admittedly more than that), this section is confined to social work operations usually identified as such: the operations of public welfare departments [34] with special reference to financial assistance sectors, at all government levels; public and private operations in the fields of child welfare, family service, and corrections; hospital and clinic services; group work; community organization; social work research; and social action. (Social workers often function within such programs as housing and others too numerous to mention; there is an increasing number of private practitioners.)

At present, the primary function of social work is the provision of social services, through governmental and voluntary agencies, to meet a wide range of human needs in a wide variety of settings. It is easiest defined by listing what it does. These services include efforts to help clients to obtain a basic economic security, but increasingly they have

---

[31] *Training for Social Work: An International Survey* (New York: United Nations, 1950).

[32] John C. Kidneigh, "Social Work as a Profession," in Russell H. Kurtz, ed., *Social Work Year Book, 1960* (New York: National Association of Social Workers, 1960), p. 563.

[33] *Ibid.*

[34] Not all public welfare is considered to be social work operation. Most agree that social work is the central professional discipline in public welfare.

been extended to people of all social levels, including those not financially dependent.

Lurie points out, "The inauguration of a national system of public assistance and social insurance measures had a profound effect on the structure and functions of social welfare." [35] Voluntary agencies were no longer considered as a basic resource for meeting problems of insufficient income. The transfer of relief to public auspices "freed social workers from a primary concern with the unsolved problems of poverty and social maladjustment. . . ."

In an effort to relieve the problems of poverty, social work operations are still directly engaged in operating specialized institutions, in administering programs of financial assistance (primarily under public auspices) to applicants who demonstrate need according to established eligibility requirements, in giving services which help clients to increase or improve management of their resources, and in meeting disaster needs. Intermediary attack on the problem includes referrals to community social work and non-social work resources. Indirectly, all operations to counteract malfunctioning or to promote the well-being of individuals or communities at least implicitly support or complement measures against poverty.

Intensified concern with research includes new approaches to the measurement and concept of need and methods of dealing with "hard core" families.[36]

In current operations accelerated recognition is being given to resumption or re-emphasizing attempts to mobilize social forces to resolve those social and economic situations that foster dependency, ill health, and mental and social maladjustments. Through its national association, the organized profession of social work has specifically committed itself to

[35] Harry L. Lurie, "The Development of Social Welfare Programs" in Russell H. Kurtz, ed., *Social Work Year Book, 1960, op. cit.*, p. 39.

[36] Community Research Associates, New York (various publications); Cora Kasius, *New Directions in Social Work* (New York: Harper & Brothers, 1954); Henry S. Maas and Martin Wolins, "Concepts and Methods in Social Work Research," in Cora Kasius, ed., *New Directions in Social Work, ibid.*; Martin Wolins, "A Base for Community Welfare Studies," *Social Welfare Forum*, 1954 (New York: Columbia University Press, 1954); Norman Lourie, "Are We Rehabilitating Public Assistance Clients?" *Public Welfare*, Vol. 20, (July 1962) pp. 170–174.

The 1962 amendments to the Social Security Act and subsequent regulations of the Bureau of Family Service, Welfare Administration (U.S. Department of Health, Education and Welfare) with respect to social study and classification of public assistance clients are particularly pertinent. Most states are now "classifying" cases to "identify" social services given which in turn bring 75 percent federal matching. The National Institute of Mental Health, the Council on Social Work Education, and the professional associations are all concerned with approaches to classification of psychosocial disorders.

identify and work toward measures to alleviate or prevent sources of deprivation. The implicit definition of poverty has been termed the "social" concept of income inadequacy: income that fails to provide for social and psychological needs as well as for the physical necessities of life.[37]

In actual operations the definition tends to be symptomological: the state of poverty being marked by such limited and insufficient food, such poor clothing, such crowded, cold, and dirty shelter that life is painful for those afflicted, and the situation is detrimental to society. The approach has been one of selective responsibility toward categories of persons whose needs are most apparent: material relief for those defined in the English Poor Laws as "impotent" gradually extended to treat others with handicaps recognized as hampering their optimum functioning. Implicit value perspectives are humanitarian mores, equality, progress, and individualism.

Friedlander points out:

> The goal of social work is to reconcile the well-being of the individuals with the welfare of society in which they live. This objective precludes that social work attempt to force the people with whom it works to accept destitution, deprivation, humiliation as given facts and to adjust to conditions that are harmful, unjust, and depriving.[38]

Efforts are therefore extended to an improvement of the environment of individuals and families receiving other aid or service.

Social work in its operations and its personnel is rooted in the middle class. Values almost inevitably include those of achievement and success, activity and work, efficiency and practicality, and external conformity. Other values or disciplines dictate compassion or tacit acceptance of failure to realize these values. In practice, reactions toward their nonacceptance are less clearly defined. In effect, some of these attitudes may be ineffective or actually deterrent to endeavors to abolish poverty. Inconsistency may also derive from the fact that professional social work operates in a variety of settings (prisons, courts, hospitals, and industry) in which the prevailing values and norms are not quite the same as those of social work. A sharpened emphasis on attacking the causes of poverty is reflected in stress on social work services and rehabilitative measures. Incongruence with norms and some sectors of society can be noted. Negative criticism of current operations and repressive punitive attitudes expressed in recurring legislative proposals such as Louisiana's withdrawal of aid from children in "unsuitable

---

[37] Helen H. Lamale, "Concepts of Income Adequacy," *Social Welfare Forum,* 1959 (New York: Columbia University Press, 1959).

[38] Friedlander, *op. cit.*

homes" and the much-publicized "Newburgh code" received scattered support. Societal norms congruent with those of social work, however, seem to be more firmly based at this time. The Newburgh code was more widely and responsibly condemned than praised. A poll reported in the *New York Times* on Sunday, January 21, 1962, reveals wide support for health and welfare proposals which are consonant with social work aims. President Kennedy's welfare message to the Congress on February 1, 1962, is a reflection that the country is ready to "scorn suspicion" and approach welfare clients with compassion and rehabilitative motives.

Insofar as these operations are confined to a residual approach of action to treat breakdowns and insofar as they eschew or fail to take action to close the gaps, they are incongruent with social work values and goals. Glaring examples are the anachronistic eligibility requirements, the disparate, inadequate financial allowances and paucity of rehabilitative services in assistance programs, and the dearth of service programs outside urban areas.

Attempts to close the gap, revealed in new legislative approaches, following the report (September 1961) of the Ad Hoc Committee on Public Welfare, appointed by Abraham Ribicoff, Secretary of Health, Education, and Welfare, are hopeful but cannot be represented as an operational result at this time. (President Kennedy's February 1, 1962, message resulted from this report.)

Non-Social Work Operations Related to Poverty

Most of the activities in the United States now dealing with the problem of poverty are not defined as social work activities. Continuing industrialization, development of natural resources, advances in technology, mushroom growth of population, and mobility have all contributed to an unprecedented growth of national income, rapid rises in living standards, and increased equality in income distribution. Efforts to combat the poverty attributable to smallness of resources include measures to increase general productivity, activities to improve the position or opportunities of wage earners (including farmers), and provisions to counteract the effect of loss of income from earnings.

Government and private business undertakings include manifold measures to increase general productivity: steps to prevent violent business fluctuations, various forms of research, promotion of full employment, area-development schemes, subsidies or concessions in the tax structure, programs of soil conservation, reclamation, and irrigation, and a variety of programs to promote education, health, and safety.

The government, labor unions, and cooperatives operate to improve the position or opportunities of income earners by numerous means, such as minimum wage laws, education and training, employment services and labor exchanges, agricultural price supports, loans at low interest rates, measures aimed against discrimination in employment based on such factors as race, religion, sex, age, and physical or mental handicap, and programs of subsidized housing.

Among provisions to counteract the financial effect of loss of income from earnings, various insurance schemes are most prominent: old-age, survivors, and disability insurance and various retirement plans and private insurance. Other resources include workmen's compensation, unemployment compensation, veteran's and railroad retirement programs, and disability benefits for selected groups. Programs for rehabilitation and for retraining also exist. (Social workers function within them sometimes in leadership positions. But social work is not the central discipline, and these projects are not known as social work activities. Yet it is still the graduate school of social work in which academic bases for some of these programs are present and are being increased.)

Non-social work operations to counteract poverty attributable to largeness of need include income-tax concessions, subsidized housing, and education for limitation of family size. Resources for medical costs and other unusual expenses include private insurance and private or public legal aid. Advertising, consumer education, and education in household management emanating from various sources seek to improve household management. Control and taxation, education, special organizations, psychiatric and counseling services, and research aim to reduce the problems attendant on addiction to alcohol or narcotics. Mental health programs have been expanded greatly.

Implicit definitions of the problem emphasize the objective aspects of poverty. Values emphasized are those of achievement and success, activity and work, material comfort, progress, and democracy. A presumption is that these operations are inevitably of reciprocal benefit to society and to the individual, and since they are society's chosen modes of meeting the problem, they must be regarded as congruent with societal norms. Some of the measures do meet resistance, in that they are believed to interfere with freedom, to disregard individualism, and to promote an equality not accepted as necessary or desirable. Others fail to meet the problem and are criticized not only for this inadequacy but also for disregard of humanitarian mores and for failure to provide equality of opportunity—societal norms that are especially dear to social work.

Consequences of Continuing of Present Program

The problem of poverty has so radically diminished during the twentieth century that there has been a temptation to assume that it could be resolved by a mere continuation of the present programs.

The prodigious economic development in the United States has made possible the highest standard of living in the world. The percentage of poverty-stricken people has decreased in recent decades. Hazel Kyrk estimates that in 1901 at least 40 percent of the families of wage earners and clerical workers were trying to live on "less than adequate" income (i.e., less than $700 for a four-person family). By 1950 (allowing for price changes) Kyrk's 1901 standard could be maintained by an average-size, urban, wage-earning family of 3.4 persons for $1700, a level below which less than 10 percent of such families lived. If vastly changed ideas of "adequacy" are ignored, it is indisputable that the objective conditions of the poor have improved.[39]

Successful operation of present programs, essentially unchanged, would probably continue to diminish certain aspects of the problem of poverty. Established insurance programs would continue to reduce the numbers of those requiring relief or other financial assistance as a substitute for earnings lost by death, advanced age, or permanent disability. A lower percentage of persons ineligible for other benefits would receive relief grants, the inadequacy of which would perpetuate impoverished dependency in a diminished proportion of the population. Anticipated expansion of general productivity and programs to improve the position or opportunities of wage earners could be expected to benefit individuals on the lowest rung of the economic ladder.

However, unless there is modification or acceleration of parts of the program, an extension of relative poverty can be anticipated. Because of continuing population growth and technical developments, including ever increasing automation, that demand a higher percentage of workers with new and greater skills, this extension would involve a growing number of persons.

Many current programs, dating back at least twenty-five years, fail to take into account some of the basic changes in the economy, sweeping social and cultural changes, and new understanding of human behavior. On the other hand, some of the programs (such as the social action aspects of social work, service, research, education, and training programs) inherently contain elements that promote change in other facets of the present program. If successful, they could lead to diminution of the problem of poverty.

---

[39] Wilensky and Lebeaux, *op. cit.*

OBJECTIVES: "THE IDEAL"

Social Change

In order to realize values of humanitarianism and the conception of a progressing, equalitarian democracy, social work strives for a society in which individuals will have the opportunity and encouragement to realize their fullest possible developments in all spheres.

For such a society the virtual abolition of poverty is an intermediate goal. It is to this goal, limited unrealistically to the United States, that this discussion is confined. Economic data support the possibility of its achievement with benefit not only to the present and potential victims but also to the total economy.

In the sixties we will have the most affluent society known to the world. Projections are that the national output of $500 billion will grow to about $750 billion; per capita income will rise from $2200 to $2900 (1960 prices). Economists assert that, barring military spending exigencies, economic growth will provide enough funds to meet the needs of all major proposed social welfare programs, including increased funds for the nonemployed, medical care under social insurance, and federal aid to education. Heller says:

> The crucial test of national fulfillment goes well beyond the restrictive bounds of economic prediction and economic policy concerning *rate* of growth. At least equally important are the *uses* of growth. Devoted to a self-indulgent scramble for material goods, economic abundance might even, on balance, intensify our many faceted social welfare problem. But, devoted in generous measure to investment in human beings—in their education, training, health and well-being—economic growth can become synonymous with human welfare.[40]

This theory is in accord with Galbraith's point of view in *The Affluent Society*, which poses the issue of social need versus private indulgence.[41] Supportive findings include those of Keyserling and the Conference on Economic Progress.[42]

This growth will not automatically relieve poverty. Achievement of such an objective requires a modification or acceleration of current programs, a flexible readiness to create new programs to meet the

---

[40] Walter W. Heller, *The Economic Setting for Health and Welfare in the Sixties* (Harrisburg, Pa.: Citizens Association for Health and Welfare, *December 1960*); "An Economic Prognosis for the Sixties," *Social Welfare Forum*, 1960 (New York: Columbia University Press, 1960).

[41] Galbraith, *op. cit.*

[42] *The Federal Budget and the "General Welfare"* (Washington, D. C.: Conference on Economic Progress, December 1959).

exigencies of rapid change, and constant re-evaluation of norms and objectives.

The social-change objective is a universal determination to eliminate poverty as a social phenomenon and to spare man from annihilation or return to utter deprivation. Official social work pronouncements support this aim.

Goals of social policy adopted by the Delegate Assembly of the National Association of Social Workers in May 1958 quote from the association's by-laws a cardinal purpose of the association:

> ... to further the broad objective of improving conditions of life in our democratic society through utilization of the professional knowledge and skills of social work ... to provide opportunity for the social work profession to work in unity toward ... alleviating or preventing sources of deprivation, distress, and strain susceptible of being influenced by social work methods and by social action.

The goals themselves define in part social work's position on the obligations of a society to individuals:

> The profession of social work is committed to the principle that democratic society exists for the benefit of its individual members. Such a society must be so ordered that its common resources are devoted to assuring to each of those members (a) opportunity for full growth and development; (b) the means for meeting economic growth needs in terms of the standards its productivity makes possible; (c) provisions of mutual aid for meeting those needs in which social interdependence is a basic factor; ... social work ... has ... a social action responsibility. ... It is their [social workers'] job to make a very complex social machinery meet the needs of its individual members in two ways: (a) by bringing to such needs the benefits of existing programs, policies and knowledge, and (b) by identifying and interpreting the areas where such machinery is proving deficient in terms of actual unmet needs.[43]

The goals contain several sections, including one on economic and labor conditions. The virtual elimination of poverty is assumed as an aim:

> Basic to all social advance is a productive economy which offers all individuals the means to an adequate income, provides the financial base for social services, and encourages creative expansion of needed goods and services within an atmosphere of freedom. Such an economy requires the optimum foresighted use of all resources and measures that assure a fair distribution of its total product. . . .[44]

---

[43] *Goals of Public Social Policy* (rev. ed.; New York: National Association of Social Workers, 1963, pp. 9–10).

[44] *Ibid.*

A complementary approach is presented in a position statement on public welfare adopted in December 1961 by the National Social Welfare Assembly, which is a central coordinating body for national social welfare agencies:

> ... essential to all social welfare programs, both public and voluntary, is the belief that in a democracy the social good and individual welfare depend upon each other. ... Social welfare plays an indispensable role in the functioning of modern democratic society. ... "Public Welfare" is the name commonly applied to those social welfare programs which function with tax support, under governmental auspices and are directed toward the specific economic and social needs of particular individuals and families. ... Public welfare is the channel through which the responsible level of government assures to individuals and families the means of meeting those special and economic needs it recognizes as basic, but for which other provisions have proved inadequate. ... Public welfare helps support a healthy society by assisting individuals in times of hardship, readjustment, and social difficulty. ... An effective public welfare policy must ... be built upon a foundation of broad economic measures that contribute to general prosperity and minimize economic hardship and social handicap for individuals. Basic to this objective is the existence of a healthy adaptive economy with production sufficient to assure jobs to all persons in the labor market and a reasonable standard of living to those who ... are not able to work. ... The cost and volume of public welfare services can best be minimized by the development of conditions and measures that prevent the needs that bring people to welfare agencies. ...[45]

The American Public Welfare Association publishes yearly a set of federal legislative objectives. These statements and the association's various publications which represent the opinions of persons working in the public welfare agencies contain similar expressions most often used as a basis for opinion-making in the field. The Social Security Act, state public welfare laws, and publications of the federal Department of Health, Education, and Welfare are important expressions of opinion and mandate.

The APWA defines public welfare as "that area of governmental services which protects individuals and families against potential or actual social disaster and helps them find the means to regain economic and social self-sufficiency."[46]

---

[45] *Position Paper on Public Welfare* (New York: National Social Welfare Assembly, December 1961).

[46] "Essentials of Public Welfare" (Chicago: American Public Welfare Association, 1953); "Legislative Objectives" published yearly by the American Public Welfare Association.

On the broader scene, the U. N. Declaration of Human Rights includes this principle:

> Everyone has a right to a standard of living adequate for the health and well-being of himself and his family, including food, clothing, housing and medical care and necessary social services and the right to security in the event of unemployment, sickness, disability, widowhood, old age and other lack of livelihood in circumstances beyond his control.

Implications

Effective determination to resolve the problem requires explicit recognition that widespread poverty still exists, general acceptance of the fact that its resolution is beyond the capacity of individuals involved, awareness that present provisions are inadequate, readiness to support and implement coordinated complementary measures, and re-emphasis on the importance of human resources.

Achievement of the objective is not consonant with those societal norms that emphasize individualism expressed, on the one hand, as the individual's right, obligation, and ability to be self-supporting and, on the other, as the individual's unassailable prerogative to dispose of his accumulated portion of the national product. It is dependent on strengthened and more fully implemented acceptance of the mutual responsibility of the individual and society. It requires recognition of current conditions in which "rugged individualism" cannot even ensure survival, much less achievement and success, in which the extended family and an open frontier no longer can be relied on as bulwarks, in which requirements for a mobile labor force nullify the virtues of stability, in which material success may be more the result of chance than evidence of the favor of God, personal competence, and willingness to work. It necessitates admission that national growth and development do not automatically redound to the benefit of all members of the community.

A concentrated effort to abolish poverty would not be incompatible with existing social work norms. It does entail resolution of differences within the field regarding approaches, priorities, timing, and the scope and function of social work. To be effective, it would require changes in organizational framework, administrative patterns, and operational methods.

Achievement of the objective requires revitalized stress on remedial steps to eradicate the causes of poverty. There are four areas of confusion present in social work thinking: confusion of scope, confusion of public and professional interest, confusion in conceptual focus, and confusion in methological priority, which must be dissipated if social work is to play a major role in dealing with poverty.

Scope. Social work and social welfare are too often misinterpreted. Social welfare composes all welfare and health activities depending all or in part on community financing (national, state, local; tax and contribution). It is a vast "humanitarian" industry made up of many administrative units which employ many professions and occupations. There are various "products" and a variety of degrees of interdependence among the units. The profession of social work (graduates of schools of social work) does not now occupy a large segment of the social welfare working force. It is questionable whether it ever will. The profession needs to grapple with this issue to determine whether a different set of relationships and roles must be developed.

Public and professional interest. This is a corollary of the scope issue. Public policy is made ultimately by various levels of public authority who are responsible to the taxpaying public. Like all citizens, social workers have a right to express themselves, but no profession can make the public policy. This is not always clear in some professional circles. An impression has been created that social work theorists are attempting to deal with public policy in terms of protecting professional interests. Although social workers can feel safe in claiming that this is not their motive, it is always a danger in any profession. The struggle between representatives of the public interest (including social workers and the social work profession) and the medical profession is a prime example. The social work profession must develop crystal-like clarity between the public and the professional interest.

Conceptual focus. Social work, by and large, is thought of in terms of fields, services, functions, methods, professional criteria, etc., which require deep consideration in living out program policy. But there is the danger that they may be operating in a vacuum unless related firmly to the end product—in this case the elimination of poverty. Thinking about such a deep social and human problem and its solution should have a number one priority. The point of departure for structure, processes, and deployment of personnel, knowledge of their causes, and a clear notion about the end results desired should be the problems to be solved. Social work needs to look carefully at its approaches to determine whether its focus, in regard to poverty, is clear.

Methodological priority. Social work is presently seeking a way toward a better understanding of the detailed processes that go into a social worker's job. From this understanding will come, hopefully, knowledge of how to plan and manage more efficiently and effectively. Applying these approaches to the question at hand, social work must determine whether they are, in their turn, related to a clear concept of the end result desired, that is, the elimination of poverty. Unless clearly related to this objective, the theoretical foundation may be erected on shifting sands.

Total View of Program Approaches

Federal legislative objectives for 1962 promulgated by the American Public Welfare Association include a basic principle:

> A democracy has the special obligation to assure to all persons in the nation full and equitable opportunity for family life, healthful living, and maximum utilization of their potentialities.[47]

Goals of Public Social Policy published by the National Association of Social Workers in 1959 point out that

> Basic to all social advance is a productive economy which offers all individuals the means to an adequate income, provides the financial base for social services, and encourages creative expansion of needed goods and services within an atmosphere of freedom.[48]

Constructive programs to attain these ends and to eliminate poverty must stem from a concept that will solve the problem rather than from one that will provide a means to mitigate its effects. Insofar as hindrances to attainment of the ideal are based on conflicting values, agreement must be sought; facts regarding the incidence and effects of poverty need to be assembled and interpreted; active efforts are necessary to consolidate the support of those who are in accord with the ideal on behalf of varied complementary approaches to solving the problem.

Programs to provide equitable resources and to combat social and psychological frustration should be constantly re-evaluated for their effectiveness in the light of changing circumstances. Just as advances in medicine and public health measures have been of general benefit, just as an increase in the gross national product raises the general standard of living and average income from earnings, so measures to secure a richer, fuller life for all would improve the lot of those in lower income brackets. Still there will be persons and groups that will not automatically share the benefits, who will require special attention. Program approaches include measures to counteract smallness of need by making available earned or substitute income, services to combat largeness of need, and facilities or services to promote optimum development.

Numerous programs aim to forestall the emergency or to counteract

---

[47] *Federal Legislative Objectives* (Chicago: American Public Welfare Association, 1962).

[48] *Goals of Public Social Policy, op. cit.,* p. 36.

the effects of poverty; some are embryonic, and most require development or modification if they are to contribute effectively to abolishing poverty (as well as some of the other social pathologies).

1. *Programs to provide adequate (equitable) resources*
   a. Income maintenance
      (1) Earnings
          (a) Measures to promote high productivity, minimize business fluctuations, promote full employment [49]
          (b) Minimum wage laws
          (c) Removal of discrimination against segments of the population
          (d) Health programs
          (e) Education, advanced programs including discouragement of dropouts
          (f) Vocational training, retraining, and rehabilitation, including special attention to minority groups, migratory or transient workers, young people, women
          (g) Day care centers and homemaker services to free actual or potential wage earners for the labor market
      (2) Substitute financial aid
          (a) Expanded, strengthened, and comprehensive program of social insurance

"The total system of social insurance . . . should protect all workers and their dependents against the major economic hazards of modern life and should provide benefits adequate to maintain a reasonable standard of living commensurate with the nation's productive capacity and sense of social justice." [50]

Pending achievement of such a comprehensive system, existing programs should be improved to ensure more adequate protection against loss of income from disability and a more realistically useful unemployment insurance program: protection for all who work for wages, an increase in benefit levels to reflect the wage level, extension of benefit periods to meet unemployment situations, elimination of restrictive disqualification provisions, and more provision for retraining and rehabilitation (see 1, a, (f) above).

---

[49] Some economists, e.g., Galbraith and Piel, present persuasive arguments against the desirability of striving to increase productivity and full employment, as presently interpreted. Since, in our society, employment (with concomitant earnings) is a major device for the distribution of wealth and also a form of desired activity, a choice between different schools of economic thought would not affect this listing and does not seem essential at this time.

[50] *Goals of Public Social Policy, op. cit.,* p. 13.

(b) Comprehensive program of adequate assistance available to any individual or family whose actual or available economic resources are insufficient to meet a minimum standard of economic and social security consistent with the productive capacity and social requirements of the nation.[51]

b. Promotion of optimum development (combat social and psychological frustrations)
(1) Casework, counseling, mental health services
(2) Information and referral services, especially in nonurban areas
(3) "Character building" activities
(4) Public health and safety programs
(5) Expanded free or low-cost recreation facilities and programs
(6) Slum clearance, urban renewal, and housing programs, including emphasis on social component
(7) Crime prevention and rehabilitation programs

2. *Programs to combat largeness of need*
a. Education for family living, including premarital counseling and household management
b. Counseling for family planning
c. Family allowances
d. Expansion or creation of programs to minimize the burdens of unusual costs, for example medical care for the aged, legal aid, mental health clinics, and homemaker services

All program approaches should include not only consideration for the well-being of the vulnerable population (groups at most obvious risk) but also for the benefit of the total society. Also the effectiveness of the program depends on many logistic factors.

The Sector Appropriate to Social Work

The scope and function of social work have not been and perhaps cannot be clearly defined. The confusion with the broader term "social welfare" has already been noted. Wilensky and Lebeaux's exposition of two conceptions of social welfare is useful. During the period between the two world wars the scope and function of social work were primarily limited within the residual concept; since then the institutional approach has become increasingly prominent.[52] Wickenden states that functionally

---

[51] Elizabeth Wickenden and Winifred Bell, *Public Welfare: Time for a Change* (New York: Columbia University Press, 1961).
[52] Wilensky and Lebeaux, *op. cit.*

social welfare can be considered as the instrument through which organized society provides assurance that (1) the recognized social needs of individuals will be met and (2) those social relationships and adjustments necessary to its own functioning will be facilitated.[53]

Within the broad field, social work is appropriately concerned with services that have direct effects on the welfare of individuals and families and has responsibility for three types of activity: (1) operations and services to help individuals, families, and groups to solve problems in relation to the social and economic forces by which they are affected and to meet needs that are not adequately met by the individual or by the family and the market economy; (2) alertness to emergent needs and promotion of "social services and institutions designed to aid individuals to attain satisfying standards of health and life," fostering "personal and social relationships which permit individuals the fullest development of their capacities and the promotion of their well-being in harmony with the needs of the community"; [54] (3) an organized effort to support or oppose politico-economic measures on the basis of critical analysis of their impact on human needs and personality development.

More specifically, social work is the social institution primarily dedicated to programs to preserve and strengthen human resources. In operation it is administrative, catalytic, critical, and supportive. In one sense its functions are residual. Unlike allied fields, such as health, education, religion, economics, and psychology, which tend to exclude all save specific aspects of the socio-economic environment from their purview, social work cannot exclude from consideration any aspect of the life of the person who seeks help in solving problems of social adjustment . . . or any of the community's other social institutions that might be of use to the individual.[55] Functioning as one of numerous normal institutions in helping individuals achieve self-fulfillment, social work is in a particularly sensitive position to support other activities which promote that goal.

In relation to the problem of poverty, social work's direct operations include a variety of services and such programs as financial assistance, casework, household management or homemaker services, substitute homes, institutional care, and consultative services to ensure inclusion of the "human angle" in programs (such as urban renewal) which have another primary focus.

In the constant effort to strengthen and promote social welfare pro-

---

53 Wickenden and Bell, *op. cit.*
54 Friedlander, *op. cit.*
55 Wilensky and Lebeaux, *op. cit.*

grams, social work has the capacity, the commitment, and the responsibility to document existing and emerging needs. Within its operational limits, it promotes programs that can eliminate problems that require the direct intervention of social work. It also has a role in organizing social planning of elements and forces that might relieve poverty. Examples include social insurance, more adaptable job-creating policies and more adequate unemployment insurance, effective job training, civil rights legislation, slum clearance and urban renewal, realistic education programs, early availability of medical care and rehabilitation services, positive provision for developmental needs of all children, and recreation and cultural facilities and opportunities.

Social work recognizes that in a democracy the social good and individual welfare are interdependent. This also requires explicit recognition of interdependence among social institutions and the entire social structure. Fulfillment of social work's functions of treatment, prevention, and promotion of positive goals requires taking a position on socioeconomic theories and proposals. There is widespread awareness of the effect on human lives of the theories of the "classical" economists and the mercantilists. The impact of Keynesian tenets is less well known. Cultural values regarding the social responsibilities of government, business, and the individual are now in flux. Publications and recommendations from such sources as the Congressional Joint Economic Committee and economists Galbraith, Keyserling, and Heller reveal some of the many directions in which social work should explore in seeking alliances in the goal to eliminate poverty. And, as previously noted, social work needs to clear up some of the confusions about its role.

RELATIONSHIP BETWEEN THE ACTUAL AND THE IDEAL

The most obvious gap between what is being done and what must be done to solve the problem of poverty is a matter of approach. Social work's focus has been primarily ideographic, confined largely to stopgap measures to mitigate the effects of poverty on individuals or groups; other institutions, using a nomothetic approach, promote programs, such as full employment insurance plus education, which, it is hoped, will be of universal benefit. A reconstituted view of poverty as a problem—a continuing phenomenon which can be eradicated—is a fairly recent development.

As Wilbur Cohen stressed in an address on April 13, 1960:

> *We need an affirmative national program to accelerate the reduction of low incomes in the United States. This problem cannot be left to natural economic forces—to economic growth—or to the impersonal*

elements of the market place. *We can, if we wish, and we must, make abolition of poverty a national goal and a national policy.*[56]

The measures being taken do not attain their own goals and need improvement and re-examination. In addition, and perhaps more important, a concerted, coordinated problem-solving effort is not operative. There is no common knowledge of the incidence of poverty. There is a lack of consensus that it can and should be eradicated and nonagreement regarding means of eliminating the phenomenon.

Although they recognize that income figures do not indicate how many are living at substandard levels, the Congressional Joint Economic Committee estimates that the substantial number of families subsisting at permanently depressed levels includes approximately 20 percent of the population. Despite the general rise in family income, since World War II the trend has been reversed for the lowest income group. In 1959 14 percent of the population (7.5 million families with incomes under $2000) received about 2 percent of the total family income.[57]

Although unemployment is not necessarily identical with low income, the facts are significant because of a tendency to equate full employment with efforts to dispel poverty. In May 1961 five million Americans, representing 7 percent of the labor force, were reported out of work. The average duration of long-term unemployment (fifteen weeks or longer) has increased sharply in recent years. (Workers displaced by technological advance or movement of industries are generally not the ones with skills in demand by newer industries; moreover, newer enterprises may not locate in the same general area.)

Social insurance standards, including unemployment compensation and public assistance, are, at best, based on minimum subsistence concepts. It is not known how many persons, including recipients of OASI, have incomes that fall below public assistance budgetary standards. Some undoubtedly are deterred from applying for assistance by such factors as pride, misinformation, or restrictive eligibility provisions. Great variation and disparity exist among states and among different categories of recipients of public assistance in eligibility requirements, in concepts of what constitutes adequacy and in the way standards are met. Speaking in 1956, Wilbur Cohen recognized that since the depression of the early thirties standards had been modified to adjust to changing prices but questioned whether they had been modified "to take account of our rising standard of living, our belief in prevention

---

[56] "Public Welfare in the Soaring Sixties," address at Central States Regional Conference of the American Public Welfare Association, St. Paul, Minn., April 13, 1960. (Mimeographed.)

[57] Publications of the Joint Economic Committee, January 1947–March 1960 (Washington, D. C.: U. S. Government Printing Office, 1960).

and rehabilitation, in the importance of protecting and strengthening family life," and whether assistance was being provided in relation to the current economy.

He pointed out that "we have 3.5 percent of the population receiving public assistance and the total public assistance expenditures are no more than eight-tenths of one percent of our gross national product." [58]

For an economy in which high productivity relies on stimulated consumption the gap is peculiarly ironic.

Resistance to Closing the Gap

In social work the major sources of deterrence to a positive effective determination to eradicate poverty are evident as cultural lag.   The reasons for cultural lag explicated by Ogburn are almost all found within the social work community.[59]

It has been pointed out that ever accelerating changes in the material culture during the present century have been swifter than they had been for the preceding two thousand or even five thousand years.

Social work (as well as other social institutions) has failed to devise social inventions to keep pace with these changes.   Mechanical obstacles include the structure and the nature of sponsorship of social work activities, statutory enactments, and agency charters. Heterogeneity within the field is marked by differences in focus, emphasis, and priorities. In view of continued personnel limitations, a dedication to the elimination of poverty as a major goal might be resisted as requiring relinquishment or diminution of development in other selected areas. Emotional values of approval have become attached to habitual ways of doing things, sometimes marked by a form of ritualism or preoccupation with the minutiae of procedure without consideration of its effectiveness as a means to and end.

The stress on individualism in social work is not always attuned to the broad approach required in solving a social problem. Emphasis on art and trained skill can de-emphasize the need for new scientfiic methodology.

Adherence to the "residual" concept of social work mitigates against efforts to shift its function and scope into harmonious adjustment with all parts of the changing culture in an organized effort to prevent, control, and eventually eradicate poverty.

The importance of services in breaking the cycle of poverty is recognized.   The fact that (for various reasons) these services are not pro-

[58] Wilbur J. Cohen, "Gearing Public Welfare to Our Maturing Economy," address to North Eastern Regional Conference of the American Public Welfare Association, Pittsburgh, September 21, 1956.

[59] William Fielding Ogburn, *Social Change* (New York: B. W. Huebsch, 1922).

vided is not adequately publicized or interpreted. This may be because of defensiveness or the nonvoiced realization that—if stressed—it could logically necessitate a re-evaluation of cherished operations and re-deployment of manpower and skills. A protective form of self-delusion may be marked in what Beck terms "the panoramic conception of prevention" which he declares "obscures the need for the painful process of actually gearing programs to solve social problems" . . . and . . . "is unnecessary and misleading." [60]

A challenge was voiced by Abraham Ribicoff, as Secretary of Health, Education, and Welfare, at the 1961 National Conference on Social Welfare:

> . . . it seems to me in the urgent national interest that you—each and every one of you—help put the "social" back into social work. . . . Stop worrying about your "professional status." Cut down your verbiage and your long-winded memoranda. Join us in the programs which we have, which we will undertake—campaigns against slums and poverty in the midst of plenty, of segregation and group tensions, of the terrors of old age. Break down the walls of artificial specialties and subspecialties. . . . Stop worrying about "intake" and whether you and I can "relate" to one another. We have work to do. Let us take a hard look at our training methods. . . . The time has come for all of us to throw out our old, stereotyped ideas. The time has come for all of us to do a lot of soul searching, to look within ourselves in the light of experience and come up with new ways to meet new problems. . . .

Outside social work also cultural lag is a major factor in deterring positive organized action to abolish poverty. Obsolescent attitudes rooted in the poverty, inequality, and economic peril of the past have become sacrosanct. Enthusiasm about the rise in the gross national product, average incomes, and general standards of living promotes confidence in the adequacy of existing institutions, and blurs awareness or recognition of the continuing existence of poverty as a social problem.

Self-protection against anxiety operates in a refusal to admit that individual initiative and existing institutions cannot provide assurance against the hazard of economic want. Stress on the values of individualism, freedom from interference, and achievement are used to perpetuate the conviction that poverty is the result of individual shortcomings or of a temporary recession in business, the insistence that the individual (taxpayer) has an inalienable right to control personally the distribution of his accumulated share of the national wealth and income. Planning and organization of social welfare services are resisted as vitiating

---

[60] Bertram M. Beck, "Can Social Work Prevent Social Problems?" *Social Welfare Forum*, 1960 (New York: Columbia University Press, 1960), pp. 180–193.

humanitarian impulses and weakening initiative. The value and necessity of investing in human capital, of developing human resources, are downgraded or denied.

Many of these beliefs and attitudes find expression or support in economic theories that accentuate the unfavorable and repressive forces in the economy. They appear as a tight-money policy which seeks to balance the federal budget by postponing essential public programs until the economy can "afford" them or stressing that they can be financed only by higher tax rates.

The Conference on Economic Progress points out:

> There is widespread and effective propaganda that this neglect of the public welfare by the Federal Budget is beneficial to the economy and the people. It is claimed that this neglect is beneficial by leaving more money in the hands of the people for them to spend for the enjoyment of private goods and services; by permitting lower tax rates or lower Federal deficits than would otherwise be the case; by avoiding the inflation which it is alleged would result from higher public outlays; and by being generally helpful to our economic strength and growth.[61]

Government subsidization of industry is firmly entrenched; the necessity of farm supports is conceded. Provision of assistance and services to individuals above the level of bare subsistence is resisted on the basis of the argument that everyone (or at least every able-bodied person) should be encouraged to solve his own problems.

Lay theorists and voters affirm the advantages of the "school of hard knocks," the efficacy of hardship in developing initiative, and the dangers of coddling the weak or encouraging "chiselers."

Support for Closing the Gap

Fundamental traditions of social work, with its roots in philanthropy and charity, support efforts to use society's resources to abolish poverty.

In the United States in the nineteenth century increasing stress on the scientific approach included efforts to document and analyze the causes of poverty. In 1886 the Honorable William Howard Neff in his presidential address at the National Conference of Charities and Correction stated:

> Prevention is better and more satisfactory than cure. . . . No one is satisfied with the mere administration of relief. Our province is to search deeper for the cause. . . . Pauperism is not a plant of American growth. . . . We must extirpate it—not by cruelty, but by kindness. . . .[62]

---

[61] Conference on Economic Progress, *op. cit.*

[62] *Proceedings, 1886*, National Conference of Charities and Correction (Boston: Press of George H. Ellis, 1886), pp. 12–18.

At the turn of the century Warner could write:

> The modern charity worker . . . now demands that ultimately justice shall precede charity, and prevention take the place of cure. It was once the accepted doctrine that prosperity and happiness were the natural results and regards of goodness, but the social worker in daily contact with the poor sees that their poverty comes from a deeper source than the vices or virtues of the individual—from sources which can be reached only by industrial and social changes. . . . In the knowledge of this fact, the charitable . . . take part . . . in the greater movement for the abolition of conditions which make dependence inevitable.[63]

Findings of surveys supported the social reform movement. Getting the facts and social diagnosis are part of social work's basic equipment. The field values its preparedness to meet existing needs, its patterns of self-evaluation, and its flexibility, and there is increasing evidence of reawakened concern with the problem of poverty and the possibility of its solution.

"Elder statesmen" at the 1960 National Conference on Social Welfare highlighted the eradication of poverty in discussing goals that should be given priority by social workers. In the following year "Toward the Elimination of Poverty" was one of the four subjects of major focus at these sessions, of which more than a dozen were specifically devoted to the problem.[64]

Reference has already been made to the policies and goals of national social work organizations. In recent years sources outside social work have assumed leadership in stressing the feasibility and desirability of measures to eliminate poverty. No listing could be exhaustive. Speakers on the subject at the sessions of the 1961 Conference on Social Welfare represented a variety of fields, including politics, anthropology, economics, education, and psychiatry.[65]

Stressing the values of humanitarianism as well as efficiency and practicality, economists have estimated the relatively reasonable financial cost and the benefit to society of eliminating pockets of poverty. Philosophers, religious leaders, and spokesmen for minority groups have added emphasis on democracy, equality, and progress. Sociologists and social psychologists test methods of research which can promote solution of social problems. Activities by organized labor include pressures to raise standards of living. Business expansion and productivity continue to narrow the gap.

---

[63] Warner, *op. cit.*
[64] *Social Welfare Forum,* 1960 and 1961 (New York: Columbia University Press, 1960 and 1961).
[65] *Ibid.*

The federal government during 1961–1962 called on experts, including social workers, for re-evaluations of present programs, which led to recommendations designed to promote the well-being of the economy and of the individual. As a result, there has been a proliferation of proposals or measures which stress the value of adequate outlays for programs that directly service individuals, such as education, health, and protection from the handicaps accompanying old age, unemployment, and poverty. President Kennedy's welfare message to the Congress in February 1962 as well as his messages on economy, trade, and agriculture were all directed, in some measure, to the goal of eliminating poverty.

Action Priorities for Social Work

In his address to the 1961 National Conference on Social Welfare Dr. Duhl posed the question, "Are we mentally prepared for the elimination of poverty?" [66]

If the aim is to be substantially achieved, the first priority for social work must be a new sense of commitment—a determination and dedication to try to solve problems superseding a focus on addition of services and treatment of symptoms. To implement such a determination, a framework for comprehensive diagnosis as a basis for differential treatment must be devised. A major task is to get rid of the notion (within and outside social work thinking) that the deviant, the abnormal, the pathological, and, in general, the deplorable always come wrapped in a single package. [67]

Within the spectrum of poverty, criteria for treatment and prevention must be established. In other words, if rehabilitative action is to be taken when a problem has occurred or to prevent one that may occur, it must be known precisely what is to be prevented. Definitions must be clarified and standards established and then applied uniformly and systematically within agencies and in the community. The concept of prevention of the onset of the problem should be documented, interpreted, and publicized. Provision must be made for evaluation and modification of problem-solving efforts. The principle of accountability should be accepted and anticipated.

The history of social welfare is replete with examples of the development of instrumentalities and services which reached the point of overlapping but did not meet needs as they emerged. At the present time new evaluations are urgently needed to determine what changes in

[66] Leonard J. Duhl, M.D., "Are We Mentally Prepared for the Elimination of Poverty?" *Social Welfare Forum*, 1961 (New York: Columbia University Press, 1961).

[67] Robert K. Merton, Leonard Broom, and Leonard S. Cottrell, Jr., *Sociology Today* (New York: Basic Books, 1959).

structure, policies, and practices within the field will best promote attainment of social work goals. In relation to the elimination of poverty, recommendations for change should be based on developments outlined in the preceding section. These recommendations could lead to some shifting of responsibility for primary activities. Consideration must be given to the appropriate and most effective divisions of financial and of operational responsibility among the three levels of government and among public and private agencies. In directing efforts to problem solving, criteria must be developed for the communitywide allocation of responsibility and the optimum deployment of skills. Thoughtful (rather than defensive) attention to negative criticism should spark fruitful self-evaluation and corrective action. Patterns of insight developed for use in service should be extended and utilized in interpretation of problems, values, and goals.

The federal government has already assumed leadership in promoting an action program for families receiving public financial assistance. This program includes more effective administrative procedures and rehabilitative and protective services and the encouragement of more effective coordinated family and community welfare services. Social work should actively support the implementation of this program, not only because it is aimed at an improvement of ameliorative and protective programs, but even more because these measures are conceived as a part of a total strengthening of community action that prevents dependency.

Pressure should be exerted toward abolition of categorical divisions, restrictions, inequalities, and inadequacies in current programs which are certainly outdated (and some of which, however expedient at the time of their inception, may never have been in accord with current values). Social work must combat all forms of discrimination so that equal opportunities are available to all.

Social work should actively participate in efforts to reverse the irrational concept that public services are a burden rather than something to be sought and purchased like any privately produced or sponsored commodity that promotes well-being. Social work does not, should not, and cannot assume sole or even primary responsibility for the elimination of poverty. It must not abrogate the responsibility it has.

As Wilbur Cohen pointed out in an address to the American Public Welfare Association in St. Paul in April 1960:

> More than ever before, matters affecting the economy, the social structure, the family, and individual aspirations will be determined by tax policies, national defense expenditures, interest and investment policies and expenditures for education, research, health, scientific advancements, and welfare. Contrary to conventional wisdom, sound

policies in these vital areas for national growth and survival are not necessarily determined by impersonal forces of supply and demand. You—and the organizations to which you belong—and your representatives in government can—and will—have a significant role to play in the decision-making process.[68]

With rapidly changing conditions, priorities for social work in relation to non-social work groups and forces are best stated less in terms of specific action than as a speedy realization of the function that social work must strengthen. Far-reaching policy decisions are being made. Whether or not they are in accord with social work goals, including the elimination of poverty, depends, at least in part, on the effectiveness of social work's awareness and active support. In recognizing social action as part of its function and in establishing goals for social policy social work admits that it must go beyond mitigation of present social handicaps and its own efforts in rehabilitation and prevention to participate in drives toward better adaptation of all social policies and institutions to changing needs and aspirations.[69] This recognition must be more extensively and intensively implemented. Social work has in Washington one paid lobbyist and some strong spokemen who maintain a critical alertness to the ways in which social institutions or policies are likely to affect individuals. Throughout the field there must be strengthened awareness of such implications, a participation in efforts to promote measures that are in accord with social work goals.

In the documentation of human need and the development of mutual obligation between individuals and their social organizations social work should assume the lead. This lead can be constructive and effective only if it takes into consideration the knowledge and competence of non-social work groups and forces. Social work is meeting a first priority by becoming more conversant and working more closely with them.

[68] "Public Welfare in the Soaring Sixties," *op. cit.*
[69] *Social Work Year Book, 1960, op. cit.*

Marital Incompatibility ▶

WERNER A. LUTZ

DEFINITION OF MARRIAGE

Everybody knows what it means to be married, yet upon reflection even so familiar a word as marriage is difficult to define precisely. Dictionary definitions tend to be merely circular: marriage is the relationship between husband and wife; husband and wife are persons related to each other by marriage.

Further reflection raises the hope that marriage might be defined as a state, an institution, and a relationship characterized by certain purposes, behaviors, and consequences. Difficulties arise immediately. Some skeptic can always point to a society in which some of the purposes, behaviors, and consequences are lacking in a social relationship which otherwise has all the characteristics of marriage as it is understood in the United States.

It becomes necessary, finally, to settle for the observation that in most or all societies, depending on the anthropological authorities cited, a social arrangement can be identified which is characterized by some of a certain set of purposes, behaviors, and consequences. The terms used by various societies for this social arrangement can conveniently be translated into the English term "marriage," as applied to a similar social arrangement in the societies of the United States and Great Britain. It should be noted at the outset, however, that the social arrangement called marriage in the United States differs in many ways from marriage as found in other societies.

Purposes, Behaviors, Consequences, and Values

In contemporary social theory a sharp distinction is drawn between purposes and consequences. The differences between what a person wishes to happen or intends to have happen and what actually does happen become the focal point for productive research. The term function is restricted to mean the consequences of the operation of a system.

41

The functions of marriage, in any society, are the events that actually follow from the ways in which marriages operate in that society.

In a discussion of marital incompatibility, however, it is necessary to remark that what people wish or intend to have happen often coincides with what actually does happen. Purposes and consequences are roughly identical. The motivations that impel individuals to marry generally correspond to the "functions" of marriage. The sociologist may find that the provision of reciprocal emotional support and gratification between the spouses and the ranking of the family in the social order are "functions" or consequences of marriage in a society. Closer clinical inspection will probably reveal that in such a society individuals enter marriage for the purpose of giving and receiving emotional support and gratification and choose partners with whom such a relationship seems possible. Moreover, individuals will tend to choose spouses of a desirable social status in the hope and expectation that the spouse's rank will be conferred on them.

There are good reasons for this correspondence between intentions and outcomes. Granted all the complex, bewildering, and frustrating interplay of forces in human affairs, human beings still possess some capacity to act rationally, to solve problems, and to adjust means to ends, whether as individuals or in association with others.

Moreover, and much to the point, such planning and problem solving are carried on within the context of value-orientations. Both individual and social goals are largely defined in terms of such orientations, and the means adopted, individually and socially, to achieve valued ends must be comfortable to values present in the society.

Throughout this discussion, the terms "value" and "value-orientation" are used in accord with the meanings attributed to them in Kluckhohn's definitions. Of value, Kluckhohn writes, "A value is a conception, explicit or implicit, distinctive of an individual or characteristic of a group, of the desirable which influences the selection from available modes, means, and ends of action." [1]

Although Kluckhohn's refined analysis of the meaning of each of the terms used in this definition would repay close study, it may suffice here to comment only on two of the component terms. A value is a conception, that is, it is, in part, an abstract, generalized idea. It may be said, perhaps, in older philosophical terms that it is a universal. It has a cognitive aspect. Further, a value is a conception of the "desirable." The distinction to be observed here is between that which is desired and that which is desirable. Any married individual may at times wish he

[1] Clyde Kluckhohn, "Values and Value Orientations in the Theory of Action," in Talcott Parsons and Edward A. Shils, *Toward a General Theory of Action* (Cambridge, Mass.: Harvard University Press, 1952), p. 395.

could have sexual enjoyment with someone other than his spouse. Limited or complete sexual freedom may be "desired." But this by no means coincides with the idea that sexual freedom is "desirable," either in the eyes of the individual or of society at large. The idea of "desirable" makes a distinction between what is right and wrong, appropriate or inappropriate, fitting or unfitting. In brief, it introduces the notions of morality and taste and the further notion of normative standards or criteria of judgment in such matters. Finally, it introduces the aspect of cathexis. Values are not matters of indifference to those who hold them, be they individuals or social institutions. A conception cannot function as an idea of the "desirable" unless someone or some group of people endows it with feeling. A value, to be a value, must be cherished or opposed. In summary, to quote Kluckhohn:

> The word *desirable*, then, brings out the fact that values, whether individual or cultural (and the line between these is elusive), always have an affective as well as a cognitive dimension. Values are never immediately altered by a mere logical demonstration of their invalidity. The combination of *conception* with *desirable* establishes the union of reason and feeling inherent in the word *value*. Both components must be included in any definition.[2]

Of the term value-orientation Kluckhohn writes, "It is convenient to use the term *value-orientation* for those value notions which are (a) general, (b) organized, and (c) include definitely existential judgments. A value-orientation is a set of linked propositions embracing both value and existential judgments."[3]

This line of reasoning leads Kluckhohn to a more concrete definition of the term value-orientation: "More formally, a *value-orientation* may be defined as a *generalized and organized conception, influencing behavior, of nature, man's place in it, of man's relation to man, and of the desirable and non-desirable as they may relate to man-environment and interhuman relations.*"[4]

Generalized value-orientations occur in two forms. They are cathected ideas in the minds of individual human beings or, to follow the language of *Toward a General Theory of Action*, organized need-dispositions which make up parts of the personalities of individuals. Shared value-orientations serve as one element in binding individuals together into various forms of social institutions: families, groups, business firms, social classes, states, nations. Value-orientations also exist in the form of systems of symbols: the "meanings" of books, the forms of graphic art, liturgies and rituals, and, indeed, every cultural artifact. Most im-

[2] *Ibid.*, p. 400.
[3] *Ibid.*, p. 409.
[4] *Ibid.*, p. 411.

portantly, perhaps, as systems of symbols, they convey the meanings of what husband and wife, parent and child, brother and sister, friend and friend communicate to each other in language and action. Value-orientations serve to "define situations" for individuals and, insofar as they are shared, for the social institutions into which human beings group themselves. Value-orientations determine what is problematical in a situation; what ends may be or should be sought; what means may be or should be adopted or avoided; what persons or physical objects may be or should be involved or let alone.

Value-orientations serve to link purposes and consequences, expectations and outcomes. A shared value-orientation determines, on the one hand, the goals and means that a society or some part of it presents to the individual as desirable. The same shared value-orientation is communicated to the individuals in the society and becomes an internalized value-orientation, an organized need-disposition, which channels and guides their selection of goals and means to achieve gratifications, avoid frustrations, and make the most of their potentialities.

If the value-orientations in society determine that marriage should result in the channeling of sexual expression within the marriage, it is likely that most individuals in the society will subscribe to this requirement. They will regard sexual fidelity as desirable. Cognitively, they will rationalize the standard to themselves. Affectively, they will define other persons than the spouse as improper sexual objects, and the value-barrier may be so strong with some individuals that such persons are not even desired. Morally, those who trespass the code will feel guilty. Above all, members of the society will, by precept and example, communicate the standard to their children.

Sources of discrepancy between expectations and outcomes, hopes and results may occur on various grounds. The very fact of internal structure in any system, whether it be a personality or an institution, imposes strains and internal conflict. For many reasons value-orientations may be imperfectly incorporated or inadequately institutionalized and so fail to serve as guides to action. Even in the simplest personalities and societies there are competing value-orientations. Value systems may function unconsciously in personalities and so be inaccessible to external influences.

In both individuals and institutions they may exist and function but be unacknowledged. Their actual influence on action may be rationalized in terms of some competing or contradictory value-orientation. Values themselves may exist as isolated standards, discrepant from organized value-orientations. Finally, value-orientations at best serve as generalized guides to action. They still leave the individual faced with concrete dilemmas. The complex variables that, in addition to value-orientations, influence his choices may well take him off in directions he does not entirely intend and which may have unhappy social consequences.

Theoretical Components of Marriage

Marriage as a social arrangement characterized by a certain set of purposes or expectations, behaviors, and consequences may be analyzed into structural and functional components.

Among the structural elements are the composition of the arrangement; its temporal characteristics; the degree to which it is related to and differentiated from other social arrangements, especially surrounding kinship groupings; the rules of locality that apply to the arrangement; and the nature and degree of its control over power and resources.

Among the functional elements are the consequences of marriage for the social placement and ranking of the spouses and their children; for the production, distribution, and consumption of material resources; for the sexual gratification of the marital partners; for social control of unacceptable impulses; for the production, nurture, and socialization of children; and for the provision of emotional satisfactions.

MARRIAGE IN THE UNITED STATES [5]

Structural Aspects of Marriage in the United States

Composition. Structurally, marriage in the United States is monogamous. No provision is made for any form of polygamy. Attempts to engage in polygamy by members of religious sects which

---

[5] The literature on marriage and the family in the United States is almost inexhaustible. Milton Yinger's paper, "The Changing Family in a Changing Society," *Social Casework*, Vol. 40, No. 8, October 1959, p. 419, provides a useful introduction to the subject and attempts to summarize the implications of some important recent studies. The author would draw attention to the following works: Nathan W. Ackerman, M.D., *The Psychodynamics of Family Life. Diagnosis and Treatment of Family Relationships* (New York: Basic Books, 1958). Dr. Ackerman's book has gained such wide attention that familiarity with it must be assumed. Norman W. Bell and Ezra F. Vogel, eds., *A Modern Introduction to the Family* (New York: The Free Press of Glencoe, Illinois, 1960). The papers in this book are selected and arranged in accordance with a systematic theoretical view of the family. The editors acknowledge their theoretical debt to Talcott Parsons and his associates. The papers themselves provide a comprehensive sociological analysis of the family. Evelyn Millis Duval, *Family Development* (Philadelphia: J. B. Lippincott Company, 2d ed., 1962). A comprehensive theoretical and factual discussion of the family in terms of its "life cycle." Victor W. Eisenstein, M.D., ed., *Neurotic Interaction in Marriage* (New York: Basic Books, 1956). The papers in this book are very useful in selecting the theoretical contributions and findings of psychoanalysis with respect to marriage. William J. Goode, "The Sociology of the Family,"

accept the practice are sternly repressed by police action. The positions of "mistress" and "paramour" are stigmatized under the pejorative terms, "the other woman" and "the other man." No rights, social or legal, attach to these positions. Throughout most of the society, lineage and legitimacy are strictly confined to the issue of a legal marriage. Adoption is accepted by most, but not by all, subcultures as a substitute way of extending the lineage. There is some limited tendency to regard the patriarchal line as of greater lineal importance than the matriarchal. Among some racial subcultures recognition as a lineal member of the family is not necessarily confined to children who are issue of a legal marriage, and the status of illegitimacy may not carry such a weight of condemnation for the mother and child.

Duration. Publicly, society demands that the partners act, on contracting marriage, as if they expect it to last until death. Provision may be made for formal, legal dissolution of marriage by annulment or divorce or for suspension of marital interaction by means of legal separation.

Grounds for terminating or suspending marriage tend to be narrowly and rigidly defined except in certain states which offer social "escape valves." The legal action is cast into the form of an adversary proceeding in which one partner is alleged to have injured the other. In many parts of the society some degree of overt or covert stigma attaches to one or both spouses involved in proceedings for annulment, divorce, or separation. A cultural myth tends to define the divorced woman as eager and available for extramarital sexual exploitation. The Roman Catholic Church, the largest single denomination in the United States, permits divorce only under special circumstances. Divorce is expensive to obtain. In the poorer strata of the social order informal separation or desertion is frequently used as a way of dissolving marriage. Remarriages are rationalized as having "common law" status, even though the law may make no provision for such status.

A formal divorce decree may not dissolve all the rights and responsibilities of the marital partners. Usually, custody of the children is awarded to one of the spouses. The other, except in cases of conduct adjudged flagrantly irresponsible or exploitative, is granted the right to visiting privileges and, frequently, periodic temporary custody

---

in *Sociology Today, Problems and Prospects*, Robert K. Merton, Leonard Broom, and Leonard S. Cottrell, Jr., eds. (New York: Basic Books, 1959), p. 178. This article makes a critical appraisal of the state of current sociological theory and research concerning the family. Robert D. Hess and Gerald Handel, *Family Worlds. A Psychosocial Approach to Family Life* (Chicago: University of Chicago Press, 1959). In an introductory chapter and a series of case studies Hess and Handel manage to communicate an understanding of the ways in which personality and the social functioning of the family interpenetrate each other.

of the children. One partner, usually the wife, may be awarded alimony from the other for the support of herself and her children.

Despite the difficulties that society tends to place in the way of the termination of a marriage, second marriage is generally regarded as permissible even in the face of prohibition or discouragement by various denominations of the Christian religion. Indeed, there is some evidence that second marriage for either spouse has relatively good prospects for success in terms of compatibility and permanence.

Differentiation from other arrangements. Sharp differentiation is drawn between each new marriage and the family of orientation of either spouse. Each spouse is expected by his partner and the larger society to separate himself socially and emotionally from ties to parents, brothers, sisters and, in large degree, unmarried friends. "Running home to mother" as a technique for handling marital difficulties is discouraged by the parents and is dealt with socially by means of humor and ridicule. The position of in-law is loosely defined and entails no legal and few social responsibilities of any degree of urgency.

Abode. Both the spouses and the society regard it as a matter of right and of common prudence for the spouses to set up a permanent joint abode apart from all other kin except the children who may result from the marriage. The social or economic necessity to live with the parents of either spouse or to take parents or relatives into the home during the early years of marriage is regarded as a misfortune. It is the policy of the federal government to make it possible for each family to purchase its own home by guarantees of mortgages and by making interest on the mortgage deductible from the family's income for purposes of taxation. In response to the increasing demand of the economic system for geographic mobility on the part of families, the couple and society accept the prospect that each family of procreation will move freely to whatever part of the country or the world seems to offer the greatest economic advantage.

Control of power and resources. Except perhaps among the rich and in some subcultures that adhere to the ways of an "old country," there are no formal expectations that either bride or groom will bring a dowry to the marriage. On the other hand, there is an expectation that "shower" and wedding presents will be given to enable the young couple to accumulate basic household goods to set up the new home. Such giving is frequently influenced more by fashion and the symbolic status values of goods than by the utilitarian requirements of the young couple. Once the marriage has been solemnized, the wife usually acquires certain legal "dower rights" in her husband's estate and the legal right to support from him for any children who may issue from the marriage.

In some respects society continues to recognize the marital partners as individuals rather than as holders of positions in a social institution. Each may possess real and personal property in his own name. Each is responsible for his own acts before the law, though neither can be required to testify against the other. Provision is made, however, to recognize their common interests through community property arrangements and the option of filing joint income tax returns.

Power, in the sense of the acknowledgment by others of one's right to control their decisions and circumstances, is severely limited in American middle-class marriages.[6] In the very uppermost strata of society marriage into a dynasty may afford access to a large measure of economic or social power. Elsewhere in the social order, however, marriage itself affords very little access to opportunities to exert power and influence.

Power and authority are also limited within the family. Except in the matter of sexual fidelity, neither spouse typically grants the other power to control his or her actions. Rather, the culture prescribes that husbands and wives cooperate and compromise in deciding on goals and on means of achieving them. Power over children is limited both legally and socially.

Functional Aspects of Marriage in the United States

Social placement and ranking. Americans adhere publicly to the value of an open society. There is some tendency to deny that placement and ranking of individuals and families occur. In somewhat contradictory fashion it is held that opportunity is or should be open to any individual to proceed upward in the social scale by demonstrating the desirable attributes. Education is held to constitute the sovereign preparation for such progress.

Actually, families are placed and ranked in terms of their possession of economic resources and their display of the cultural symbols of such possession, their color, ethnic background, and religious affiliation. Strong pressure is exerted on individuals and families to move upward. At the same time, strong barriers are erected against such movement. The degree to which upward movement is actually possible is not well known. The barriers are especially strong against members of the nonwhite races. They are less so but still of considerable rigidity with respect to ethnic background and religious affiliation. They are least so with respect to the attainment of the marks of high economic status. One of the most vicious aspects of the American class system is the

---

[6] For a penetrating discussion of the concepts of power and authority, *see* Samuel Mencher, "The Concept of Authority and Social Casework," *Casework Papers,* National Conference on Social Welfare (1960), p. 126.

tendency to stigmatize and stereotype as constitutionally inferior the members of races, ethnic groups, and religions to whom opportunity for social advancement has been denied.

In American marriages the social placement of the wife and children predominantly follows that of the husband and father. In view of the social isolation and geographic mobility of the family of procreation in the United States, married couples can often dissociate themselves from the status of their parents. If opportunities are available, the married couple may achieve a new and higher status than was possessed by their families. The result of such movement may be further isolation of the marriages of each generation. In a somewhat different form isolation may occur today between husbands and wives when the husband, stimulated and enriched by his experiences in a complex occupational world, "moves beyond" the wife he chose as a young man.

In general, families of orientation prefer that their daughters "marry upward." It is acceptable for sons to "marry downward" but preferably not so far downward that embarrassing social notice is taken of the status difference between the young people. Families of orientation tend to prefer that their sons and daughters marry within the racial, ethnic, and religious groups. Marriages across racial lines are bitterly and even violently opposed.

In American marriages there is a tendency for the role of the wife to include responsibility for patterned attitudes, values, and behaviors which demonstrate and symbolize, maintain, or increase the social status of the family. In the upper range of the class structure this aspect of the wife's role may become almost ritualized in its grades and types of activity. Here belong the spectacular (or unobtrusively rich) patterns of expenditure and consumption: the participation in Junior Leagues and assemblies, the charity balls, the sponsorship of the arts. In the upper middle and middle classes activities similar in type though different in content are delegated to the wife; there is, perhaps, greater emphasis on activities that carry civic responsibility. In the lower middle class church activities become prominent. In the lower classes the prestige-maintaining role of the wife is not so marked, but she is often expected to be clean and neat as a sign of respectability.

At points the function of maintaining and demonstrating social placement merges into the economic functions of the family. This merging function is seen in the wife's determination of the consumption patterns of the family in accord with the standards of the social class to which the family belongs or aspires. It is openly recognized at the executive levels of business and the officer levels of the armed forces that a wife's social graces contribute in important ways to her husband's professional and economic advancement.

Economics and housekeeping.   The "ideal type" of division of labor between husband and wife prescribes separate economic tasks for each. He is expected to participate actively in the economic system to earn money to support both and to provide funds for achieving their common goals. She is expected to remain at home to perform the instrumental tasks necessary to maintain a household and to set the patterns of consumption for the family within the income provided by her husband. In addition, she is expected to carry on the noneconomic but indispensable activities necessary to the nurture and socialization of the children.

This division of labor has altered so radically during the last two generations that some sociologists hold that a new basic pattern of division of economic labor is emerging. Today wives more frequently than not expect and are expected by their husbands and by society to engage in economically oriented activities outside the home for various purposes at various stages of the life cycle of the family.

Shifts in the older pattern of division of labor between husband and wife have resulted in some blurring of the sharp distinctions between their roles. If the wife expects and is expected at various stages and crisis periods to take over some of the responsibility for providing income, the husband expects and is expected to share in the performance of the instrumental tasks of running the household. Some aspects of the interchange and sharing may extend into the function of nuturing and socializing the children. These newer patterns should probably not be regarded as evidences of diffusion or reversal of roles unless they are markedly exaggerated or there is evidence that the husband and wife perceive them as uncomfortable or humiliating. Many couples probably regard the new arrangements as opportunities for sharing and cooperation.

Sexual gratification.   Values and behaviors with respect to sexual gratification show many contradictions in American marriages. The over-all public value prescribes that each marital partner have sexual intercourse only with the other. Virginity is expected, especially of girls, before marriage. Public mores tend to restrict sexual experience to necking, petting, and genital intercourse. As a rule, it is expected that the husband's wishes will prevail over the wife's with respect to times and occasions.

Divergencies from practices sanctioned by public morals, even though forbidden by law, are so widespread that it must be recognized that other sets of values than the public ones exist in society and are recognized among intimates who adhere to them. In general, not too much of an issue is made of virginity for either sex. On the whole, the tendency seems to be in the direction of the expectation that a prudent wife will not make too much of an occasional infidelity on her husband's part and will certainly not terminate her marriage if the circumstances are not forced on her attention and if he otherwise supports her, gives her marks of respect, "loves" and understands her, and is a good father to their children. Less tolerance is permitted of infidelity in the wife, but she does not necessarily reap bitter and irrevocable retribution in a destroyed marriage and a blasted reputation, especially if she can rationalize her action on the grounds of having been "in love" or can make a case that her husband was, for some reason, unavailable.

Sexual values and practices seem to vary from class to class and from subculture to subculture. There is a tendency to stereotype members of lower classes and stigmatized racial and ethnic populations as sexually lecherous, promiscuous, and virile. There is no evidence that such stereotypes have any basis in fact. Indeed, it is more likely that members of the stigmatized populations, having sustained impairments in psychosexual development, may seek and experience sex in ways related more to dependency, security, and identity than in the mature ways that Freud subsumed under the concept of "genitality."

There is some tendency to conduct sexual relationships within a cultural convention in which the man asks and the woman grants sexual access. The convention is qualified in several ways. Even though the husband may be expected to ask, nevertheless he has a "right" to sexual gratification from his wife and she has a "duty" to grant it. The phrasing of the sexual aspects of the marriage in terms of right and duty is probably more heavily underlined in lower- than in middle- or upper-class marriages. There is some evidence that women of the upper-lower or "working class" regard sexual intercourse as disturbing and egodystonic. In the upper middle and upper classes opportunities and wishes for sexual gratification may be somewhat impaired by heavy professional demands on the time and energy of the husband. Some studies suggest that members of the middle and upper classes are more tolerant of and interested in nongenital forms of sexual enjoyment than are members of the lower classes.

Sexual *mores* seem to vary among the different religions and denominations. Members of various ethnic groups still adhere to and seek to enforce definitions of moral sexual behavior derived from their cultural backgrounds.

Social controls. Several psychological mechanisms seem to assist in the achievement of social controls by means of marriage. Cross-identification of the marital partners produces the not uncommon phenomenon of their personalities' becoming increasingly alike over the years. An abundance of emotional support and gratification seems to facilitate the development of stronger sublimatory capacities. A sense of "belonging" may arise from the individual's being accepted by his partner on the basis of ascription rather than achievement, and out of the sense of belonging may come the ability to use energies in the service of reciprocally defined acceptable goals. The marital relationship, further, provides a safety valve for the expression of sexual and aggressive impulses within the marriage. Many such expressions are displaced from persons and institutions in the larger society, in which such expression would bring penalties, and are discharged on the marital partner. Husbands and wives learn to recognize such displacements for what they are and to tolerate them up to a point.

In American marriages of the middle class social control is in part an outcome of the way marriage is institutionalized around the value of sharing, cooperation, or, to use the term which caricatures the value, "togetherness." By the time a young man and woman marry, their basic personality structures have already been formed. Marriage can hardly be expected—though it often is—to alter the substrata of unconscious infantile wishes, defense mechanisms, and superego pressures or "lacunae." Middle-class culture does strongly recommend, however, that the partners view their marriage as a joint venture. In accordance with a more generalized value of the culture, they are required to set long-range goals for the marriage and to adopt instrumental plans for achieving them. The goals include upward social mobility and economic and professional advancement.

Middle-class culture permits the discharge of some aggressive energy within the marriage. The expression of the aggression must, however, be confined to words or to symbolic acts. Direct physical assult, even a slap, is regarded as humiliating and intolerable. This aspect of marriage can exert considerable strain on the partners during the first few years, for it runs counter to the idealized expectation of "understanding" and "love" and to the value of cooperation.

The concept of goals and the value set on "togetherness" are much less influential in lower-class marriages. Goals tend to be short range: the purchase of material products valued in the subculture. The sexes take much of their recreation apart from each other, so that there is less opportunity for interaction and cross-identification. The lower-class culture permits the discharge of a good deal of aggression within the marriage, and it may take forms of physical assault without attendant feelings of humiliation and outrage.

Variations occur among social classes and ethnic groups with respect to the ways in which certain kinds of impulsive, exploitative behavior are defined and handled. In general, lower-class wives regard drunkenness in their husbands as behavior to be deplored and punished but tolerated. Lower middle-class wives probably regard excessive drinking as sin. Upper middle-class wives tend to regard it as an illness. Similar differentials probably exist with respect to gambling, homosexual activity, morals offenses against minors, and related forms of acting out. Much research is needed in the ways in which wives perceive and respond to evidences of dishonesty in business practices on the part of their husbands.

Children. Concern for children is one of the most prominent characteristics of the culture of the United States. Society expects parents to want children, though it accords them the right to determine for themselves their number and spacing. Childless couples are pitied, and the single child of a marriage is regarded as having been deprived of the opportunity for a full family life.

It is probably safe to say that most marriages in the United States are contracted with the hope and expectation that the couple will have children. With the development of research on fertility and modern contraceptive devices, marital partners in industrialized Western societies such as the United States have, probably for the first time in human history, some reasonable assurance that they can have children or not have children as they wish. As a result, variations appear with respect to the number and timing of children. During the period of the Great Depression of the 1930's one or two children was the optimum number desired. The tendency since World War II has been toward earlier marriages and the hope for three or four children, born within a few years after the marriage. Concern is expressed for what is regarded as the optimal spacing of children. There are many variations in patterns of hope and expectation among the subcultures of the United States with respect to childbearing. Young couples who desire advanced graduate and professional education tend to regulate the timing of pregnancy in relation to the economic demands of prolonged higher education. Among some religious denominations artificial contraception is prohibited. In the lower class the responsibility to decide on the use of contraception is delegated to the man.

The hazards of bearing children are lower than ever before in history, for advances in modern medicine have decreased the risk to life and health for both mother and child. In the larger cities provisions for medical insurance and for free or low-cost prenatal clinic care and delivery have decreased the economic burdens of bearing children.

The situation is less happy in many rural areas and in the economically disadvantaged sections of the United States. Doctors and hospitals may be far away or altogether lacking. The expectant mother may have to use the services of a midwife. Some states conduct training programs for midwives to serve in rural and disadvantaged areas.

Within the marriage, the husband is expected to meet his pregnant wife's needs and even to cater to her whims. She expects such attention from him and regards it as a sign of his love and understanding. On the other hand, the husband of a pregnant wife, especially as the time of her delivery approaches, is culturally regarded as a slightly ridiculous figure of fun. There are innumerable jokes about the "pregnant father" and about doctors "never having lost a father." The prospective father's legitimate and understandable worries are overlooked.

The culture of the United States not only recommends that married couples have children, it requires them to love the children, to care for them, and to support them until late adolescence or early adulthood. Moreover, this nurturing should be carried on in a separate joint abode, with few forms of support from other kin and few financial resources available except from the earnings of the husband and frequently the wife. The climate of American culture is one in which parents are held responsible for the development and behavior of their children but are afforded relatively little help in carrying out their responsibilities. The home is, in a sense, a nest of intense emotions and interactions, with much attention focused on the children, who easily become the symbolic embodiments of every ungratified wish, every internal conflict, every cultural hope or disappointment of the parents.

Parents are expected to sacrifice their own interests for the sake of providing a desirable kind and amount of nurture and socialization for their children. Abandonment, desertion, and neglect are given legal definition, and, although these definitions or their implementation are usually confined to the physical care of children, penalties may be imposed on parents found guilty. Neighbors are reluctant to make formal legal complaint that children are being neglected, but the social instruments of gossip and ostracism can be used as powerful weapons to enforce parents to care for their children in accordance with class, ethnic, and religious norms.

Education is culturally defined as the pre-eminent means to social and economic advancement, and the society of the United States has devised an educational system that puts great emphasis on the symbols of social mobility. Parents are expected to manifest great interest in the educational careers of their children. The educational system does not express the values and goals of the lower classes. Lower-class parents become involved in the conflict between the school and the child as he manifests behaviors that reveal protest against an educational process which is socially meaningless to him. Middle-class parents become involved in the competition for grades and offices as symbols of social status.

The social isolation of the family of procreation and the limiting of its positions to husband and wife, father and mother, and son and daughter result in close emotional associations between parents and children. They may conceive close attachments for one another, make intense cross-identifications, or, on the contrary, have to defend themselves against attachments and identifications that are too intense and too threatening. Difficulties between spouses are easily displaced onto children, and the family can be broken down into complex systems of offensive and defensive alliances. Children become the symbols of the parents' identity, accomplishments, and failures.

Parents are held responsible by society to impose controls on the primitive aggressive and sexual behaviors of their children. At the same time, the means of control legally and socially delegated to the parents are limited. Parents are frequently left in the position of having to resort to cajolery, bribery, and manipulation to enforce the controls demanded by society.

Emotional satisfaction. In the culture of the United States individuals are expected to find their major experiences of emotional support and release from tension within the family. Other social institutions seem to provide individuals with fewer opportunities for emotional gratification than they may have done in the past. The family has become a relatively small, socially isolated, tightly knit group. It is under heavy social pressure to advance its status in the community. It can count on no assured income. Husbands and wives are directed to seek sexual satisfaction only from each other. They are enjoined to place the well-being of their children above their own, and they are held responsible for the behavior of their children in the social world outside their own.

Under these circumstances, each husband and wife becomes the one person most available to the other as a source of release and support. The culture defines the spouse as the most appropriate person. The society is so organized that in actuality the spouse is the most available person. It comes as no surprise then that in American marriages the emotional stakes are high and that the issue of whether support and release are afforded pervades every other function of the marriage.

There is a general tendency among Americans to idealize marriage as a relationship in which unending love and emotional support can be realized. American men and women expect their spouses to love and "understand" them. Understanding seems to mean a sensitive, perhaps intuitive, perception of the partner's needs and wishes and an unfailing, unquestioning response of sympathy, support, and approval of his needs if not his actions.

There are probably some differences between the sexes in the ways in which this expectation is phrased and experienced. Wives tend to say that they want to be "loved." They prefer that their husbands express this love verbally. They observe his actions, sometimes uneasily, for signs of love or a falling off of love. Husbands seem to put greater emphasis on being "understood." They are less articulate than their wives and more accepting of behavioral evidences that the relationship possesses the desired qualities.

There is some evidence of differences among social classes with respect to the demand to be loved and understood. Women in the lower classes seem to be able to isolate reality from fantasy. They learn to accept and live tolerably with the husband who, on the whole, is faithful, does not drink too much, and brings home his pay. They reserve for the realm of daydream the image of the understanding, exciting lover set forth in the magazines and television programs especially designed for them. Women of the middle and upper classes may be less sucessful in reconciling themselves to the differences between the ideal lover and the real husband and may exert a greater strain on the husband to approximate the ideal in his behavior.

The cultural emphasis on the desirability and possibility of love and understanding in marriage may be conceived as part of a larger cultural complex which defines and shapes the relationship between the sexes. Emphasis on the uniqueness and worth of the individual personality constitutes an element in this larger complex. Each individual feels and is accorded by society the right to feel that he possesses a total identity irrespective of his several attributes. Each individual wants and has a right to be loved and cherished as an integral personality different from all other personalities. A man may respect his own economic potentialities or abilities, but he does not want to be loved merely because he is or is likely to become a good provider. A woman may be aware of and respect her sexual attractiveness, but she does not want to be loved merely because of this. If either marital partner believes that he is valued solely because of some single attribute, he feels degraded. The husband in question tends to feel that his wife is a "gold digger" who values him only as a "work horse." The wife in question tends to feel that her husband is "oversexed" and really thinks of her as a harlot.

The cultural emphasis on romantic love as a criterion for the selection of a marital partner may be seen as a part of this total complex. Adolescents and young adults search themselves anxiously to assure themselves that they have an attractive personality. They perform all sorts of rituals, engage in all sorts of exercises, try on all sorts of roles to develop a sense of their own identity. At the same time each seeks the one person of the opposite sex who is "meant for" him. Once he or she is found, it is expected that there will be a total involvement of the two young people in each other's needs and hopes. The blissful stage of being "in love" is felt to be a prelude to a lifetime of reciprocal gratification and emotional support in marriage. True, more experienced and prudent parents and friends often feel called on to warn the young couple that "marriages are not made in Heaven." But the need to advance the caution betrays the fact that both the elders and the young people can understand how it can be felt that they are.

Romantic love is not, of course, the only criterion for the selection of a spouse. The point is that the society as a whole thinks that, whatever other criteria are adduced, it is desirable that a prospective bride and groom be in love with each other. There is a tendency to regard other, more prudential motivations for selecting a spouse as important but of lower value than love. Great attention is paid to the ways in which other criteria and motivations are phrased. The weightings given to the value of the total personality and to romantic love tend also to define and re-enforce the expectation of love and understanding in marriage. Although it is generally recognized that romantic passion will fade, it is hoped and expected that out of passion will grow tender love that will increase over the years as the two spouses learn to know each other more intimately.

DEFINITION OF MARITAL INCOMPATIBILITY

A typical dictionary definition of incompatibility describes it as "inability to live together harmoniously or get along well with each other." Obviously, then, marital incompatibility is the inability of husband and wife to live together harmoniously or get along well with each other.

Subjective unhappiness. In one perspective this definition refers to a feeling of subjective unhappiness or dissatisfaction by one or both spouses with some aspect of the marital role performances of the other or with the appearance in the marital relationship of interactions that reciprocally and circularly re-enforce the sense of subjective unhappiness. Clearly, this approach to an understanding of marital incompatibility reflects disappointment of the expectation that the marriage provide reciprocal release of tension and a reciprocal sense of emotional support for the two partners. When this expectation is not met, the marriage is incompatible. Given the weighting on this function of marriage in the United States, it might be supposed that social provision could be made to deal with marital incompatibility by studying the incidence, distribution, and causes of overt expressions of unhappiness in marriage. This is true as far as it goes.

Unfortunately for the hope of providing simple social solutions, marital incompatibility, in the sense of subjective disharmony, is not always expressed overtly and simply. There are a number of reasons why this is so.

In the first place, marital partners are not always aware of their subjective dissatisfaction with the marriage. The roots of the dissatisfaction may be bedded deeply in the history and structure of the personality. The behavior that is so distressing in a spouse may be so because it unconsciously symbolizes old deprivations and degradations for his partner. The emotional issues may be bitter, and conscious awareness of them may be too threatening to bear. The unhappy husband or wife may defend himself against such awareness.

In still more complicated fashion a husband or wife may tolerate and even enjoy subjective disharmony in marriage because the current state of affairs seems better than any conceivable alternative. Marriages are rarely broken nor is help sought to save or improve them on the basis of an arithmetic summation of "goods" and "bads." Marriages are lived. Often they are tolerated. Narcissistic self-esteem is partly gratified and partly wounded. Dependency needs are partly met and partly frustrated. Submission is made to the seemingly tyrannical domination of the partner because rebellion is felt to be too hopeless or too dangerous. Guilt and impotence may be experienced, but underlying the guilt may be a secret sense of naughty satisfaction. Reciprocal bonds of sadistic and masochistic interaction may become so strong that they are unbreakable despite the torment they create. And always there is the old adage: "The devil you know is better than the devil you don't." Breaking up the marriage poses a frightening prospect.

Moreover, not too fine a point must be made of the issue, whether marital incompatibility or something else is the "real problem." As long as the spouses are unable to render each other a satisfying degree of release from emotional tension or a satisfying degree of emotional support, there is a problem of incompatibility in the marriage. The causes may lie in the remote fastnesses of childhood history. The sense of unhappiness with the marital partner may be displaced from other social relationships into the marriage or displaced from the marriage into other social relationships. In any case, the influence of the causative variables on the marriage must be taken into account in building a social program for dealing with marital incompatibility.

Cultural variations. There is no single simple standard of behavior that is regarded or felt by married people as evidence of lack of interest and support on the part of their spouses. Rather, there are important subcultural variations in the United States with respect to these perceptions and feelings. Some of these variations follow the lines of social classes. A working-class wife would probably not think that she and her husband were incompatible merely because he took most of his recreation apart from her. An upper middle-class wife, on the other hand, might well regard her husband's going out in the evening without her as evidence of disinterest and neglect. This same upper middle-class wife might, with relative contentment, put up with her husband's late hours in his business or profession and his extended trips away from home as long as she remained convinced that he was occupied with his vocation. She would regard his absence as evidence of his effort to help the family get ahead. Her own willingness to bear her loneliness would constitute her contribution to that joint effort.

There seem to be differences, too, between the cultures of men and women in the United States with respect to what is felt to be lack of interest and support from the marital partner. Women seem to value verbal expressions of endearment and affectionate gestures more highly than men do. Married women may regard the lack of such expressions from their husbands as evidence of lack of "love." At best, American women tend to put up with their husbands' unresponsiveness with resignation. American men, on the other hand, tend to feel embarrassed in expressing their passionate or affectionate feelings verbally. They accept as evidence of "love" in themselves and their wives the steady performance of vocational or household duties, the responsible handling of money, and the faithful carrying out of parental tasks.

There are differences in what is felt to be emotional support, or its lack, at various stages of the family life-cycle. During the stages of consummation of the marriage and early reciprocal adjustment both partners expect that their interest will be largely concentrated on each other. During the wife's first pregnancy, both she and her husband want and expect the evidence of tenderness to take the form of interest in her as a pregnant wife. Following the birth of the first child, the marital partners can, for a while, accept the displacement of support and interest from each other to the child. At some peril, however, does the American father or mother permit this displacement to continue too long or too exclusively. At some point, husband and wife want some portion of the interest returned to themselves. If it is not, the continued displacement is felt as marital incompatibility. At a later stage of the marriage evidence of emotional support is felt in the common devotion of both partners to consolidating or raising the social status of the family. If either partner fails to contribute his part, the husband through bringing in the necessary income or the wife through the proper performance of symbolic duties, the failures may be taken as evidence of lack of emotional support. When the marriage is finally brought to an end as a system of concrete interactions by the death of one of the partners, a continuing sense of emotional support may be derived from retrospective memory of the association and from the tangible resources and symbolic keepsakes that one partner has left behind for the other. If these legacies are missing, there may be some sense of disappointment in the marriage.

Finally, there are subcultural differences with respect to the willingness to make marital unhappiness known to persons or agencies outside the marriage. In general, wives, more of whose total sphere of interests is occupied by marital concerns, are more willing to seek outside help than husbands, whose interests are more sharply divided between family and work. To the wife, failure of the marriage may be equated with total failure as a person. To the husband, failure of the marriage may, if admitted, reflect on the sense of personal adequacy he has build up in the business world. In some ethnic groups it is a mark of personal worth to seek professional help with a marital problem. In other ethnic groups personal worth accrues from "handling things within the family." To reveal to others that one cannot handle one's marriage is to reveal one's shame to the world. Subcultural variations with respect to class, race, ethnic origin, and religious affiliation also determine the nature of the resource from which help is sought and the kind of help that is acceptable. Clearly, these differences must be taken into account in devising a comprehensive plan for dealing with marital incompatibility in the United States.

Structural-functional disorder. The concept of marital incompatibility need not be and should not be limited to subjective disharmony in the marriage. The provision of reciprocal emotional support and release from tension is only one of the expectations and functions of marriage. Structural breakdown of marriage may be considered a severe consequence of dysfunctional operation of the marriage and therefore a consequence of incompatibility. Inability of the spouse to meet the expectations and carry out the various functions of marriage by means of complementary effort may be considered as a form of incompatibility, that is, as a form of disharmony and of inability to get along well together. It is highly likely in the United States that such structural or functional inadequacy in marriage will be accompanied by feelings of unhappiness. Indeed, these evidences of inadequacy may be the major clues to subjective marital disharmony. But even when subjective dissatisfaction is not present, and cases of the kind do occur, the society has a stake in the functional efficiency of marriage as a social institution.

Structural Forms of Marital Incompatibility

Divorce. The most dramatic evidence of the structural breakdown of marriage, the evidence that seems to cause the most widespread concern in society, is the statistics of divorce.[7] There is no doubt that the

---

[7] A good summary of the statistical incidence of divorce in the United States

rate of divorce has been increasing in the United States, especially since the end of World War II. Approximately one quarter of all first marriages end in divorce. The greatest incidence of divorce occurs during the first five years of marriage. If the statistics for annulment and legal separations were added to those of divorce, the rate of structural breakdown of marriage in the United States would be even higher.

The response of society to the increasing divorce rate raises the problem of stability versus compatibility as relative criteria for assessing the well-being of the institution of marriage in the society of the United States. The need for stability is an expression of the cultural value that it is desirable that marriage continue until the death of one partner. Compatibility, in one of its meanings, expresses the value that it is desirable that marriage provide a satisfying sense of emotional support in the relationship of the partners. Some religious denominations prohibit their members access to divorce or refuse to solemnize remarriage of a divorced person. Some legal authorities and legislatures permit only limited grounds for divorce and continue to force the action into the form of an adversary proceeding in which one of the parties must be adjudged guilty of offending the other. Such policies and measures tend to give exclusive weighting to the value of stability at the expense of the value of compatibility.

It is doubtful that an approach to the problem of marital incompatibility which, in effect, denies the existence of the problem can attain results other than those that have already been achieved. The consequence of an extremely rigid and restrictive policy on divorce is to drive incompatible spouses to seek other means of dissolving their marriages. Such alternative means often involve collusion, the dissipation of resources, the exacerbation of an already bad interpersonal relationship, and the formation of extramarital liaisons which society regards as undesirable.

The counterargument is that easy divorce would cause the breakdown of morals and marriage in the society. It is, of course, questionable whether divorce followed by remarriage is more immoral by any reasonable standard than conspiracy to present false evidence or than the degradation, according to current cultural values, of an extralegal, quasi-marital relationship. As a matter of fact, there is both statistical and clinical evidence that second marriages following divorce tend to be both

---

over the period from 1920 to 1960 may be found in "Trends in Divorce and Family Disruption," reprint from *Health, Education and Welfare Indicators* (Washington, D. C.: National Vital Statistics Division, Public Health Service, U.S. Department of Health, Education and Welfare). *See also Statistical Abstract of the United States*, 1963, Tables 49, 79, 80, and 81.

stable and compatible, so that there can hardly be a serious question of a widespread breakdown of morals and marriage.

Perhaps access to divorce, guarded as it increasingly tends to be with prior access to counseling services, offers greater opportunity for marital stability and compatibility than does the continuation of an unwanted and failing marriage. Perhaps the problem for this "social problems" project is to devise ways of decreasing the number of unhappy first marriages. How and where can social workers intervene in the social scene to help people make better first choices and so avoid the unhappiness, the stigma, and the expense of divorce?

Divorce, the legal termination of the marriage, is in some ways the most clean-cut form of structural dissolution of a marriage. It is true that many divorced people remain emotionally tied to their former spouses for some time. On the other hand, there is a finality about the process that makes it possible for many people, with or without help, to live through a mourning period which eventuates in emotional detachment from the former partner.

Assuredly, children of divorced parents have additional emotional complications introduced into their lives. This aspect of divorce is not discussed here, since this discussion is limited to marital incompatibility.

Separation and desertion. Other forms of structural alteration or dissolution of marriage which are of frequent occurrence in the society of the United States present many hazards for the individuals involved. These forms include informal separation and desertion. Unfortunately, valid and reliable statistics concerning their incidence are unavailable. Caseworkers familiar with the caseloads of family courts, public assistance agencies, family and child welfare agencies, and medical and psychiatric clinics would probably agree that the incidence of all the structural consequences and functional forms of marital incompatibility is great enough throughout American society to warrant social concern. In a sense, informal separation and desertion may be considered as "the poor man's form of divorce," since they are so widely resorted to by members of the lower class in preference to more expensive and cumbersome divorce procedures.

Separation and desertion lack many of the safeguards provided by divorce. They can be initiated impulsively, even without the knowledge of the marital partner. They are seldom accompanied by planning for the continuance of financial support or for care of the children. They often constitute episodes in a succession of separations and reconciliations. Neither the deserter nor the deserted spouse is left free to enter into a stable succeeding marriage.

Not infrequently one or both of the separating spouses has made an arrangement to set up a liaison with a third person. Such liaisons may range in stability from casual adulterous affairs to long-lasting quasi-marriages which the partners justify to themselves as "common law marriages." When such a liaison is set up before the separation or desertion from the legal spouse, it may constitute an unacknowledged form of polygamy. Whenever the liaison is established, whatever qualities of stability it may possess or lack, it is still defined culturally as an adulterous relationship. Although it may be tolerated by society, it affords no social supports for either partner. Whatever security it affords to the partners arises entirely from their emotional attraction to each other and from the economic advantages that the union may offer.

Problems in the membership of the family. The sharp distinction drawn between one family and another gives rise to certain characteristic forms and issues of marital incompatibility which are usually thought of as "in-law" problems. Other common forms and issues involve the places of stepchildren and adopted children in the family.

The "in-law" problem may emerge during the later stages of courtship after the prospective spouses have gone through the initial stages of the process of differentiating out a new family of procreation and developing its identity. The problem may become fullblown in the first years of marriage. Reciprocal complaints of interference or of emotional and social withdrawal are common on the part of the young spouses and of the in-laws on either side in the marriages that experience early separations, desertions, and divorces.

At issue are all the structural and functional decisions that the young people must face to make their marriage a going concern with an identity of its own: when to marry and how; where to live; who is to live in the new family; what the style of life is to be with respect to social placement; whether the young wife is to work; how she is to conduct her household; after whom children are to be named, how they are to be raised, and what authority and privileges are to be granted to grandparents; how shortcomings and transgressions by either spouse are to be handled.

Problems in relationships with in-laws may persist for many years, often accompanied by running battles and hostile truces. Ultimately, these relationships take on the character of an unhappy equilibrium. Some families of procreation never differentiate themselves completely from one or the other of their background families of orientation. Two or more families of parents-in-law, sons- and daughters-in-law, and brothers- and sisters-in-law may share a two-family or apartment house or live in proximity in a neighborhood. There may be much pooling of the performance of various family functions. The emotional relationships may be relatively amicable or quite ambivalent. Problems of marital incompatibility may emerge in later stages of family life when the issue arises of taking one or more aging parents-in-law into the home or of supporting them financially elsewhere.

Relationships between a stepparent, his spouse, and her children by a former marriage may become an issue in a second or third marriage. Marital partners have become so sensitive to the mythology of the "bad stepparent" that they often "lean over backward" to avoid such problems, but the underlying potentialities for marital discord may still exist and be given indirect expression. Relationships with adopted children may also precipitate or be used to express various aspects of marital incompatibility. Whenever these relationships with step-children or adopted children become an issue between the spouses, the question of their right to a place in the family is raised.

Marital incompatibility that involves questions of the membership of the family and of relationships with other families is typically manifested in problems of role definition and in overtly or covertly coercive patterns of interaction between the spouses. As differences develop over the questions of who has the responsibility to do what, role conflict, diffusion, and reversal ensue. Typically, one of the spouses is attempting to be a husband or wife in one family and to continue, at least in part, to be a son or daughter in another.

Certain emotional issues are of frequent occurrence. Unsatisfied and unresolved dependency needs in a young husband or wife lead to a turning back to a parent for gratification. The young spouse then feels abandoned, jealous, and resentful. A young married person may unconsciously split his parental images into "good" and "bad" mother or father parts and conceive his parent-in-law to be the "bad" mother or father. He, or she, may project some of his own undesirable qualities onto the parent-in-law. He may unconsciously ready himself to fight out once again the old issues of authority or emancipation.

Parents-in-law, too, may inject real emotional issues into the relationship. They may, in fear of losing some part of themselves, attempt to interfere in the new marriage. They may need to retain a married son or daughter as a child. They may, especially as they grow older, try to obtain gratification of their own dependency needs from their married children and their spouses. They may even unconsciously conceive the spouses of their married children as sexual objects and once more experience oedipal wishes and oedipal rivalries in disguised forms.

Functional Forms of Marital Incompatibility

The forms taken by the functional aspects of incompatibility are largely determined by the cultural phrasing of what is to be expected of marriage. The ways in which husband or wife perceive and judge the relative failure of the marriage depends on what the culture has taught them to expect and require of marriage.

Social placement and ranking. One important form of marital incompatibility consists of actual failure on the part of one or both partners to carry out their responsibilities to maintain, improve, and demonstrate to the larger society the social status of the family. In more subtle form incompatibility occurs when either partner misunderstands or misinterprets the efforts of the other with respect to this function.

In the light of the content of the cultural complex of social status and mobility, marital incompatibility takes a characteristic form. In reality, or in the perception of his wife, the husband fails to work in a vocation that bears the marks of the social status she thinks the family should possess. He fails to make enough money to purchase the desirable symbols of status. He fails to manifest a wish to get ahead or he is too negligent in pushing himself forward vocationally. He does not manifest sufficient interest in the social and recreational activities necessary to maintain or advance the status of the family or he buries himself in some hobby of no status value. In reality, or in the perception of the husband, the wife may fail in the performance of her symbolic roles by lack of proper "taste" or by inattention to matters of personal appearance and dress, decoration and management of the home, activities as a hostess, and the conduct of civic responsibilities.

Economics and housekeeping. Economic issues underlie a great deal of marital incompatibility in the United States. Although the economic system may provide an ever increasing abundance for most families, it never represents real economic security, except perhaps for the few who are rich. Few families can really count on the continuance of their income through the vicissitudes of the business cycle, the advances of automation, and the sickness of the earner. For the many families at the lower end of the economic scale, the members of depreciated races and ethnic groups, the sufferers from chronic ill health and crippling mental and emotional disorders, the less intelligent, and the poorly educated, the economic issue is still one of survival. Public assistance affords a scanty and, after all these years, degrading bulwark. For families in the middle and, perhaps, upper ranges of the economic scale the cultural pressure to maintain and advance social status may cause a degree of economic insecurity as great as, or greater than, the threat to survival. Interruption or cessation of the usual sources and amounts of income may force the family to lower its standard of living and thereby suffer a severe loss of self- and, perhaps, public esteem.

The forms and consequences of marital incompatibility with respect to the economic aspects of marriage are complex and pervasive. As in all functions of marriage, difficulties in the economic realm are interlocked with those in other realms and with the particular emotional needs and defenses of the marital partners. It may be no exaggeration to say that almost every case of marital incompatibility in the United States reveals some aspect of disharmony in the management of the economic affairs of the family.

When the husband loses his employment or when his earnings are felt to be inadequate, the most common alternative is that the wife seek employment. Many American families have adopted this measure as an accepted, long-term solution to economic difficulties. Despite its immediate financial advantages, it may result in some impairment of the ability of the wife to perform her other roles in the home. Complicated patterns of reversal, ambiguity, and diffusion of the husband-father and wife-mother roles may ensue.

Serious incompatibilities may develop in the allocation of economic resources and the responsibility for the performance of the instrumental tasks necessary to keep a household going. There are wide variations among social classes, races, and ethnic groups with respect to the answers to these questions: to whom is money given and for what purposes; who is responsible for the purchase of what items and the payment of what bills; who is dutybound to do the cooking, the washing, the cleaning; who should take care of the car and the yard. As long as husband and wife agree on the allocation of resources and the differential responsibility for the performance of the instrumental tasks, no incompatibility exists. In many marriages, however, such agreement is lacking. Failure of communication and understanding between husband and wife about these matters is common. To the extent that it occurs, it constitutes a form of marital incompatibility, and its consequences constitute some degree of breakdown in the marital system.

Sexual relationships.   Disharmony in sexual relationships, whatever its causes, constitutes in itself a serious disappointment of expectations and has deleterious consequences for other marital functions. Sexual incompatibility is expressed in its simplest form when one spouse feels and, perhaps, complains that the other does not provide sexual gratification as frequently, at the times and occasions, and in the forms expected. A somewhat more complex form of incompatibility consists of the complaint that the partner does not respond fully enough in sexual relations. The complaining partner feels that his sexual performances and attractiveness are unappreciated and devalued. It is more frequently, perhaps, the husband who complains that his wife keeps herself inaccessible or that she is unresponsive, but the same complaint by the wife against the husband is not unusual. More typically, however, the wife, especially in lower-class marriages, is likely to complain that her husband does not prepare her for intercourse, confines himself to immediate physical satisfaction, and leaves her feeling devalued and ungratified, physically and emotionally.

The asking-granting convention places in the hands of each spouse a strong and commonly used weapon. The husband can hurt the wife by demanding what she regards as too much or too little. The wife can punish him by persistent refusal or by making her consent conditional on his acceding to her wishes in other matters. The convention that the woman must wait to be asked and the pressures on her to conform to the public code of respectability play into and, indeed, may have helped to develop the emotional tendency of many American men to separate in their minds the image of the wife as a "good" woman, that is, a woman uninterested in sex and an inappropriate object, from the "bad" woman with whom sex can be enjoyed. Finally, the discrepancy between the public sexual code and the unacknowledged sexual codes of various subcultures may give rise to some uneasiness between the partners. In the early stage of marriage they may be unsure of their partner's wishes and expectations and may not know the meanings of cue behaviors. The problem may be somewhat more difficult for them if they come from different subcultural backgrounds. If they are relatively mature people emotionally, this problem may be expected to die down as they become more accustomed to each other and as each comes to identify with the other's values or to modify his own.

Either partner may signal the existence of sexual incompatibility by turning outside the marriage for satisfaction. This may, on the part of either husband or wife, range from casual flirtations to open and acknowledged infidelity. When such episodes go beyond casual attentions to members of the opposite sex, they are usually symbolic of many other kinds of incompatibility in the marriage than the sexual.

Children. Marital incompatibility may take the form of disagreements over whether to have children or the number and timing of children. Although frankness and the sharing of hopes in this matter undoubtedly help, it is still true that it is difficult to deal emotionally with a hypothetical situation. Even though the couple may have had intercourse before marriage, as many couples do, marriage itself and the sharing of a joint abode introduce the likelihood of more frequent intercourse, often more impulsive and under more casual conditions. A seemingly settled agreement concerning children, arrived at before marriage, may break down when the partners are confronted with the real prospect of the wife's pregnancy and of parenthood. The requirement of the American culture that each family provide for its own economic needs by means of work whose steadiness is unassured makes each child an additional economic risk for the family. Although this risk falls more continuously on the husband, its potential threat is even greater for the wife. If the marriage should break up or the husband become seriously ill at some future time, she is likely to have to bear the major responsibility for providing for the children as well as for raising them. The real economic risks of having children may become embroiled with unconsciously rooted emotional fears. Anxiety or guilt or fixation on pregenital wishes may make it impossible for either spouse to tolerate the prospect of fatherhood or motherhood.

Nor does contraception offer an unexceptionally simple answer to the problem. It may be supposed that no two relatively mature young people would marry each other in the United States today if one adhered strongly to a religious prohibition on the use of chemical or mechanical means of contraception and the other favored their use. But many young people are not so mature as they think. And it is difficult in the throes of a romantic love affair to realize the depths of one's ethical convictions. The announced belief that one will give up one's own wishes for the sake of one's partner may be accepted too literally. The real intention to change the convictions and behaviors of the partner may be unacknowledged or, if announced, may not be heard. Moreover, even if the husband and wife agree ethically on the use of contraceptive devices, they may find after marriage that discrepancies in taste arise concerning the relative acceptability of various methods.

The interplay of cultural values, emotional needs, and defenses produces some rather common forms of marital incompatibility with respect to the bearing of children. Real wishes and convictions, unacknowledged or concealed before marriage, may emerge into the open. Arguments over the number and spacing of children are common. The partner who is afraid may engage in inexhaustible delaying tactics. The partner who wants the child may make every affectionate gesture a prelude to possible impregnation. Every occasion for intercourse may become loaded with fear, anxiety, guilt, or anger. The partner who wishes to use contraception may try to force his wishes on the other. The reluctant partner may "forget" to employ the device or may feel and express disgust. Actual pregnancy may be followed by demands of either partner on the other for greater physical and emotional indulgence, or it may be followed by the couple's drawing apart.

Perhaps the clearest example of marital incompatibility related to the function of nurturing and socializing children occurs when, in reality or in the perception of one of the spouses, interest in the marital partner is withdrawn and transferred to one or more of the children. The one spouse's emotional preoccupation with a child and the other spouse's jealousy are well known. This situation is most likely to develop when one or both of the spouses are needy, dependent persons who turn to the children for emotional gratification that the other spouse does not or cannot give.

A similar but not identical form of marital incompatibility is present when one of the spouses consciously or unconsciously casts a child into a marital role. Situations are well known to social workers in which a wife makes a quasi-husband of one or more of her sons, turning to them for financial and emotional support. She may also seek sexual gratification from the sons, usually in symbolic or aim-inhibited ways. All this may occur while her husband is in the home and with or without his consent. Relationships between father and daughter in which the father turns to the daughter as a quasi-wife are also well known. Here the father asks for emotional support and often the performance of household tasks that his wife would usually provide. Cases of actual sexual relationship between father and daughter, sometimes with children resulting, are more common than are cases of mother and son incest. The wife may be present in the home and may either object or abet the father-daughter relationship.

Social controls.   The most flagrant cases of marital incompatibility seem to occur in those situations in which spouses behave toward each other in a manner that violates public decency, scandalizes neighbors, and, perhaps, breaks the law. The behaviors associated with serious alcoholism, physical assault on the partner, and "forcing" the partner into prostitution are illustrative. The broad culture condemns attack and exploitation of these kinds. Even those subcultures that permit such behaviors in some degree set limits on how far they should go.

Such behaviors by one or both partners in a marriage indisputably constitute forms of marital incompatibility with respect to the reciprocal enforcement of social controls. Close study often reveals that they gratify primitive wishes and serve to ward off internal anxieties and fears. Moreover, the behavior of the suffering spouse often discloses evidence that he or she provokes the acting-out behavior of the other, thereby achieving vicarious satisfactions of his or her own primitive needs. The reciprocal recriminations followed by sentimental sessions of forgiveness and promises never to do it again serve to relieve the guilt of both partners. Such partners are often bound to each other indissolubly, as the repeated pattern of separation, complaint to court, and reconciliation shows. Rarely is professional help extended to the acting-out partner successful unless the other partner can be helped. The cycle of interaction must be interrupted.

Emotional satisfaction.   Expectations of one's self and of one's marital partner with respect to carrying out the various functions of marriage are organized into patterns of interrelated values, attitudes, and behaviors. These expected patterns comprise the roles of functional importance to the marriage. Difficulties erupt between husband and wife when discrepancies of several sorts occur. In the performance of a role the partner may manifest values, attitudes, and behaviors different from those that his spouse expects. In the performance of a role a husband or wife may manifest different values, attitudes, and behaviors from those that he expects of himself. Either partner may find himself lacking in understanding of what is required in a role by the surrounding culture, by the spouse, or by himself. In a happy and effective marriage the respective roles of husband and wife are defined in complementary, interlocking fashion, based on "division of labor" agreed to by each. Discrepancies may occur in the ways in which the partners wish to define the division of labor, and complementarity may break down. The several forms of discrepancy may become rigidified into various dysfunctional patterns of role definition and performance. Husband and wife may reverse their roles in one or more of the functions of marriage, and ambiguity in expectation and performance may come to characterize them. Roles may be so defined that the partners become locked in open and perpetual conflict, and their important aspects may go unperformed.

Every discrepancy in definition, every failure of complementarity, every dysfunctional crystallization of roles is a potential source and focus of emotional conflict between the spouses. The discrepancies, failures, and rigidities induce tension within the partners and a decrease in their ability to sustain each other's self-esteem and sense of being "loved."

Roles are actually defined and performed and support and release from tension are actually provided or withheld in the interactions that constantly exist between husband and wife. Spiegel's concept of "techniques of induction" sets forth a classification of the kinds of behaviors that enter into destructive interactions between individuals as one person attempts to exercise control over another. These include coercing, coaxing, evaluating, masking, and postponing.[8] The meanings of most of these terms are probably self-evident.

Social interaction cannot be completely understood in terms of the actions of only one partner or even of both partners considered separately. Cottrell's paradigm of social interaction outlines the reciprocal processes that occur.[9] A husband does not merely react to his wife's

[8] John Spiegel, "The Resolution of Role Conflict within the Family," in Milton Greenblatt, Daniel J. Levinson, and Richard H. Williams, *The Patient and the Mental Hospital*, (Glencoe, Ill.: The Free Press, 1957), p. 545; reprinted in Bell and Vogel, *op. cit.*, p. 361. Spiegel also includes role reversal as one of these techniques, though in a somewhat different sense than implied by the term elsewhere in this discussion.

[9] Leonard S. Cottrell, Jr., "The Analysis of Situational Fields in Social Psychol-

use of some technique of induction. He gauges his initial proposal or explanation to her in terms of his expectation of her response. He, himself, may at the outset seek to coax her in the expectation that she will try to coerce him. Indeed, a kind of gamesmanship, a plotting of grand strategy, can take place as the process becomes elaborated. Each prepares and regulates his own responses in terms of how he expects to respond next to the response he expects to receive or invoke from his partner. When interaction reaches this stage, a feedback process is taking place within each individual.

Clearly the use of such techniques in such complicated ways to attempt to alter the other's unsatisfactory performances of marital functions has serious emotional consequences for both partners. Ample opportunity is provided to attack and be attacked. Internal tension in both is likely to rise. Any sense of giving or receiving emotional support is lost or submerged.

In a sense, the concept of interaction may be restricted to the process of the exchanges between marital partners, whereas the concept of communication takes account of the content of their exchanges. The "message" that a husband intends to communicate to his wife may be quite different from the "message" she receives. It has already been suggested that American men and women may differ from one another in the extent of their wishes and abilities to communicate verbally about "love." Members of the lower class tend to think that talk is useless or pretentious as a means of sending and receiving messages in social interaction. Members of the middle class, on the other hand, rely largely on verbal means of communication. Members of some ethnic groups are verbally expressive to the point that they do not always expect their verbalizations to be taken as literal and serious indications of their intentions. Members of other groups are essentially taciturn, expecting their intentions to be communicated by subtle behavioral cues.

Unfortunately for persons who are trying to communicate with one another, the behavioral cues to meanings reveal many cultural variations. A facial expression or gesture by which a young husband of one culture may intend to convey mild disapproval may be interpreted by his wife of another culture as a sign of anger or disgust. Similarly, a facial expression or gesture which she uses to communicate affection may be interpreted by him as a sign of unfeminine sexual forwardness. Every young husband and wife, even though they are the products of identical backgrounds, have to learn how to send and receive messages during the early period of the marriage, since each of their respective

ogy," in A. Paul Hare, Edgar F. Borgotta, and Robert F. Bales, eds., *Small Groups. Studies in Social Interaction* (New York: Alfred A. Knopf, 1955), p. 57.

families of orientation has inculcated in its son or daughter its varieties of the general culture of communication.

Discrepancies between husband and wife in the interpretation of messages become perceptions of failure on the part of the partner to offer emotional support and release from tension. The problem becomes further complicated when misunderstood communications contribute to discrepancies in reciprocal role definition and to ineffective performance of marital functions. When consciously adopted masking techniques and unconscious wishes and defenses enter into marital communications, the potentialities for the partners to hurt and to be hurt are boundless. Social workers know that a part of every "marital problem" consists of a breakdown of reciprocally helpful communication between the partners.

Summary

In this discussion of marital incompatibility the term has been taken to mean disharmony between the spouses or their inability to get along well with each other in the reciprocal and complementary performance of one or more of the functions of marriage. Subjective dissatisfaction with each other, what is usually called marital unhappiness, has been regarded as inability to provide each other with relief of tension and emotional support. This function is, for cultural reasons, of special importance in American marriages. Incompatibility with respect to it usually pervades incompatibility in the reciprocal and complementary performance of the other functions. The basic processes by means of which incompatibility develops are disorders in role definition, interaction, and communication.

CAUSES OF MARITAL INCOMPATIBILITY

Causes of marital incompatibility will be discussed under the following headings: causes inherent in culture and social structure; causes inherent in individual personality; situational and transitory causes; and causes inherent in existing institutions designed to cope with the problem.

There is some overlapping in the assignment of causes of marital incompatibility to one category or another. Some of this overlapping occurs by design. Social institutions are built on and give expression to cultural values, which exert their influence largely by the ways in which they are expressed and enforced by social institutions. Therefore in this discussion a deliberate attempt is made to play back and forth between cultural values and their institutionalized expression as variables causing marital incompatibility. Some of the overlapping develops because the complexity of the causes and their manifold effects make it necessary to refer to them now in one perspective, now in another. Finally, it is a point of emphasis throughout the discussion that *sociocultural variables and variables operating within individual personalities exert a continuous influence on one another.* What is perceived by the individual is simultaneously determined from both directions. It is indisputable that there are differences between what is and what is perceived and that what is influences and alters what is perceived. It is just as indisputable that what is perceived influences and alters what is. To specify this point at every turn would extend the discussion endlessly, but it must be assumed with respect to everything that is said.

Causes Inherent in Culture and Social Structure

Man seems to have three basic modes of experience: cognitive, appreciative, and evaluative.[10] In the first mode he observes, abstracts, generalizes, and tests. As a result of these intellectual operations he acquires intellectual knowledge of situations. In its purest forms the cognitive mode is exemplified in scientific method and rational problem solving. The most general characteristic of the cognitive mode is partialization. In the use of himself to acquire knowledge man tries to suppress feelings and values that might bias his intellectual operations and to rely on the use of his intellectual capacities alone. In observing and manipulating the world he partializes out those aspects of experience that are significant for his immediate purposes, whether theoretical or practical, and sees experience in terms of partialized abstract concepts. In the appreciative mode man tries to relate to the totality of an event in a total way. He seeks awareness of all his own ideational, affective, and evaluative responses to the event and in it an immediate revelation of all its attributes and meanings. In a sense, he tries to butt up against events or to immerse himself in experience. The product of the appreciative mode is understanding. The distinction between the product of the cognitive and appreciative modes of relating to experience is summed up and elaborated in the German philosophic terms, *Erkenntnis* and *Verstehen.* The evaluative mode consists of man's attempts to judge experience and to develop criteria that will serve as guides to future action. Values and value-orientations are the end products of this mode. The most generalized values, those that serve as criteria for evaluating other values, figure as moral standards and are regarded as especially binding on action.

The three modes of relating to experience can be disentangled only theoretically. Cognitive processes are often attended with and sometimes

---

[10] The basic idea that man has these three basic modes of experience and that his values are of these three kinds is taken from Parsons and Shils *Toward a General Theory of Action, op. cit.* The idea is set forth and explored in a number of perspectives throughout the book. The author of this paper is, however, responsible for the particular emphases and applications given to the idea here.

vitiated by appreciative and evaluative processes. All appreciative experiences contain elements of intellectual thought and evaluative judgment,
even though individuals make strenuous efforts to dispel them and to
relate to events in an immediate, total way. All evaluation necessarily
includes thought and feeling.

Predominance of the cognitive mode. The most predominant
and general characteristic of the culture of the world in the twentieth
century is the emphasis placed on the "desirability" of the cognitive as
opposed to the appreciative or evaluative mode of approaching and
dealing with experience. The reciprocal and accelerating development
of scientific method and knowledge has constituted the very heart and
essence of the cognitive cultural complex. Its spectacular success in both
the theoretical and practical realms has generated a self-perpetuating
and expanding process of cultural dissemination, so that the methods
and results of science have pervaded every area of man's experience.

By contrast, interest has been withdrawn from the appreciative and
evaluative modes of dealing with experience. Neither has been able
to develop processes that can compete with science in making energy
available for man's purposes or in solving problems of physical health
and economic production. With respect to problems of political and
social organization and mental and emotional illness, the contributions
of scientific method and knowledge have been less spectacular but they
have been more effective and predictable than methods developed out
of an appreciative or moral orientation.

Interest in the appreciative mode has not, of course, been abandoned.
Indeed, a case could be made for the proposition that the fine arts, the
purest product and expression of the appreciative mode, are in a more
flourishing condition than ever before in human history. It is probably
true that a larger proportion of the people of the United States than
of any other people in the world participate in artistic activity and
devote time to the appreciation of the arts. The same cannot be said
when man himself is regarded as the object of his appreciative mode
of experience. Our culture seems to take little delight in man's capabil-
ities and excellencies. Indeed, his potentialities are often denied, and
he himself is regarded as an object of disgust or despair. In many parts
of Western society man is regarded as secondary to political or economic systems and may be manipulated and even destroyed in their
interest.

The evaluative mode has undergone a similar cultural depreciation.
Religion, one characteristic expression of the evaluative orientation,
formerly underwent a period of eclipse. Despite evidence of a more
recent revival, candid members of the clergy are not sure whether the
increase in church membership and attendance represents a real re-

surgence of faith and conviction, a deplorable retreat into innocuous respectability, or a retreat from the seeming implications of science concerning man's nature and fate.

Certainly it is true in the United States in the mid-twentieth century that moral values fail to provide a sure guide to conduct. There seems to be little disposition to accept without question any particular form of moral imperative, whether a supernatural God or a humanistic ethic. The most ambitious and influential attempt by formal religion to recapture and dramatize a religious, moral orientation to experience is seen in certain aspects of existentialism. Yet existentialism introduces canons of thought which affront people thoroughly imbued with the cognitive, scientific mode of dealing with experience. Worse yet, existentialism seems to serve the purposes of a nihilistic retreat from the world quite as well as it serves the purposes of religion and ethics.

Bureaucracy.[11] The cognitive cultural complex, both in its more purely scientific form and in a more generalized form that emphasizes the desirability of applying rational methods and standards to problems of social and economic organization, has produced the modern economic and political bureaucracy. With the recognition of this fact, one of the major immediate causes of marital incompatibility inherent in the culture and social structure of the United States becomes explicit. Economic bureaucracies, by their very size and relative efficiency, are able to enforce their means and ends in opposition to the functional requirements of an unorganized mass of isolated marriages and families.

The consequences of the structure and operation of an economic bureaucracy reach into the heart of the family, since the employees of the bureaucracy, at every level of the bureaucratic hierarchy, are also the husbands and wives in marriages. The goals of advancement in the hierarchy and greater financial remuneration presented by the bureaucracy to managerial employees become integrated with and instrumental to the achievement of the social status goals of the family. The structure and operation of the bureaucracy thus exert pressure on the middle-class family to advance in social status. For employees in clerical positions and in the factories the bureaucracy may, though it does not necessarily do so, confine the worker to a routine job that offers little or no opportunity for advancement and that impairs his sense of individuality and self-esteem. The bureaucracy defines all its component offices and employee roles in terms of the functionally signif-

---

[11] The author is not aware of specific studies of the effects of bureaucracy as such on family life. This is surely an area of interaction in which many variables are operative. Most of the studies available seem to deal with specific consequences for the family of employment of members of the family in bureaucratically organized economic systems.

icant requirements of the job. An employee has a right to his job only as long as his performance meets the requirements of the bureaucracy. No person is indispensable. Many persons can, at least potentially, perform any given job. Formal remuneration is confined to salary or wages and to certain symbols of status attached to particular jobs. Many economic bureaucracies have introduced measures to humanize the relationship between employer and employee. In every economic bureaucracy an informal network of relationships exists to relieve tensions, provide emotional support, and increase the individual employee's sense of his identity and self-esteem. Nevertheless, all of these arrangements are distinctly ancillary to the formal system itself, and many of them are dispensable. The basic characteristics of the system are such that it provides little or no opportunity for the release of personal tensions and little emotional support. Many bureaucracies, and all bureaucracies under conditions of strain, tend to increase the tension of the worker and to withhold support. When the worker moves back into his marital role, he is likely to require an even greater measure of support and release from his spouse.

The economic system.[12]   The economic system also contributes to marital incompatibility by reason of some of its more purely economic characteristics, more or less independently of its bureaucratic structure. Although Weber's formulation of the relationship between the Protestant ethic and capitalism may be true historically, it is highly questionable whether the contemporary economic system in the United States operates in terms of any ethic or, indeed, any value other than the ones it has itself generated. The basic value that guides the operation of the economic system asserts the precedence of the right of the system to make a profit over the right of every other interest in society. The value-orientation of the system reveals itself in a number of ways as a special instance of the exaggerated cognitive value-orientation of the contemporary world. Its theoretical base is still grounded on an overly abstract, partialized concept of the individual as an "economic man," that is, a hypothetical creature who can judge accurately what his economic interests are and who is free to act in terms of those interests. The economic structure, as a system, is interested in only this aspect of man, whether as entrepreneur, laborer, or consumer. Any attempt on the part of government or other organized interests to force the system to take account of man's other institutional requirements or of his appreciative and moral value-orientation is met with resistance.

---

[12] An analysis of the economic system as a structural-functional system will be found in Talcott Parsons and Neil J. Smelser, *Economy and Society* (Glencoe, Ill.: The Free Press, 1956). The particular emphases and interpretations set forth here are the responsibility of the author.

The abstract, partialized view of man contributes to the depreciation of the self-esteem of the individual worker and increases his need for support and recognition within his marriage. The economic system always bargains sharply and enforces its "rights" down to the last clause in the finest print in the contract. It accepts only a narrow range of responsibility toward its workers. It pays the wages or salary agreed on only as long as the system needs his labor. Thus, as husband, he has no security in the source of his income. The increase of automation in industry exacerbates this basic insecurity. The threat falls most heavily on the least skilled and least educable workers.

The system can regulate the nature and amount of its products and its prices solely in terms of its own goals and functional requirements, irrespective of the needs of the families that must use its products. It can locate plants and offices in accordance with the economics of its own operations, without regard to the needs of the families in a community for employment.

The system itself operates in erratic and only grossly predictable ways. Perhaps to death and taxes may be added the certainty that business will have its ups and downs, the "downs" being unemployment which, at least in the present, is not entirely compensated by an increase of employment during the upswings. Nor in the last decade have the recessions been accompanied by a corresponding lowering of prices. The worker as husband or wife is caught in the vicious trap of concomitant increases in unemployment and rises in prices.

One of the most destructive consequences for the family of the effort of the system to recognize only profit-making as a legitimate aim is the failure of the system to accept institutionalized responsibility for the education, health, and welfare requirements of the population. There has been a reluctant recognition that elementary and secondary education should be paid for out of tax funds, but the recognition has been extended only partially to governmental support of higher education. A similar situation exists with respect to governmental support of hospitals and medical care: partial support is provided, but many gaps exist. The problem is much worse with respect to governmental support of social welfare. Spokesmen for the economic system stigmatize welfare services as "handouts" and the recipients of such services as "reliefers" and "chiselers." They refuse to recognize the range and complexity of the welfare services that are needed and advocate that the problems with which the services are designed to cope be dealt with by coercive methods.

The representatives of the economic system tend to regard the system of privately supported educational institutions and health and welfare services as preferable to the publicly supported ones. The privately

supported institutions are regarded as having the voluntary characteristics of economic free enterprise and are, in great measure, free of
governmental "interference." Nevertheless, the economic system does
not fully accept institutionalized responsibility for their support. As a
consequence, most public agencies and institutions are chronically under-
financed and poorly staffed. Private agencies and institutions may be
better financed and staffed, but they are, characteristically, relatively
small operations which cannot meet the total needs of their geographical
area for the type of service they provide.

The cost of production of some of the resources and services needed
by families is proportionately very high. Housing is an outstanding
example. The cultural requirement of a separate abode for each family
of orientation presents the economic system with a demand for the
production of a large number of relatively small units of housing, all
with much the same facilities. This need would seem to be of a kind
that the American economic system, with its emphasis on mass production, could meet easily and cheaply. Other economic and cultural factors
in the situation, however, such as scarcity of land in urban areas,
restrictive work rules set by the unions in the building trades, and an
adherence by builders to the use of traditional materials and designs
have made housing costly.

Similarly, health care has become expensive. Modern medical care
requires costly instrumentation and must be technically supported by
costly research. For various reasons, both cultural and economic, families are requesting hospitalization rather than care at home and
physicians are acceding to this demand. Physicians themselves seem to
be conducting their practices more within the value-orientation of commercial business than within the traditional value-orientation of professional service. They restrict or refuse to make home calls. They tend to
locate in the downtown areas of cities or in middle-class suburbs, in
which their prospective income is higher, thus leaving many poor and
less urban areas inadequately provided with medical services.

Despite its adherence to a narrowly conceived profit-making orientation, the economic system, in some areas, admits other cultural values,
some of whose consequences contribute to marital incompatibility.
Some business firms conform to the culture of the surrounding community with respect to various forms of racial and ethnic discrimination. Some participate in the cultural complex that disvalues the older
person. Some share in the general cultural definition of the acting-out
person who has been arrested and convicted as a "criminal" or "ex-con"
who can never again be trusted. The consequence of the implementation of all these values is restriction of employment opportunities for
husbands and wives. It is only fair to state that many business firms

have moved along with the larger society and have even, on occasion, given leadership in changing these discriminatory values and practices.

In the twenty years following the passage of the Wagner Labor Relations Act in 1935 union membership expanded spectacularly in the United States. The new unions which made up the CIO seemed for a time to be challenging some aspects of the basic value-orientation of the economic system. They not only made the same demands as the AFL unions but they demanded greater job security; they pressed for so-called "fringe benefits," that is, various forms of insurance for the worker and his family against the hazards of unemployment, sickness, and old age. When they insisted on paid annual vacations, they were, in effect, protesting against the tendency of the economic bureaucracies to treat the worker as an automaton. In some of their abortive demands and proposals they challenged some of the basic theoretical assumptions of the economic system. The proposal of the United Automobile Workers that the companies reveal the details of their financial positions as groundwork for bargaining constituted an assertion that large-scale economic enterprise has responsibility to other interests than those of the owners and managers. The demand of the same union for a guaranteed annual wage placed the worker in a different theoretical as well as practical relationship to his employer. Within their own organizations many of these unions provided educational, health, and welfare services for their members and their families. Throughout this period these unions presented to the American public the clearest and most effective case for a shift in the value-orientation of the economic system. They were asking that appreciative and moral values be introduced into the system. Since families in the United States are oriented at least as much to these values as to the efficiency values of the exclusively cognitive orientation, the unions were speaking in the interest of the families of the United States.

During the last seven or eight years the voice and the actions of the unions have decreased in fervor and in effectiveness. Total union membership has declined as the working population has risen. Perhaps, as some observers maintain, unionism has less intellectual, emotional, and moral appeal to the educated technician who is replacing the semiskilled worker in the industries of the country. Perhaps it is true that the gains that unions sought for the semiskilled have been won for the highly skilled. Those who most need the gains for which the unions have fought are the unskilled, and they have rarely been able to act in their own interest as well-organized and disciplined union members. Moreover, as individual unions increased in size, they, too, to a degree, have adopted a bureaucratic and hierarchical form of organization. The power and influence of the individual union member, his sense of mission, and awareness of his identity as a union man have diminished. Some union leaders have succumbed to the temptation to engage in corrupt practices, and some unions have fallen into the hands of venal leaders. The spokesman for the business interests, including most of the press, has been avid and able to seize on these examples of corruption and portray them to the country as evidences of the corruption of the whole union movement. Unions and the federations of unions have quarreled among themselves and vitiated their own effectiveness. The sad result of the decline of aggressive and effective unionism has been that the family has lost the major champion of its interests within the economic system. In a sense, this decline may be regarded as one of the more general causes of marital incompatibility.

It would be incorrect to assess the influence of the economic system on the family as only destructive. Certainly the family has benefited from the vast increases in productivity of the economic system. To this extent, the operation of the economic system serves as a primary preventive of marital incompatibility. Yet as Norman Lourie's paper on poverty demonstrates, a substantial proportion of American families continue to live poverty-stricken lives, with all the sad consequences of poverty for individuals and families.

Government. In many ways in the United States the effect of government, especially the federal government, on the family is beneficial. The government can and does operate within the appreciative and evaluative as well as the cognitive value-orientation. It can and, to a limited degree, does attempt to arrange that the functional requirements of families as well as those of the economic system are met.

Nevertheless, government in the United States does exert some destructive influences on the family and this contributes to the occurrence of marital incompatibility. These influences are the consequences of the size of government, its bureaucratic form of organization, its political form of organization, the way in which it relates to the needs of the citizenry, and the authority of government and the position of the United States in world affairs.

The government of the United States has asserted publicly and eloquently over a long period of time that the individual, as a citizen, has the right and the ability to determine the policies and practices of the government. "Of the people, by the people, and for the people" affirms a deeply held value. When such a government becomes so large and unwieldy that the individual citizen can no longer make his voice heard, the consequences for his self-esteem and sense of justice are most unfortunate. In the United States the result has been a kind of resentful apathy—a sense of being manipulated and exploited and in some quarters support of various leaders of the "lunatic fringe." This devastation of public morale and self-esteem places a heavier burden on marriage to provide emotional support and release of tension.

For most people the stereotype of bureaucracy is the governmental agency, so enmeshed in "red tape" that it cannot perform its proper duties or take individual differences into account. The consequences of massive, hierarchical, bureaucratic organization of government are rigidity of operation, delay, and emphasis on formal rules. Governmental institutions and agencies, especially those that provide education and health and welfare services and therefore come into direct interaction with families, have been able to mitigate many of their traditional bureaucratic attributes. Nevertheless, some formal structure of regulations always remains, and families in the throes of a crisis are likely to be especially sensitive to it.

Government in the United States is organized politically in two separate but interlocking ways. First the legislative, executive, and judicial functions are organized independently of one another. Each of these functional organizations tends to be jealous of its own prerogatives and to compete with the others for power and influence. When the system is operating at its worst, any interest of the people, including the interests of families, may be lost sight of in the pulling and hauling among the various legislative bodies, executive offices, and courts. Second, government is organized on federal, state, and local "levels." Competition among them for power, influence, and popular support is severe. Each appeals for legitimation to a strong historical tradition: the founding fathers, states rights, and local control of local affairs. Each has to impose taxes and each has the responsibility and the opportunity to spend public funds. All interests, including the interests of families, are likely to suffer from attempts of government to retain control at one level or to pass on responsibility for taxing and spending to another level.

In making policy the legislative bodies and executive agencies, at every level of government, tend to respond to the pressures of organized interests rather than to the needs of unorganized individuals. "Lobbying," the organized attempt to influence governmental policy making, has become a major factor in the conduct of both private and public affairs. Unfortunately for themselves, the institutions of marriage and the family are not organized as interests to influence government. Many types of organization speak for marriage and the family, and many try to use the emotional appeal of marriage and the family to influence the government to act, but the institutions of marriage and the family have no direct access to government.

Strictly speaking, it is incorrect to say that the authority inherent in government bears hard on marriage and the family or contributes to the causation of marital incompatibility. Some bureaucratic officials and some judges overreach themselves in the use of authority by reason of their own insecurities. On the whole, however, the American governmental system seems to be participating in the cultural trend which recommends that the imposition of authority be withheld whenever possible.

The difficulty with authority resides not in government but in the family itself. There is a strong cultural tradition in the United States, going back perhaps to the circumstances that led the early settlers to come here, that all governmental authority is inherently unjust and that flouting it is permissible when it can be done safely. The American husband or wife approaches the public school, hospital, or governmental social service agency with a wary eye. He will reveal only as much of his affairs as he must to get what he wants. He will go his own way to the extent that he can. This tradition and its consequences in attitudes and behaviors make it somewhat more difficult to provide public health and welfare services directly to people than to provide similar private services.

The consequences of the position of the United States and of the dilemmas confronting the United States in world affairs bear heavily on marriage and the family, both directly and indirectly. Directly, the military draft forces postponement of careers and marriages. The calling up of reserve units separates husbands and wives. The effects on marriage are not only economic. The caseload of the Home Service Division of the American Red Cross reveals the broader consequences. Immature wives, deprived of the emotional support of their husbands, suffer crippling anxiety and fail in the performance of various marital and maternal functions. Immature or emotionally crippled husbands use military service as a means of fleeing from the marriage or become involved with other women at some distant military post.

The indirect effects are harder to identify and evaluate. American families seem to live through the successive crises and the alternations of triumph and despair with a good deal of aplomb. Yet there have been occasional mass outbursts of feeling approaching panic. There may be grounds to suspect that the perils of the international situation are exerting a continuous strain. If this is so, the consequences are likely to be manifested in marital relationships, since it is those relationships that bear such a heavy responsibility to provide people with emotional support and release from tension.

Law. To discuss government and law apart from each other is to make an artificial distinction. Government operates by enacting, administering, interpreting, and enforcing laws. The distinction is one of perspective. In a discussion of the relationship between government and marital incompatibility emphasis is placed on the general characteristics of government. In discussing the law and its relationship to marital incompatibility emphasis is placed on particular bodies of law that pose conditions within which families must function.

Divorce laws reflect the cultural ambivalence toward formal termination of marriage. In many jurisdictions the legal grounds for divorce are narrowly conceived. In a few jurisdictions they are written so broadly that they create a tragic and humiliating farce. Divorce laws take the form of an adversary proceeding in which one spouse seeks divorce on the grounds that the other has injured him. It is beyond the competence of the writer to judge whether divorce laws should be uniform throughout the United States. The idea seems to make sense, but perhaps there are cultural variations among people in various parts of the country that would justify different grounds for divorce. What can be affirmed is that divorce laws should be written and administered in ways to protect the dignity of the spouses.

Laws that require husbands to support their wives and children are often written, interpreted, and enforced in ways that exacerbate incompatibility in already unhappy and deteriorated marital situations. Alimony laws seem to provide opportunities for divorced spouses to continue to wreak vengeance on each other. Surely it makes little sense to force a husband to continue to perform the one marital function of financial support when all other aspects of the marriage have broken down. Surely a more dignified and stable way can be found to provide financial support for divorced women.

Residence laws that withhold public services and benefits from persons legally defined as nonresident in a state or community may save money for the governmental jurisdiction that imposes them, but they contribute to the misery of the most disadvantaged families in American society: the families of migrant workers and of unskilled workers who seek better employment opportunities. Laws that permit discrimination in housing and employment on grounds of race exert a similar destructive effect on the most disadvantaged families in the society.

It is, perhaps, in this same cultural context that the laws and policies which set standards for public assistance should be discussed. No matter how these laws and standards are phrased, public assistance provides little money to needy families. The grants support life and physical health if the recipient families manage them well. Indigent families are required to manage their funds more efficiently than everyone else in the population. The opportunity for some margin, some cushion, in the use of money is a powerful antidote to strain in interpersonal relations and intrapersonal conflict. The starkness and monotony of poverty contribute to despair and help to break down whatever abilities married people may possess to perform the various functions of marriage, including the rendering of reciprocal emotional support and recognition.

If this seems to be a plea for the waste of public funds, it should be pointed out in rejoinder that "waste" is an ambiguous term. What to the school board is waste of money on "frills," to the school principal is expenditure on facilities to educate the child in social living. What to the business-oriented legislative body or public welfare commissioner is waste of public money to support the lazy and immoral elements of the population is to the recipients a meager allowance that provides no margin and no motivation for trying to reorient their lives toward financial independence. Public assistance agencies are, in general, confined within a rigid economic orientation that defines standards in too rationalistic a way. Certainly business firms that operate within the economic system impose no such rigidities on their own use of funds, as practices in the handling of expense accounts demonstrate. Nor need public assistance itself operate only in this narrow, ungiving way, as the policies and practices with respect to old age assistance in some states show. The culture of the United States seems to disvalue poverty so severely that it provides institutionalized means to punish the poor for being poor.

Related to the high value placed on the right and ability of the citizen to determine the policies of his government is the recognition of his right and responsibility to determine the major issues of his private life. Responsibilities, however, are emphasized rather than rights. Failure to perform his responsibilities is defined as morally wrong. When his inability to support himself and his family or to make a go of his marriage becomes a matter of public knowledge, the public, before assisting him, has a prior interest in finding out who is at fault in the situation, who failed to meet his responsibilities, and how. This moral value-orientation underlies the legal approach to divorce, separation, and crime. It also underlies the persistent tendency in the administration of public assistance to hold the unemployed worker responsible for his condition. This moral value orientation is derived from the major religion of the Western world but constitutes a special interpretation of the ethical implications of that religion. It is a heritage of the Protestant ethic and is incongruent with the understanding of human behavior and social problems derived from the modern behavioral sciences. As the dynamic behavioral sciences and restrictive morality compete for supremacy in ordering the public services, the agencies of government can manifest only internal conflict and confusion of policy in dealing with such problems as marital incompatibility.

Most illegal offenses that husbands and wives commit against each other are misdemeanors and bring fines or relatively short sentences. Some spouses, however, do commit felonies on each other, and many spouses, usually the husbands, commit felonies outside the marriage. There is no uniform code of sentences for given offenses. The laws of the different states set different sentences for the same offenses, and judges of the same court differ widely in their sentencing practices. In general, federal courts impose longer sentences than state courts. Long sentences, of course, break up marriages and families either informally or, when the spouse seeks divorce, formally. Whatever constructive influence the spouse might have been able to bring to bear on the rehabilitation of the offender is lost. It is, perhaps, pertinent to remark here that only in a few jurisdictions has probation and parole work developed to the stage in which it has a real and effective orientation to the whole family of the offender.

Discriminatory value-orientations. Certain aspects of the culture of the United States that contribute to the causation of marital incompatibility must be discussed independently of the particular ways in which they are institutionalized. These broad value-orientations permeate many different kinds of institutions, including marriage and the family. The ones discussed here are the culture of social class; racial, ethnic, and religious discrimination; devaluation of the aged; and anomie. Note has already been taken of the ways in which each of them exerts a destructive influence on marriage and the family, both from within and without.

The material and symbolic manifestations of class status permeate all institutions. Society exerts pressure on and offers inducements to the family to advance its social class status, as it withholds resources and opportunities that will enable the family to achieve the advancement. Some barriers between classes may be more difficult to pass than others, and, as already noted, there is a tendency in American society to punish the poor for being poor. On the whole, however, class barriers can be maintained by denying opportunity to families and individuals lower on the scale, by the altering of the symbols of higher status as members of the lower orders of society take on these symbolic behaviors and possessions, and by the social strategies of physical separation, stereotyping, and ridicule. The system is not entirely closed. Advancement can be achieved, at least with respect to the economic aspects of social class status, and partial initial acceptance of the newcomer to a higher social class status is often followed by total acceptance of the next generation of his family.

The culture of racial, ethnic, and religious discrimination enforces more stringent exclusion of members of the devaluated categories of people. The barriers are higher, in some cases approaching the exclusiveness of a caste system, in that intermarriage between members of different categories is legally or socially forbidden. In addition to the social strategies employed for maintaining the class system, cruder, crueler strategies are employed; strict prohibition of social interaction by setting up separate, parallel institutions; physical expulsion or removal from the community; and physical violence. Although there has been some diminution in the social comprehensiveness and severity of racial discrimination, the gains have been won only by hard, often heroic effort, and setbacks and outbreaks of the crueler forms of enforcing racial discrimination have been frequent.

During the last twenty years the culture of ethnic and religious discrimination in the United States has tended to become milder, though it has by no means disappeared. It has increasingly come to resemble class discrimination with respect to withholding access to opportunity and to the social strategies employed to maintain the separation and identity of the several ethnic and religious categories. There is a tendency to identify categories of people regarded as objectionable as racially rather than ethnically or religiously different.

The cultural devaluation of the aged, and to some extent the middle aged, is much milder than the cultures of social class or racial, ethnic, and religious discrimination. It is manifested predominantly in the economic and sexual spheres of life. Employment is terminated at some arbitrary age, usually sixty-five. Opportunity for new employment begins to decrease in the forties. Sexual interests of persons in their fifties are regarded as slightly ridiculous. Sexual interests of people over sixty are regarded as unseemly or their existence is denied. As a consequence of the cultural devaluation of middle age, unemployment of a middle-aged spouse constitutes a far more serious problem for the marriage than does unemployment of a younger person. The sudden cessation of employment at sixty-five not only reduces income sharply; it also poses a threat to the sense of identity and self-esteem of the retired worker and demands a greater measure of support and forbearance from his spouse. The depreciation or denial of sexual interests among the elderly makes it more difficult for widows and widowers to begin a courtship, to carry it through to remarriage, or to obtain acceptance of the idea of remarriage from their grown children.

It is being said on many fronts that the society of the United States is suffering from anomie, or normlessness.[13] It is alleged, both at home

---

[13] The basic papers concerning anomie are, of course, to be found in Robert K. Merton, *Social Theory and Social Structure.* See especially the second edition (Glencoe, Ill.: The Free Press, 1957) Chapter 4: "Social Structure and Anomie," p. 131, and Chapter 5: "Continuities in the Theory of Social Structure and Anomie," p. 161. Reference should also be made to the psychoanalytic interpretation of the same phenomenon in individuals in Alan Wheelis's *The Quest for Identity* (New

and abroad, that Americans, as individuals and in their various social institutions, manifest a lack of purpose, a lack of conviction about moral values, and an absorption in the pursuit of money and selfish, brutish pleasure. That some degree of normlessness of this kind does exist in the society of the United States can hardly be questioned. It is more difficult to determine how widespread it is, how deeply it has permeated individual and institutional life, how much it has vitiated the ability of Americans to solve their domestic and international problems, and how much the current situation is different from the past. The evidence available on both sides of the question is necessarily partial and impressionistic.

How is the evidence to be summed up and what verdict should be reached? Middle-aged critics who compare the United States of today with the country of their youth in the 1930's and 1940's probably miss the sense of high purpose in fighting the wars against depression and fascism. Critics who are slightly older and can remember the 1920's may not be so convinced that the morals and sense of purpose of the American people have degenerated to any marked degree. When the American culture of today is set against the background not of its own immediate past but of the broad sweep of history and cultures, it is not immediately apparent that American society is less self-consciously purposeful or less devoted to the pursuit of high ideals.

On the other hand, it does seem to be true that there has been some slackening off in the sense of purpose, some increase of questioning of basic values, some loss of confidence as a people, and some deterioration of morale among adolescents. The value problem in American society should not be denied. Adherence to a cognitive orientation alone means that only knowledge scientifically derived, with emotions and values excluded from scientific study, is regarded as a legitimate influence on action. Even though such knowledge suggests a course of action that runs contrary to the feelings or values of an individual or a group of people, it is still legitimate to pursue it because feelings and values should not be permitted to influence action. Such a viewpoint permits people to be used as instruments in the pursuit of goals without regard to their individual welfare. Since all men, even scientists and administrators, have feelings and values that insidiously intrude themselves into professionally scientific study and scientifically based administration, they create the monstrous situation in which people are manipulated in the name of scientific truth and efficiency to permit governmental and economic systems to achieve ends that are really determined by the emotions and the values of the manipulators. With the

York: W. W. Norton, 1958). The reader will find many clear parallels, too, in the various works of Erich Fromm.

increase of size and efficiency that science has produced in governmental and economic systems, the individual and his family may be unable to resist such manipulative processes.

Summary

In summary, many of the values on which American society is built affirm the worth and dignity of the individual, motivate him to the pursuit of goals consistent with that view, and provide him with a firm sense of purpose and individual identity. On the other hand, the attempt to take over into the field of human relations in unmodified form the exclusively cognitive orientation suitable for the study and manipulation of the physical world has presented a rationalization for monolithic theoretical systems and has produced a pseudo-scientific emphasis on efficiency. As manifested in the economic system, this orientation has resulted in a tendency to closure and permits the manipulation of people in the interests of the system regardless of their desires and values. As a result, the values and the sense of identity of individuals have been impaired. The problem for the individual has been compounded by the size of the governmental and economic systems with which he has to cope and his consequent inability to identify or influence the sources of power and decision making. The operation of the social class system and discriminatory values and practices with respect to race, ethnic background, and religion have also produced a diminution of personal values, a blurring of the individual's identity, and destructive modes of adaptation to the situation. In the situation of the United States today there are potentialities for the development of a fuller, more purposeful life for the nation and all its people, yet there are potentialities for an increase of resentment, apathy, and drift.

Causes Inherent in Individual Personality [14]

Despite all the sources and kinds of assault to which marriage is subjected from the culture, the economy, the state, and the society, marital compatibility does not depend on any prescription of mental or emotional health. No degree of mental retardation or any specific form of psychopathology necessarily leads to marital incompatibility. The nature of the interaction between the partners is the key to the intrapersonal causes of marital compatibility or incompatibility. As long as the partners' needs are satisfied in the marital interaction and as long as each can compensate for the shortcomings of the other in the performance of the various functions of marriage, compatibility can be achieved. Not all functions may be performed to the satisfaction of both partners or of

[14] The formulations in this section depend on a general familiarity with the literature of psychoanalytic theory and its applications in social work. Certain works have been found especially helpful. These include Beatrice Simcox Reiner and Irving Kaufman, *Character Disorders in Parents of Delinquents* (New York: Family Service Association of America, 1959).

society, but the total outcome may be more satisfying for everyone concerned than dissolution of the marriage.

Many marriages are incompatible partly or mainly because the emotional needs and the modes of adaptation of the two partners do not "fit." To understand how and why the personalities of marital partners may fail to complement each other, attention must first be directed to some aspects of the structure and function of personality that are especially trying to other people. The basic cause of the difficulty is the way in which the personality is organized to cope with the needs and fears induced by pregenital fixations.

Pregenital fixations. The pregenital fixations, even though they are not so severe that they result in identifiable psychopathology, produce character traits that can be troublesome to the marital partner in the intimate interactions of marriage. The person with a strong narcissistic fixation tends to be self-centered and insensitive to the feelings and needs of others. He has little capacity to identify with others and perceives them only as objects to be manipulated in his own interest or as extensions of himself. He acts as if the world is or should have been created for his needs and purposes. He demands that the marital partner and the children revolve around him as the center of their universe. Although he may be overburdened with guilt over some issues, he may be quite heartless and free of guilt about others. The use of projection, one of his most characteristic defense mechanisms, makes him attribute his own sexual wishes and hostilities to others. As a result, he is often suspicious of the (to him) patently tempting and hostile world in which he lives.

The individual with strong oral receptive fixations tends to cling to others and to demand support and gratification from them in either an actively or passively hostile way. His needs are insatiable, and his capacity to tolerate frustration and delay is extremely limited. Nothing the marital partner gives is quite enough to satisfy him. His whining demands and his ingratitude exhaust the patience of his spouse, who tries to introduce realistic limits into the relationship or who retaliates by withholding any gratification at all. The dependent spouse, in turn, is thrown into a panic and increases his demands. To the dependent person, other people are essentially objects to be squeezed and sucked for his own sustenance. He is starved for what he calls love. His superego, poorly developed, permits him to exploit others. Often he incorporates other people so totally that he engulfs them and destroys their individuality. When they disappoint him, as inevitably they must, he turns rapidly from the disappointing person to a new one who seems to promise "love" and gratification.

The person with strong oral sadistic fixations builds on top of his dependency needs a set of biting, attacking, sarcastic character traits. No person with these fixations can trust the world. The oral-sadistic person attacks before he is attacked. He cannot trust his spouse or give the spouse credit for good intentions. He is likely to be rejected by the outer world because of his hostility and to make his family a parade ground for all his grudges.

All of these orally fixated people suffer from underlying depressive feelings. Basically, they feel worthless and abandoned. Sometimes they suffer consciously from depression. They are then impatient and demanding or sunk into themselves and inefficient in the performance of their duties. Others spend much of their lives avoiding conscious awareness of their underlying sense of emptiness, worthlessness, and loneliness. Their defensive activities take the form of various kinds of acting out, including drinking and infidelity to the marital partner.

Persons with strong anal fixations present several types of character traits. In one type, in which the underlying anal wishes are given expression in ill-disguised symbolic form, the person frankly enjoys messiness and disorder. The predominant fixation is at the anal expulsive level and an impulsive, angry quality characterizes his interactions with other people. Often he frankly tries to dominate them without regard to their needs or wishes. When the fixation is more at the anal retentive level, the individual is cautious, stubborn, and passively controlling of others. He is penurious about money, and he saves and hoards various kinds of trifles. He, too, tends to defend himself by means of projection, so that he is suspicious and hostile in his relationships with other people, including his marital partner. His emotions are withheld, and his conscious emotional life is thin and restricted. He cannot give, and he is suspicious of accepting anything offered to him. All persons with strong anal fixations have difficulty with the authoritative aspects of human relationships. They tend to see an intent to control them where no such intent exists. When the anal expulsive fixation is the stronger, the person wages an open and everlasting battle against his spouse, his employer, his children's teachers, and the representatives of government. When the anal retentive fixation is stronger, he is likely to protect himself against what he regards as unjust exploitation by stubbornness and argumentativeness.

Neurotic traits. Persons who move as far in their development as the oedipal level but who are unable to pass through the oedipal experience successfully may develop neurotic character traits. Later, in response to the impact of threatening or seductive life experiences, they may suffer from neurotic anxiety followed by the development of neurotic symptoms. On the whole, however, it is the neurotic character traits that are most important today in contributing to marital incompatibility.

Since these traits manifest regressions from the oedipal to the pre-oedipal points of fixation, they resemble the various traits described. There are differences, however. If the person is able to experience the oedipal conflicts as such, his ego will have become firmer, more flexible, and better integrated than it would have if his development had been arrested at the earlier levels. He will not act so entirely in terms of the pleasure principle and the repetition compulsion. Reality will exercise some control over his actions. He will, moreover, have developed a superego by identification with the oedipal aspects of his experiences with his two parents. The pre-oedipally fixated person will have incorporated only partial precursors of a superego. Consequently, the person who has developed as far as the oedipal phase will experience guilt and signal anxiety instead of the terror that characterizes the inner experience of the pre-oedipally fixated person.

The person who, in the face of inability to move successfully through the oedipal experience, has regressed to the phallic level, suffers from problems of sexual identity. The man unconsciously experiences castration anxiety, against which he protects himself with defenses of repression and denial. As long as these defenses hold, he may present himself to the world as a person who is timid in his relationships with both men and women. He may be unable to make the most of his abilities in the vocational world. He may be an ineffectual, somewhat impotent lover. On the other hand, he may have developed a set of essentially counterphobic defenses. Then he will seem to be the daredevil who takes unnecessary risks in his occupation and who proves his masculinity to himself in an endless series of affairs with other women.

The woman who regresses from the oedipal to the phallic level also uses the defenses of repression and denial. Unconsciously she feels herself, as a woman, to be injured and ugly. Consciously she feels an insatiable need to be loved and to prove to herself that she is whole and desirable. She may, like the man, be driven into activity to deny her anxiety. She may try to become a better man that her husband and so become the tragic but destructive figure of the castrating woman. She may retain her seeming femininity but be driven through an interminable series of unsatisfactory love affairs in which she unconsciously symbolically deprives each lover of his penis and captures it for herself.

When the regression is to the anal levels, the well-known obsessive-compulsive character traits are seen. The interplay of the defenses of reaction formation, isolation, and undoing produce the picture of the overconscientious, meticulous person who worries about money and time, who is over conciliatory and apologetic in his relationships with other people, and who also manifests the anal characteristics of stubbornness and active or passive attempts to control other people and all the events of life. For these people life is a constant series of preparations and few consummations. In both their emotional and sexual relationships they are guarded, withholding, and controlling. They are literal and pre-occupied with detail to the point that they drive freer individuals into a frenzy, but they are often able to find positions of high status and abundant remuneration in an occupational world which at certain levels puts a premium on efficiency and the ability to perform routine tasks.

All these character traits result from various combinations of fixation, regression, ego defenses, over- and underdeveloped superegos, difficulties in making identifications, and patterns of object choice. The various elements of personality structure and function enter into the causation of marital incompatibility because they lead to patterned modes of adaptation in social interactions and in the conduct of the affairs of life that are immature, ineffectual, and exasperating to others. In psychoanalytic terms, motivation and behavior are characterized by the pleasure principle and repetition compulsion rather than the reality principle.

Pregenital fixations and regressions result in the perpetuation and predominance of the needs, wishes, and terrors of infancy and childhood over the needs of the marital partner and the functional requirements of the marriage. These needs and wishes are insatiable; the terrors are overmastering. The capacity to tolerate frustration or delay is low.

Little or no superego develops to impose inner prohibitions or exploitative behavior. If aspects of superego do develop, they are so harsh in their demands on the ego that it must repress and deny them so that it can act as if they did not exist. The ability to conceive and pursue ideals remains rudimentary.

Defenses of the ego. The primitive ego defenses necessary to ensure some degree of internal comfort, equilibrium, and integration of the personality are difficult for the marital partner to cope with in the intimate interactions of marriage. Primitive incorporation by his partner gives a spouse a feeling of being swallowed up and obliterated. Confronted with projection, he is blamed and held responsible for motives and actions of which he is innocent. The use of denial by his spouse leaves him wondering, in puzzlement and exasperation, how she can possibly fail to see the nature of her own characteristics and actions when they are so plain to him. Repression in her confronts him with insensitivities and failures of perception, blanks in her feelings and inhibitions in her actions he can neither understand nor change. Reaction formation results in exaggerated protestations of love, an artificial kind of compliance, and extremes of self-sacrificing behavior that are patently false. Isolation produces a divorce of feeling from action he cannot understand: she is calm when she should be angry but becomes violently angry when the occasion for her anger seems trifling. She seems to divide up her life into impenetrable segments, so that what she learns in one experience she cannot use in another. Undoing causes her to engage in petty rituals, in word and deed, which are annoying but which she cannot give up.

Difficulties in identification make the spouse insensitive to the needs of the partner and the children. She may seem to go her own way regardless of their pleas. She may seem unsure of who she really is in the sense that she reveals no constant identity on which they can count.

Object-choice. Difficulties in object-choice take several forms. She may treat husband and children as if they were things to be pushed or moved at her convenience. She may relate only to a part of her spouse. She may see him only as a provider, in which case he may feel that he is being exploited. She may consider him an unreasonable tyrant, with the result that he may feel that an injustice is being done to him. She may use him only as a sexualized male, so that he may feel depreciated as a total man and, perhaps, somewhat ridiculous. She may relate to him as if he were her father or her mother, leaving him wondering when they are ever going to break away from her family. When the husband is the one who has difficulties in object-relationships, he may become so dependent, so clinging, and so passive that his wife will realize, with anger and disgust, that he is making a mother of her. He may see her as a termagant and tyrant, his "warden" or his "ball and chain," leaving her feeling depreciated and resentful at this picture of herself. He may treat her only as a female animal, demanding intercourse without tenderness; she may often complain with resentment that he treats her as if she were a prostitute.

Personality disorders. Any or all of the basic structural and dynamic difficulties outlined above may become so exaggerated that truly pathological personality disorder may result. Many of the patients and clients seen by members of the clinical professions suffer from such personality disorders. The theory has been advanced that the circumstances of modern life, that is, the cultural, political, economic, and social variables described in the preceding section, combine to produce personality disorders which present, in extreme degree, the motivations and behaviors already described. They are inadequate or unstable, or immovably passive, or their behaviors are characterized by a driving, guiltless exploitation of every person and every situation they encounter. Their marriages are shambles, often held together only because of some interplay between the partners of sadistic and masochistic needs or because of fear of trying to go on without anyone to depend on to meet their needs.

Self and identity. The ego is the product of the interaction of constitution and experience. The qualities of the ego functions of perceiving, interpreting, judging, and acting, at any given time, are the result of the interplay of these basic capacities of the individual psyche with the biologically determined and historically molded instincts and energies. One of the qualities of ego functioning is self-awareness. The human being does not behave entirely as if he were driven by forces inside and outside himself. He reflects on the nature and consequences of these forces for himself. In more abstract terms, the concept of the self or identity acts as an intervening variable in the operation of the personality system and in the interactions of the personality with the outside world. In recent years the attention of the clinical professions has been directed toward an attempt to understand the concept of self or identity. The clinical observations and theoretical formulations that have resulted have provided a common ground of interest with social psychology which has, for a long time, studied this concept and its functions in human motivation and behavior.[15] Much work remains to be done, both empirical and theoretical. On the empirical side not enough is known about how people see themselves as a result of their biological characteristics, their particular forms of life experience, and the various cultural, political, economic, and social milieus in which they live. Not enough is known about how their varying perceptions of themselves influence their actions. On the theoretical side, the concept of self or identity cannot be fitted neatly into the structure of personality as it is set forth in psychoanalytic theory.

Many aspects of marital incompatibility are illuminated by an understanding of the ways in which an individual perceives himself in the

---

[15] Limitations of space preclude a more intensive exploration of the contributions of ego psychology to the understanding of marital incompatibility. For an introduction to the concept of the autonomy of the ego, the reader is referred to the following works: Joseph E. Lipschutz, "A Brief Review of Psychoanalytic Ego Psychology," *Social Casework*, Vol. 45, No. 1 (January 1964), p. 3; David Rapaport, "The Autonomy of the Ego," *Bulletin of the Menninger Clinic*, Vol. 15, No. 4 (July 1951), p. 113, and "The Theory of Ego Autonomy: A Generalization," ibid., Vol. 22, No. 1 (January 1958), p. 13.

More thorough discussion of the subject will be found in the articles of Hartmann, Kris, Loewenstein, and Beres, Lustman *et al.*, in the successive volumes of the *Psychoanalytic Study of the Child*. The papers comprising David Rapaport's *Organization and Pathology of Thought* (New York: Columbia University Press, 1951) set forth the theoretical background for the newer ego theory. The concept of identity is developed by Erik H. Erikson. Among the major works are "The Problem of Ego Identity, *Journal of the American Psychoanalytic Association*," Vol. 4, (1956), pp. 56–121; "Identity and the Life Cycle", Selected Papers, in *Psychological Issues* (New York: International Universities Press, 1959), p. 18. *See also* the recent report of a student research project at the School of Applied Social Sciences, Western Reserve University: Elizabeth G. Meier, "An Inquiry into the Concepts of Ego Identity and Ego Diffusion," *Social Casework*, Vol. 45, No. 2 (February 1964), p. 63.

marital role. The elucidation of correspondences between the solution or failure of solution of various developmental tasks of the individual and the components of his sense of identity contribute depth and consistency to our understanding. Erik Erikson has done the major work on this problem. He has shown how the vicissitudes in the development of the sense of being able to trust oneself and others, in feeling that one can control and command the major issues of one's life, in perceiving clearly how one is boy or girl, in developing a sense of being able to do skillfully what the situations of one's life require, and in feeling that one fits into some significant career pattern—all are preparations for embarking with sureness and self-esteem on the intimacy of marriage.

Summary. Incompatibility does not necessarily occur because the structure and operation of one partner is in some degree inadequate. Incompatibility is, by definition, a matter of disharmony between the partners in performing the functions of marriage. It is a problem in social interaction.

The real danger which inadequacy in the personality poses for marital compatibility is that it induces processes of selective perception, interpretation, reinforcement, and avoidance in social interactions. In damaged personalities these processes are, of course, incorrect, misguided, and doomed to disappointment of their aims. In the interaction of courtship they raise false hopes. The disappointments occur later in the marriage itself, when neither spouse can live up to his partner's expectations. Each tries to reinforce in the other responses that will meet his own needs and to inhibit responses that are frustrating to him. Since the reinforcements and inhibitions miss the mark of the partner's real, underlying needs, incompatibility results.

Crises and Disasters

For the purposes of this discussion, crises as causes of marital incompatibility are defined as culturally, politically, economically, or socially induced situations which interrupt the usual pattern of functionally significant arrangments between the partners.[16] They can usually be

---

[16] The following are the major items that deal with the concept of crisis: Daniel H. Funkenstein, Stanley H. King, and Margaret E. Drolette, *Mastery of Stress* (Cambridge, Mass.: Harvard University Press, 1957); Karl Menninger, "Psychological Aspects of the Organism under Stress," *Journal of American Psychiatrists Association*, Vol. 2, Part I, "The Homeostatic Regulatory Function of the Ego" (January 1954), p. 57; Part II, "Regulatory Devices of the Ego under Major Stress" (April 1954), p. 280, discussion pp. 166–175; Howard J. Parad and Roger R. Miller, *Ego-Oriented Casework Problems and Perspectives* (New York, FSAA, 1963); Charlotte G. Babcock, "Inner Stress in Illness and Disability," p. 45; Howard J. Parad, "Brief Ego-Oriented Casework with Families in Crisis," p. 129; Howard J. Parad and Gerald Caplan, "A Framework for Studying Families in Crisis," *Social Work*, Vol. 5, No. 3 (1960), p. 5; Lydia Rapoport, "The State

anticipated if either of the spouses has sufficient intelligence, education, interest, and energy to maintain a working knowledge of his community. If they can be anticipated, steps can be taken to avoid them or to lessen their impact on the marriage and the family. If they are not anticipated and prepared for, they may be experienced as disasters. On the whole it may be said that the severity of the impact of such crises increases in proportion to the degree of actual incompatibility or of potential causes of incompatibility. Insofar as marriages are compatible, the partners tend to develop actual and anticipatory techniques for solving problems and maintaining compatibility under strain. Insofar as marriages have been characterized by incompatibility, prior efforts to solve problems have resulted in breakdown in performance of the marital functions and in interpersonal friction. The specific ways in which incompatibility will appear or be increased during a crisis depends on the nature of the strains and deprivations that the crisis imposes and the ways in which these strains and deprivations are perceived by the partners in the light of their personalities and in which each spouse evaluates his partner's responses to them.

Military draft. The first culturally and politically induced crisis that is likely to confront young married couples in the United States today is the drafting of the husband into military service. Whether the wife remains at home or accompanies him to the vicinity of his station, the draft interrupts the usual marital arrangements for the achievement of social status and economic goals, the division of labor between the spouses, and arrangements for bearing, nurturing, and socializing children. If the wife stays behind, the draft interrupts the usual arrangements for the provision of emotional support and sexual gratification and may confront either or both spouses with the fear that the partner will not exercise control over his or her sexual impulses during the period of separation.

The impact of military service on marriages is exacerbated by the fact that the United States is technically at peace. Many, if not most, spouses regard military service as unwarranted by the political situation and as unjustly imposed on their particular marriage. In time of war both spouses are likely to define the call to service as legitimate and to respond with better morale and more effective problem-solving measures.

Layoffs, shutdowns, and strikes. Layoffs, shutdowns, and strikes constitute economically induced crises insofar as they can be anticipated. Since the wage earner usually remains at home during the period of unemployment, the major consequences may be in the interruption or

of Crisis: Some Theoretical Considerations," *Social Service Review*, Vol. 26, No. 2 (1962), p. 213; Rhona Rapoport, "Normal Crises, Family Structure and Mental Health," *Family Process*, Vol. 2 (1963), p. 68.

reduction of income. A long period of unemployment may result in a lowering of the standard of living and of social status. In some marriages the presence of the husband in the home during his normal working hours may result in mounting strain between husband and wife. Much depends on how they define the situation. Participation by the husband in a strike which both define as just may raise the morale of both for a while. The wage earner's position as the undeserving victim of a layoff or shutdown may bind the partners together. Ultimately, however, if unemployment continues, the husband's self-esteem will decrease, and his defensive rationalizations are likely to cause irritation between the spouses. Ultimately, too, the wife's willingness to continue to provide emotional support for her husband throughout the crisis will depend on how she sees him performing the substitute economic function of looking for work. The husband's presence in the home may also result in greater opportunities for sexual gratification. For a while both partners may regard this as delightful, but ultimately, if he does not return to work, the wife is likely to feel that her husband is lazy and oversexed and he is likely to see her as withholding and punitive. The husband's presence in the home may also result in rearrangements of the patterns of nurturing and socializing the children. The initial period of "having Daddy at home" may be an opportunity for him to have closer association with the children. In the long run, however, if he does not return to work, the wife is likely to reproach him either for interfering in her handling of the children or for neglecting his responsibilities in their care and discipline.

Mobility. Occupational mobility, in the sense of moving to a new job in a new neighborhood, city, or state, constitutes an economically induced crisis of increasing incidence in the United States. When the move is voluntary on the part of both partners and when it brings vocational promotion, a greater income, and, perhaps, an increase in social status, it may be experienced as an enriching and gratifying challenge. Even under these circumstances, however, some aspects of potential difficulty are inherent in the situation. Moving requires the finding of a new home. It may entail creation of new patterns in the use of time, in travel, in the expenditure of money, and in domestic arrangements. When there are children, a move always raises the question of the quality of the schools in the new locality. Moving to a distance results in the interruption of sources of ancillary emotional support from relatives, friends, and religious and recreational facilities. If the husband has to precede his wife to the new location, the couple may be separated for some time, and the usual patterns of providing emotional support and sexual gratification are interrupted.

Economic mobility may occur under much less happy circumstances.

It may be enforced on the family by the exhaustion of mines or soil or by the shutdown or transfer of a major business or industry. A job may have been offered or obtained in a new community, but it may afford no increase in vocational or social status or pay. Indeed, it may afford less of all three, and the wage earner may, in addition, have to bear the whole financial burden of moving his family to the new community. In even more desperate circumstances the worker may have no specific prospects of a job elsewhere and may set out, alone, or accompanied by his family, in the hope of finding work. Sometimes he may go to a new community to which relatives and friends have preceded him and where they hold out hope of employment. At other times, the worker, with or without his family, may set out on an aimless search from one locality to another, not knowing what he will find. In all these circumstances mobility constitutes a severe crisis for the family. It is attended with all the hazards cited above in more fortunate movings, but the interruption of every marital and family function is intensified and the potentialities for the development of severe marital incompatibility or even for the formal or informal dissolution of the marriage by desertion, separation, or divorce are increased.

The limiting situations of economic mobility, namely, the occupational patterns of the migrant worker and emigration to another country, have some additional characteristics of their own. They contain abundant potentials for marital incompatibility and for the breakup of marriages. The migrant agricultural worker, in following the crops, may be reasonably assured of finding employment, but his wages are low, and he and his family are defined by the communities they enter as intruders, useful only for economic exploitation. They are excluded from the social life of the community except for certain bars, gambling joints, and houses of prostitution. Their children are not welcomed in the local schools. The writer is not familiar with the forms of social organization that migrant workers and their families develop among themselves. The emigrant may leave his country for political as well as economic reasons. He may be fleeing imprisonment or death. Under these circumstances detailed planning for the emigration may have been impossible. Whatever the causes of emigration, the husband may have to leave wife, children, and other relatives behind, not knowing what will happen to them. The process of reuniting the family in a new country is difficult and wearing, not only for economic reasons, but because of immigration quotas and other similar kinds of restrictions. Once the husband and wife are separated, they may never be reunited. Whether or not they emigrate together, in entering the new country they encounter a new culture, often with a different language, government, economic system, and cultural definition of marriage and the family.

Not infrequently, the emigrant is defined in the new country as economically and culturally undesirable. Economic and social opportunities are limited and social barriers are placed in his way. He may be isolated into a ghetto with others of his national and cultural background and denied access to the larger society.

In many ways the Negro, Indian, or Puerto Rican who tries to move from his place of origin to the large industrial and commercial cities of the United States is faced with the same elements of crisis as the emigrant. In some ways his situation is worse because he is already known as a member of a culturally defined, depreciated category of people.

In all these types of mobility the movement becomes a crisis that poses severe threats to the continuance of the marriage or to whatever degree of compatibility a couple may have achieved before the move.

Urban redevelopment. Urban redevelopment functions as a culturally and economically induced crisis for many families who are confronted with the requirement that they give up their homes so that new buildings and parks can be built on the site. Much urban redevelopment takes place in the downtown areas, on their immediate fringes, or in the deteriorated areas spotted elsewhere in the city. The older residences in these areas may be crowded slums, their occupants members of the culturally denigrated and economically deprived minority groups. When residents are forced to move, they often have to crowd into existing slums or into deteriorating neighborhoods which are soon converted into new slums. Forced moving of this kind exert a strain on the various aspects of marital compatibility.

The problems of the older couple forced by an urban redevelopment program to give up a home in which they may have spent most of their married life are tragic. Sometimes the renting of rooms in a house in an old, deteriorating neighborhood may constitute the major source of income. Possessions in and associations with the house and the certainty of being known and respected in the neighborhood may constitute invaluable sources of emotional support as the social isolation of old age approaches. The confrontation of the crisis may strengthen rather than loosen the marital bond between the spouses, but the experience of living through the crisis exacts a toll on their emotional and physical health.

Retirement. The prospect and experience of retirement may constitute a crisis for married couples. How well they will weather it depends largely on their ability to support each other and to make tolerable alternative arrangements for housing and expenditures. If the seeds of marital incompatibility have been sown beforehand, the prospect of retirement may induce irrational spending of savings, injudicious disposal of the home and belongings, an increased and insupportable dependence on each other, and acting out in the form of quarreling, a search for new sexual partners, and drinking.

Unforeseen catastrophes. For the purposes of this discussion transitory causes of marital incompatibility are defined as unforeseen circumstances whose impact may induce reactions of stress in the marital partners as individuals and impairment of the various aspects of marital compatibility. The distinguishing characteristic of this kind of experience is that it is not anticipated, cannot be prepared for, and comes as a shock. The severity of the impact increases in proportion to the intrapersonal vulnerability of the spouses and to the degree of actual or potential incompatibility in the marriage beforehand.

These stress-inducing events have been defined as transitory because of the nature of the reactions of individuals in responding to them. First comes a stage of shock and alarm, often marked by severe anxiety and suspension of the ability of the ego to perceive the situation correctly. The immediate response of the ego may be in the form of regressed, undifferentiated reactions, including somatic signs of distress, helpless pleas for aid, or random actions. In the second stage the ego attempts to recover mastery of itself and of the disastrous situation. The efforts at recovery, often overcompensatory in nature, consist of anxious, compulsive activity, denial of threatening aspects of the situation, and suppression or displacement of feelings. In the third stage the ego achieves some relatively stable level of dealing with the situation. It may regain its former patterns of problem solving, or it may achieve higher levels of integrated functioning, or it may have to settle for more regressed, undifferentiated, and infantile ways of functioning. When the third state is reached, the new or regained ways of functioning become part of the characteristic mode of adaptation of the individual. The situation has lost its transitory aspect and has somehow been integrated into or excluded from the basic fabric of experience and adaptation.

Individuals differ markedly from one another in their thresholds of tolerance for various kinds of strain. An event that may constitute a disaster for one person and induce a severe stress reaction may by another person be perceived and handled as one of the expected vicissitudes of life.

The effect of a disaster on marital compatibility depends on the respective thresholds of the partners for that type of experience, on the availability of cooperative techniques for handling emergencies, and on the ways in which each partner evaluates his spouse's response to the situation and to the partner.

Certain types of public disaster, involving many people, are not uncommon in the United States. They include fires, floods, airplane crashes, and multiple automobile accidents, any of which will produce reactions of shock in the most stable of individuals taking part in them and in their spouses who witness or are informed about them. Once the shock reactions begin to pass, the efforts of the egos of the victims to master their own reactions and the situation itself may be assisted by a realization that the disaster has affected other people as well as themselves and their families.

In any circumstances of disaster the ability of the spouses to communicate a warm but unobtrusive sense of emotional support constitutes a manifestation of marital compatibility. Resentment over the spouse's continued reaction of shock, withdrawal into himself, excessive emotionality, and ineffectual behavior may precipitate more lasting forms of marital incompatibility.

Causes Inherent in Existing Institutions

It can probably not be credibly maintained that existing institutions designed to cope with marital incompatibility actually contribute to its causation. By contrast, for instance, it can be upheld that prison systems actually contribute to the causation of crime by placing the guard in a position in which he cannot exercise discipline without condoning and participating in illegal activities by the inmates. Of institutions designed to cope with marital incompatibility it can be said that some of them in some aspects of their functioning tend to increase existing marital incompatibility.

Some examples have already been mentioned. Presumably one of the indirect, if not direct, responsibilities of public assistance agencies is to help prevent or alleviate marital incompatibility by providing financial support to families when income from their usual sources is not available. Marital incompatibility may be exacerbated when eligibility for public assistance is defined and administered in narrow, rigid ways; when grants are kept so low that they impair the health of the marital partners or precipitate disagreements between them over the ways in which the inadequate funds should be used; when the bureaucratic interests of the agency, allowed to take precedence over the needs of the clients, result in delayed responses to requests and inconvenient ways of providing assistance; and when residence laws are imposed that heighten the burdens of the mobile family.

Marital incompatibility is aggravated when courts, governmental agencies, and voluntary agencies charged with providing protection for women and children will accept only the grossest physical evidence of abuse and put an exaggerated weighting on the formal continuance of a marriage at the cost of provoking greater friction. Public assistance and child welfare agencies and hospitals, which are required by law or policy to withhold from clients all available information on planned parenthood services, contribute to the precipitation or encouragement of marital disagreement in the decision to have children. Courts charged with jurisdiction over divorce, separation, and nonsupport help to increase marital incompatibility by implementing the judicial process in ways that are humiliating to the people who appear before them.

All agencies, public and private, that come into contact with families tend to worsen relations between husbands and wives when they fail to provide suitable training for their workers so that problems of marital incompatibility may be quickly identified, when they use ineffectual referral processes, and when they adopt such narrow interpretations of agency function that they cannot move out toward troubled, inarticulate people.

Some private agencies and clinics help to raise the barriers of social class and racial and ethnic discrimination by restricting their clientele. The location of the office, the way in which the waiting room is furnished, and the dress, manners, and speech of the staff may make it clear to clients who are members of disadvantaged groups in the population that this agency is not meant for them. Since social class strivings and racial and ethnic discrimination are such powerful factors in causing marital incompatibility, the agencies may fairly be charged with having contributed one more blow to the self-esteem and to marriages of these people.

Non-social work institutions designed to meet the problem of marital incompatibility also engage in practices that tend to exacerbate the very problem that they are supposed to help solve. Discriminatory practices and symbols occur in psychiatry, psychology, marriage counseling, and the church. Newspapers, magazines, radio, and television assume and are granted responsibility for helping people with marital problems by means of articles, columns of advice, dramatizations, panel discussions and other means. Many of these presentations are knowledgeable and sensitive. Others, however, are rash, unthinking and permeated with hasty moral judgments or are candidly irresponsible. In more subtle fashion these media, and stage and screen as well, tend to present marriage to the American public in an unreal way. In some cases the standard of living of families is shown as far higher than it could possibly be. In other cases adultery is presented as a spicy, naughty adventure. Almost all complex problems of marital incompatibility are solved with a rapidity and ease that smack of magic. No one knows whether any of these shortcomings actually do any harm to readers and audiences. Certainly, however, they do no good in undertakings in which much could be accomplished.

Interplay Between External and Internal Causes
Marital incompatibility consists, in the last analysis, of specific concrete

actions by real people and their internal thoughts and feelings relating to these actions. The actions of each partner function as cues that evoke the thoughts, feelings, and actions of the other. Neither responds entirely in terms of the current meanings of these actions. Neither merely reacts to the other. Rather, the reason why a husband interprets his wife's action as a cue and attributes meaning to it is that it is already a symbol of that meaning in his memory.[17] Perception and interpretation are determined in part by complexes of memories of past experiences which are charged with feelings and values. Unconscious complexes of memories of childhood experiences are of special importance, since they influence perception and interpretation of the actions of other people but are not themselves corrected by new experiences. They continue therefore to exert a distorting influence on perception and interpretation.

A member of a social category defined by the dominant culture as undesirable is not hurt only because the majority discriminates against him. Nor is he hurt only because the dominant group restricts his opportunities and then defines him as unworthy because he does not display the attributes he could achieve only by the use of the denied opportunities. His own sense of unworthiness is not entirely the result of his resigned acceptance of this evaluation. Finally, his anger and sense of injustice are not entirely a response to ill treatment. All these reactions occur, but they are only the reactive components of his response.

They are elaborated and complicated by the internal structuring of his perceptions and interpretations. His sense of himself is comprised in part of identifications with his parents who themselves as members of a minority group felt unworthy. He therefore bears within himself a sense of his own unworthiness. Moreover, his ego ideal is, at bottom, composed of identification with unworthy parents, so that even in achieving the approval of this ideal his ego is settling for "second best." If parents with whom he identified felt angry and unjustly treated in their interchanges with the dominant group, he, as a consequence of identification, is internally prepared to feel angry and unjustly treated in such interchanges. All these aspects of his identifications influence his perception and interpretation of the actions of others as confirming his internalized expectations.

The influence of racial discrimination on the self-image, perceptions, and interpretations constitutes only an illustration. Similar results follow from all the cultural, political, economic, and social causes of

---

[17] For elaboration and illustration of this idea *see* Barbara Gray Ellis, "Unconscious Collusion in Marital Interaction," *Social Casework,* Vol. 45, No. 2 (February 1964), p. 79.

social problems. Of crucial importance is the way in which the attenuation of values, confusion of identity, and depreciation of self-esteem are transmitted from one generation to another. The sense of anonymity, of being the helpless instrument of irresistible and inaccessible social and economic forces, of injustice and anger, of apathy, of despair that conformity to any value system will make life more rewarding, all may have been experienced reactively by adults, as the cultural, political, economic, and social causes began to exert their influence. As these adults become parents, however, their helplessness, blurred sense of identity, and normlessness are presented to their children as models for identification. As the children identify with these aspects of the parents, confusion and normlessness are built into the personality structures of the children. The resulting damage will continue from generation to generation unless changes in the external society and culture intervene to break the cycle and afford new generations more effective models of identification.

The nature of the processes by which personality is formed has consequences for programs of social action designed to change the cultural values and the political, economic, and social arrangements that contribute to the causation of problems such as marital incompatibility. Such programs can alter the external influences that cause, exacerbate, and perpetuate the problem, but they cannot produce the immediate solution of the problem. People whose personality structures have been built on identifications with parents who suffered from the problem will continue to perceive and interpret current situations as if the causative variables were still operating and will thus perpetuate the problem itself. The immediate cessation of all depreciative and discriminatory behaviors and social arrangements would not prevent the people affected from continuing to act as if depreciation and discrimination were still being practiced or members of the "power structure" and dominant majorities from continuing to perceive and interpret actions of depreciated peoples and minorities as evidences of inferiority. Complete dissipation of normlessness and discrimination would take several generations to accomplish.

MARITAL INCOMPATIBILITY AS A SOCIAL PROBLEM

The purpose of the "social problems" project of which this discussion forms a part is to develop an approach to the control of certain social problems at a local level. The following distinction was made between social problems and individual problems:

> The term "social problem" as used in this project is limited to those problems which are manifested by family, group, or individual behavior which require intervention by the organized community in order

that the community may continue to function. It does not include problems manifested primarily by a state of being, thinking, or feeling.[18]

The question was raised at a meeting of the consultants to the project whether marital incompatibility should be considered a social problem within the definition quoted. The summary of the discussion follows:

> There is a conceptual problem in defining marital incompatibility. Is it a social problem or an individual problem experienced by many yet not a priority social work concern on the basis of values, magnitude, and consequences? It is only in recent history and in a few Western cultures that marital incompatibility has been considered a problem. Our task is to look at the context within which it is defined as a problem.
>
> One view expressed in the group was that any problem engendering unhappiness, and capable of being helped by social work, is a social problem. In this context marital incompatibility would be a social problem. However, the majority of the group firmly believed that while such a problem might be a social work concern, it would not necessarily be a social problem.[19]

The present discussion has, perhaps, begged the question by defining marital incompatibility as a social problem, that is, as disharmony in the social interaction between the marital partners with respect to the performance of the major functions of marriage. Subjective dissatisfaction, that is, "a state of being, thinking, or feeling," with the person or behavior of the marital partner was accepted as one aspect of marital incompatibility, but this was subsumed under the general marital function of reciprocal provision of emotional support and release from tension. It was recognized that this function of marriage is given especially heavy weighting by the culture of the United States. On the other hand, it has been argued throughout the discussion that no aspect of marital compatibility is solely a matter of individual "being, thinking, or feeling." Every aspect is the consequence of an intricate social interaction between the spouses.

The argument, however, should be carried further. It is stated that a social problem must be a "priority concern on the basis of values, magnitude, and consequences" and that it is one that requires intervention by the organized community in order that the community may continue to function.

This formulation seems to imply that the marriages in a community are not a part of the community. Such a position seems untenable by

[18] "Minutes of the Meeting of Consultants" (to the project) held at Western Reserve University, February 24–25, 1961, p. 1.

[19] "Minutes of the Meeting of Consultants," held at Western Reserve University, September 22–23, 1961, p. 20.

any common or reasonable definition of the term community. If community is defined as a geographic locality, then the number and the
characteristics of the marriages in the community constitute some of
its most important demographic data for political and economic purposes. If community is defined as an area of common interests, surely
the interest of the married people in their marriages constitutes one of
the most widespread and deeply felt interests in the community. If
community is defined as a set of social institutions bound together by
common values, then surely the marriages constitute one of the most
numerous kinds of institutions in the community and reflect the values
of the community. It has already been demonstrated in the discussion
of marriage in the United States and the causes of marital incompatibility, that the general values of the community determine the structure
and functions of marriage and that the particular forms of marital incompatibility most common in the United States are determined, in large
measure by the requirements set upon marriage by the culture.

It may be said, then, that marriage is an integral part of the community. If widespread marital incompatibility occurs, then the community is, in some measure, ceasing to function adequately, and intervention by the organized community is necessary.

The question of the incidence of marital incompatibility in the United
States has not been discussed at length. The increasing divorce rate
suggests that a great deal of marital incompatibility exists. The experience of workers in the clinical professions, the widespread testimony
of the public media of communication and, finally, the inclusion of
marital incompatibility in the "social problems" project, all testify to a
sufficient incidence of marital incompatibility for it to be a matter of
social concern. It is therefore proposed that in terms of the definition of
social problem given here marital incompatibility constitutes a social
problem.

VALUES

Cultural Values in Support of Marital Incompatibility

The general values in the culture which support the existence of marital
incompatibility were identified in the section on causes inherent in
culture and social structure.

Cultural Values in Opposition to Marital Incompatibility

Many value-orientations and values in American culture oppose the
existence of marital incompatibility and many of them are effectively
institutionalized.

Humanistic orientation. At the highest level of generalization
the cognitive, scientific mode of experience does not necessarily imply

an inhumane, instrumental orientation toward man in all its aspects. Rather, it underlies the viewpoint of the modern nonbehavioristic sciences of man, which asserts that man's behavior is determined by a complex interplay of many kinds of variables, that man and his behavior can be understood, and that man is capable of development and change. It serves as a value-orientation when it states further that the application of knowledge to the solution of man's problems and the furtherance of his potentialities is desirable.

The modern sciences of man, at least in their more dynamic forms, tend to accept the appreciative and evaluative modes of man's experience as data to be studied and understood. By a process of cultural diffusion, the orientations to be studied tend to influence the orientations of the students. The appreciative aspects of clinical methods of study are used to supplement the more rigorous, positivistic methods that emerge from the cognitive method alone. Value-orientations are recognized to provide guides as well as hindrances to the study of man. Methods and data reciprocally supplement one another until gradually a body of knowledge emerges in a form that can be converted into humane social policies. For purposes of convenience, this value-orientation, which accepts the appreciative and evaluative as well as the cognitive aspects of man, is called the humanistic orientation.

Religious values. Nor have the value-orientations derived from Christianity and Judaism been solely condemnatory of man. The narrow Puritanical ethic is not the only one that can be derived from Christianity. The emphasis on understanding instead of judgment brought over from the dynamic sciences of man, on love and the withholding of judgment in the Christian gospels, and on justice in Judaism can be brought into ethical harmony. All three affirm the worth and dignity of the individual.

Political and social values. At a less abstract level of formulation, certain value-orientations exist in American society as special cases of the affirmation of the worth and dignity of man and of the conversion of the existential proposition that man is capable of change and development into the value statement that he should be helped to develop his full potentialities. One of these value-orientations is political and social democracy: the proposition that man participate as fully as his capacities permit in the formulation and administration of the policies that influence his welfare. Another is the political value-orientation that asserts that it is the responsibility of the government to provide for the general welfare. A third is the value-orientation that states that cultural plurality is desirable and, as a corollary, that members of identifiable races, ethnic groups, and religions should be afforded full opportunities and resources to develop their own patterns of living. A fourth value-orientation is based on the objective finding that women are different from but in no way inferior to men. This value-orientation proposes that women be afforded full opportunities and resources to develop their potentialities. A fifth, similarly based on objective findings, states that children are neither small adults nor savages but undeveloped human beings who should be provided with the opportunities and resources necessary for their full development.

Supporting these value-orientations is another of different historical origin, namely, the proposition that all authority be limited. This value seems to underlie the American tendency to identify with the underdog and the willingness to act generously in various ways to assist him. It is important to recognize that all but one of the value-orientations and values outlined above could probably obtain fairly general assent in the American population. True, every assenter would have private reservations about their universal applicability and would adhere to different or contrary values with respect to certain kinds of behaviors and certain groups of people. The exception in the list is, of course, the value-orientation that asserts the desirability of cultural plurality and of the consequences following therefrom. This would probably not obtain general assent, even as an abstract ideal. It should be noted, further, that no general value-orientation concerning the social responsibility of the economic system has been included in the list. Although minorities of various kinds are prepared to assert such a value, no such proposition would obtain general assent in the United States today. "Business is business," that is, a closed system, is still the prevailing existential statement and value-orientation.

Consequences of the values. At the next lower level of generalization it is possible to determine how these value-orientations become converted into more specific values that stand opposed to marital incompatibility. In general, the placing of a high valuation on the appreciative mode of human experience and the more specific value of cultural plurality tend to remove from marriage the burden of having to seek higher social status. These two and the values set on democratic political and social participation and on the right of the individual to achieve his full potentials stand in opposition to the barriers of race, ethnic identity, and religion and therefore to the ways in which these barriers exert destructive influences on marriage. The emotional support and release from tension found in marriage are maintained by the high values placed on democratic participation and on women. Greater permissiveness and greater self-determination in sexual matters are buttressed by the appreciative value-orientation that is accepting of all of man's characteristics, by the democratic right of the individual to participate in the decisions affecting his welfare, and by the higher valuation of women. The same values and, in addition, the higher value placed on children support the right of the family to plan the number and timing of children. All these values, of course, support the more permissive and encouraging methods of nurturing and socializing children; the same values, with the exception of that placed on children, ensure that the parents will not become nonentities in the family. None necessarily supports the authoritative imposition of social controls on the acting-out spouse; indeed they tend to enjoin the spouse to be tolerant and patient in the face of exploitation. On the other hand, they do reinforce whatever guilt the acting-out spouse may feel because of his escapades. The higher valuation of women has tended to make of the woman a partner rather than a household drudge and to open to her the opportunity for fuller use of her capacities in the vocational world.

No mention has been made of the value-orientation that requires government to concern itself with the general welfare. Obviously this value, affirmed in a decision of the Supreme Court, undergirds the various grants and services government provides to foster marital compatibility.

In many families adherence to and faith in Christianity or Judaism provide a substratum of conviction concerning values that influences marital compatibility. In such families the ethical values are explicitly and verbally formulated in prayers and in supportive and restraining injunctions concerning conduct in the various family roles. Insofar as these religions emphasize the worth of the human being in the eyes of God and the cherishing aspects of interpersonal relations their values are supportive of marital compatibility.

Presumed Values of Social Work

Values opposing marital incompatibility. Social work adheres predominantly to the humanistic value-orientation at all levels of generality. This, in the broad society, opposes the existence of marital incompatibility. It has been discussed in detail in the immediately preceding section.

Social work gives greater emphasis to some of the component values of the orientation and less emphasis to others than does the general culture. For social work the basic and encompassing value is phrased as "the worth and dignity of the human individual." Almost equal rank is assigned to a value phrased as "the right of individual self-determination" and to another phrased as "confidentiality." Actually the last two values are derivatives of the other major values—the worth and dignity of the individual and the right of the individual to participate in decisions that affect his own welfare. Although these two derivative values tend to oppose the existence of social problems such as marital incompatibility, the tendency of some social workers to treat self-determination and confidentiality as unconditioned values sometimes leads them into practical and theoretical dilemmas.

Social work probably gives greater weight to the values set on women and children than does the general culture. It may also have a greater tendency to assign a negative value to personal and institutional manifestations of authority. In its ideals social work adheres more strongly to the value of a completely open society and is much more opposed than is the general culture to the pressures for social class mobility and racial, ethnic, and religious discrimination. On the other hand, except in the direct practice of casework and group work, social workers do little to effect changes in these values or in their social expressions. Social work tends to support a good deal of sexual freedom between marital partners. In their informal jesting social workers often seem to advocate complete sexual freedom for everyone, whether inside or outside marriage. In their professional practice they take a more conservative position, grounding their thinking largely on diagnostic rather than on philosophic variables. Social work differs markedly from the general culture in advocating that the economic system assume greater responsibility for the welfare of the population and in supporting governmental services of every conceivable kind.

Values supporting marital incompatibility. The problem here is to distinguish those values, overt and covert, that may fairly be said to inhere in the whole profession and to constitute parts of its total value-orientation from those that are held by individual members or segments of the membership of the profession. The differences could not be established validly without extensive and intensive study. Separation of the two by any other means is necessarily somewhat arbitrary and reflects the biases of the observer. This is true of the separation effected here. Certain value-orientations and values are assumed to be characteristic of the whole profession and are discussed in this section. Others are assumed to be characteristic only of segments of the profession and are discussed in another section in connection with programs and services.

The existence of marital incompatibility and of other widespread social problems is supported by a peculiar derivative of the humanistic value-orientation which recognizes the worth and dignity of man and his capacity to change and develop. The derivative constitutes an exaggeration of some aspects of the total value-orientation at the expense of others, and in its more extreme forms forces its holder into the trap of believing that because something is desirable it is also achievable. This distortion or exaggeration, whether acknowledged or not, asserts that since man should always be held to be worthwhile and his dignity respected and since it is desirable that his capacity to change and develop be fostered, it is also desirable that he should be dealt with, under all circumstances, in ways that will promote his potentialities for constructive change and development. What drops out of the picture is a frank facing of evidence that some individuals and institutions do not want to change and develop constructively and that some cannot. Some differ so widely and forcefully from social work in their philosophical definition of the nature of man and their ethical concept of what constitutes constructive change that reconciliation of their ends and means with those of social work is impossible. Other individuals and institutions more or less candidly pursue selfish ends by exploitative means, regardless of the consequences to other people.

Social work as a profession is permeated with this distortion of its basic value-orientation. It emerges in the uncritical practical precept that every statement and every program should be couched only in positive terms. Frank, public opposition to or negative criticism of an individual, an institution, or a program is regarded as undesirable. It is defined as a denial of the worth and dignity of the opponent, as an obstruction to his potential for constructive change and development, and as a manifestation of hostility in the social worker.

Community workers are especially guilty of susceptibility to this distortion of the humanistic value-orientation. Sometimes they seem to think that the mere fact that they are able to call the organized opposition to constructive programs of social welfare "the power structure" constitutes sufficient justification for failing to come to grips with it. The community worker is sometimes rendered impotent by what he conceives to be his professional value-orientation. On the one hand, he cannot oppose. This solution entails serious risks for him as an individual and is not supported by the distorted value-orientation of the profession. Therefore, he takes refuge in the rationalization that he is seeking to affect the philosophy, aims, and methods of various segments of the "power structure" by recognizing the worth and dignity of its members and by trying to influence their potentialities for constructive change and development. He cannot afford to recognize that the philosophy, aims, and methods of many leaders in a community may be different from his, sometimes on high philosophic and ethical grounds, sometimes on the grounds of candid self-seeking.

This same distortion of the humanistic orientation is found in the practice of casework. The problem emerges most clearly when casework is introduced into protective, correctional, and other frankly authoritative settings. As the problem is usually defined, the caseworker is said to be unable to accept the authority necessary to the conduct of these programs. This constitutes one element in the situation. Difficulty in accepting authority is not, however, the whole problem. The caseworker may perceive that the acting out of a spouse or parent is having seriously destructive consequences for the marital partner or for the children. He may see that a probationer or parolee is unable to refrain from illegal acts. Yet the caseworker is reluctant to ask for intervention by a court or to recommend remand to a court or correctional institution. This reluctance arises in part from the distortion of the basic value-orientation. The social worker believes so strongly that individuals should be helped to change and develop constructively that he confuses desirability with feasibility. His values sometimes becloud his diagnostic acumen.

Sometimes the boards of agencies make it a matter of policy or administrations make it a matter of accepted practice to refrain from calling on authoritative supports when they are indicated. The most damaging consequences for individuals, families, and communities occur when agencies will not publicly acknowledge that they have such policies or practices but nevertheless fail to refer to authoritative agencies or use authoritative methods when the situation demands. Consequently, complicated processes of manipulation go on among agencies as one attempts to induce another to take the necessary action. Sometimes deplorable situations in families and communities continue indefinitely while the agencies jockey with them or avert their attention entirely.

Another aspect of the humanistic value-orientation of social work may contribute to the particular form the distortion of values just discussed assumes in social work. This is the orientation of the profession to feminine values. In many of its consequences the assertion of the worth and potentialities of women makes possible some of the most distinctive and socially effective contributions of social work among the professions. It is fortunate for the American people that the women in social work, and the male social workers who share the feminine orientation, can be satisfied with slow, patient, understanding work and with slow progress judged in essentially pragmatic terms. In one respect, however, the feminine orientation plays into and buttresses the tendency among social workers to confuse what is desirable with what can be achieved. As Sigmund Freud pointed out, women differ from men in the content and operation of their superegos. Women are less concerned with justice and with generalizations. They are more concerned with piece-meal, everyday experience. These characteristics enter into the value distortion under discussion. Because of the feminine orientation of social work, the social worker is inclined to go along with practical situations, buttressed by the conviction that constructive change can occur but overestimating the potentialities for such change. The consequences of this distortion in the humanistic value-orientation have been fortunate in limited ways for social work and for the people it serves. The profession, in its several component practices, has taken refuge in an elaboration of knowledge and technique for dealing with the problems of individual persons, families, and groups. Much knowledge has been gained about how to work at these levels.

On the other hand, the consequences of the distortion in the humanistic value-orientation have, in their wider aspects, been unfortunate for the profession and for its clientele. To overestimate the "good will," in terms of the values of social work, of persons and institutions not at all committed to the values and goals of social work can lead only to frustration and defeat. It is no accident that social work has tended to give only lip service to its responsibility to participate in political and social action. Moreover, the failure of community work or social policy formulation and administration to develop theory and practice comparable in sophistication and effectiveness to those of casework and group work has not occurred because caseworkers and group workers are more intelligent or better educated. The failure is there because in the fairly recent past social work with social problems at the various levels of government and community organization has been vitiated by the discrepancy between the real nature of the variables at work and the social work estimation of what those variables are. The results have been velleity and a form of normlessness among social workers. The sharp self-image and public image of social work in the early twentieth century has become blurred. Then the leaders of social work correctly assessed the values, motives, and goals of their opponents and stood up to them courageously. Today, social work, as a consequence of its unrealistic interpretation of its basic value-orientation, questions its own goals, pursues theoretical fads, wastes its energies in endless, critical self-examination, and always, finally, retreats to the pursuit of more knowledge of individual situations.

The assertion has been made that social work adheres to the American value that dictates distrust of authority. Unquestionably the formal and informal implementation of this value in the past has caused difficulty for social workers and their clients. There has been too much tendency to condone destructive acting-out behavior, which has impaired effective work in marital situations as well as in other problems. There is abundant evidence that social work has largely overcome this problem and that social workers are now better prepared—culturally, psychologically, and intellectually—to handle authority in constructive ways. The more interesting question today is why this cultural tendency to identify with the underdog has not led social workers into more effective action on the broad political and social fronts. The basic reason, in the opinion of the writer, is the countervailing effect of the distortion in the basic humanistic value-orientation already discussed. Protest among social workers at social injustice is voiced, but action is inhibited. Local chapters of NASW devote endless hours to preparing position statements about social problems. The materials prepared for the delegate assemblies of the NASW contain impressive indictments of the social injustices of American society. Then nothing happens because social workers must always start where the client is, work within the situation, try to develop the potentialities of the participants to make constructive contributions, and so forth.

Perhaps the major manifestation of the inability of social work to deal effectively with social problems at any other level than that of the individual case or small group is the defensive perception and evaluation of the profession which have evolved. Social workers spend a great deal of time and effort insisting to themselves and to the public that they have a profession. They try to explain away the shortcomings of social work on the grounds that it is a young profession. In one sense this is true. In another it is not. It is true that social work has emerged as an identifiable, institutionalized profession only since the mid-nineteenth century. In that sense it may be considered young. On the other hand, all the modern professions have developed their character-istic ways of defining problems, the scientific knowledge for dealing with those problems, and the modern technical methods of solving problems during the same period. In this sense social work is no younger than its sister professions. Social workers also expend great effort in trying to identify the characteristics that distinguish their pro-fession from allied professions. On the one hand, they manifest an excess of deference in the company of physicians, psychiatrists, sociol-ogists, and anthropologists; on the other hand, they evince a narrow provincialism in their practice and in their education. This profes-sional provincialism is offensive to other scholars and professionals and to the general public. All perceive the insecurity that underlies it. The social work profession blocks itself off from the free interchange of ideas during a period when the most rewarding and exciting work is being done through the sharing of interdisciplinary perspectives.

Since the social worker cannot comfortably feel that he is a member of a true profession, he does not carry his profession where it belongs, namely, inside himself. Few social workers have internalized their profession as doctors and lawyers have. Rather, social workers tend to place the profession elsewhere and then attach their loyalties to what-ever institution embodies the profession for them. Most social workers see the profession as the agency, and as a consequence they develop a narrow professional identification with the agencies in which they are employed. The tendency is reinforced by the bureaucratic attributes of these agencies, which convert the professional social worker into an employee. This subservience obstructs efforts to draw knowledge from sources outside the agency or to work effectively toward the solution of social problems on a community-wide basis.

CURRENT RESOURCES AND SERVICES FOR DEALING WITH MARITAL INCOMPATIBILITY

Services and resources other than social work are discussed first because many of the social work services are administratively attached to non-social work resources or are used as the means of purveying these resources to the public. Specific social work services and their characteristics are discussed in a second section. In both sections the presentation is organized in terms of the major functions of marriage and the major forms of marital incompatibility that occur in the United States.

Many of the services provided by the various levels of government in the United States share certain characteristics because of certain cultural, political, and economic variables. These services include public assistance and child welfare, the courts, and the correctional agencies. All are organized as bureaucracies and, despite the best intentions of administrators, tend to manifest in their dealings with the public the characteristic narrowness in the definition of eligibility for resources and services and delay and rigidity in making decisions. They lack adequate financing. They are forced to employ workers, including social workers, who are inadequately educated to carry out their responsibilities. Turnover of new staff may be high, whereas older, less competent persons tend to remain on staff for many years. Great expenditures of time and money for in-service training are often vitiated in their effects by this pattern of turnover of staff, since workers who can make use of the training leave the agency and those who remain cannot use it. Many of the untrained workers deal with their client-families in terms of the less constructive values of the American culture: the overweighting of the individual's responsibility and the underweighting of his rights, negative moral judgments on behavior, and various, more or less subtle forms of discrimination. The agency is inaccessible to influence by its clientele and, in turn, finds its sponsoring administrative and legislative bodies in the higher echelons of the structure of government somewhat inaccessible. Some, though by no means all, of these agencies are subjected to various forms of "politicking."

The private or voluntary family agency—the major contribution of social work to the solution of problems of marital incompatibility—is discussed in a separate section. Since the voluntary family agency defines its functions as responsibility for helping with all aspects and types of family problems, it is not referred to in the discussion of resources and services available for the separate aspects of marital incompatibility, for such separate references would be endlessly repetitious.

General Resources and Services for Specific Problems

Membership of the family. Help to young people in guiding themselves through the mazes of the cultural patterns and social inter-actions of dating, courtship, and romantic love to the selection of a marital partner is provided by a wide variety of institutions. Public high schools and public and private colleges offer courses in marriage and family living. Many have the objective of influencing behavior as well as of providing information. From time immemorial clergymen have offered guidance with these problems in their pastoral function. Many clergymen conduct classes for prospective spouses, and many are insisting on several pastoral sessions with each young couple before consenting to perform the marriage ceremony. The new specialization within the ministry of pastoral counseling offers both educational pro-grams and group and individual counseling. Psychiatrists and psychol-ogists also provide individual and group therapy or counseling. News-papers, magazines, and books turn out an inexhaustible amount of educa-tion, guidance, and counsel. Radio and television offer occasional serious programs on the selection of a spouse.

In general, it is probably true that most of these resources and services are conceived within the framework of the humanistic value-orientation. Different emphases enter into the various kinds of resources. Ministers, acting in their pastoral function, are more likely to introduce specifically religious and moral concepts and values. Those who act as pastoral counselors are more likely to ground their work on a psycho-dynamic orientation to human behavior. Psychologists and psychiatrists are likely to explain problems in the selection of a marital partner as manifestations of some aspect of psychopathology. Educational courses may have an essentially academic orientation. The quality of the education and advice provided by newspapers, magazines, radio, and television varies widely. Some of it is conceived on the basis of sound knowledge and is presented responsibly. Some is ignorant in content and sensational in presentation. Variations from the general cultural orienta-tion are most likely to be found in books. On the whole, the more responsible and professionally skillful forms of premarital education and counseling from these sources are likely to be available in the forms and places to which members of the white race, the middle class, and the dominant ethnic groups have access.

The solemnization and registration of marriage are performed by magistrates and ministers. Civil ceremonies are often hurried and lacking in dignity, for the officer who performs the ceremony may be unknown to the couple. Marriage by ministers is performed under a wide variety of circumstances. The religious marriage ceremony constitutes a public display of the social status of the bride's family, and the wedding reception may be more important to everyone than the ceremony itself. Nevertheless, there is a better chance that the couple will know the minister and that the ceremony will be performed with dignity if it is conducted under religious or quasi-religious auspices.

Responsibility for dealing with problems of desertion or separation and the often attendant problems of physical protection and nonsupport is placed in the judicial system. In very deteriorated marital situations public intervention may precede appearance before a court. In the larger cities jurisdiction over these problems may be lodged with a separate family court. In other places a justice of the peace at the first level of intervention or a judge of a county court at the second level may have jurisdiction. The way in which the judicial officer defines such problems and the values he brings to bear in dealing with the marital partners probably depends as much on the particular judge as on any other factor. His conduct of the case may be grounded on a broad, dynamic understanding of people and problems, or it may be judgmental, moralistic, and interlarded with unacknowledged personal emotional involvement. If such cases are heard in a family court, there is a likelihood that a casework service will be attached by the court, but it does not necessarily follow that the casework service will be highly professionalized.

When either marital partner takes steps to sue for divorce, contact is made with individual lawyers. The law itself takes the viewpoint that lawyers have a responsibility to save marriages if possible. Many lawyers make a conscientious effort to effect a reconciliation between spouses seeking divorce. Some undertake to counsel the couple; others refer them to marital counseling resources. When lawyers act in this way, their definition of the problem and their value perspectives are in accord with the basic humanistic value-orientation underlying the helping professions. If the lawyer's efforts fail or if he conducts his practice from the beginning out of a legal orientation to the problem, then his definition and value perspective are different. He acts as if the client and his spouse know what they want and are responsible for their actions. He undertakes to represent his client and seeks legal evidence to uphold his client's suit before a court. The basic theoretical orientation of the divorce court is like that of the lawyer. The court is called on to weigh the facts and to adduce the relevant aspects of the law.

Some divorce courts try to bring about reconciliations between the partners, either directly or by referral.

When the structure of a marriage is temporarily interrupted by the drafting or enlistment of the husband in the armed services, the chaplaincy is available as a non-social work counseling resource. The chaplain's orientation to the marital problems of man is likely to be much like that of the civilian minister, tempered by the chaplain's greater familiarity with the husband's perspectives in marriage. He is likely to share the humanistic value-orientation toward marital problems.

Abode of the family. The culture expects each married couple to set up its own home but does not require or expect that the family or friends of either spouse will contribute more to its initial establishment than the giving of shower and wedding presents. Furniture is expensive. From the very beginning of the marriage most young couples have to mortgage their futures through installment buying for furniture and household goods. At this point and forever after in their lives they are subjected to the pressures of commercial advertising and sales techniques to increase their purchases.

The building and sale or rental of houses and apartments are commercial ventures. Purchase is, almost without exception, financed by means of a mortgage. The federal government maintains a policy of encouraging the purchase of houses and implements it through the FHA and the Veterans Administration which guarantee mortgages. The cost is high, and the guarantees are made only up to a figure that permits the purchase of a relatively modest dwelling. Both federal and local governments participate in the building and rental of low-cost housing projects, in which rental units are provided at relatively moderate cost. On the other hand, there are some knotty problems associated with these projects. They are usually built on land cleared of slums, and the building causes the displacement of families and the creation of new slums. The projects themselves are so spare and grim in their architecture that many families find them unattractive. The projects therefore tend to draw the most disadvantaged families in the community. If a predominance of families of depreciated status moves in, the issue of segregation arises. White families or families of "desirable ethnic" background may be reluctant to move in because living in a project becomes a sign of depreciated status. Members of the depreciated categories of people may refuse to move in for essentially the same reason. They regard the projects as systems of social segregation.

Social status. The educational system makes available to families the primary means for social and economic advancement. Outside the regular curriculum for elementary, secondary, and advanced education, the system offers an abundance of courses of all kinds, general and technical. The non-social work organizations which have directly attacked the class structure have been the Marxist political parties whose value-orientations are objectionable to social work because they represent the cognitive orientation in its most rigid and inhumane form.

Most non-social work resources for lowering racial, ethnic, and religious barriers take the form of "cause" movements and organizations. On the other side of the picture, there are many organizations which seek to preserve racial, ethnic, and religious identity as a matter of pride in the face of general depreciation of the group by the larger community.

Economic maintenance of the family. At the federal level the policy of the government in countering the economic cycle of recession and inflation varies from administration to administration, as does the vigor and comprehensiveness with which such a policy is pursued.

Unemployment insurance constitutes the major source of replacement of income when employment ceases. The trend is toward increase in the amount provided and extension of the period of eligibility. Not all workers, however, are in covered employment, and dependence on unemployment compensation entails, for most families, the use of other financial resources or reduction in the standard of living. Unions have been able to obtain provision by industry of supplementary unemployment benefits, but this is a hard-won and unstable gain.

The American culture still defines savings as the most desirable source of income when employment ceases. It is true that American savings banks report great savings by the American people, but the amount of the debt for installment purchases and for mortgages is also very large. The culture of saving is, moreover, a part of middle-class life. The desirability of saving is not so thoroughly accepted in the lower class.

Commercial loans are resorted to by many families to augment current income and to deal with crises. This is the form of borrowing available to lower-class families, since the only collateral required is a chattel mortgage on household goods and car or a garnishee against wages. The small loan companies manifest the exploitative aspects of the economic system in their most patent forms. Interest is extremely high and the rate of interest and the existence of other charges are often concealed from the family. The companies have successfully opposed effective governmental regulation. Available to the lowest social and economic levels of the population are the services of the "loan shark," the modern version of the usurer. Middle-class families can resort to commercial banks for loans, since they are more likely to possess the kind of collateral required, namely, stocks, bonds, or real estate which they do not wish to liquidate.

The economic resource that constitutes the "floor" under the family is public assistance. It is debatable whether it should be considered a social work program. The most recent policy of the federal government defines the program as one designed to assist families to regain a state of self-maintenance whenever possible and provides that skilled case-work be made available for this purpose. State public welfare laws tend to announce the same purposes. In some communities devoted, intelligent efforts are made by county commissioners, boards, and administrators to achieve these objectives and to employ such means. In other communities the problems that bring families to the need for public assistance are defined in terms of willful laziness and immoral conduct. The public assistance program is conceived as an illegitimate drain on an economic system which has no responsibility except to provide profits for owners. Public assistance grants are called "hand-outs" and are provided in such degrading and miserly ways as to constitute just that.

Resources to protect husband and wife in their roles as purchasers and consumers are meager and inadequate. The important fact is that consumers are not organized, whereas producers, middlemen, and sellers are. There are federal, state, and local laws to protect the con-sumer against exploitation in the form of dangerous and adulterated products, fake advertising, usury, and substandard housing, but the economic system vigorously opposes governmental efforts to retain, to extend, or to enforce these laws. The consumer-cooperative movement is small and ineffectual, and the business community has been successful in inducing government to impose on it a form of taxation that further impairs its usefulness.

The school system provides courses and entire curricula in home-making, home economics, and nutrition, and nutritional consultants are available in various kinds of health and social agencies. Scholar-ships have been made available from many sources to enable young men and women to pursue advanced education and technical training. Various industries provide such scholarships in their own technical fields, and the federal government underwrites education for a number of profes-sional fields. This whole movement is promising, but its benefits accrue largely to the most intelligent and to those who are already fairly well educated. Governmentally sponsored training programs are only now being provided for the great number of citizens whose basic intellectual gifts are more limited, who lack usable occupational skills, and whose motivations are impaired by hopelessness and inability to conceive attainable vocational goals.

Emotional satisfaction.   Non-social work resources for problems of this kind include a host of clergymen, pastoral counselors, marriage counselors, psychiatrists, and psychologists, the educational courses, formal and informal, and writings in the press, magazines, and books. Informal groups meet in churches, schools, and homes to discuss personality, marriage, and family living. Leadership and teaching are sought from every available professional who is willing to give or sell his time. In general, the cultural value-orientation that underlies these efforts is humanistic, with the qualifications and exceptions already noted.

Sex.   In the American culture father and mother still bear first responsibility to instruct their children in the "facts of life." More educated, sophisticated families make a point of doing this thoroughly and with complete emotional freedom. In lower-class families and among some ethnic groups there is a good deal of reticence in discussing sex between the sexes or between generations. It is assumed that boys will learn about sex from other boys and girls from other girls. If the girls do not learn about it before marriage, their husbands will show them. Obviously the cultural orientation underlying such practices regards sex, in some way, as dirty or evil. Increasingly, however, the formal educational system is assuming responsibility for providing sex education in high schools and colleges. Physicians also constitute a major resource of counsel as well as of treatment in sexual matters. How they handle them probably depends largely on their own value-orientations and emotional freedom. Clergymen, too, are a resource to which families turn when confronted with sexual problems. Here, again, the ways in which the problem is handled depend on the orientation and emotional freedom of the clergyman as well as on the beliefs of his church. Confession and penance may be required as a prelude to absolution. On the other hand, the clergyman may feel he can and should engage in a more humanistically oriented counseling process. Many modern clergymen try to integrate the two approaches.

Having children.   American husbands and wives can now decide whether to have children, how many, and at what intervals if the technical information and treatment necessary to carry out the decision are made available to them. Medical advances have been made in the problem of sterility, but economic and emotional problems remain. Diagnostic studies and treatment are expensive. Some sterility seems to be psychogenic.

Even greater advances have been made by medical science in developing a range of safe and effective contraceptives. The long-hoped-for oral pill is now a reality. The family physician is the major resource of middle-class families for education and individualized examination with respect to contraception. Unfortunately, education in contraceptive knowledge and techniques is not yet a regular part of the curriculum in all medical schools. The Roman Catholic Church continues its moral prohibition on the use of mechanical or chemical means of contraception but permits the "natural" methods of rhythm or abstention from intercourse. The states retain laws prohibiting the dissemination of contraceptive information or devices under various conditions. The commercial drugstore and the peddler remain major sources of contraceptive devices for lower-class families and for unmarried people.

The privately sponsored Planned Parenthood centers in the major cities constitute a resource for examination and treatment of problems of sterility and of responsible provision, under medical supervision, of contraceptive devices. The centers, under the leadership of their national association, have engaged in efforts to take the story and the techniques of planned parenthood to families in the lower classes and to minority groups. They engage in aggressive social action against prohibitory laws, and they seek ways of obtaining recognition and support by government, at the three levels, of the need for family planning throughout American society. They also sponsor and conduct relevant research.

Once pregnancy has occurred, private physicians, nurses, prenatal clinics, and hospitals supply the needed medical resources. Private insurance plans such as Blue Cross and Blue Shield provide funds for delivery and aftercare, and public funds provide this care for indigent families.

Maintenance of social controls. Relatives and friends constitute the first line of defense in the family when one of the spouses begins to drink heavily, gamble, stay out late, or to assault the marital partner. The clergyman and physician constitute the second line of defense. All of these resources are expected to dissuade, scold, and threaten. If they fail, the physician is expected to find a physical cause for the acting out. The various orientations and procedures that clergymen and physicians bring to the handling of these problems are of the same kind already discussed with respect to their handling of other problems. If the drinking assumes serious proportions, Alcoholics Anonymous is regarded as a resource. The value-perspective of this organization seems to be a combination of the humanistic and a specifically supernatural religious value-orientation. The psychiatrist is regarded, perhaps, as the next line of defense. He sees himself, of course, in the humanistic orientation.

The police, the courts, and the correctional system are the last resort. They may be drawn in earlier if the acting out involves assault on the wife or physical or sexual abuse of the children. The police themselves may intervene if one of the spouses has committed illegal acts outside the family.

Crisis and disaster. Officers and chaplains in the armed forces provide some counseling, advice, and access to material resources for servicemen whose induction or continued service causes problems in their marriages or families. Such services may be given within a generally humanistic value-orientation, since this orientation has, to some degree, influenced the military system. Underlying it, however, is the military orientation which defines the individual first as a soldier, whose primary responsibility is to his country and his service. The requirements of the military system may make it necessary for officers and chaplains to withhold some forms of emotional support and to regard as inadmissible privileges some requests which in civilian life would be granted in the interest of the marriage or family. In time of war a host of established institutions and informal social arrangements extend services to members of the armed forces and their wives, but these are withdrawn during times of technical peace.

Unemployment insurance constitutes the major replacement of wages during a layoff from work or the shut-down of a business or factory. The economic system has successfully opposed payment of unemployment insurance to strikers so that the question whether a cessation of employment during a labor dispute is a strike or a lockout by the employer is often bitterly debated between management and labor. Unions try to build up funds in advance to provide strike benefits to their members.

There are few non-social work resources available to families confronted with the problems attendant on mobility. Travel agencies, public transportation, and moving companies, for those who can afford to use them, are commercial operations. Some churches, especially in middle-class urban neighborhoods and suburbs, maintain committees of members to locate and visit newcomers to the community to invite them to visit and join the church. Civic clubs and bridge clubs are likely to spring up in new suburbs and serve as a way of bringing newcomers together. Commercially operated welcome wagons offer bonuses and bargains to newcomers to encourage patronage of the local markets. Disadvantaged families who move into a slum or a deteriorating neighborhood receive no organized welcome. If they are migrant workers who follow the crops, they are assigned to a ghetto maintained by local employers. If they are migrants aimlessly seeking work and a place in which to settle, they may find sanctuary in a slum or trailer camp. Sometimes they are greeted by the cold injunction of the police to "keep moving." Temporary resources are set up by the government, often under the administration of the church and of social work, to meet some of the needs of refugees from the episodic political upheavals in other countries.

Increasing attention is being focused on the needs of the aged as the proportion of older persons in the population of the United States increases. Medical research has developed new knowledge of the physiology of aging. Clinics and hospitals provide more inpatient and outpatient services for older patients suffering from acute and chronic disorders.

Old age and survivors insurance constitutes the basic economic resource for the retired worker and his family. The amounts received, if unsupplemented from other sources, provide for a low standard of living. Business firms offer contributory or noncontributory pension systems as inducements to valued executive and professional personnel. The more enlightened companies set up pension systems for all office personnel. Unions demand pension systems for industrial workers as a part of the union contract and seek to protect their workers by a rigid insistence on seniority in layoffs. Middle-class persons are able to purchase limited annuities from insurance companies. Despite these arrangements, many persons, chiefly the unskilled and marginal workers and their wives, are uncovered by any pension system.

Savings, for persons who have been engaged in well-paying businesses and professions, constitute an important supplement to income from pensions but may not be a sufficient resource for total support. Sale of the family home to enable the retired couple to move to smaller quarters may provide an access of usable capital. Contributions from adult children, though common, may be a drain on the income of the donors and are a manifestation of affection and concern rather than a major increment to the income of the retired couple. Public assistance in the form of aid for the aged or old age assistance is the last financial resort. In some states organized groups of the aged have forced some relaxation of the rules of eligibility for old age assistance and some increase in the size of the grants. In general, however, the financial plight of the aged couple dependent on old age assistance is bleak.

Until the last few years the commercial building industry showed little interest in the housing needs of retired couples. More recently, housing developments for the aging have mushroomed in the warmer parts of the country. Still more recently, relatively luxurious, semi-institutional, semiprivate apartment houses for the aged have been built in a number of sections of the country. Purchase of an apartment in one of these buildings requires considerable capital and is limited to those families who have savings or money from the sale of the family home. Among the lower classes and the disadvantaged groups elderly people have to move in with married children or subsist in dreary furnished rooms on the support afforded by public assistance. Nursing homes for the aged are usually conducted as commercial ventures. Residential institutions conducted by religious organizations and fraternal lodges often require the aged individual or couple to deed over all their financial resources to the institution. The county home may be available to those who cannot manage for themselves but have no funds. It is usually a bleak place in which the indigent aged can live out their days in a deprived and meaningless routine. Some aged persons end in state hospitals, even though they are not psychotic, because they are ill and alone and there is no other place to send them. In county homes and state hospitals aged spouses may be separated.

Loneliness and a sense of being unwanted are the great burden of old age. The best antidote is grandchildren, but they cannot meet all the need for companionship. Many resources exist to help the aged individual or couple find companionship and sources of emotional support. Programs usually stress recreational activities and events, since these, like all recreation, may offer release from tension, an increase in self-esteem, and a sense of identity in the exercise of individual talents and capacities. Churches and schools organize groups of the aging for these purposes. In communities in which retired couples live together, they themselves provide opportunities for companionship and recreation.

The medical profession, of course, bears the major responsibility to care for the medical aspects of accidents but few resources are available outside social work to lighten the consequences for the marriage and the family. Privately operated insurance schemes such as Blue Cross and Blue Shield provide protection for families who can afford them, but they are expensive and their cost is constantly increasing. Families whose wage earners have unstable employment may be unable to afford such policies, may not have access to them through their places of employment, or may not be able to keep them paid up on a continuous basis. Some industries pay the premiums for workers, but for blue collar workers this arrangement is likely to constitute part of a union contract. It would not be available to unorganized, unskilled workers. Private insurance companies do a large volume of business in accident and illness insurance policies, but policyholders sometimes find it difficult to collect benefits and companies may refuse to keep policies in force after an accident or illness.

Workmen's compensation is available to workers injured in covered employment and this helps to support their families through the period of unemployment until the wage earner recovers. If the wife is the one who is injured, the consequences for the family may be very serious, financially as well as emotionally. No governmental insurance is available to cover the cost of having her household duties performed in some alternate manner, nor is money available from workmen's compensation.

The federal government has, during recent years, supported a policy of providing vocational rehabilitation and retraining for workers unable to perform their previous occupational skills and for those whose skills are no longer in demand. When resources for rehabilitation and retraining are available, they constitute one kind of economic bulwark for the family, but workers in rural areas and small towns may have to travel such a distance for these services that their use is made impractical.

Governmental insurance against the consequences of illness is limited to "long-continued" disability under the Old Age, Survivors, and Disability Insurance program of the Social Security Act. Private insurance is expensive and not always available. Professional, clerical, and unionized workers may be protected with provisions for sick leave, some portion of pay, and return to the job. The unskilled, those in unstable employment, those employed in very small businesses, and the self-employed "small business man" may have no financial protection against the hazards of illness.

Clergymen traditionally are assigned the responsibility for visiting the sick and disabled and for advising them and their families. Arrangements for transportation for spouses to visit their partners in the hospital are usually left to family and friends to provide. Emotional support and practical counseling when a spouse or other member of the family dies is also the traditional responsibility of the clergyman, supplemented by other relatives and by friends. Funeral services remain a commercial operation. Funerals are conducted within the value-orientation of the economic system, though attempts are made to disguise this orientation under a cloud of sentiment. Their expense to the family is increased when some undertakers play on the guilt of the bereaved and because families sometimes regard the degree of ostentation of the funeral as a mark of the social status of the family, a social pattern common in some ethnic groups.

Old age and survivors insurance provides a minimal income to widows with children below the age of eighteen. If no other income is available, the surviving family must live on a very low economic and social standard. Private insurance constitutes the main financial bulwark of the family against the death of the wage earner. Its most advantageous form, a continuing annuity, is very expensive, and most families have to settle for conventional life insurance. Families with small incomes can purchase only so-called industrial insurance, the most expensive kind to buy.

Social Work Resources and Services for Specific Problems

The basic resources that the profession of social work can bring to bear on the problems of marital incompatibility are its professional methods: casework, group work, community work, administration, and research. Social work operates within the humanistic value-orientation and reveals the cultural problems previously described as characteristic of the profession at the current stage of its development.

Membership of the family. Social casework, under social work administration, with premarital problems is provided in a few voluntary agencies which focus on the problems of adolescents and young adults. Such casework may be of high technical quality. Unfortunately, even in the cities in which it is provided, the amount available to the public is quite limited. Some assistance of this kind is provided by caseworkers in private practice, usually in conjunction with a psychoanalyst or psychiatrist. Public assistance or child welfare agencies may offer their services in premarital interviews with young people seeking or obviously in need of such help, but the goals are often limited by the scant time and restricted skills of the workers, who will more characteristically try to refer their clients to a voluntary family agency. Caseworkers in psychiatric clinics do some premarital counseling with patients. Consideration of plans for marriage may be one of the subjects dealt with by a state hospital worker as part of planning for discharge or followup after discharge.

Some group work agencies provide help for adolescents, through the medium of the group, with problems of dating, courting, and selection of the spouse. The actual group work is usually carried on by an untrained volunteer or a student under the supervision of a trained, experienced group worker.

Among the courts that deal with problems of separation, desertion, and nonsupport, those organized under the law as family courts are most likely to have a casework department attached to them. Unfortunately, most of these departments are staffed by untrained workers and reflect the basic characteristics of such public agencies. A few have attained a high degree of social work professionalization. In general, the degree to which the caseworker's findings and recommendations influence the judge of a family court depends largely on the real competence of the social worker. In jurisdictions that do not provide for a separate family court, and this includes the small towns and rural areas of the country, any available "casework" is done by overworked, untrained social workers who also serve as probation officers for juvenile cases. Not infrequently their background is in police work. Some of the more progressive ones are experimenting with the use of group work.

Social workers have not entered into private practice in association with lawyers as they have with psychiatrists. Consequently, spouses who go to a lawyer's office for a divorce have no access to the social worker unless the lawyer refers them to a social agency. The same may be said of social work in the courts which have jurisdiction over divorce. If the court is one in which other family cases are heard, a casework staff may be available. Otherwise, access to a social worker depends on the value-orientation of the judge and his knowledge of agency resources.

Abode of the family. Social work is associated with the problems of the abode of the family only in indirect ways. There is no social work agency to which a husband and wife may turn for help in assessing their resources or the availability of other resources for the rental or purchase of a home, the cultural and social characteristics of a neighborhood, as these might relate to their own tastes and needs, or their indecisions about the selection of a dwelling. A caseworker in a voluntary family agency, a medical or psychiatric social work department, a public assistance or child welfare agency, or a court may discuss any of these problems with a family as one aspect of its total problems; but social workers are not usually seen as a first line of resource with respect to housing problems.

Similarly, social workers have not generally been introduced into housing projects, though the initial and continuing problems of social adjustment of families in the projects are often burdensome to themselves and their neighbors. Governmental housing agencies take the position that the residents in a housing project should not be considered apart from the dwellers in the surrounding neighborhood. The same social services should be available to the residents of the neighborhood and the project. Therefore residents with problems are referred to the social agencies in the community.

Social status. There are, as far as the writer knows, no social work organizations or social work programs in other organizations whose purpose is to try to alter the class structure of the United States. Some group work and community work programs have gained access to lower-class people at the neighborhood level to help them to fight publicly and effectively against the class barriers which deny them opportunity to education and economic advancement. The writer does not know the extent to which professional community work or group work are employed by the "cause" agencies which struggle against racial, ethnic, and religious discrimination in the United States: the American Civil Liberties Union, NAACP, Urban League, and B'nai B'rith. If they are not, it is to the shame of social work.

Economic maintenance. Professional social work has been represented in the councils which have shaped basic federal policy concerning social security and public assistance and in the administrative and consultative posts through which the federal government has given leadership to the states concerning their programs of public assistance. On the whole, however, this leadership has been timid and has permitted economic and bureaucratic considerations to convert local public assistance programs into "dead ends" for many of the families who have had to ask for assistance. The same may be said for social work administration at state levels. At the local level, the visitor's position is often defined as a casework job; but the local public assistance department often typifies the governmental bureaucracy at its worst in its narrow interpretation of eligibility, its formalism and rigidity, its submergence in paper work, and its overworked, unmotivated, untrained staff. To do casework under such conditions is impossible. What can be done is demonstrated in the occasional project in which a selected group of cases is isolated for concentrated skilled casework.

The program which the Community Research Associates takes into public assistance agencies raises a number of ethical and theoretical questions. It defines the relative responsibility of the agency for dealing effectively with various problems entirely in terms of the concern of the community. How the community is defined and who speaks for the community are unanswered questions. The CRA approach renders the public assistance agency vulnerable to the demand of any powerful minority that some particular category of clients be singled out as the object of special concern. Moreover, the diagnosis and classification of cases is left in the hands of untrained workers. Despite these shortcomings, the CRA plan does provide for a differential classification of cases in terms of defined criteria of seriousness and amenability to casework treatment. It does confront the agency and the worker with the responsibility to work effectively with its clients, and it does provide means to use available skill and time differentially and in the cases in which they are most likely to produce effective results.

The inability of public assistance agencies to grant assistance to men on strike reflects the influence of the closed economic system on public policy. Rigid and punitive policies concerning eligibility for ADC demonstrate the effect of an authoritarian, moralistic value-orientation on human problems.

Homemaker and day-care services, under social work administration, and both public and private auspices, are available in limited amounts in some communities. These services provide for the care of the children while the mother is away at work.

Neither casework nor group work is available in business firms or factories to provide direct help to the wage earner with problems in his family background or in his relationships with his fellow-employees which may affect his performance on the job. A few attempts have been made, but they have not been reported fully in the literature. Nor have business and industry, from their side, sought to introduce social work into the economic system. The reason seems quite obvious. The value-orientations of the economic system and of the profession of social work differ so markedly that each tends to distrust the other. A close working relationship within the framework of the business corporation would probably be intolerable to both.

Casework was welcomed into the welfare programs of some of the more progressive unions during the most flourishing period of the union movement. Interest seems to have died down on both sides, as the unions have been beset with troubles and as social work has become more cautious and tentative.

Emotional satisfaction. The provision of highly skilled social work for marital problems of this kind is the heart and soul of the work of the voluntary family agency. The technical process involved is casework treatment, based on study and diagnosis, addressed to the motivations and behaviors of the spouses in their complementary roles, interactions, and communications in the marriage. Although material resources of dynamic significance to the marital interaction may be made available, the major process used in treatment is casework interviewing. In very recent years promising results have been achieved by interviewing spouses together or by working with groups of husbands and wives. Some casework and group work with this aspect of marital incompatibility are performed in psychiatric clinics, in medical social work departments, and are provided by courts. Much of the private practice of casework seems to relate to this aspect of marital incompatibility. Since the issue of emotional support and release of tension in the marriage is involved indirectly in all aspects of marital incompatibility, all social workers who deal with any problems of functional significance to the marriage exert an indirect influence on the ability of the partners to give each other support and release.

Some social agencies and individual social workers have acted as consultants to newspapers and magazines and to radio and television stations interested in articles and programs on marital incompatibility. Individual social workers have written articles on the subject for popular consumption. They have taught courses on marriage and family living in schools and colleges and have led discussion groups in churches and other institutions.

Sex. Casework with marital problems is now accepted by Planned Parenthood centers as an integral part of their responsibility to the community. Concern with sexual relationships and pregnancy motivates engaged or married couples to go to the agency initially. In other agencies in which various aspects of marital incompatibility receive direct attention, help with the cultural, social, and emotional concomitants of the sexual relationship may be supplied.

Having children. Casework help with the cultural, social, and emotional variables that influence the wish to have children is offered by the caseworker in voluntary family agencies, by Planned Parenthood centers, by psychiatric and medical social workers in clinics, by workers in adoption agencies, and by workers in private practice. The motivations underlying emotional blocks to impregnation in either husband or wife are often deeply unconscious and very complex. Psychoanalytic or psychiatric treatment may be the therapy of choice.

Nurture and socialization of children. Programs designed to provide social work help with the developmental problems of children are not discussed in this presentation. Casework and group work in child guidance clinics, child welfare agencies, and schools may attempt to effect healthier interaction between parents or to repair various deteriorated marital functions, but the effort is made in the interests of the child. Two aspects of social work in the educational system with some relevance to the problem of marital incompatibility are discussed.

The purpose of social work in the school system, as it is defined today, is to identify and alter those physical, intellectual, cultural, social, and emotional variables in the child, in the school, and in the family which impair the child's ability to make the most of his opportunities as a student. Such work is desperately needed on a far wider scale than is possible with the social work resources available. Such work, however, is essentially remedial. Can social work be employed in the school system in a preventive way? One of the most significant social attributes of the school is that it has access to every child for five days a week for eight years or more of his life.

The value-orientation within which education is provided in the United States defines one of the major purposes of formal education as preparing the child to participate effectively as a citizen in a democratic society. The school accepts responsibility for the development of the child's social as well as his intellectual potentialities. Despite the recent reinvigoration of the intellectual aspects of the curriculum, the other purpose has not been entirely given up.

There are two aspects of the socialization of the child in which social work might participate effectively if it could win its way into the heart of the school system instead of remaining more or less isolated in a remedial function. The one aspect is the preparation of children to use democratic ways of solving problems; the other is the preparation of children to assume the marital roles. Social group work seems to be the method of choice for dealing with the first of these problems.

With respect to the second, it should be noted that a whole series of boy-girl relationships is played out in school and college, from the first tentative notice of and defensive withdrawal from each other through all the stages and manifestations of "going steady," dating, and courtship. What an opportunity for the social caseworker and group worker to move into the school itself to help the youngsters to perceive and evaluate each other correctly and to assess and correct their exaggerated emotional reactions!

Maintenance of social controls. What has already been said about social work in the courts applies to social work with those aspects of the breakdown of social controls in marriage in which one partner has the other arrested or complains about his behavior before a court. If the partner is incarcerated or placed on probation, the casework is characterized by the general features of social work in adult corrections. Direct casework with acting-out marital partners is a subject of intensive study in all agencies which deal with marital problems. During the early stages of the work, the client's conduct may have to be held in restraint by the imposition of the external controls inherent in the worker's authority as representative of society. Voluntary family agencies are providing a great deal of casework help of this kind. Casework with alcoholics has not been successful in general agency practice, but the literature reports some fairly promising results in specialized clinics for alcoholics.

Crisis and disaster. Major responsibility for providing help to families with problems consequent on the drafting or enlistment of the husband in the armed forces rests with the Home Service Division of American Red Cross. The agency itself is founded on congressional authorization and has a semiofficial status in dealing with the armed forces in the interest of servicemen and their families. In the larger cities the Home Service Division is a professionalized family agency. Its communications system enables contact to be made immediately with any American military post in any part of the world, and information can quickly be transmitted between the member of the armed forces and his family concerning the welfare of both. Casework is available to the wives of servicemen and to the servicemen themselves while they are home to help them meet the various family problems, including those of marital incompatibility.

The Army and the Air Force maintain staffs of trained social workers with officer rank, many of whom are stationed in hospitals and disciplinary barracks. Others are assigned to various kinds of mental hygiene and morale services and are in a position to help servicemen and their wives with problems of marital incompatibility. The medical and psychiatric hospitals of the Veterans Administration have staffs of trained social workers, much of whose work is related to the social and emotional components of physical and mental illness, but some aspects of marital incompatibility are dealt with.

The writer is not aware of any agency whose major purpose is to provide social work for persons discharged from their positions or unemployed because of the closing of a business or factory, temporary layoffs, strikes, and lockouts. Some of the progressive unions formerly engaged caseworkers to deal with the family problems of their members, and counseling with reference to the consequences for the family of discontinuance of employment fell within their purview. The writer does not know whether any union continues to provide such counseling service today. Spouses whose marriages are affected by various forms of marital incompatibility precipitated or exacerbated by interruptions of employment are likely to go to or be referred to the voluntary family agency.

Under the auspices of the affiliates of the National Travelers Aid Association, casework is provided for mobile families. As patterns of travel have changed, the sign on the desk in the railroad station is now appearing in bus stations and airports and even, in a few places, beside the main roads leading into cities. Some public child welfare departments are also taking casework and the material resources it can provide into the camps of migrant workers. The national office of the Planned Parenthood Association has also provided services in some of these camps. Indigent families who enter a new community usually turn to the department of public assistance for financial help, but residence laws are likely to prevent their receiving more than temporary emergency assistance. Arrangements have been set up in some states to provide for the return of such families to their places of residence or legal settlement. Little systematic effort is made to effect such return, unless some administrator, legislator, or newspaper tries to dramatize the charge that a disadvantaged minority group is pouring into the community for the sole purpose of obtaining public assistance. For mobile families and individual transients the shelters and kitchens of the Salvation Army or other missions, municipal shelters, or, as a last resort, the jails may ward off starvation and exposure. These resources are mentioned here because, except for the jails, sometimes someone on the staff is designated as a social worker. These workers are untrained and operate out of the religious orientation of the particular mission or the often judgmental, suspicious, and ungiving orientation of the municipal authorities.

Social work assistance for the problems of marital incompatibility of the aged is not provided under separate agency auspices. The voluntary family agencies sometimes designate one or more workers to specialize in these problems, and the larger agencies may set up a special unit or project for this purpose. Problems of marital incompatibility are dealt with as one aspect of the total situation of the family. Public assistance agencies provide financial assistance and make referrals of aged clients to other health and welfare agencies for help with specific medical and social problems. Social workers in medical and psychiatric clinics and hospitals may deal with the marital problems of the aged as they are related to their physical, mental, or emotional ill health. Some institutions for the aged are highly professionalized and their staffs include competent social service departments, but many provide no social work at all. Settlement houses organize Golden Age clubs for which they provide group work leadership, usually undertaken by volunteers under the supervision of trained professional group workers.

When a family is temporarily disrupted by accident or illness and obtains medical treatment in a hospital or clinic in a large city, highly proficient medical social casework may be available to help with the social, emotional, and economic consequences for the patient and his family. Even in metropolitan areas, however, not all hospitals have medical social work departments, and, when they are present, these departments do not necessarily "cover" all medical "services." In general, too, physicians and patients are less willing to use medical social service if the patient is in a private room and is a private patient of the physician. This reluctance or aversion is a manifestation of the tendency of well-to-do and middle-class people to think of social work as appropriate only for the poor and deprived. One of the more promising developments in dealing with the sick is the home-care program. Medical social work to the patient and his family is one of the integral services.

Caseworkers are likely to take part in modern programs of vocational rehabilitation, but the availability of such social services is still limited. Social group work with patients or with the spouses and other relatives of patients is being introduced into progressive hospitals. Medical social service departments in hospitals in smaller cities may be staffed by untrained workers. Their services may be limited to help with immediate, practical problems of finances and household management.

When illness takes the form of mental or emotional disturbance, and the patient attends a psychiatric clinic or enters a state hospital, the services of the psychiatric social worker are required. The variations of focus and quality in psychiatric social work are very great. Both casework and group work may be used to help the patient and his spouse accept his need for treatment and to help them prepare for his discharge. Contemporary psychiatric social work is becoming increasingly family-oriented and is assuming more responsibility for offering casework and group work with the interrelationships between the illness and the frequently present marital incompatibility of the partners. On the other hand, much psychiatric social work still tends to be oriented exclusively toward the patient. Spouses may be seen only at admissions and on visiting days, and the contact may be limited to questions and answers regarding the progress of the patient. Psychiatric social work in many clinics and hospitals is highly professionalized. In other hospitals, especially in state hospitals remote from large cities, it may be performed by untrained workers and consist mainly of admissions interviews and routine contacts with patients and relatives.

The American family does not turn immediately and directly to the social worker for support at the time of the death of a member of the family. The family may know the medical or psychiatric social worker because the deceased had been ill before his death. The family may apply to the public assistance agency because of economic needs consequent on the death of the wage earner. The caseworker usually has access to bereaved families only because they ask for or are receiving help with some other problem or some other consequence of the death of a member of the family.

It seems likely that barring some unforeseen changes such as a war or a major depression marital incompatibility in the forms it now takes will increase in incidence and intensity. The major dimension in which the deterioration will take place is an increase in the manifestations of normlessness in the society at large and in normlessness and loss of a sense of identity in individuals. Spouses will commit less of themselves to marriage because there will be less of themselves to commit. The new "companionship" marriage may become a rather casual association of two people who stay together or drift apart as whim and circumstance dictate.

Social work programs will become more specialized and more refined technically. The casework available to families will be better casework, but a smaller proportion of families will be able to take advantage of it. Public assistance will continue to struggle with its internal value-conflicts, and its program will vary in objectives and methods as the restrictive economic and bureaucratic orientations on the one hand or the humanistic orientation on the other gain temporary ascendance. Courts and correctional systems will not alter their basic orientations, but more social workers may enter them and cause more internal conflict. Group workers will be introduced into the family agencies, hospitals, and clinics in increasing numbers and will find some surcease from their present fears by becoming involved in technical refinement of their skills. Community workers will continue to come to terms with the "power structure," but there will be no changes in the basic orientations of communities with respect to their social problem. Social work leadership in the National Association of Social Workers, in the administration of governmental departments, and in voluntary agencies and federations will continue to be timid and ineffectual. The schools of social work will continue to refine their curricula and to attract mediocre students who are looking for security in their jobs and "good supervision."

The Voluntary Family Agency

The voluntary family agency is the social work institution that bears the major responsibility in any community in which it exists for dealing directly with the problems of families. It discharges this responsibility in three ways. First, most of its resources of skill, time, and money are used in its program of direct casework service to families. In the last few years experimental attempts have been made to provide direct service to clients in groups. Second, the agency accepts the responsibility to participate in social action, including attempts to influence legislation and to alter the broader cultural, political, economic, and social circumstances which are damaging to the families in the community. Third, the agency undertakes research in the causation of family problems and the effectiveness of methods of alleviating them.

As the embodiment of a voluntary organized effort on the part of a segment of the citizenry to deal with a problem independently of the government, it reflects a strong and important aspect of the culture of the United States. Such organized voluntary efforts seem to be almost an anachronism in the mid-twentieth century when the tendency is to seek governmental organization of and support for efforts to cope with social problems. Since the days when the older family agencies emerged from amalgamations of smaller benevolent societies and began to assume their present institutional identity, they have maintained an "open door" policy at intake. The definition of the purposes of the agency has been kept sufficiently flexible so that any family in the community could take any problem to the agency. Up to the time of the depression of the 1930's, the private family agencies provided financial assistance to families for purposes of maintenance, but this service was surrendered to the public assistance agencies when it became evident that governmental funds were necessary because of the magnitude of the problem of financial need. In the past other services have been provided by family agencies and then turned over to other agencies as the need became so great or the service so specialized that it warranted provision under separate institutional auspices. Throughout, however, the private family agency has maintained the "open door" policy and the concomitant orientation to the total family and all its needs and requirements.

The fact that the family agency conceives and performs its work on the basis of this total orientation is one of the reasons why its work with marital incompatibility has to be discussed apart from the work of other agencies. Casework in the family agency seeks to identify the causes of all the problems in the family and it takes account of the ways in which these causes influence the performance of the various marital and family functions. Casework treatment is provided for threats to the structural unity of the family and for all the problems of incompatibility in social status, economic functioning, emotional support, sexual gratification, decisions about having children, parent-child problems, and breakdowns in reciprocal social controls. Indeed, the artificial separation of marital incompatibility from other aspects of family problems in the "social problems" project has brought critical comment from staff members of family agencies with whom the writer has discussed this presentation. To a person, they asked how marital incompatibility could be discussed independently of the problems between parents and children or among children.

Voluntary family agencies have, over the years, played a major part in the development of casework as a refined technical process and they continue to do so. The family agencies in the larger cities engage only graduate social workers as members of staff and maintain high standards of performance. A considerable amount of agency time is devoted to improving the quality of its casework service through various programs of study and consultation. The voluntary agencies in the smaller cities and those that have been set up in the more remote parts of metropolitan areas have been unable to maintain such high standards. It is sometimes necessary for them to employ untrained caseworkers.

Structurally, the voluntary agency seems to have worked out a happy solution to the problem of organizing professional services. Bureaucratic structure is kept at a minimum in an effort to free the caseworker to do his basic job—casework with families. In recent years there has even been an alteration in the role of the supervisor, the key person in the hierarchy of the family agency. Greater emphasis is placed on the worker's responsibility for independent competent practice, and record keeping is held to a minimum. A basic statistical form prepared by the Family Service Association of America serves most purposes and is relatively easy to fill out.

If the family agency has the orientation, the professional knowledge and skill, and the structure to enable it to deal effectively with family problems such as marital incompatibility, why does so much marital incompatibility continue to occur? Several reasons are apparent. Even the largest voluntary family agencies are small operations, given the size of the task that confronts them. An agency with a staff of thirty case-workers cannot provide casework for all the maritally incompatible couples in a metropolitan area of two million people. Family agencies either have long lists of clients awaiting service or they have to close intake periodically. Neither the funds nor the staff are available to meet all the needs that exist in the community. Many people can take help only on their own terms. When marital incompatibility is the problem, one spouse often asks the caseworker to make the other behave differ-ently. The other spouse frequently denies that a problem exists and re-fuses to see the caseworker. The behavior of a person who cannot be interviewed cannot be changed. The only avenue of approach left open is to offer to work with the spouse who has come to the agency. This is likely to be less effective than work with both, but, whether it is or not, the spouse who came initially may refuse to participate in the casework process on this basis.

Many people with marital problems are too hurt and too fragile to sus-tain any contact with the caseworker at all. They may be able to come in once or twice to tell about their troubles in their marriages, but they become frightened at the seriousness of the problems which their own words reveal. They have to flee, so that they can continue to deny that there is anything really seriously wrong with them or their marriages. Family casework has acquired more understanding of how to move out toward such hurt people and to sustain them during the initial stages of a contact, but not all of them can be reached.

Certain questions can be asked about ways to make family casework more available and more effective, but the answers are not immediately apparent. Would not the solution of the problem of lack of funds be to turn to the government? Then existing agencies could be enlarged and new agencies established in places in which the service is not available. Yes, that could be done, but at what cost? The field of voluntary social work itself represents one of the important strengths of the community. For reasons already discussed, the citizen in America feels that govern-ment is remote and beyond his control. If voluntary family social work becomes a governmental function, does not another manifestation of the citizen's sense of identity and autonomy pass out of his control?

Granted that that question can be answered satisfactorily, would not resort to governmental support so alter the character of the agency that the casework service itself would be drastically altered? One of the strengths of the voluntary family agency is its ability to keep its eye on its main task, the provision of a casework service of high quality for family problems. It has been able to remain singularly free of the bureaucratic elaboration that consumes so much precious time and that rigidifies professional service. Once the government enters the picture, bureaucratic organization and bureaucratic control systems become a part of the way of life.

Cannot voluntary casework service be made available in places and in ways that will make it more accessible to more people? Some family agencies have made the attempt. Outposts have been established in suburbs. Caseworkers have been placed in nursery schools, public schools, settlement houses. On the whole, these efforts seem not to have been singularly successful, and agencies have tended to withdraw from them after trial periods. This does not imply that the agencies should not continue to seek ways to get closer to the people whom they wish to serve. It does imply that the public as a whole or in its various cultural subdivisions does not always "see" the family caseworker as a person who can help.

Cannot the voluntary family agency be more aggressive in its social action program, so that some of the causes of family distress can be dealt with at the source? The agency is limited here by its nature and sponsorship. It represents an effort of people committed to the socio-economic status quo to alleviate some of the unfortunate consequences of the current values and organization of the society and economy. There are limits to the ability of the agency to participate in attempts to change the basic values and institutions without losing its sources of support.

Not infrequently other agencies and individual social workers perceive the family agency as somewhat remote from the mainstream of social work endeavor in the community. Complaints are made that the agency does not assume the leadership in interagency efforts to solve local problems to which its unquestioned competence entitles it. Family agency workers are said to be reluctant to participate in the activities of the local chapter of the National Association of Social Workers. The agency is said to refuse to accept referrals which other agencies believe it should accept. The administration and staff of the family agency are always quick to reject these charges. They point to a formidable amount of social action carried on. They disclose many activities which staff workers perform in the community under the auspices of the agency itself. They maintain, with justice, that the caseworkers in the agency must retain the right to accept or reject referrals on the basis of their own diagnostic thinking.

Despite these disclaimers, the impression often persists that the administration and staff of the family agency comprise a closed system in which internal morale and pride in membership are high. It is the impression of the writer that staff members of family agencies do possess more loyalty to the agency and pride in the agency than do the staff members of many other agencies. Their value-orientations tend to be derived from the field of family casework rather than from social work or even social casework as a whole. Three reasons for this restriction of professional horizons can be suggested. It is a defensive reaction, sometimes overtly acknowledged, against the overestimation of psychiatric social work current in the profession. More significantly, it constitutes a refuge in technical competence in the face of patent evidence that the profession of social work has not dealt effectively with the broad and pressing social problems of the community and cannot do so. Finally, it is a manifestation of the fact that the high standards of competence demanded by the agency result in a process of selection by the agency and self-selection by candidates for positions in the community of competent, highly motivated caseworkers intensely interested in family casework.

GENERAL PROPOSALS FOR ACTION

The proposals in this section are couched in general terms for two reasons. First, the problem of marital incompatibility and the other major social problems of the times are inextricably mixed together in causation and in influence on one another. Proposals to deal with one problem must take account of proposals to deal with all the others. Specific proposals can be justified only when all problems are taken into account. Second, since many of the major causes of marital incompatibility reside in the basic value-orientations of the society, as expressed in large complex social systems, proposals for dealing with them must include recommendations for action at the broadest level of social organization. The writer, who is a social caseworker, has limited competence to recommend specific programs of action at this level of social organization.

It is desirable that the profession of social work assume once again the original and traditional responsibility accorded it by society. This is the responsibility to try to achieve the solution of social problems by removing or altering their causes, whatever their nature, whether cultural, political, economic, or social values and organization or intrapersonal values, emotions, and ideas. It has always been assumed by society that in the selection of its goals and means social work would be guided by a humanistic value-orientation.

Marital incompatibility is ultimately caused by certain value-orientations and their derivatives to which the value-orientation of social work is opposed. These pejorative value-orientations are the dehumanized version of the cognitive orientation which makes instruments of human beings and the discriminatory value-orientation. The derivatives of the dehumanized cognitive orientation are the size, remoteness, and inaccessibility of the political system, the operation of the economic system as a closed system which recognizes no accountability to any noneconomic interest in society, the operation of the social class system in the interest of the economic system, and bureaucratic formalism, rigidity, and devotion to efficiency of the bureaucratic system as an unconditioned value. The discriminatory value-system operates by placing human beings in disvalued categories, evaluating them in terms of the characteristics attributed to the category rather than as individuals, and attributing to them, as inherent characteristics, the shortcomings that are the consequences of the discriminatory practices themselves.

The derivatives or ways of operation of the two pejorative value-orientations may be classified roughly into two categories. In the first category belong the closed economic system, that aspect of the social class system that is expressive of the economic system, namely, the denial of opportunity for upward mobility and the discriminatory social practices. All these social arrangements are highly institutionalized. They are politically, economically, and socially powerful. They excite and mobilize deep, often irrational, emotions in their adherents. They can be ruthless in action. They are often made to function as "causes." They will not yield to direct attack unless more powerful forces can be mobilized against them.

In the second category belong the size, remoteness, and inaccessibility of the political system, bureaucratic formalism, rigidity, and devotion to efficiency, and that aspect of the social class system that consists of symbolic rites, possessions, and behaviors. None of these is powerful as a "cause." None tends to call forth deep or irrational feelings in their supporters. All are susceptible to many forms of influence. It is significant that each is the subject of a large body of satire and humor, whereas all the items in the first category are generally considered too grave or too sacred to be the subject of humor.

This general classification does not hold for all manifestations of the two sets of social arrangements. Business tycoons are sometimes the butt of satire, though the consequences of their more ruthless actions are not. On the other hand, some devoted bureaucrats can make a "cause" out of a regulation, and some symbols of upper-class status are worshipped with what seems to be almost irrational ardor. The most portentous general consequence of the pejorative value-orientations is their destruction of other values and of the sense of identity and purpose in individuals. The processes by which this destruction takes place have been explained.

The most significant fact about the current value-orientation of social work, with respect to its potential for changing either of the pejorative value-orientations or their derivatives, is that it is itself a distortion of the humanistic value-orientation which it pretends to be. The nature of this distortion has already been discussed. Goals are rationalized as achievable because they are desired. Countervailing forces are discounted, leaving the social worker in a position in which he can work comfortably and interminably in his accustomed way to develop potentials when no potentials exist. A nice project in social work research would consist of an attempt to determine whether this distortion is itself a form of normlessness, the product of the derivatives of the pejorative value-orientations.

Components of a Program of Action

A program of action for dealing with all causes of marital incompatibility would have to include programs to achieve the following:

1. Alter the distorted value-orientation of social work.
2. Increase the social responsibility of the economic system.
3. Bring government closer to the people it serves.
4. Humanize the operations of bureaucracies.
5. Alleviate the pressures on individuals and families to engage in ceaseless strivings for upward mobility.
6. Make opportunities for desirable upward mobility available to individuals and families who need them.
7. Destroy the discriminatory value-orientation and the social arrangements that proceed from it.
8. Provide services for marriages in which incompatibility exists.
9. Influence social work education to adjust to the new value position.

The components of the program, except the first, are not listed in the order of priority of action. Each has to be made specific with respect to the community in which it will be carried out, the institutions to be altered or created, and the concrete actions to be performed to achieve the goals.

1. Alter social work's value orientation. This first component is clearly the responsibility of the profession of social work itself. Under the existing organization of the profession, the National Association of Social Workers, the National Conference on Social Welfare, and the Council on Social Work Education might be expected to provide the necessary leadership. In view of the suggested value position for social work, it would be important to try to engage the participation of those friendly critics from other disciplines and professions who charge social work with being timid and ingrown, narrow in its outlook, and overly preoccupied with technique and the making of records.

2. Increase the social responsibility of the economic system. The second component of the program cannot be carried out by the profession of social work alone. Social work must find allies both inside and outside the world of business. Two considerations are important. Social work must not confuse its enemies with its friends. Many powerful leaders and exponents of the current economic system do not agree with the value position of social work. Social work must not try to pretend that they do and invite them into its councils. Second, to achieve the goals of this component of the program social work will have to sacrifice some of its respectability and economic security.

The major objective of this part of the program, with respect to marital incompatibility, would be an effort to induce the economic system to guarantee security of income to families. Clearly, this aim could not be accomplished by requiring the individual business firm to guarantee jobs and wages to its employees for life. It could be accomplished by altering the basic philosophy of the public assistance program, so that the emphasis would be placed on maintaining and developing the potentialities of individuals and families rather than on requiring them to furnish proof of indigence. Grants should be based on helping people maintain a socially desirable rather than a minimal standard of living. In determining the size of grants, an attempt should be made to maintain or improve the standard of living of the family. Money should be made available to families during periods of crisis, even though their usual source of income has not been interrupted.

3. Bring government closer to the people. The third component of a program of action depends on the concerted efforts of many different kinds of associations of citizens and the participation in the effort of many professions. The contribution of social work would include several strategies. Social workers have succeeded in humanizing certain aspects of governmental bureaucracies in which the social workers exert an influence on policy and practice. They have helped to conduct the interactions between the bureaucracy and its clients in an individualized manner. Social workers in governmental bureaucracies in which their advocacy of individualized treatment of the clients is rejected need to be more aware of their responsibility to their clients and less willing to accede to the demands of the bureaucracy itself for treating people in routinized ways. This strategy constitutes perhaps only a special case of the application of two of the criteria for defining fields of social work practice enunciated by the Subcommittee on Fields of Practice of the NASW Commission on Social Work Practice. These criteria specify that "there is actual or potential compatibility of the goals of the organization and social institution(s) and of social work" and that "there is involved a contribution by social work to the character and goals of the social institution." [20]

---

[20] "Identifying Fields of Practice in Social Work," by the Subcommittee on Fields of Practice, NASW Commission on Social Work Practice, *Social Work*, Vol. 7, No. 2 (April 1962), p. 9.

A second strategy would consist of a deliberate effort by the various institutions and levels of social work leaderships to become more aware of the *political* aspects of social work goals, proposals, and programs and to intervene in political processes more effectively. Social workers seem to adhere to the common American belief that public problems can best be solved if they are removed from the political arena to the more rarefied and presumably purer atmosphere of science and the professions. Such an attitude is questionable on the grounds of both policy and practice. With respect to policy, the issues of public welfare, whether in a general or specific sense, are the business of the public, and politics is, in a very important sense, the means of conducting public debate and public solution of public problems. With respect to practice, the American party system, with all its machinations, is an unavoidable reality. When programs that affect large numbers of people are at issue, the party system becomes one of the effective variables in determining the outcome.

Clearly other strategies must be and can be devised. The two sketched above illustrate the basic recommendations, namely, that social workers at all levels of practice become more sensitive, more knowledgeable, and more active politically.

4. Humanize the operations of bureaucracy. The fourth component of the program does not seem quite so formidable, complex though the undertaking undoubtedly is. Few people, even bureaucrats, defend the rigidities of the bureaucracies as desirable in themselves. Social workers have a great deal of relatively successful experience in this particular task and have achieved some notable success in some of the public assistance and child welfare agencies. What is required to achieve the goals of this part of the program is systematic, public demonstration and criticism of the dehumanizing effects of the bureaucracies in business, education, and government.

5. Alleviate pressures to strive for upward mobility. The achievement of the goals of the fifth component must be sought on several levels. Social work should participate more openly and more vigorously with whatever allies it can find in education, the clergy, and the communications media to expose the facts, the tragedies, and the absurdities of the race upward. Social workers should as individuals and in their professional institutions speak clearly and incessantly for humanistic values. Further, social work must practice what it preaches and take the consequences. Executives should protest against the use of their boards and committees as symbols of social class prestige. Community workers should seek ways of gaining entry to middle- and upper middle-class suburban communities to help the residents define and deal with their community problems in terms of humanistic values rather than in terms of the symbolic affirmation of class status. Group workers and caseworkers need to become more aware of the ways in which strivings for the symbols of upward mobility enter into the problems of their clients.

6. Make opportunities available for desirable upward mobility. The conduct of the sixth component of the program requires the alteration of some of the values that some social workers hold. Some of the lower-class social patterns tend to brutalize individuals and to prevent the development of their potentialities. There is no virtue in being verbally inarticulate just because inarticulateness is a characteristic of the class to which one happens to belong. If the point can be granted, it can then be said that to achieve the goals of this part of the program social work of a vigorous nature will have to be carried on at the community level, in cooperation with many "cause" movements, to open up opportunities for the disadvantaged. Group workers and caseworkers can do something of this nature with groups and individuals, but the main push has to be at the community level.

7. Destroy discrimination. To achieve the goals of the seventh component, social work must ally itself publicly and vociferously with the organized "cause" movements and the unorganized citizens of good will who are battling racial discrimination. This is a battle, and many individual social workers are engaged in it. The profession itself is not. At the level of organization of services the profession must refuse to admit discriminatory practices, whether overt as in some sections of the country or covert as in others. Expediency must not be accepted as a plea for delay. This battle can be won.

8. Provide services for couples whose marriages are incompatible. The eighth component raises some knotty problems. The major problem is how to reach married people who are psychologically or socially inaccessible or who do not "see" the agency as a resource for help with their marital problems. The answer, of course, is a service that can reach into all neighborhoods, all social classes, and all racial and ethnic groups, a service that can be "seen" because it is nearby and because it is performed by a profession known to be concerned about marital incompatibility and about the injustices which give rise to it.

The review of available social work services also shows that although the counseling service is potentially comprehensive, certain issues that contribute to marital incompatibility are not usually conceived, either by social workers or by married couples, as being within the purview of family social work. The potentials for group work with young people in the schools and colleges on the problems of early social relationships between the sexes have been mentioned. Such work would constitute a first step in preparing young people for marriage. Young couples do not ask for nor are they likely to receive help in the selection of a home. Mobile families and migrant workers seldom turn to the family social worker for help with the dislocations that mobility enforces on them. Family social workers are not called in after accidents or in anticipation of death.

Similarly, material resources are not available for many of the natural crises of married life. There is no provision that enables young couples to furnish a home. Many of them cannot afford to do so. There is no provision to guarantee continuance of income at the level to which the family is accustomed, regardless of the vicissitudes of individual companies or jobs. There is no adequate provision of homemaker services during the illness of the wife. There is no adequate provision to finance the cost to the family of fertility studies, of strikes, of moving to a new city or neighborhood, of accidents and illnesses, of retirement, or of death.

The counseling services under the authoritative auspices of courts and probation departments are utterly inadequate in quantity and quality to meet the needs of those marriages in which social controls have broken down. A desirable program to meet these needs is not easy to devise. Nevertheless, a program will be outlined. It may serve as a basis for discussion out of which a sounder proposal might emerge. The program consists of three parts.

First, the basic counseling service, using casework and group work with families, will consist of a voluntary family agency with a board of directors. Persons drawn from the social classes, races, and ethnic and religious groups which appear in the caseload of the agency should be among the membership of the board. Voluntary contributions for the support of the agency should be supplemented with grants from the local, state, and federal governments. The relationship between the agency and the government should be somewhat like that between the schools of social work and the National Institute of Mental Health. The government should be responsible for presenting a concrete plan for the use of the money, and the implementation of the plan should be left in the hands of the agency. Great freedom should be allowed the agency to adjust its program as the needs of the community require. The focus of the counseling service should reside not in a district office but in the worker. Implementation of the new value position of the profession should produce workers whose profession is within themselves, not in the agency. These workers would regard themselves, and the agency would regard them, not as staff members or employees but as professionals who are contracting their services to the agency. Supervision would be available for inexperienced workers. Others would be held accountable for the quality of their work. Consultation would be available to them on request.

Centers would be established throughout the city in which the worker might hold interviews and receive telephone calls and mail if he wished. He would not, however, be required to work in the centers. Rather, he would be encouraged to locate the counseling services in places in which potential clients might "see" them: churches, schools, local clubs, shopping centers, places of business, suburban municipal buildings, housing projects—wherever, indeed, the people who live in the community go in the course of their normal patterns of living. The worker should be a part of the local scene, as familiar as the neighborhood family doctor. The worker would seek the sponsorship of local clergymen, principals and teachers in the schools, justices of the peace, doctors, dentists, business men, and women active in local civic affairs. The worker would receive referrals and would seek out potential clients. Several workers, including a community worker, would form a team to provide leadership to residents in local neighborhoods to deal with the local conditions affecting their marriages, their homes, and their families.

The second part of the program would consist of the provision of services and money to alleviate the crises of family life. It is suggested that the major specific goals of the second, third, and fourth components of the over-all program, namely, influencing the economic system, the government, and the bureaucracies, be focused in an effort to have the public assistance program at the federal, state, and local levels of government converted into a family welfare program. The family welfare department should assume responsibility to guarantee to all families the continuance of income at the level set by the usual earnings of the wage earner or wage earners in the family. Whether the department should seek to raise the level of living of economically deprived families is a moot question. Achievement even of the first objective would be revolutionary in the United States. The department should, further, provide funds to families to enable them to weather the crises of life without exhausting their savings. The nature of these crises has already been noted.

Both the counseling services and the financial grants should be extended to newcomers to the community, to mobile families, and to migrant workers. Workers under contract to the family agency would be assigned the responsibility to seek these families out, make the services and grants known to them, and offer counseling service and necessary financial assistance. The grants of the family welfare department would not supplant the current family maintenance programs such as unemployment insurance. The voluntary family agency would have a responsibility to participate in efforts by the community to have the standards for these programs raised to appropriate levels.

The third part of the program of family services would consist of systematic, vigorous efforts by centrally located professional representatives of the agency, in cooperation with other interested institutions and individuals, to change the value-orientations and expand and improve the social work services of the courts and correctional system. These activities would constitute additional concrete steps in the conduct of the second, third, and fourth components of the general program.

The question will be raised about the cost of this program of services for families. It would be far more expensive than the current programs, but social work must not permit it to be evaluated in terms of financial cost alone, for that would constitute a surrender to the value-orientation of the economic system. The important answer to the question is that the program is likely to decrease the amount and severity of marital incompatibility in the community. When it really "takes hold," it will counter the trend toward normlessness, since more people will find first in their workers and then in their spouses someone with whom they can identify in a constructive way. In the long run the program will be cheap because, in conjunction with similar programs to deal with other social problems, it will produce a better motivated and more productive citizenry.

9. Influence social work education to adjust to the new value position. No comments will be made here about specific content of the curriculum, for that will have to be developed when the total recommendations of the NASW project on social problems emerge. The most important change in the educational program will consist of the announcement of the new value position as the focus around which the educational program will be built. The correction of the distorted value-orientation of social work will free social work education, just as it will free the agencies, from preoccupation with traditional arrangements and with the current emphasis on inculcation of course content rather than on teaching as a joint effort of teacher and student to learn the answers to questions of professional concern to both. Several specific changes can be anticipated. As social work makes common cause with a broad range of disciplines and professions, the educational barriers in the schools will be lowered. If pastoral counselors, teachers, and students of business administration and public administration need to know the same things about human beings and their social arrangements and about ways of influencing human situations to humanistic ends, then all these students might study together. Eventually, perhaps, the new and broader profession that underlies all these professions may emerge.

It can be anticipated that students and teachers will work together more closely than they do under current educational arrangements. The artificial distinction between the classroom teacher and the field instructor will disappear. The teacher will teach in the field and in the classroom. Perhaps some of the other distinctions will also disappear. It can be predicted with some confidence that workers will not identify themselves as caseworkers or group workers but will think of themselves as social workers who can work effectively with clients singly or in association with other clients. What rapprochements may take place among community work, social welfare policy, and administration cannot be accurately foreseen at this time. Certainly they will not continue to be locked off from one another as they are now. A very risky surmise might be that social work will pass through a stage in which it is seen as composed of two interrelated efforts, the one designed to deal with the problems of social functioning of small systems and the other designed to influence the structure and functioning of large systems. The small systems segment would consist of efforts to understand and help people deal directly with the problems in their own lives. It would include the methods now known as casework and group work, but it would not conceive of them as two discrete disciplines. Rather, the focus would be on ways of reaching people with problems, on understanding those problems, and on bringing to bear whatever methods might offer some hope of alleviation. The large systems segment of the profession would be concerned with influencing the various forms and levels of social, political, and economic organization in the interest of the welfare of the individual members of the society and their families. It would comprise those parts of social work now known as social welfare policy and organization, community work, and administration. Best of all, perhaps research will grow out of the need to learn more about the results of a new venture and about ways of proceeding more surely in the future.

The new value position and its consequences in action should attract to the profession students with different characteristics from those who now seek admission. The newer students will be more idealistic and more radical. They will have more energy and they will be brighter. They will be less concerned with "psychiatric" social work and more concerned with social work. They will seek opportunities to try out ideas rather than "good supervision." They will probably be harder to teach, for they will be more inquisitive and more challenging of the teachers' statements. They may even do some reading! Perhaps the new venture in social work will produce better teachers, teachers who

, are less timorous and defensive of their specialties and less pre-
occupied with routines.

Feasibility of the Proposed Program

The new program will not receive easy acquiescence within the profession. Too many leaders of the national organizations are tearing
off in all directions at once, pursuing grants and conducting projects, in
a frenzy of unfocused activity. So many projects are started. So few
are brought to satisfactory completion. Many administrators in public
and private programs are deeply imbued with the distorted value-orientation of present-day social work. They find safety in getting along with
the "power structure" and in bureaucratic controls. Many educators
have built their reputations on jealously guarded specializations. The
new venture would deprive them of their badges of status. Many workers find real enjoyment in the elaboration of casework and group work
technique. They can recognize the need for bolder approaches, but
they will not want to be called on to give up comfortable ways of working.

The sources of opposition outside social work will be formidable.
Once the spokesmen for the economic system and for the discriminatory pressure groups smell what is in the wind, they will rally to the
attack. Attack, however, need not imply defeat. Indeed, some attack,
on the grounds of value differences, might be good for social work.
It might stimulate lethargic commitments. The greater danger lies in
the apathy, normlessness, and uncertainty of identity of people of good
will in the community. The most chilling question that can be asked
of the new venture is "What difference does it make?"

It is hard to predict where sources of support might be located within
the profession. Individuals rather than national organizations, agencies,
or schools come to mind. As a teacher, the writer hazards the guess
that first-year students would love the new venture; second-year students would be troubled by it; advanced students would try to pick
the logical holes in it.

Support from outside social work might come from one unexpected
source—the universities that contain schools of social work. Social
work seems to make little sense to administrators of universities. Under
all the fine talk, they ask, "What does social work do? Why does it
profess to deal with social problems and then talk only about working
with individuals?" "Why is the school of social work so remote from
the sociology department and so close to the department of psychiatry?"
The universities might be made uncomfortable by the new venture, but
they seem able to tolerate a good deal of discomfort and criticism.
What they cannot tolerate is obfuscation.

Other sources of support may be found in political organizations; in some unions and among some city councilmen, federal representatives, and senators. Some administrators and consultants in the state bureaucracies will lend support, for they are caught between official indifference from above and pressures for more purposive action from below.

With respect to specific priorities for action, the initiation of efforts to alter the distorted value-orientation of social work must come first, for nothing else can take place until some social workers have adopted the new value position. The publication of the report of the NASW project and of the component papers should probably constitute the first step. The chairman's summary and the papers themselves should emphasize again and again the desirability and feasibility of a shift in the value-orientation of the profession.

The second step should be to engage competent social workers to test the feasibility in the least unpromising communities of initiating programs such as that proposed for a new type of family social work service. The reference here is to the first of the three steps of the proposed programs. The second, the establishment of a public Department of Family Welfare, will probably be more difficult of accomplishment, since it involves a radical change of policy within the Department of Health, Education and Welfare and, in all probability, will require congressional approval. The third step is receiving attention in a number of communities now.

Following the feasibility study, a well-publicized conference, led by social workers convinced of the necessity for the new venture, might be convened to affirm the new value position and its consequences for action. Sponsorship of this conference by the National Conference on Social Welfare might be advisable if such sponsorship could be obtained.

The fourth step, immediately following on the third, would be to assemble a public meeting in each city in which a project similar to the institution of the family social work program might be feasible. The process of assembling and conducting the conference would help to locate sources of support in the local community. The whole venture might be strengthened if several such proposals were presented to the public in the same city.

To try to work out further plans of even this degree of specificity at this point verges on fantasy. So much depends on the recommendations concerning approaches to the other social problems included in the project. For similar reasons, no specific proposals will be made concerning research. It should be evident that much will have to be learned to carry the new venture into action. The major theoretical question underlying the whole proposal is one to which no answer is yet, in the writer's knowledge, available. *How can a state of normlessness in a community be reversed?* If the writer's hypotheses about the relationship between individual normlessness and apathy, on the one hand, and the social consequences of the value problems deriving from the two pejorative value-orientations are incorrect, then the whole basis for the recommendations is destroyed. The question needs to be tested. Pending such a test, however, the indications for the linkage seem sound. They are sustained by the theory cited in the body of the presentation. It seems justifiable then to make one final recommendation:

Let's go!

Child Neglect ▶

ELIZABETH G. MEIER

THE PROBLEM

An analysis of the professional capacities, obligations, and rights of social workers to intervene in the social problem of "child neglect" requires examination of its professional competence: (a) to bring about changes in the circumstances and the behavior of individuals; (b) to plan, organize, administer, and coordinate social services; and (c) to affect those social values and influence those parts of the social structure that are related to the problem of child neglect.

But before such an analysis can be undertaken, other questions must be raised. What is "child neglect"? Does the neglect of a child constitute a "social problem" under any and all conditions? If so, are the services of social workers essential in all such circumstances? If not, does the profession have an obligation to intervene, even in circumstances in which such neglect does not constitute a social problem?

Three hypothetical situations may make these questions more graphic.

1. In X community, a very small village in a remote mountainous area in this country, all of the children except one are well cared for by their parents. This six-year-old boy is cared for so poorly that it can be predicted that he will die unless he is given better care. It is also known that he has a physical ailment which, if he is kept alive, will require periodic hospitalization and expensive medical care. It is further known that this child has very limited mental ability, and it is doubtful if he will ever be able to do more than fifth-grade work in school. The village is located in a very poor state. Each visit of the state child welfare worker to this remote community would cost the taxpayers at least $50, taking into account the worker's salary and traveling expenses.

Is this child experiencing child neglect? Do his circumstances constitute a social problem? Is the situation the legitimate concern of social work?

2. In Y the population of twenty-nine thousand persons includes ten thousand children under the age of eighteen. An omniscient citizen knows these facts about fifty children, all living with one or both parents in this small city. Ten children are steadily losing weight because they do not get enough to eat. Ten children are beaten every day by their parents, and they usually carry welts and bruises on their bodies. Five others are being taught to pick pockets by their fathers, and five are living in houses of prostitution with their mothers. Five children have medical problems for which their parents refuse to provide medical care, since this would be against their religious principles. Five children are sent to school only irregularly by their parents. Finally, there are ten children who are provided with food, clothing, and shelter of excellent quality. They are sent to the best schools—but their parents wish they had never been born.

The citizen who in his omniscience knows all of this is also an unerring prophet. He knows for a certainty that even though nothing is done to bring about changes in the present circumstances of these children, thirty-eight of the fifty will nevertheless become socially productive adults. Only eighteen of them will in adulthood be problems to the community.

Do the circumstances of all fifty of these children constitute a social problem for the community? Or do the circumstances of only some of them present a social problem? Is it the business of social work to be concerned about any or all of these children and their parents?

3. The hypothetical situation of community Z requires the reader's indulgent willingness to suspend ordinary principles of economic growth, development, and population shifts. Let us suppose then that Z has few economic resources and no way of increasing those it has. The economic situation has worsened because of a rapid increase in population within the last few generations. Very recently infant and child mortality rates have increased sharply, and many of these deaths have been caused by physical neglect. Someone has figured out that if these exceedingly high mortality rates continue the economic circumstances of the community will improve markedly within the next ten years, since there will be many fewer persons to consume the goods produced.

In this situation is neglect of these children a social problem? Would improvement in the quality of child care and the subsequent reduction in mortality, which, in turn, would lead to increasingly difficult economic conditions, constitute a social problem? Would social workers be able to operate within this situation, and, if they could, to what ends would they direct their knowledge and skills and how would their values be expressed?

These hypothetical situations in the communities of X, Y, and Z call attention to the fact that any approach to the question of social work intervention in the problem of child neglect must take into account that the profession is identifiable not alone by its knowledge nor yet by its skills or its values. Rather, knowledge, skills, and values are inextricably interwoven, and professional activities are expressive of this integration.

What Is "Child Neglect"?

The phrase "child neglect" may be used in a fashion purely descriptive of a quality of care which someone, somewhere, at some time regards as inadequate to the child's needs, or may be used definitively by a court of law which has been given jurisdiction to determine whether a child alleged to be neglected is indeed experiencing child neglect.

In discussing professional "authority," Greenwood writes:

> Extensive education in the systematic theory of his discipline imparts to the professional a type of knowledge that highlights the layman's comparative ignorance. This fact is the basis for the professional's authority. . . . The client's subordination to professional authority invests the professional with a monopoly of judgment. When an occupation strives toward professionalization, one of its aspirations is to acquire this monopoly.[1]

In defining the condition of child neglect, the variable meanings of the term, in particular, that the determination of the condition of neglect leading to a change in the child's legal status is dependent on the judgment of a court, clearly indicates that in matters of child neglect the profession of social work exercises no "monopoly of judgment." Thus it becomes necessary to explicate the legal meaning of "neglect" and to recognize that social work does not play a solo role in relation to the social problem of child neglect.

The profession may, and frequently does, act in concert with other dominant social forces which hold congruent values. The more challenging questions are these: has the profession any knowledge, skills, and values that are uniquely its own—different from the knowledge, skills, and values that other forces in the community could use to assess and deal with child neglect? And does the profession possess knowledge, skills, and values that contradict these other social forces and, if so, what is its obligation to make use of its professional equipment to exert pressure in opposition to that exerted by other social forces? Thus it becomes necessary to examine points of congruence and incongruence

---

[1] Ernest Greenwood, "Attributes of a Profession," *Social Work*, Vol. 2, No. 3 (July 1957), pp. 45–48.

between the approach of social work in regard to child neglect and the approaches of other forces concerned with the problem or those that help to create the problem.

"Neglect" Laws

Neglect laws by their existence denote that extrafamilial forces have been given the right to use definite and predictable sanctions against individuals if some aspects of their intrafamilial behavior, in this instance the behavior of parents toward their children, are unacceptable to the community. This right, exercised by the state, is contrary to the "natural rights" of a parent in regard to his child. Judge Gill, discussing the "legal nature of neglect" states

> . . . by the filing of a neglect petition seeking the custody of these children on behalf of the state, the petitioner is, in effect, declaring that those fundamental individual rights must stand forfeit to the community interest in raising up well-bred, well-trained citizens for the maintenance of society. Caseworkers in the field of neglect have too often assumed that the familiar words, "the best interest of the child" give the court the right to invade the family circle. These words are a legal syllogism which in truth must govern the actions of the court, but only after its right to determine what, in effect, is best for the child has first been established. This right flows from the "venerable common law doctrine of *parens patriae* which declares the state to be the ultimate guardian of every child with a vested interest in his well-being. . . ." [2]

The point is not to be overlooked that "vested interest" implies the self-interest of the state in the child, not necessarily an interest predicated on the child's needs.

The foregoing paragraph might suggest that there is one law in regard to child neglect. Such is not the case nor could it be in a republic comprised of 50 states, each of which has the constitutional right to deal with matters of intrastate significance. Consequently, neglect laws vary, but any neglect law must embody these elements: (1) the definition of a child; (2) identification of the persons qualified to petition the court who allege that a child is being neglected; (3) specification of the meaning of neglect; (4) description of the nature of the legal procedures to be followed and identification of the court of jurisdiction; and (5) a statement of the ways in which the court may dispose of the neglect petition before it.

Even the definition of a "child" varies from state to state. In some states, for example, the protection of the neglect law is extended to "a

---

[2] Thomas D. Gill, "The Legal Nature of Neglect," *National Probation and Parole Association Journal*, Vol. 6, No. 1 (January 1960), p. 3.

child" up to the brink of his majority, age twenty-one, whereas in others, a "child" passes from its protection when he reaches the age of sixteen. Other states range between the six-year differential.[3]

Similarly, the conditions that constitute neglect are variously defined, but rather characteristically the laws cite these circumstances: (1) inadequate physical care; (2) absence of or inadequate medical care; (3) cruel or abusive treatment; (4) improper supervision; (5) exploitation of the child's earning capacity; (6) unlawfully keeping the child out of school; (7) exposing the child to criminal or immoral influences that endanger his morals. The definitions of "neglected child" used in the Alabama and New York State laws, quoted below, are fairly typical.

> ... (2) The words "neglected child" shall mean any child, who, while under sixteen years of age is abandoned by both parents, or if one parent is dead, by the survivor, or by his guardian, or custodian; or who has no proper parental care or guardianship or whose home, by reason of neglect, cruelty, or depravity, on the part of his parent or parents, guardian or other person in whose care he may be, is an unfit or improper place for such child; or who is found begging, receiving or gathering alms, or who is found in any street, road or public place for the purpose of so doing, whether actually begging or doing so under the pretext of selling or offering for sale any article or articles, or of singing or playing on any musical instrument, or of giving any public entertainment or accompanying or being used in aid of any person so doing; or for whom his parent, parents, guardian or custodian, neglect or refuse, when able to do so, or when such service is offered without charge, to provide, or allow, medical, surgical, or other care necessary for his health, or well-being; or whose parent, parents, guardian or custodian, permits such child to engage in an occupation or calling contrary to the provisions of the child labor law of this state; or whose parent, parents, guardian or custodian fail, refuse or neglect to send such child in accordance with the terms of the compulsory attendance law of this state; or who is in such condition or surroundings, or is under such improper or insufficient guardianship or control as to endanger the morals, health or general welfare of such child; or who is not being reared or cared for in accordance with the provisions of any law, regulation or ordinance for the education, care and protection of children; or who for any other cause is in need of the care and protection of the state.[4]

---

[3] *See Huston's Social Welfare Laws and Supplements* for neglect laws. Examples of variations in age are these: Alabama, Georgia, New York, and Pennsylvania laws protect up to the age of 16; Florida and Michigan up to 17; Arizona, Colorado, Idaho, and Illinois until 18; Arkansas and California until 21.

[4] From *Huston's Social Welfare Laws and Supplements*, Vol. I, section pertaining to Social Welfare Laws of Alabama from 1936 supp. code, Chapter 100, Section 3528.

From *Huston's Social Welfare Laws and Supplements*, Vol. 2, section pertaining to the Social Welfare Laws of New York, Art. 11, Sec. 104:

... (c) A neglected child shall mean a child (1) who is without proper guardianship, or (2) whose parent, guardian or person with whom the child lives, by reason of cruelty, mental incapacity, immorality or depravity is unfit to care properly for such child, or (3) who is under unlawful or improper supervision, care, custody or restraint by any person, corporation, agency, association, institution, society or other organization, or (4) who wanders about without lawful occupation or restraint, or who is unlawfully kept out of school, or (5) whose parent, guardian or custodian neglects or refuses, when able to do so, to provide necessary medical, surgical, institutional or hospital care for such child, or (6) who is found in any place the existence of which is in violation of law, or (7) who is in such condition of want or suffering or is under such improper guardianship or control as to injure or endanger the morals or health of himself or others.

The frequency with which these items are found within the laws suggests that these are the elements of child care which are important, *in the interests of the state.*

There is a further assumption: the laws imply that in these aspects of child care there are *norms* of parental behavior and that it is possible to identify a level of care below which parents shall not be permitted to fall with impunity. Nevertheless, the paradox of neglect laws is that they teem with adjectives and adverbs—"properly," "improper," "necessary," "unfit," "insufficient," "inadequate"—thus requiring a judgment to be made by the court in each specific instance of alleged neglect to determine whether the child is indeed neglected. But the *norms* of child care are derived from community standards which vary from place to place and change from decade to decade; and it would be most surprising if the ideas of child rearing and of appropriate parental behavior idiosyncratic to the presiding judge did not sometimes influence the presumably objective decision of the court in the actual interpretation and application of the law.

Norms are related to real or presumed knowledge concerning the effects of certain conditions on children, the consequences of parental behavior toward children, and the means to correct conditions that exist. Thus the meaning of "neglect" is subject to change as knowledge changes. Removing children from the custody of their parents because they refuse to permit certain types of medical care most clearly illustrates this point. Parents have been cited as neglectful because of their refusal, on the basis of religious principles, to permit a child to have a blood transfusion, which, according to medical opinion, the child needed. Yet this "need" would not have been a cause for court action had a child experienced the same health problem a few decades ago, before the technique of transfusions had been developed. Recognition of a "need" and the definition of that which is necessary must sometimes await the invention, development, and availability of that "necessity." Similarly, ideas concerning discipline change. Punishment regarded as "cruel and abusive" today might in some instances have been regarded in an earlier era as consistent with the honored adage of "spare the rod, spoil the child."

The Alabama law quoted earlier is particularly interesting in that its high degree of specificity makes clear that norms for parental behavior are also related to the norms and expectations established by law in regard to institutions other than the family. Thus failure to send a child to school "in accordance with . . . the compulsory attendance law" constitutes neglect, as does disobedience to the "provisions of the child labor law." A further point of interest is contained in the phraseology which describes as neglectful those parents who fail or refuse to provide necessary medical or surgical care when they are able to do so or "when such service is offered without charge."

Such portions of laws clearly illustrate that although "parental rights" have been infringed on by law, concepts of parental responsibilities have also changed. True enough, parents of today are expected to obey and cause their children to obey the compulsory education law, but, unlike the parents of the early periods of our history, they are not expected to educate their children themselves or to make their own private arrangements for such education. Neither is the father expected to provide occupational training for his son nor to apprentice the boy to some other individual for such training. Similarly, today's parents who use home remedies to effect medical cures are likely not to be regarded as knowledgeable and resourceful as they might have been in the past, and in some circumstances they might even be regarded as neglectful. Indeed, in some ways the test of parental adequacy is based on the parents' willingness and ability to use available extrafamilial services in behalf of the child rather than on their personal attributes.

Nevertheless, as already pointed out, when a neglect law is applied, two highly important legal principles are placed in opposition—the doctrine of the parents' "natural rights" to the guardianship of their child and that of the doctrine of *parens patriae*, the state's ultimate guardianship of the child. Each court decision that involves a change in the custody of a child because of neglect by his parents represents a case in which the natural rights were infringed on and the state's right to ultimate guardianship of the child was invoked. From these two opposing principles a somewhat different translation sometimes emerges, with the interpretation being given that the state, acting on the *parens patriae* principle, acts in behalf of the child. This translation shifts the opposing principles from parents' rights versus states' rights to parents' rights versus child's rights. The judge is a highly important figure in making this translation.

In their study of nine communities across the country Maas and Engler found that in some communities "parental rights" were characteristically regarded as of greater importance, whereas in others the "rights of the child" were given precedence. These authors relate such differences in judicial behavior to three factors: (1) codification and consistency of laws, (2) remoteness of legal and welfare worlds, and (3) religious, economic, and cultural influences restrictive on the judge's freedom of action. They conclude

> this . . . combination—lack of newer welfare opposition and direction plus older legal and cultural restraint . . . typified our parents' rights communities. By contrast, a combination of welfare opposition and/or legal recodification plus relative freedom from older legal and cultural restraint typified our more child's rights communities.[5]

In summary then:

1. There is no national uniform neglect law, but each state has its own.

2. Within such variation, there is great similarity in the types of behavior designated as constituting child neglect.

3. Laws assume the existence of norms for parental behavior.

4. Norms for parental behavior vary from time to time and from place to place.

5. Judicial decisions, expressive of application of the law, may reflect an emphasis on one or the other of two opposing legal principles —"parental rights" or "rights of the child."

Social Work Concept of Child Neglect and of Parental Care

The varieties of social work *action* which may be undertaken when a condition of child neglect exists or when there is danger that child neglect may occur are a matter for detailed discussion in subsequent pages. Similarities and contrasts between social work *values* which cause the profession to oppose child neglect and values of other forces in the community in regard to this problem are likewise discussed later. Here the concern is with the profession's contribution to the definition—to the concept—of child neglect. Foregoing pages have limited its use to the

---

[5] Henry S. Maas and Richard E. Engler, Jr., *Children in Need of Parents* (New York: Columbia University Press, 1959), p. 316.

legal phrase, but the term is also employed in the professional records, the case records, of caseworkers.

It would be erroneous to suggest that the social worker's meaning of child neglect is contrary to the meaning encompassed by law. Rather the meanings given to the concept by social workers and the definitions stated within the laws and expressed in judicial decisions have much in common. This is to be expected, since many of these meanings are derived from common sense and, as previously stated, from community norms of parental behavior. Both social workers and the courts are influenced by this knowledge of community norms. Furthermore, the juvenile court, usually the court of jurisdiction in neglect cases, is in itself a creation which was intended to express social as well as legal values. Gill speaks of the juvenile court as "a new union of the law with the behavioral sciences. . . ." [6] Also, in the process of working together on the same situations, court personnel and child welfare workers have affected each other—the meanings of law in regard to child neglect have influenced the caseworker's thinking and behavior and the meanings of social work have sometimes become infused into the judicial point of view.

Nevertheless, if the knowledge and value base of the profession of social work has distinctive attributes, then it is to be expected that its interpretations and assessments of human behavior and its proposals for remedying situations when that behavior becomes problematic would also be somewhat different from the assessments and proposals advanced by other forces in the community. Were this not true, it is doubtful that social work could claim an identity of its own. It is to these differences in emphasis that attention is now directed.

As already implied, when a situation of child neglect is dealt with by law, the law presumes that the burden of proof falls on the person or persons alleging neglect, not on the parent or guardian allegedly neglectful. A further assumption is that the natural right of the parent to the custody and guardianship of his child will not be disturbed unless it is shown that he has fallen below the minimum standards acceptable to the community. Evidence must be given that the conditions to which the child has been subjected have been harmful to him in the ways in which the law specifies. In a strict interpretation of law only behavior which is overt and observable can be a matter of concern. Law cannot be concerned with the causative factors or with predictions of future behavior.

In contrast, a fundamental concept in social work is that behavior is caused. It is the business of social work, particularly in the practice

---

[6] Gill, *op. cit.*, pp. 1–2.

of casework, to have the knowledge and skill to understand that there are many causes of inadequate care of children or of injurious behavior toward a child by his parents. These are but a few examples: indifference to a child's needs because the parents are overburdened and their energies are depleted, ignorance of the needs of children, ungovernable impulses symptomatic of the parents' mental illness, and brutality which expresses the neurotic consequences of the parents' own early deprivations. Further, it is social work's business to know as well as to value the capacity of the human being to grow and change. Differential capacities for growth and development are recognized. Nevertheless, the social worker starts with the premise that most parents wish to be adequate parents to their children and that they will make use of help extended to them so that they may become better parents.

These social work concepts, that behavior is caused and that individuals are capable of growth and change, are closely related to the cherished social work value that individuals shall have the opportunity to develop their capacities fully, not just to the minimum required by the community. This would include the adult's capacity for parenthood and the child's various capacities for physical, intellectual, and emotional development. Consequently, social work is likely to assess the quality of child care along a continuum, ranging from care that is below the minimum required by the community to that which provides maximal opportunities for development. Furthermore, unlike the intervention of law, social work intervention is not restricted to those children experiencing neglect in the legal sense nor to those parents who are neglecting them.

Differences in the concept of child neglect as defined by law and as regarded by social work also emerge in respect to the emphasis placed on various aspects of child care. Since the social worker's training and education sensitizes him to the importance of the emotional sustenance of the child as a factor in later personality development, it is understandable that its absence, "emotional neglect," would be regarded as being particularly damaging.

The Child Welfare League of America's publication *Standards for Child Protective Service* makes this observation:

> Most neglect legislation was written when physical neglect was the primary, if not the only, type of neglect recognized as such. Knowledge of emotional needs of children was meager, and laws did not specifically define emotional neglect. Interpretation of existing statutes in the light of current knowledge can be expected to liberalize existing laws. At present, it is often difficult or impossible to provide protection in the courts for children suffering from emotional neglect,

even though many neglect laws could be interpreted to encompass emotional neglect.[7]

The following comments bear on the practice of protective agencies in coming before the courts. Mulford writes:

> Our dilemma is that, while we recognize the harmful effects and the insidious cruelty of emotional deprivation and neglect, we have not reached the point of using this knowledge constructively and successfully in legal action. If our present statutes can be interpreted to include emotional neglect, then the problem would seem to be at the level of court interpretation and acceptance of evidence which is not stated in physical terms. Most protective agencies bring into court cases involving extreme emotional deprivation, but base their case on evidence involving physical factors which is readily accepted by the courts. Some courts do recognize emotional neglect and use evidence in this area constructively to help children.[8]

Put more bluntly, in some instances the worker presents to the court evidence to effect the child's removal, an action the worker deems necessary, but the data used as evidence are not those that the worker regards as crucial in determining the necessity for such action.

Although the plea for including specific phraseology covering emotional neglect within the law is heard from some child welfare quarters, opinion concerning its advisability is divided.

The judicial opinions quoted in the *Children's Bureau's Standards for Specialized Courts Dealing with Children,* as well as its own formulations therein, stress the importance of safeguarding the legal rights of parents as well as children. "It is a principle of our society that where such rights are limited, they can be so limited only in accordance with due process of law." Furthermore, the grounds for legal intervention "should be specifically and clearly delineated in the statutes. Whenever the state seeks to intervene, it should be required to show that those conditions do in fact exist with respect to a child and that its intervention is necessary to protect the child or the community or both.[9] Hazards to rights safeguarded by "due process of law" have been identified as arising from the admission of testimony in children's courts that would not be acceptable as evidence in other courts and in

---

[7] *Standards for Child Protective Service* (New York: Child Welfare League of America, 1960), p. 8.

[8] Robert M. Mulford, "Emotional Neglect of Children: A Challenge to Protective Services," *Child Welfare,* Vol. 37, No. 8 (October 1958), p. 24.

[9] *Standards for Specialized Courts Dealing with Children,* U. S. Children's Bureau Publication No. 346 (Washington, D.C.: U. S. Government Printing Office, 1954), pp. 6–7.

the assumption of judicial authority that, however benign in purpose, would not be tolerated in other parts of the judicial system.

From another source, and in another connection, it is pointed out that the court's use of services in behalf of persons appearing before it because of family problems (including child neglect) "must never intrude in such a way as to do violence to the integrity of the legal process." The administration of family justice must be "legally impeccable." [10]

Inclusion in neglect laws of phraseology pertaining to emotional neglect might well leave the door open to decisions even more likely to be affected by individualistic notions of the meaning of the phrase.

A further consideration suggests the inadvisability of including emotional neglect as a cause for court action. Neglect laws are intended to be corrective in their effect. The court expects that the neglected child removed from the custody of his parents and placed in the care of an agency will then be a "cared-for child." It is reasonable for a court to expect an agency to be able to give assurance that a child in its care will be adequately fed and clothed, properly supervised, not subjected to cruel and abusive treatment, will be given needed medical care, and will be sent to school—opposites of conditions of neglect currently covered by most laws. However, emotional sustenance or satisfaction, love, affection—or whatever phrase might be used to designate the opposite of emotional neglect—is dependent on the development of a relationship between the child and the adults in whose care he is placed. Furthermore, the child's emotional well-being is affected by continuity of relationship, by his sense of security, and his feeling sure that he is cherished by adults.

Foster children, unfortunately, frequently experience replacements. At the present stage of inaccurate knowledge of how to "match" foster children to foster parents, no agency can undertake to guarantee against the contingency of replacements. If children were removed from the custody of their own parents on the basis of emotional neglect and subsequently experienced rejection by foster parents and replacement, the question might well be asked whether this constituted cause for the child to be brought before the court again on the basis that now the agency in whose custody he had been placed had subjected him to emotional neglect. When children are placed in those types of institutions in which the opportunities for developing a close relationship with adults are poor, emotional neglect might well be regarded as a continuing part of their experience—while in the care of an agency. It would seem questionable indeed to include as a basis for

[10] Bernard C. Fisher, *For the Family in Court* (New York: Community Service Society of New York, 1956), pp. 28–29.

neglect conditions that the law is in no position to correct by the child's removal from the home.

None of the foregoing, however, is to be interpreted as a repudiation of the importance of emotional satisfactions to the child nor to underestimate the significance of social work's contribution in keeping consideration of the child's emotional needs in the foreground. One aspect of the special knowledge of social work is that of understanding the meaning of social relationships (including familial relationships), and one aspect of its skill is that of helping individuals develop and maintain more effective and more satisfying relationships. This is part of the profession's job. Unless it wishes to abrogate its claim to the special knowledge, skills, and values which set it apart as a profession, it cannot expect to have its job done for it by legal fiat. Some of the ways in which social work activities might more nearly approximate its claim to special competence in these areas, as it pertains to problems of child neglect, are explicated in the last section of this paper.

The preceding pages have pointed out social work's contributions to the concept of neglect, distinguishing it from the legal concept. But "the profession" does not think, feel, evaluate, or draw conclusions. These things are done by social workers—members of the profession. Social workers, in their interpretation and application of concepts, like the judges, who interpret and apply laws, are affected by the norms of the community, by changing knowledge concerning the needs of children, and by their idiosyncratic interpretations of the meaning of neglect. This is likely to occur because neither "capacity for parenthood" nor "parental neglect of children" is a unitary concept. Parents ineffectual in some aspects of parenthood may be effective in others. But a child is an indivisible person and in determining whether he is neglected, the effect upon him of the parents' abilities and disabilities are weighed together. Different conclusions will be reached if workers disagree among themselves in regard to the different weights to be attached to the various attributes of parenthood.

In summary, then, social work's knowledge has contributed to the concept of child neglect in the following ways:

1. The social worker is likely to assess the quality of child care along a continuum ranging from care that is below the minimum required by the community to that which provides maximal opportunities for development. Social work intervention is not limited to those situations that could be legally defined as neglect.

2. Professional knowledge includes understanding of causative factors in child neglect.

3. Social work recognizes and values the capacity of the human being—including the neglectful parent—to grow and change.

4. Professional knowledge recognizes various facets of child care and emphasizes the importance of emotional satisfactions. Hence "emotional neglect" is regarded as having serious consequences for the child.

Nevertheless, it is the point of view of this paper that the concept of "emotional neglect" should not become incorporated into the legal definition of neglect.

VALUES

It can be assumed—generally speaking—that the law, social work, and the community as a whole are all opposed to child neglect, but the opposition may arise from group values that differ; the methods advocated for reducing the problem may vary among groups; and the willingness to pay the cost of preventing and correcting conditions of child neglect may not be present in equal degree among all of the individuals and groups who deplore such conditions. This does not necessarily imply sharp differences in values among groups. They are likely to overlap. Furthermore, social work would not be supported by the community unless its activities were acceptable to at least a considerable segment of the community's population.

Perhaps the most elemental consideration in the community's opposition to child neglect is its desire for its own perpetuity. The social group needs to protect its young if the group is to survive. The dependence of the human young is a biological reality, and a child whose physical needs are grossly neglected will die. If a sufficiently large number of human young within the group failed to survive, the group's survival would be threatened.

Social work also favors survival of the group; but, in addition, the profession expresses the value of the worth and dignity of the individual. This value is difficult to explain, and some attempts at definition seem to be but a restatement of the same idea, merely substituting the nouns, "worth" and "dignity," with other synonymous nouns. Nor am I able to do any better. Perhaps something can be gained, however, from Edith Hamilton's discussion of the essence of Greek tragedy. She writes:

> . . . it is illuminating to consider our everyday use of the words tragedy and tragic. Pain, sorrow, disaster, are always spoken of as depressing, as dragging down—the dark abyss of pain, a crushing sorrow, an overwhelming disaster. But speak of tragedy and extraordinarily the metaphor changes. Lift us to tragic heights, we say,

and never anything else. The depths of pathos but never of tragedy. Always the height of tragedy.

The dignity and the significance of human life—of these, and of these alone, tragedy will never let go. Without these, there is no tragedy. To answer the question, what makes a tragedy, is to answer the question wherein lies the essential significance of life, what the dignity of humanity depends upon in the last analysis. . . . It is by our power to suffer, above all, that we are of more value than the sparrows. Endow them with a greater or as great a potentiality of pain and our foremost place in the world would no longer be undisputed. Deep down, where we search out the reason for our conviction of the transcendent worth of each human being, we know that it is because of the possibility that each can suffer so terribly.[11]

Perhaps the social worker, too, when speaking of "the dignity and worth of the human being" shares Edith Hamilton's concern for his capacity for suffering as a constituent part of his humanity. Hamilton, however, conceives of tragic sufferings as being limited to those of great soul, and she would admit only some human beings into that exclusive circle capable of tragic feeling. She writes:

Tragedy's preoccupation is with suffering. But, it is to be well noted, not with all suffering. There are degrees in our high estate of pain. It is not given to all to suffer alike. We differ in nothing more than in our power to feel. There are souls of little and of great degree and upon that degree the dignity and significance of each life depend. . . . Tragedy is enthroned, and to her realm those alone are admitted who belong to the only true aristocracy, that of all passionate souls. Tragedy's one essential is a soul that can feel greatly. Given such a one and any catastrophe may be tragic. But the earth may be removed and the mountains be carried into the midst of the sea, and if only the small and shallow are confounded, tragedy is absent.[12]

Social workers would not limit the applicability of the concept of the dignity and worth of the human being to those persons fulfilling the requirements of Edith Hamilton's definition of the tragic soul. Instead, the social worker would encompass other forms of suffering, less than tragic, as attributes of humanity. It seems likely, too, that the social worker would regard the capacity for joy as a human attribute which together with the capacity for suffering give dignity and worth to the individual.

Belief in the human being's capacity to suffer and to experience joy is then perhaps the kernel of the value concept of the worth and dignity

---

[11] *The Greek Way to Western Civilization* (New York: New American Library, 1961), pp. 166, 168–169. (Reprint of original hardcover edition published by W. W. Norton and Company, 1930.)

[12] *Ibid.*, p. 169.

of the individual. Consider again the example of the little boy in X community who is neglected—sorely neglected—to the extent that he would not be likely to survive if he were to remain in his present circumstances. That child is not needed for the community's survival. Furthermore, if he is provided with better care and thus enabled to survive, his limitations are such that he is not likely to contribute very much to that community's productivity. In fact, if he were to live, he would be a continuing expense to the community. From these points of view, his death would not represent a loss. But this one little boy with his capacity for joy, however circumscribed by his physical pain, embodies the dignity and worth of the individual. Permitting him to die by withholding these services would be a corrosion of the human values expressed in social work.

Community Z presents a different problem. Admittedly, the fictitious circumstances devised are hardly likely to be found in that combination in any community. However, it is quite probable that within the recent past there have been cases in which value judgments required by the circumstances were not too dissimilar from those implied in the fictional community of Z. In wartorn starving communities inadequate relief supplies from external sources sometimes placed on relief workers the agonizing responsibility for deciding whether the supplies should be divided among all children within the community, with the consequence that none received enough food to ensure healthy growth and development, or whether some children—those who were the healthiest—should be given adequate amounts of food for survival so that they might become the nucleus for a new generation of healthy, vigorous citizens.

Value judgments concerning behavior toward children are sometimes inextricably interwoven with other values made explicit in the customs and mores of the community. In James Michener's novel *Hawaii* one of the characters expresses the point of view that the ancient custom of brother-sister marriages among Hawaiian royalty had values of conserving and consolidating the prestige and prerogatives of the royal line and that the system worked well—provided the society was not "squeamish" about throwing into the sea the defective infants born from such unions.[13]

The singularity of the circumstances of the one neglected child in community X also touches on the question whether the profession shall limit its attentions to those matters identified as "social problems" by the community. The idea of a social problem carries a certain quantitative implication. Only when a certain number of similar situations

---

[13] James Michener, *Hawaii* (New York: Random House, 1959).

become troublesome to a community, or endanger the safety and well-being of others, is the phrase "social problem" likely to be applied. But, again, if social work's belief in the value of the individual is to be expressed, its attention cannot be restricted to problems that by their sheer weight of numbers constitute social problems. Unfortunately, as far as child neglect is concerned, this is a purely academic question. There is no doubt that the quantity of child neglect qualifies this problem as a social problem. In 1960 juvenile courts in the United States disposed of an estimated 131,000 dependency and neglect cases. The number of cases disposed of by courts does not necessarily reflect the number of children who, in truth, are neglected. For example, the number of cases disposed of in rural courts is at a rate of 1.3 per 1000 child population, whereas in urban courts the rate is 2.7 per 1000 child population, more than twice as high. It can be surmised that the greater visibility of the neglected child in urban areas contributes to this differential. It cannot be assumed that the proportion of children who are neglected is that much smaller in rural areas.[14]

In earlier pages the law's opposition to child neglect was explained on the basis of "the community's interest in raising up well-bred, well-trained citizens for the maintenance of society." [15]   Maxine Virtue designates an even more specific basis for the doctrine of *parens patriae*. She writes:

> The law, which abhors a vacuum, has developed several doctrines for bringing judicial authority to bear upon the child in need of management other than that supplied by his parents. These are usually lumped together under the phrase, *parens patriae*, which, in the broadest possible terms, signifies the right of society, through the agency of any court of competent jurisdiction, to exert whatever authority is necessary in order to protect the child and to prevent him from becoming a public charge.[16]

Social work has no quarrel with these expressed values. It, too, is in favor of children being adequately cared for so that their capacity for social productivity will not be jeopardized. Undoubtedly, many children have been removed from neglectful parents and placed in foster homes on the assumption, implicit or explicit, that they were likely to turn out to be better citizens than if they remained in these

---

[14] *Juvenile Court Statistics, 1960,* U. S. Children's Bureau Statistical Series No. 65 (Washington, D.C.: U. S. Department of Health, Education, and Welfare, 1961), pp. 13–14.

[15] Gill, *op. cit.,* p. 3.

[16] *Basic Structure of Children's Services in Michigan* (Ann Arbor: American Judicature Society, for the James Foster Foundation, 1953), p. 162.

neglected homes, that is, it was in the interests of the community to remove them.[17]

From this the question posed by community Y arises. If it were possible to know which types of neglect and combinations of neglectful experiences suffered by which kind of child were certain to cause adult social nonproductivity and, on the other hand, which kinds of combinations of factors would nevertheless permit the children to mature into socially productive adults, would then the community be likely to seek corrective action in behalf of the first group of children only? If only the value of protecting the community were to be expressed, this then might very well be the consequence of such precise predictive knowledge. Social work values, to the contrary, hold that the child is a human being in his own right as well as a future adult citizen, and as a child he has the right to relief from distressful circumstances and the right to satisfying experiences.

Frequently, action in behalf of a family of neglected children is not taken until one child of that family comes to the attention of the community's institutions, notably the school. That particular child may have suffered neglect throughout his preschool years, and his younger siblings, under school age, may also be neglected. But until his entrance into school, his needs receive scant attention from the extrafamilial institutions. Sometimes this is the consequence of his not having been "visible." Conditions of his neglect were less apparent when he was not in almost daily contact with interested adults other than his parents. But sometimes action is delayed until the child enters school, simply because his poor care has not troubled anyone else. At the time that he enters school parents of other children become concerned about their children having contact with the neglected child, who may be dirty, smell, have infectious diseases, or use language and express ideas that they do not want their children to hear. These neglected children may also be thought of as encouraging other children to take part in behavior disapproved of by their parents.

In other words, the "value" expressed here is that well-cared-for

---

[17] Interesting enough, this assumption has never been tested by research in this country. In Finland such a study was undertaken. One of its findings was that a smaller proportion of these children removed from neglectful homes and placed in foster homes and institutions for dependent and neglected children manifested problem behavior as adults than the proportion of such adults found among the older siblings of those children who remained in their neglectful homes throughout their childhood. However, an interesting point is that a high proportion among the older group also did *not* manifest problem behavior. *See* Salo Reino, *Kunnahinen Iastensuojelutyo Sociaalisen Sopeutumisen Kasuattajana* (Municipal Child Welfare Work as Promoter of Social Adjustment), summary of study in English in book (Suomi, Finland: Vassa, 1956).

children should be protected against "contamination" by neglected children. Social workers would disagree to a greater or less degree with this value. First of all, the neglected child should be protected for his own sake. Second, this value leads to discriminatory behavior on the part of other adults and children who exclude the neglected child from their association and set him apart as undesirable. These behaviors are, in themselves, damaging to the neglected child. He, perhaps even more than the well-cared-for child, needs association with his peers and the friendly attention and interest of extrafamilial adults—the minister, the corner policeman, the storekeeper, and particularly the teacher.

In a democratic society equality before the law could be expected to be a value expressed in the operation of neglect laws. This would include equal protection of parental rights and the rights of children, regardless of the economic circumstances of the family. Certainly, this value would be consistent with social work values. There has been a great deal of progress since the early days of our history when children whose parents or whose widowed mothers were unable to keep them were "bound out" by indenture to other families or were placed in institutions. Thus the children of parents who were poor were much more likely to be separated from their families. The injustice of this was not sharply challenged until the twentieth century. The first White House Conference on Children, held in 1909, provided a new ideal with its avowal that children should not be removed from their own homes for reasons of poverty alone. More than twenty-five years later the provisions for Aid to Dependent Children, under the Social Security Act, did much to bring reality to this ideal.[18]

But even today it is likely that the parental rights of parents in need of financial assistance are less well protected than are those of parents in more favorable economic circumstances. The increase in the number of illegitimate children born in this country and the fact that a significant proportion of children receiving the benefits of Aid to Dependent Children are illegitimate is admittedly a problem in itself. Similarly, the social cost of broken marriages is another separate topic. The concern of this paper, also another separate topic, is that punitive measures adopted in some states against unmarried mothers in need of public assistance creates inequities before the law. Such measures which cause illegitimate children to be ineligible for public assistance result in some of these children having inadequate food, clothing, and

---

[18] As provided for under the Public Welfare Amendments of 1962, the Aid to Dependent Children program is now known as Aid to Families with Dependent Children (AFDC).

shelter—conditions of "neglect" in law which then make the parent vulnerable to court action.

It is probable that legally married but economically deprived parents are more likely to have neglect laws invoked against them than are parents not so disadvantaged. Sometimes the community assumes that parents receiving economic aid are to be subjected to rules and regulations not applicable to other parents. The American Public Welfare Association in 1952, in its Statement of Principles, enunciated the principle that the receipt of public assistance was not to be the basis for application of extra-legal sanctions. "Personal and family problems involving possible compulsion, such as desertion, nonsupport, or the removal of a child from the home, should be handled as with other citizens through the courts or other legal channels." [19]

Further, the grinding harassments of constantly doing without the things that are needed and the small daily discouragements and disappointments that poverty-stricken parents suffer deplete the energies of parents and render them less able to meet the social and emotional needs of their children. One of the most obvious characteristics of a child is his quality of need—he needs things, physical care, affection, encouragement, teaching, and continual looking after.

If one of the values of law is that its protections are applicable to the economically deprived, the obverse of this is also true. Its restrictions and sanctions are applicable against those in economically favored positions. With this the values of social work would also be in agreement. A child who is neglected must not be deprived of the law's protection just because his parents are well-to-do.

Basic to these considerations is the matter to which attention has already been drawn—the legal principle of the natural rights of parents. This is a value of law as well as a principle. The social work concepts and values of the client's "right to self-determination" and of the child's right to and need for parental care and affection parallel the legal value of the natural rights of parents. It would be expected that when social work activities express these concepts and values professional efforts would be directed toward maintaining the child's home, just as in the conservative approach of law the removal of children from their parents' custody is undertaken with reluctance.

However, as noted throughout this paper, the legal rights of parents "stand forfeit" to community interest. Similarly, the social work value of the "right to self-determination" is not limitless. It does not encompass the right of an individual to behave in ways injurious to others.

---

[19] "Essentials of Public Welfare: A Statement of Principles," *Public Welfare*, Vol. 2, No. 1 (January 1953), p. 5.

Nor is the child's need for and right to parental care absolute, without regard to the quality of that care.

Certain similarities and contrasts between the values of social work and those of other forces in the community have been drawn in relation to the problem of child neglect:

1. Many of the values pertaining to adequate care of children or its opposite, child neglect, are shared by many forces in the community, including social work.

2. The community opposes child neglect in order to ensure its own perpetuity. Social work is likewise concerned with group survival but also places value on the individual.

3. The community opposes child neglect on the premise that ill-treated children are less likely to become good adult citizens. Social work shares this concern but also holds that the child, as a child, has a need for constructive experiences and a right to be protected against destructive experiences, whether or not they adversely affect his adult behavior.

4. The community opposes child neglect because the presence of neglected children may be damaging to well-cared-for children. Thus the neglected child is likely to be "isolated" from other children or pressure is exerted to remove him from the group. In some respects this is contrary to the social work value that all children need association with their peers.

5. Equality before the law, regardless of the economic circumstances of parents, is a social work value. Sometimes communities exert pressure against the economically disadvantaged parents, particularly if they are receiving public assistance, holding them accountable in regard to care of their children in ways in which parents not receiving assistance are not held accountable.

6. Social work shares with the community the recognition that the "right to self-determination" is not limitless.

DIFFERENCES BETWEEN SOCIAL WORK VALUES AND ACTIVITIES

In a preceding section the statement was made that although a judge's right to intervene in a situation alleging child neglect is based on the determination that the care of the child is below the minimal quality required by community standards, the social worker, on the other hand, is more likely to think of the quality of the experiences of children as ranging along a continuum from that care which is grossly inadequate (extreme neglect) to that which provides the child with maximal opportunities for development. Furthermore, social work activities are not restricted to those circumstances at the extreme lower end of the continuum.   On the basis of values held by social work, some of which have been described, it should be possible to range certain types of life experiences—relative to neglect and to parental care—that children might have along such a continuum.

Immediately, obstacles arise. In the material following only a few points along such a continuum are suggested, with full awareness that in actuality a much larger number would be needed to cover "typical" kinds of experiences of children. A more real dilemma is that it would be difficult to secure agreement among social workers, even among a group limited to child welfare workers, about the order in which the midrange of experiences should be placed. With these hazards recognized and with no attempt to designate exactly comparable factors in each of the described types of experiences, these possible points on the continuum are suggested:

1. The child is of legitimate birth. He lives with both parents throughout his childhood. They are economically secure, healthy, capable of giving him affection, and respected in the community. The child has free access to the educational, recreational, and religious institutions of the community.

2. The child is of legitimate birth, but because of death or divorce one parent is absent from the home. He continues to live with one parent with whom he experiences continuity of relationship. Resources for supplying physical and material needs are adequate, and he receives affection from one or both parents. His parents have a secure place in the community.

3. The child lives with one or both of his own parents throughout his childhood. Because of economic problems, health problems, or personal limitations the parents need one or more of the specialized social services of the community to supplement or to strengthen their parental capacities, such services being required for a greater or lesser period of time. Such services might include public assistance, homemaker service, child guidance services, school social work, or protective casework services.

4. The child has parents who provide inadequate care. He is temporarily removed from the custody of his parents and placed in a foster home. Rehabilitative work with the parents makes it possible for them to resume his care after a brief placement experience.

5. The child, legitimate or illegitimate, has parents who will never be able to provide adequately for him. He experiences no neglect or only a brief period of mild neglect, following which, at a very early

age, he is placed for adoption within a situation such as described under (1).

6. The child experiences major neglect in his own home for a considerable period of time, following which he is placed in a foster home, where he receives good care and affection and where he remains the balance of his childhood.

7. The child experiences major neglect in his own home for a considerable period of time, following which he is placed in foster home care, which involves placements with a series of foster parents who provide care and affection of varying quality.

8. The child experiences major neglect for a considerable period of time, following which he is placed in an institution for dependent and neglected children, where he remains for the balance of his childhood.

9. The child has those kinds of experiences, either in his own home, in foster home care (or both), or within the community setting which cause him to become emotionally disturbed or delinquent. At this point he is perceived as being dangerous to the community or his behavior is too disruptive to be tolerated within a family setting, whereupon he is placed in an institution for delinquents or in a treatment institution.

10. The child within his own home has destructive experiences in that they do not provide him with satisfactions nor do they equip him to become socially productive. However, his reactions to these experiences are not such that the community perceives him as a danger. Therefore he is permitted to continue to live within the destructive environment.

It seems reasonable to suggest that to the extent that social work's values pertain to the clients to be served, those values are rooted in the profession's ideas regarding the kinds of experiences individuals need, should have, or have a right to have in order that they may have personal satisfactions and be socially productive individuals. It would also seem reasonable to expect that the activities of social work would be directed toward ensuring, insofar as possible, that children be given opportunities to have these experiences in the upper range of the continuum and to prevent them from needing to endure the damaging types of experiences placed at the lower end of the continuum.

When incongruities exist between the profession's values and the directions in which it extends its energies to intervene in problems of child neglect or to provide constructive experiences for children, explanations are in order. Such incongruities might arise from a variety of sources:

1. The values of social work might be incompatible with those of other forces in the community, which are more powerful and therefore are able to thwart the profession in its desire to help make available to persons those experiences it deems valuable.

2. The values of social work might extend beyond the outside limits of the knowledge and competence of the profession to help create those conditions and to help bring about the kinds of experiences for individuals that are explicit or implicit within its values.

3. It may be that a proportion of the practitioners of the profession lack the competence to effect the intentions of the profession as a whole, as expressed in its values.

4. The values of social work, as expressed in its literature, its codes, and in the formulations of professional leaders, demonstrate that contradictory values exist within the profession concerning the phenomenon (in this instance, child neglect) under consideration.

5. Professional values pertaining to matters other than the phenomenon of child neglect, contraindicate, deflect, or interfere with the pursuit of those activities that would bring about the experiences for children which the values would define as desirable.

6. Social work activities which were developed to intervene in social problems (in this instance, child neglect) as they existed in an earlier era become institutionalized and resistive to changes that would render them more effective in dealing with changes in the nature of the problem in the current era.

Looking then to the continuum of the types of experiences, ranging from very constructive to very damaging, let us consider a few examples of the kinds of activities which would be expected from social work to bring about those constructive experiences, for more children, to prevent child neglect from occurring, and to intervene in situations in which child neglect is already present—and if such activities are not being undertaken, let us attempt to locate the cause of the incongruity between values and actions.

Emerging Social Needs Versus Institutionalized Services
Item (6), identified as a factor that creates incongruity between professed values and social work activities, needs further elaboration as it pertains to problems of child neglect. The lag between the emergence of a new social welfare need and the development of services to meet that need is well recognized. However, it may also be true that once the service does develop it becomes institutionalized and the service itself creates a barrier to the recognition of new problems which could be dealt with more effectively by new types of activities. Professional energies are directed toward developing and perfecting skills

to administer the service and attention is thus withdrawn from evaluating changes in the social conditions out of which the need originally emerged. Equally important, new knowledge of ways to deal with problems may be incorporated into practice at a very slow rate, if use of such knowledge required radical changes in the structure of services or in habits of work. To examine this factor of institutional lag as a deterrent to the development of effective means for intervention in problems of child neglect requires a brief summary of historical developments in child welfare.

Undoubtedly, there have always been some children who could not be reared by their own parents because of parental death, illness, or inadequacy. A chapter of the Old Testament might be regarded as a portion of the "case record" of one foster child who made quite a name for himself in his adult life—Moses—and who needed to be hidden in foster care to protect him against oppressive persecution. (*See* Exodus II, verses 1–10.) The Elizabethan Poor Laws of 1601 specified that children whose parents could not provide for them became the responsibility of local officials. In the American colonies the system of indenture was taken over from the English Poor Laws. Later, institutional care was frequently provided, either in public almshouses or in children's institutions established under religious auspices. The New York Children's Aid Society, established in 1853, is credited with being the founder of the foster home care movement. In the next half century, many other agencies of a similar nature were established.

In that era many of the children who were placed were orphans or half orphans. In New York City thousands of homeless waifs roamed the streets. They begged for their food or scavenged for it among the refuse. In New York City, as in other Eastern cities, such children were scooped up from the city streets by the newly formed children's societies and were sent to the Middle West in trainload lots. Communities were notified in advance that a trainload of children would be arriving so that families wanting children could come to the public square, the church, or the courthouse to select a child from among those available. Predominantly, children were placed in "free homes," a quasi-adoptive arrangement in which it was intended that the placement would be permanent.

This method of providing for children who could not be cared for by their own families was responsive to a variety of factors. The social fact of the high proportion of orphans among the placed children already mentioned not only produced a need for foster care but influenced the form of that care. Long-time care was an obvious need in many situations. Another social and economic fact was that in an agricultural economy a child is an economic asset, not a liability. The child sent to a farm home could be expected to earn his salt. From the point of view of the agencies, the benefits of "wholesome" life on a farm, with plenty of fresh air and good food, were made available to the child who had had nothing but the misery and poverty of life in a city slum. Theoretical knowledge of the era directed scant attention, or none, to the psychological factors involved in the child's placement. Equally limited was the understanding of some of the psychological factors involved in parental neglect when neglect, rather than orphaning, caused the need for placement.

Foster home care, paid for by an agency or a governmental unit, was a later development, responsive to changing social factors and the changing knowledge base for practice. One of the recommendations of Sophie van Senden Theis's study of former foster children, published in 1924, was that boarding care be used more extensively for children who were not yet ready to "settle down" in free homes immediately following removal from their own.[20] When foster families took children into their homes on the free home placement basis, with the expectation of rearing children as their own, the satisfactions they derived from having a child were deemed sufficient compensation for his care and the older child earned his own keep. When, however, a foster home was to be used prior to free home placement, then the idea of paying board for the child's care in the temporary arrangement was consistent with the philosophy. Furthermore, the need for more supervision of the child's care subsequent to placement was recognized and agencies felt more secure regarding their right to supervise if board were being paid.

In the meantime, too, the middle western states had shown their displeasure with the practice of eastern agencies, who sent children into their localities without supervision or follow-up, burdening officials with the problem of dealing with the consequences when the placements did not work out satisfactorily. Various states passed laws requiring agencies to obtain permission for interstate placements or to post a bond or exerted other kinds of restrictive pressures. These regulations sealed off some of the opportunities for free home placements a half continent away from the child's original home in the predominantly rural areas where children were an economic asset.

The mental hygiene movement, too, had its influence in bringing about greater awareness of the emotional needs of children and of the importance of early familial influences and relationships. Recognition that the child carried with him the impact of earlier experiences undermined the expectations that a change in environment would automatic-

---

[20] Sophie van Senden Theis, *How Foster Children Turn Out* (New York: State Charities Aid Association, 1924), p. 120.

ally bring about desirable changes in a child. Parental behavior, too, came to be seen as a product of the parents' own life experiences.

Although the removal of children from their own homes "for reasons of poverty alone" had been condemned by the first White House Conference on Children in 1909, mother's aid laws, passed by many of the states between that date and the provision for Aid to Dependent Children in the Social Security Act of 1935, often were highly restrictive in their operations and frequently were local rather than statewide in their application. The development of the OASDI and the ADC programs made increasingly unnecessary the foster care placement of children whose fathers had died or who were absent from the home for other reasons, and whose placement in an earlier era would have come about "for reasons of poverty alone." However, as implied earlier, even today the hazard of being neglected remains greater for the children of poverty-stricken parents whose energies are depleted by their struggles against economic pressures—and low ADC budgets in many states make it necessary to count recipients of this form of help among these struggling parents.

On the whole, however, children placed in foster care today are coming from quite different familial circumstances than in an earlier era. There are very few orphans and even fewer half orphans in foster care today. No data on a national basis are available on this point. Some child-placing agencies have examined their own case loads, often finding that as few as 5 percent of the children are orphans or half orphans. Children whose custody is removed from their parents are likely to be committed as "neglected children" rather than "dependent children," and they have had the kinds of experiences designated within the neglect laws which were described in an earlier section. Voluntary placements too (*not* involving court action) are likely to be on the basis of the parents' request because of broken-home situations, problems within the child himself, or temporary emergency situations.

While these changes in the type of foster home care, in the kinds of circumstances bringing about placement, and in the theoretical formulations concerning such care were coming about, institutional care of children has also continued to be used.

This brief excursion into the history of child placement has been taken in order to provide the background for identifying some of the ways in which this particular form of welfare service has become institutionalized, then sometimes operating as an antichange agent against the development of more appropriate means of meeting social problems. In institutional care of children the service is literally "institutionalized" into brick and mortar and stone. It is difficult, indeed, to change the function and services of an institution once it has been brought into being. However, the institutionalization of child placement is not restricted to the child placement facilities which are, in literal truth, institutions.

The kinds of forces which brought about the development of foster care resources (both institutional and home care) had the secondary effect of developing "child welfare" as a field of social work practice, distinct in itself and apart from "family welfare" and "family casework." Furthermore, child welfare was for all practical purposes tantamount to "child placement," since this was the predominant method used to promote "child welfare."

This particular aspect of the institutionalization of child welfare services—the equation of *child placement* with *child welfare*—is referred to again in later paragraphs as a factor in furthering or hindering the development of professional activities and services to intervene in the social problem of *child neglect*.

Economic Measures Safeguarding Family Versus Deprivation of Children

If the well-being of parents and the security of the family, including economic security, are such important safeguards for children, as suggested by the points on the continuum set forth earlier, then one would expect the profession to be particularly interested in those economic measures that safeguard family life, particularly those designed to benefit children.

Family allowances. In view of this, it is odd that the family allowance system, as known in many European countries and as established in Canada, does not seem to have stimulated the interest of social workers in the United States to any marked degree.

Dr. Eveline Burns has chided social workers in this regard:

> . . . while our ignorance of this almost universally adopted approach to the economic needs of children is not so abysmally great as it was ten years ago, the first reaction of social workers (to the family allowance system) is still likely to be hostile. Certainly there is no evidence of any burning desire to explore responsibly the potentialities for America of this new instrument for social welfare. Lest it should appear that Americans are unique in this respect, it should also be said that in Canada, too, the impetus for children's allowances did not come from social workers, but from the economists and politicians.[21]

True enough, one of the Forums of the Golden Anniversary White House Conference (1960) "commended study of a system of family al-

---

[21] Eveline M. Burns, "Social Welfare Is Our Commitment," in *The Social Welfare Forum, 1958* (New York: Columbia University Press, 1958), p. 8.

lowances and, by a 125 to 35 vote, came out for a program of children's allowances—which will offset the inverse relationship between income and size of family." [22]

Nevertheless, neither the events before nor since that conclave have suggested steady consistent interest. In the 12-year period from January 1950 through December 1961 *Child Welfare*, the publication of the Child Welfare League of America, carried no article specifically related to family allowance systems. *Children*, the publication of the Children's Bureau, so titled since 1954, published one such article, "Canada's Family Allowances in Retrospect," in 1957.[23]

A variety of causes may be postulated for this lack of interest on the part of the profession. Admittedly, professional education does not and could not be expected to equip social workers to devise and set into operation a national family allowance system. For this the knowledge and skills of economists, political scientists, and other governmental experts are required. Nevertheless, the social worker could be expected to recognize the values for family life that other countries have found in such systems and could be expected to speak out for the values that a similar system might have in this country. This requires that the professional strength in values be matched by strength in facts—information about the economic and geographical location of children, about population trends, about family income in relation to family size, about the limitations in current income tax provisions that are intended to benefit taxpayers responsible for dependents, about variable per capita income among the states. It may be that social work educators do not provide sufficient stimulation to help students make connections between (1) "social problems" as taught in undergraduate study or within the context of social work education and (2) the values they are expected to incorporate within their professional behavior.

Additional causes may be operative. The family allowance system may express values that run counter to other deeply ingrained values derived from the culture but not necessarily consistent with professional values. This culture continues to stress the importance of economic self-sufficiency of the family unit, but although this value has remained relatively constant the concept of the "family" has shifted markedly. Both the resources and the responsibilities of "the family" have contracted from those of the extended family to those of the nuclear family. To a certain degree, income tax deductions for dependent children and taxes for education, laid alike on parents and the childless, are in-

---

[22] *Conference Proceedings*. Golden Anniversary White House Conference on Children and Youth, March–April 1960 (Washington, D.C., 1960), p. 138.

[23] George F. Davidson, "Canada's Family Allowances in Retrospect," *Children*, Vol. 4, No. 3 (May–June 1957), pp. 83–88.

fringements of the principle that parents are wholly responsible for economic support of their children. It is a long step between these measures which in their effect decrease the amount of money that will be *taken from* persons who are rearing children to a family allowance system in which money is given to parents.

Some of these value premises are implicit in the minority statement of that White House Conference forum, cited above, whose majority came out in favor of family allowances. The minority stated: "There is no proof that a system of child allowances is necessary if present social insurance and public assistance programs are improved. A child allowance system would drastically increase the involvement of government in family life." [24]   This statement, it will be noted, is problem-focused and evokes those programs that operate in behalf of the individual or his family when some particular circumstance in family life occurs—the death of the breadwinner (Old Age and Survivors' Insurance), his death, absence, or incapacitation (ADC), or lack of adequate income from other causes, such as unemployment (General Assistance). It is true that these programs do provide benefits and assistance for large numbers of children. Nevertheless, the vast majority of children do not live in families in which these circumstances have occurred. The minority statement eschews or avoids directing its attention to the principles on which family allowance systems are based—extension of benefits to families, not because of special problems, but on the basis of more equitable sharing of the economic burden of child rearing, redistribution of economic resources, and the desirability of government taking some small measure of responsibility for improving those opportunities for children that are dependent on economic adequacy of the family.

Economic protection for the children of migrant agricultural workers. Of all the groups of children in this country who might be identified as disadvantaged, the children of migrant agricultural workers are probably in a worse plight than any other group. These are the children who with their parents "follow the crops," starting from the South and making the trek northward along the eastern seaboard and from the Southwest to the Northwest, with some of each group fanning inward to the interior states of the country, harvesting first one crop and then another. Many of these children live in makeshift housing, have inadequate medical care, and are deprived of schooling. Important as these problems are, they are secondary to the migrant family's hazardous economic circumstances, although some are a product of the basic economic problem.

---

[24] *Conference Proceedings, Golden Anniversary White House Conference on Children and Youth, op. cit.,* p. 138.

In *The Harvesters, The Story of the Migrant People,* Louisa Shotwell has identified the strong political power exerted by agricultural growers' associations and farmers' groups to block the enactment of state laws which would protect the economic rights of farm labor.[25] Paradoxically, minimum wage legislation and other legal protections, applicable alike to migrant labor and locally available workers, would likely cut down the number of migrant workers, since such laws would remove some of the economic incentive for growers to employ, under exploitative conditions, labor imported from other states or from outside the country. Often, with current conditions, in order for a family to earn enough to survive at the piecework rates paid, even small children are put to work in these "factories in the fields" under conditions which have long been outlawed by child labor laws that protect the urban child.[26] The circumstances of many of these children of migrant families would undoubtedly be defined as "child neglect" even in a strict legal interpretation of the phrase, that is, if anyone were sufficiently concerned to bring their circumstances to the attention of a court.

A variety of factors contribute to the incongruities between professional values and professional activities in regard to the problems of these children. Pressure groups opposed to change are stronger than those working to effect improvement. Further, because of the migratory nature of the parents' employment these children do not "belong" to any community in any of the states through which they move. Remnants of the concept of local responsibility for local needs—and *only* local needs—continue in force under those conditions in which the cost would be borne locally if services were instituted, even though these same localities and states are willing to forego this principle in those instances in which the practical effect of doing so is that of securing federal reimbursement for a portion of the cost of those programs shared by the federal government. Some states and localities within states have developed programs of welfare, health, and educational services in behalf of migrant families, but these efforts are spotty.

Not only do these migrant workers and their children not "belong" in the sense of permanent residence, but they are also often members of minority groups—Puerto Ricans, Negro families from the South, Spanish-American families from the Southwestern states, and the Mexican workers from across the border. With reference to dependency and foster care, Maas and Engler have pointed out that "where norms are

---

25 Garden City, New York: Doubleday & Co., 1961.
26 *See* Florence Taylor, "On the Child Labor Front," *Social Service Review,* Vol. 22, No. 1 (March 1948).

ordinarily applied differently to different categories (segments) of people, the norms of dependency will be applied separately within, and relative to, each segment." [27]

The same might be said about standards by which child care and child neglect are measured. Put baldly, it matters less to the community if a bronze-skinned Spanish-American baby dies in a migrant farm labor camp because of medical neglect than if a white baby dies from similar causes within the city limits of a county seat or state capital. The problems which the comings and goings of large numbers of transient families create for communities are real, and the difficulties and complications of providing adequate services should not be underestimated. The public health resources of a community, adequate for the normal population, may be quite inadequate to provide maternal and child health services for an influx of seasonal workers, to inspect the housing facilities of the labor camps, and to check on the water supply and sanitary arrangements. The teachers in the local schools would have a difficult time maintaining educational standards for the local children if they were also faced with the task of dealing with a considerable number of migrant children who would enter the classroom with an indeterminate amount of previous education and who would be pupils there for only a few weeks before moving on to yet another school in another state, where the next crop was ready for their parents to harvest.

Again it is necessary to emphasize that regulations to ensure adequate housing, health services, and educational facilities—important as they are—are secondary to adequate protection of the economic rights of migrant workers. Unless the consciences of the citizens of states are aroused more effectively than has yet been the case, it seems likely that powerful political forces will continue to block needed legislation that would provide economic protection and that only federal legislation will serve this end. Similarly, insofar as the varieties of services mentioned earlier are concerned, states and localities need federal help in order to be able to supply them. Government-sponsored housing and government-sponsored transportation would eliminate two of the ways in which migrant workers are exploited by being forced to pay exorbitant rents for shacks and by being carried at high cost from one site of employment to another in crowded unsafe vehicles. It may be, too, that services need to be as mobile as the persons they serve. It is possible to conceive of "mobile units" of doctors, dentists, nurses, nutritionists, teachers, recreation workers, chaplains, and social workers who, like the migrant workers, would "follow the crops."

---

[27] Maas and Engler, *op. cit.*, p. 289.

Services To Strengthen Parents Versus Inadequate Care of Children

The location of the various points on the continuum of child care, suggested earlier, ranging from maximal opportunities for development to child neglect, carries the implication that all things possible should be done to strengthen, augment, and supplement parental resources and capacities to help parents to provide adequate care for their children.

Some of the social additives to family resources might include protective services and other casework services, day care, and homemaker service. One would expect that a large portion of the resources and energies of child welfare programs would be directed to their development and use in behalf of children. However, of the great majority of children served by child welfare agencies as of March 31, 1959, only 39 percent were in the houses of parents or relatives, 43 percent were in foster family homes, and 18 percent were in institutions or elsewhere.[28] No comparable figures are available concerning the living arrangements of children served by voluntary agencies, but it is likely that the proportion in their own homes would be even less than among public agencies.

The over-all objective of this paper is to examine the ways in which the profession of social work, through it knowledge, skills, and values, can intervene in the problems of child neglect by working with individuals and groups, by the structuring of services, and by its impact on social values and the social structure.

In each of these areas of operation reasons may be adduced for the incongruities between the professed value of keeping the child in his home and the expressed predominance of professional activities related to the child who has already been removed from his family. Limitations in the profession's knowledge and skill in working with certain types of problems constitute one deterrent to the greater use of protective casework and other casework services in behalf of children living with parents who are allegedly neglecting them or who are having difficulty in providing adequate care.

Bertram Beck has identified the current confusion in equating "aggressive casework" with "protective casework service." He has pointed out that the former refers to techniques of the casework approach and casework treatment, whereas the latter defines an area of service which, once so defined and accepted by an agency as its function within the

---

[28] *Child Welfare Statistics 1959*, U. S. Children's Bureau Statistical Series No. 60 (Washington, D.C.: U. S. Department of Health, Education, and Welfare, 1960), p. 7.

community carries with it certain kinds of obligations.[29] A protective service must be responsible for determining the facts when children are reported to be neglected, and it must retain responsibility for the case situation until the protection of the children has been assured. Such assurance may come from the determination that the complaint was baseless or from the discovery of neglectful conditions which were corrected as a consequence of rehabilitative work with the family or, in some instances, of the removal of the children when such work with the family did not prove effective.

Although, as Beck warns, the area of protective service must not be equated with aggressive casework, he also points out that in many instances in which protective service is required aggressive casework techniques are also appropriate. The fact that in many locations protective services are an unclaimed area of service may be related to the profession's limitations in knowing how to apply the developing knowledge about such techniques and about the persons and problems for which they are appropriate.

Among parents who are neglectful or in danger of becoming neglectful of their children there are those who are simply overwhelmed by external pressures, those who are unknowing of standards expected from them in a community whose ways are strange to them, those whose physical stamina is unequal to the task of child rearing, those reacting to their children in terms of their own unresolved conflicts and unmet needs within their own past or present circumstances, and those who are mentally ill. There are also likely to be a considerable number of parents with defects in ego development who are diagnosed clinically as character disorders and whose behaviors are those of "acting out" their impulses in contrast to the inhibitions and the symptom formations of neurotic persons. Knowledge concerning neurotic difficulties learned from psychoanalysis has become well integrated into casework knowledge and has been translated into casework skill in helping those individuals who are guilt-ridden and conflicted, who have low self-esteem, and whose psychological defenses against impulses and affects interfere with their functioning. On the other hand, psychoanalytic contributions to ego psychology which illumine the nature of character disorders are less well integrated into professional knowledge and less well translated into skills. Fortunately, however, there is reason for optimism because the body of social work literature concerning such problems is growing.[30] As the theoretical formulations become clearer, the kinds of treatment techniques required become better understood.

---

[29] "Protective Casework: Revitalized," *Child Welfare*, Vol. 34, Nos. 9 and 10 (November–December 1955).

[30] *See*, for example, Beatrice Simcox Reiner and Irving Kaufman, M.D., *Character*

Nevertheless, it can be expected that "retooling" for work with persons with these kinds of difficulties will cause difficulties for the social worker. Otto Pollak has identified some of the ways in which certain aspects of the professional social worker's training are antithetical to his task of bringing about those changes that lead to more effective social functioning by persons with the diagnosis of character disorder.[31] Permissiveness, acceptance, guilt-relieving techniques, and explorations of the client's early deprivations—attitudes and techniques of value with the neurotic—are ill-advised for the person with ego defects who may require limits, may need to be taught that certain kinds of behavior are expected from him, and to incorporate a sense of responsibility for his behavior, and who must be given extensive help in learning to understand and to cope with current reality.

Perhaps in less direct ways, as well, some of the traditional emphases of casework serve the client poorly in cases of child neglect—whether or not the parent has a character disorder. Appreciation of the great influence of the past on the client's attitude and feelings, and the emphasis on the client-worker relationship per se as a therapeutic experience, may sometimes blind the caseworker to current reality pressures which in themselves, regardless of the client's past, produce tension, conflict, and a sense of personal disorganization. Underestimating the degree of distress that current pressures may cause leads to a comparable underestimation of the amount of help that practical services—day care, homemaker service, and the educational help of the public health nurse and the home economist—could provide. Furthermore, these services are not supplied by automation. People perform them. There may be times when the caseworker will feel that the therapeutic value of the relationship can be diluted by the introduction of the homemaker, the nursery school teacher, the nutritionist, or the nurse into the case situation.

The degree to which child welfare services have been institutionalized into agency structures that emphasize placement of children has already been considered in earlier pages. When foster care, rather than service to the family, is the predominant method for intervening in situations of neglect or in circumstances that might lead to neglect, opportunities

---

Disorders in Parents of Delinquents (New York: Family Service Association of America, 1959) ; Isabel Stamm, "Ego Psychology in the Emerging Theoretical Base of Casework," in Alfred J. Kahn, ed., *Issues in American Social Work* (New York: Columbia University Press, 1959), pp. 80–109; Alice Overton *et al.*, *Casework Notebook Family-centered Project* (St. Paul: Greater St. Paul Community Chest and Council, 1957) ; Kenneth Dick and Lydia Strnad, "The Multi-Problem Family and Problems of Service," *Social Casework*, Vol. 39, No. 6 (June 1958), pp. 349–355.

[31] "Treatment of Character Disorders: A Dilemma in Casework Culture," *Social Service Review*, Vol. 35, No. 2 (June 1961), pp. 127–134.

are not used for developing and learning to apply skillfully the resources
that supplement and strengthen parental capacities.

There are hopeful signs that public welfare services of the future will
be restructured to close the gap between those approaches that have
been designated as "child centered" and those that are "family centered." [32]   At the national level a new Bureau of Family Services has
been constituted to bridge the former administrative split between Aid
to Dependent Children programs and programs of the Children's Bureau.

This structural change is paralleled by a new emphasis on rehabilitation as one of the key concepts of public welfare. Vocational training
and upgrading of work skills are objectives in work with individuals.
Policies are being re-examined to evaluate their impact on the individual,
not only in his current situation but also as they affect his future opportunities. In this connection Senator Abraham Ribicoff, when Secretary of the Department of Health, Education and Welfare, made two
highly specific suggestions. He urged that states permit a portion of the
earnings of adolescents to be excluded from public assistance budgets so
that their own personal needs might be met more adequately and so that
they might set aside some of the money for future educational needs.
A comparable suggestion was made with reference to the earnings of
parents receiving supplemental help. Such policies may have great
constructive value, particularly for adolescent children in families receiving public assistance who hithertofore have suffered from policies
that inflict on them the indignities of poverty and that stifle their aspirations for achieving education.

President Kennedy, himself, in his message to Congress on welfare
programs, February 1, 1962, made this statement:

> Although Federal law permits, it does not require states to take into
> account the full expenses individuals have in earning income. This
> is not consistent with equity, common sense, or other Federal laws
> such as our tax code. It only discourages the will to earn. In order
> to encourage assistance recipients to find and retain employment, I,
> therefore, recommend that the Act be amended to require the states
> to take into account the expense of earning income.[33]

It remains to be seen what states and localities will do to implement
this new optimistic spirit which perceives service and rehabilitation as
key concepts in public welfare. Obstacles exist. The undersupply of
professionally trained social workers is a difficulty that cannot be over-

---

[32] Elizabeth Wickenden and Winifred Bell, *Public Welfare: Time for a Change*
(New York: Columbia University Press, 1961).

[33] *New York Times* text of President Kennedy's message to Congress on reforms in
welfare program, February 2, 1962, p. 10.

come quickly. However, much can be done to increase the effectiveness of the agency-trained worker by adequate in-service training. Such preparation for the job, plus the inspiring new conception of the role of the public welfare worker, are forces that may decrease the high rate of staff turnover from which many public welfare departments suffer.

Staff shortages have also been a factor in defining the content of efforts to intervene in problems of child neglect. No method has been devised to determine what percentage of families in any given community are likely to need one form or another of social work assistance in behalf of their children. The rate of children per 10,000 child population who do receive child welfare casework service from state and local public welfare agencies is 51 for the country as a whole, but within the continental United States the rates vary from 175 in the District of Columbia to 6 in Texas. Other rates are California 39, Michigan 10, Mississippi 118, New York 68, Ohio 62, and Wyoming 28.[34] It is not certain whether the units of count are exactly the same. Also, there is no way of knowing whether the highest rate, 175, is "too high" and the lowest rate, 6, is "too low" or whether both are too low to meet the need that exists. What is known is that many public child welfare divisions and private child welfare agencies are pressed for service beyond the capacity of a limited staff. They find themselves confining service to those situations that are most serious. By that time, placement of the children may be the only feasible plan. Welfare programs are frequently in the position of the boatsman who is so busy bailing water out of his boat to keep from sinking that he cannot take time out to make the repairs that would stop the flooding.

To prevent child neglect before it occurs, a different approach is needed—that of identifying the circumstances that are potentially threatening to the welfare of children: economic inadequacy, health problems in one or both parents, mental illness or convalescence from mental illness after hospitalization, separation or divorce of parents, unmarried parenthood, large families with limited income, and families new to a community in which the ways of living are quite different from those to which the family has been accustomed—these are some of the circumstances to which it is likely that the hazard of child neglect is greater than in other kinds of familial groups. Obviously, this is not to say that children in all such families are being neglected. Rather it is only surmised that the probabilities are greater.

This suggests that the concepts of "aggressive casework," "assertive casework," and "reaching out" need to be extended to case finding. One practical implication is that organizations, institutions, and agen-

---

[34] *Child Welfare Statistics 1959, op. cit.,* p. 7.

cies dealing with problems of physical and mental health, housing, and population trends need to develop greater awareness that the specific problem with which they are confronted may have its impact on family life and the care of children. Greater coordination of services is called for. Possibly, too, a neighborhood approach is needed with social service stations as numerous and as readily accessible as branch post-offices and public schools. Personnel of these stations would be knowledgeable about the problems of the neighborhood and would supply some types of services. Equally important, they would serve as referral sources for more specialized services.

According to Alfred Kahn, the profession has failed to take into account changes in the social scene which call for corresponding changes in the role of social welfare services in a modern community. Among the social trend data he cites are these: disruption of family life for many children because of high divorce and separation rates, the large numbers of illegitimate births, the high rate of geographical mobility, and the increasing extent to which women with children under eighteen are employed. Challenging the current perception of social welfare services Kahn writes:

> . . . social welfare services tend to be seen by the American public and by social workers as both residual and as therapeutic; that is, they are considered to fill the gaps in "normal" institutional functioning and to help individually those who fall by the wayside in the flow of human living. The assumption is that able, competent, "normal" (and moral?) people manage alone or obtain family help but do not need assistance and many forms of welfare services. It is this assumption that affects attitudes toward those who do need services, the character of available service, and their quality. . . .
>
> An opposing view of social welfare in increasingly emerging, which may be called the "institutional" view. . . . Is it not possible, given the social trend data . . . that we need a much larger "institutional" (or perhaps, "developmental") emphasis in child care? Communities provide educational resources, libraries, hospitals, public recreation and much else because the character of modern life is such that adequate socialization, development, and protection cannot be provided by the typical family. Has the time not yet arrived to add to this listing such services as day care, homemakers or home helps, family life education, vocational counseling—to mention several possibilities? The crucial issue is whether knowledge of the social scene now enables us to predict the need for such resources on a large scale. Is it not clear that the typical family cannot be expected to manage alone? [35]

---

[35] Alfred J. Kahn, "The Social Scene, Social Science, and the Planning of Services for Children," *Social Work.* Vol. 7, No. 3 (July 1962), pp. 5–6.

The foregoing pages have identified some of the factors in the present level of skill of services to individuals, in the structuring of those services in these agencies, and in the changes in the social scene with which the profession has not kept up to date. These factors operate to bring about incongruities between social work activities and those social work values that would be expressed by intervening in problems of child neglect by other means than the placement of children.

Welfare Measures Versus the Impact of Family Breakdown on Children

Several references have already been made to the Aid to Dependent Children program. Along with the other public assistance programs, it is, of course, an income maintenance program. However, it must also be identified as the program that represents some of the social costs of family breakdown.

As the Old Age and Survivors' Insurance program has expanded, it has provided benefits for an increasing proportion of the children whose fathers have died. Consequently, children receiving ADC because of the death of their fathers have been reduced in numbers. In late 1958, among the 2,142,396 children receiving ADC there were only 10.3 percent whose fathers were dead. The fathers of 26.1 percent were incapacitated; 61.5 percent were those whose fathers were absent from home.[36] The 61.5 percent is further subdivided into these groupings: divorced or legally separated, 12.9 percent; separated without court decree, 8.7 percent; deserted, 18.5 percent; not married to mother, 15.7 percent; imprisoned, 4.7 percent; absent for other reasons, 1.0 percent.[37]

An even greater number of children *not* receiving ADC are living in homes in which the father is absent. Characteristically, the family incomes in families headed by women—whether receiving public assistance or self-supporting—are lower than those of families headed by men. Thus these children, to a greater degree than the children whose fathers are present in the home, are deprived of material advantages.

Equally important, the full burden of the tasks of child rearing, unshared by a spouse, falls on the mothers of these children who are thus more vulnerable to the pressures that lead to inadequate care. Furthermore, the father's absence, in itself, is a distinct loss to the child. On

---

[36] The difference between the sum of the percentages given and 100 percent is 2.1 percent, which includes children whose fathers are in the home as caretakers because of the death, absence, or incapacitation of the mother.

[37] Robert H. Mugge, *Characteristics and Financial Circumstances of Families Receiving Aid to Dependent Children, Late 1958*, Public Assistance Report No. 4 (Washington, D.C.: U. S. Department of Health, Education and Welfare, Bureau of Public Assistance, N. D.), pp. 16–17.

these various counts, then, the child whose parents are divorced, separated, or unmarried is exposed to a greater hazard of having less than average opportunities for development. Nonetheless, the conception of ADC, regardless of some of the shortcomings in the program, must be regarded as a highly constructive force that makes it possible for children to remain in their own homes. Hopefully, modifications in policy, indicated earlier, will make its effects even more beneficial.

The fact of widespread family breakdown remains. Reuben Hill writes, "The United States is one of the few civilized countries of the world which has not yet formulated an explicit family policy in which a coherent program for families can be built. The federal government, having ceded the issues of family life to the states, has taken little initiative in promoting programs of family betterment." Some of the many measures Hill recommends are family life education, uniform marriage and divorce laws, and counseling services within domestic relations courts.[38]

It may be expected that the recommendation for the further development of counseling services within courts dealing with divorce cases, if followed, would prevent some marital breakups and thus protect additional children from the consequences of family disruption. Such services would also safeguard the interests of children when their custody was at stake.

However, these measures directed toward individual family situations are not likely to reduce the family instability arising from forces in the social structure. Such deterrents to family stability are experienced with particular force and by a disproportionately large number of the Negro population. Hylan Lewis points out that the "heavy wave of professional concern and popular preoccupation with social class values, tastes, and behavior has had telling and, on the whole, favorable effects on the Negro community and the Negro family." Recognition of class differences in the Negro community has weakened the stereotype of racial characteristics and has paved the way for an examination of the economic and social forces that influence behavior, values, and aspirations. Lewis regards efforts to change "practices or circumstances affecting Negro family life" as a reflection of

> public and professional awareness of the threat and social costs involved as well as increasing recognition that such non-middle-class behavior is a result of neither inherent racial nor immutable class characteristics. They show the desire, if not the "need" to grant

[38] Reuben Hill, "The American Family Today," in Eli Ginzberg, ed., *The Nation's Children—The Family and Social Change*, Vol. 1 (New York: Columbia University Press, 1960), pp. 103, 104–107.

middle-class potentialities to Negro families; and, frequently, to implement their attainment—both under segregated and unsegregated conditions—with public and private funds.[39]

The study of families receiving ADC in late 1958 points out that "although less than one-tenth of all families in the nation in 1958 were non-white, over two-fifths of the families receiving Aid to Dependent Children that year were non-white." This disproportionate representation of Negro families is related to several factors. In 1958 the median income of nonwhite families amounted to only 51.2 percent of the median income of white families. The rate of unemployment among nonwhite persons was twice as high as among white persons in 1958, the comparison being 12.6 percent in the former group and 6.1 percent in the latter. Furthermore, the nonwhite man was in a relatively more disadvantaged economic position than the nonwhite woman. In 1958, 22.4 percent of all nonwhite families had female heads, compared with only 8.6 percent of all white families.[40]

The greater likelihood that the Negro woman can be the stable wage earner within the family group puts her in a better position than the man for assuming economic responsibility for the children. Although, as pointed out earlier, an increasing number of women in the population as a whole is in the labor market, it nevertheless remains an assumption—and value—in the dominant culture that the man will be the primary wage earner and that the economic unit of the family will consist of father, mother, and children. Among Negro families, on the other hand, economic pressures favor the mother-children family unit, which results from higher rates of divorce, desertion, and illegitimacy.

Goal-Directed Foster Care Versus Foster Care Drift

It could be anticipated that cases of child neglect leading to the removal of children from their own homes would decrease sharply if some of the measures discussed in preceding sections of this paper were put into effect. Nevertheless, it is altogether probable that some children would continue to need foster care no matter how well developed these other services might be.

The question then is, what constitutes adequate care after a child is placed and what constitutes "child neglect" on the part of placement agencies? In the following paragraphs we are not then dealing with the direct day-by-day care of the child and his experiences with foster parents, cottage parents, his peers, and the community; rather the concern is with the "neglect" or "care-ful-ness" of the long-range planning for which agencies have responsibility.

---

[39] Hylan Lewis, "The Changing Negro Family," *ibid.*, pp. 130–134.

[40] Mugge, *op. cit.*, p. 14.

Although there is considerable emphasis in child welfare literature that currently foster care is of a "temporary" nature, the fact remains that a large proportion of children remain in long-time foster care.[41] For some children long-time foster care is an appropriate plan, but it is essential that such arrangements be the result of constructive long-range planning rather than simply a drift into long-time care by default.

Early diagnosis of the family situation followed promptly by rehabilitation work with parents would make it possible for some children to be returned to their own homes. In other situations early diagnosis would lead to the conclusion that adoption was a suitable plan with the consequence that a larger number of children could be given the advantage of adoptive placements.

Social structure and cultural values influence attitudes toward foster children and toward adoption. Since agencies operate within the social structure, their practices are influenced by these forces. For example, there are many more white childless couples who wish to adopt a baby than there are white babies available for adoption; on the other hand, there are many more Negro babies than there are Negro couples who wish to adopt them. If this were a society in which the factor of race was relatively unimportant in shaping the attitudes of persons toward one another, it would be possible to think in simple terms of babies needing parents and couples wanting to adopt babies, with the consequence that fewer children would grow up without parents of their own and fewer couples would be disappointed in their quest for a child. (Of course, this argument is somewhat specious, for if this were a society free from racial discrimination there probably would not be such a marked difference between white and Negro illegitimacy rates.) Some agencies at the present time are placing babies of mixed Negro and white parentage in white adoptive homes, but the number of such placements is limited and highly selective.

It is quite possible that agencies have been more conservative in the matter of "matching" racial and nationality backgrounds than adoptive parents themselves would expect or require. Since World War II considerable numbers of Americans have adopted children in Europe, and men of the Armed Forces and their wives who were stationed in the Orient have adopted Oriental children and brought them back to this country. Agency-sponsored and agency-supervised international adoptions have now increased. These facts may have contributed to the present tendency for agencies to re-examine their thinking concerning "matching" of nationality and racial background as a prerequisite for placement. Policies of this nature are being replaced

---

[41] Maas and Engler, *op. cit.*, estimate that among the children studied in the nine communities, half would remain in foster care for the balance of childhood.

by pragmatism and the attempt to identify the characteristics needed by adoptive parents to be able to adopt children from backgrounds markedly different from their own.[42] The special project undertaken jointly by the Bureau of Indian Affairs and the Child Welfare League of America for the placement of American Indian children in white adoptive homes is an example both of a breakthrough in this regard and of the continuing need to take cultural attitudes into account.[43] These Indian babies, "first Americans" who were born on reservations in states of the Central Plains area and the Southwest, are not "adoptable" babies in their home states. There they are members of a fairly sizable minority group which is economically, socially, and educationally deprived, and undesirable characteristics have been attached to the stereotype of the Indian. In the East, on the other hand, the concept of the American Indian has become somewhat romanticized and these babies are "adoptable."

The same social and economic factors that contribute to high rates of illegitimacy among Negroes also operate to reduce the number of families within this group who regard themselves able to adopt children. Thus the "surplus" of babies needing adoptive homes and the "undersupply" of such homes are in part products of the same causes.[44] Agencies are making some progress in modifying their policies and in developing techniques that will be more effective in increasing the number of adoptive homes among the Negro populations of communities.[45] Some traditional standards for adoptive families are clearly based on norms of family function derived from the dominant white culture, as, for example, the standard that the adoptive mother is not to be employed outside the home. Impersonalized procedures and forms and regulations perceived by Negro couples as rejective and threatening are being replaced by a "reaching out" approach to potential adoptive couples.

The definition of the "adoptable child" is gradually being extended

---

[42] For further discussion on this point, *see* Alma Jenkins, "Some Evaluative Factors in the Selection of Adoptive Homes for Indian Children," *Child Welfare*, Vol. 40, No. 5 (June 1961) ; Letitia Di Virgilio, "Adjustment of Foreign Children in their Adoptive Homes," *Child Welfare*, Vol. 35, No. 9 (November 1956) ; *Adoption of Oriental Children by American White Families* (New York: Child Welfare League of America, May 1960) ; Margaret A. Valk, "Adjustment of Korean-American Children in Their Adoptive Homes," in *Casework Papers, 1957* (New York: Family Service Association of America, 1957) ; Lloyd B. Graham, "Children from Japan in American Adoptive Homes," *ibid.*

[43] Arnold Lyslo, "The Indian Adoption Project," *Child Welfare*, Vol. 40, No. 4 (May 1961), pp. 4–6.

[44] David Fanshel, *A Study in Negro Adoption* (New York: Child Welfare League of America, 1957).

[45] Mildred Hawkins, "Negro Adoptions—Challenge Accepted," *Child Welfare*, Vol. 39, No. 10 (December 1960), pp. 22–27.

to include any child who is legally free for adoption and who is capable of responding to a relationship with adoptive parents, regardless of age, existence of a physical handicap, or some degree of intellectual limitation.   However, any of these conditions requires some modification of agency policies and practices that affect adoption placements.   The older child, for example, needs much more casework help than the baby in becoming part of a family group, since he already has a concept of himself as being a part of some other family or of being derived from some other family.[46] The criterion of adoptability usually is that the older child already has relationships that are meaningful to him.   Thus, paradoxically, it is only the child who will experience some suffering in the loss of preadoption relationships who is adoptable.   Agencies are learning that it is sometimes neither appropriate nor necessary to maintain the policy that the child placed for adoption shall not have continued contact with the previous foster parents.   Nor is it always necessary to maintain the sharp dichotomy between "boarding parents" and "adoptive parents."   Progress is being made in planning, in some instances, for boarding parents to adopt the child already in their care.

These developments must be strengthened and expanded if placement agencies are to be able to regard themselvs as guiltless of "child neglect" of a most profound nature, that of needlessly depriving a child of parents who claim him as their own.   The fact that these developments in adoptive practice are the topics discussed frequently in child welfare literature of the last decade is encouraging, but, at the same time, it points up the fact that these changes are still regarded as noteworthy— not yet taken for granted.

Some children in foster care will not be adopted and will not be returned to their own homes.   They will need foster care over a long period of time.   The most obvious criterion of "care-full" or "neglectful" planning by agencies is whether these foster children have the type of placement most suited to their needs.

There are great variations among communities and states in the proportion of children in foster homes compared with the proportion in institutions.   These data in themselves strongly suggest that children are still being given that form of care which happens to be available rather than the form of care needed.   The preceding section which dealt with the institutionalization of placement—removal of the child from his own home—as the predominant method of intervention in child neglect can be applied also to the rigid maintenance of the particular type of foster care, institutional care, or foster home care that predominates in any given community.

---

[46] Jacqueline McCoy, "Identity as a Factor in the Adoptive Placement of the Older Child," *Child Welfare*, Vol. 40, No. 7 (September 1961), pp. 14–18.

The structure of foster care service within a community may hinder or facilitate the probability of a child's receiving the particular type of foster care he requires at any given time. In some communities a high degree of specialization exists among agencies; some provide only foster day care, institutional care, foster home care, temporary care, or adoption services. Such specialization may have the advantage of furthering the development of a high degree of skill in that particular area of service, but it predisposes the child welfare community to the disease of red-tape sclerosis, symptoms of which are the dulled percep-tions of the changing needs of the child as his circumstances change and inertia in seeking those services that he needs. The effect of this disease on the children involved is child neglect. For example, there are agencies that are set up to provide only temporary care, but by an agency-centered definition. Children are cared for in these agencies and then passed on to another for replacement. From the child's point of view there is nothing "temporary" about foster care. To him it has meant being uprooted from one foster home and adapting to another. A contrary hazard exists in that children are fitted into the service of a specialized agency and not referred elsewhere when circumstances change. For example, if changed conditions in a foster child's own family cause him to become adoptable, unless the placement agency providing foster care also has adoption placement readily available within its own range of services it may fail to seek that service from another specialized agency within the community.

Whenever policies and practices become agency-centered rather than child-centered, child neglect is likely to be the consequence.

Integration into the Community Versus Placement in Institutions

Experiences of the kind that lead to a child's commitment to an institu-tion for delinquents and those that lead to placement in an institution for emotionally disturbed children were deliberately grouped together when in earlier pages a continuum of experiences ranging from those providing maximal opportunities for development to those constituting neglect was postulated.

This was done with full recognition that the status accorded by the profession to the professional worker in the treatment institution is usually immeasurably higher than that accorded to the worker in the institution for delinquents. Out of this sharp difference there is only blurred recognition that these children share the common fate of having been regarded as so much trouble to others or to themselves that they were removed from the fabric of community living. There is the second problem that the kudos extended to the worker in the treatment institution and the profession's high regard for the services in such institutions eases the conscience of the profession and deflects its members from examining factors in the structure of social welfare services and in professional practice that contributed to the failure to intervene earlier or more effectively to prevent the eventual designation of these children as unfit to take part in the normal processes of family and community living.

The potential of a third problem is inherent in this situation. The high status accorded by the profession to the types of knowledge and skills of the workers in these treatment institutions might lead to the illogical assumption that the social value of that particular type of service should be given a comparably high rating in the range of social welfare services. This conclusion might in turn cause members of the profession to have unrealistic expectations of the benefits to be derived from the service, to use the service indiscriminately, and to urge expansion of these resources without careful evaluation of community needs and priorities among needs. Fortunately, there are counterforces operating against this third problem. Personnel of treatment institutions become aware of the futility of institutional therapy unless, on the child's discharge from the institution, changes in the familial situation, community situation, or both permit the therapeutic gains to be maintained. The related facts that care in treatment institutions is extremely expensive and that fewer children can be served in the facilities available than there are requests for service has had the salutory effect of causing the profession to create other resources to meet the needs of emotionally disturbed children. Foster home care plus outpatient psychiatric clinic treatment and other auxiliary aids to foster parents and to children is one such approach. Day care provided by treatment institutions is another.

Obviously, the fact that a child is emotionally disturbed means that something has gone awry in his development, sometimes because of constitutional factors but more often, it is believed, because of his experiences. Frequently causes of the child's distorted feelings toward himself and toward others are posited within the familial relationships. Therapy is directed toward treatment of the resultant gaps in development.

However, having experiences in the cultural institutions of the community, such as the school and the church, becoming aware of the political and commercial institutions, and learning how different kinds of behavior are expected in different settings—all of these, as well as familial experiences, contribute to the child's development, for good or for ill. They affect him as soon as he has contact outside his familial group, but the particular values to be derived from these different types of experiences vary according to the child's level of development. The specific experiences appropriate to each stage are different, and those of each level provide the foundation for those that come next, each according to its "season." The child removed from family and community is for that period of time relatively isolated from these community forces, and this may bring about other gaps in development, productive of other problems, when once again he returns to community living.

CONCLUDING STATEMENT

Child neglect has been examined as a legal concept which defines a quality of care below the minimum expected by community standards. This assumes that there are community norms of adequate child care. However, norms vary in time and place and are sometimes applied differentially along ethnic and social class lines. Legal intervention is limited to those situations in which care falls below the minimum.

Social work, on the other hand, is not so limited, and one of the values of the profession is that of helping individuals achieve maximal development. To accomplish this end, it could be expected that professional intervention would be directed toward helping make available to individuals those experiences most likely to contribute to such development. Moreover, on the bases of knowledge of the needs of children and of social work values, it would be expected that major efforts would be directed toward safeguarding family life by economic and social measures and strengthening and supplementing parental capacities when such assistance was needed to ensure adequate protection and care of children. Yet placement of children away from their own families remains a predominant method for intervening in instances of child neglect.

This contradiction suggests that not all professional realities would be accounted for within a claim that social work's knowledge, skills, and values always operate as a coordinated and integrated force in the profession's activities in behalf of individuals and families, in its structuring of services, and in its attempts to influence the social values of the community. Within each of these three planes of professional behavior, possible causes for the discrepancies between professed values and professional activities in regard to child neglect have been located and examined.

There are reasons to believe that gains in professional knowledge and skills, as well as patterns for the realignment of social welfare services now being worked out on a national level for public welfare services, will help bring about more effective intervention in those situations in which there is the potential threat of child neglect.

Of great importance, too, are the intimations of changes in the social scene. The last two paragraphs of the late President Kennedy's message to Congress on welfare programs read as follows:

> ... communities which have tried the rehabilitative road—the road I have recommended today—have demonstrated what can be done with creative, thoughtfully conceived, and properly managed programs of prevention and social rehabilitation. In those communities, families have been restored to self-reliance, and relief rolls have been reduced.
>
> To strengthen our human resources—to demonstrate the compassion of free men—and in the light of our own constructive self-interest— we must bring our welfare programs up to date. I urge that the Congress do so without delay.[47]

The President's words are altogether consistent with the dual aims of social work—improved social productivity and increased capacity for personal satisfaction. They are also resonant of the recent Presidential emphasis that it is necessary for the country's progress that talent be discovered, recognized, and developed and that opportunities for such development be afforded to children.

Great might for social change is embodied in this approach. In the past, when men were needed to serve their country in wartime, their racial and nationality backgrounds and their class derivations came to be of relatively less importance in evaluating their usefulness. Perhaps in the future a child's capacity to develop will be regarded as an equally valuable asset to the nation, regardless of those currently divisive factors of race and class that now permit the application of variable norms of child care in determining whether he shall be offered opportunities for maximal development.

When the child's needs and rights become the nation's imperative, fewer children will suffer child neglect.

---

[47] *New York Times*, February 2, 1962, p. 10.

Deterioration of the Inner City ▶

LAWRENCE K. NORTHWOOD

The purpose of this paper is to work out a method of analyzing the social conditions that exist in the residential areas adjoining the central business districts of cities. The desired goal is to be able to point to the social conditions that have become, or are likely to become, "social problems." In particular, we are interested in the problems of the "inner city" that are amenable to amelioration or solution by application of professional social work.

To accomplish the assigned task, the following procedure is employed. In the first section of the paper four major concepts are defined in sufficient detail to permit forward movement: social conditions, social problems, social work, and the inner city. In the second section we are plunged into an analysis of empirical studies of social conditions existing in the inner city. The third section is a brief description of the traditional and current interest of organized social welfare in the cause and cure of its social problem conditions. This is followed by two sections that deal analytically with lines of amelioration through what is called "the small-area approach." The fifth section discusses the "housing problem" and some lines of social welfare amelioration. The final section is a brief summary of the findings placed in the framework of directed social change.

DEFINITION OF MAJOR TERMS

Social Conditions

Social conditions usually refer to a steady state of organization of persons, things, events and relationships existing in reality. Since these conditions are produced and modified by mankind, they are called *social conditions*. However, in large part, social conditions are independent of any single individual and his perceptions. They are the "given" in which life occurs. This concept of social conditions is akin to Durkheim's "social facts" and Ruth Benedict's "patterns of culture." [1]

Social Problems

From time to time certain social conditions come to be identified as "social needs" or "social problems." These are the social conditions that cause discomfort to members of a group or threaten the continuance of the group in its steady state of organization. Defined negatively, a need usually refers to a *lack* of something, which lack contributes to the discomfort of members of the group. A problem usually refers to the *presence* of something, which presence contributes to the discomfort of members of the group. The absence of a good thing may be just as deleterious as the presence of a bad thing. The conceptual distinction between a "need" and a "problem" is frequently lost. The distinction, however, is not of great importance in this paper.[2] In any case, it is evident that in order to have a genuine social problem there must be real social conditions, identified as "bad" by some group members. Arnold Rose underlines this point: "The conditions are not inherently good or bad, but people define them as problems or not problems." His definition of social problems would seem to be very useful here:

> Social problems [are] conditions which affect sizeable proportions of the population, which are out of harmony with the values of a significant segment of the population, and which people feel can be improved or eliminated.[3]

I have minor points of disagreement with this definition. For instance, some conditions such as suicide need affect only a few persons to be considered a social problem.

Social Work

In this paper there are comments about social work, social workers, professional social workers, social welfare agencies, social welfare institutions, social services, and the like. I follow the lead of Wilensky and Lebeaux, Kahn, and Cohen in the use of these terms. In general this means that social work is an occupational specialty practiced in

---

[1] Emile Durkheim, *Rules of Sociological Methods;* Ruth Benedict, *Patterns of Culture* (New York: Penguin Books, 1947).

[2] Council on Social Work Education, *Concepts of Prevention and Control; Their Uses in the Social Work Curriculum* (1961) ; Mary E. MacDonald, "Social Work Research: A Perspective," in Norman A. Polansky, ed., *Social Work Research* (Chicago: University of Chicago Press, 1960), p. 11.

[3] Arnold Rose, "Theory for the Study of Social Problems," *Social Problems*, Vol. 4 (1957) pp. 189–199.

social welfare agencies, which are one type of organizational structure for the provision of services broadly grouped together under the term "social welfare institution." [4] The social work functions are these:

> ... in helping individuals in their social roles in all areas of individual and group living. . . . In addition to staffing direct services, social work devotes a substantial proportion of its professional and lay energies to the identification and recognition of needs which emerge in society as a whole or in social subgroups, with changing social conditions. Social work articulates the need, studies its characteristics and its implications. Social work plays its role, along with other professions and citizens at large, in assuring the creation of institutional structures (sometimes but not always social welfare services) for need satisfaction and, where appropriate, assuring legal guarantees of need satisfaction, that is, assuring the translation of needs into rights.[5]

According to this definition, the functions of social work extend beyond the provision of services to individuals and groups who are adversely affected by social problem conditions. It is also the function of social work to attempt to correct these conditions, both by direct services to the client and indirectly by the establishment of policies, laws, and organization for their control and elimination. Social work thus conceived is concerned with directed change and social planning as well as with "help" for the less fortunate and adaptable members of a dysfunctional social system.[6]

Social work is seen as just one segment of the occupational categories within the social welfare institution and is itself divided into specialties based on most usual methods: caseworkers, group workers, community organizers. The term "professional social worker" is restricted to the person who has received a professional degree from an accredited school of social work.

The Inner City

The inner city refers to a zone of land that circles the central business district of the metropolis, extending outward toward the city boundaries.[7] The reference is not to the land per se but to the people who live on the

---

[4] Nathan Cohen, *Social Work in the American Tradition* (New York: Dryden Press, 1958) ; Harold Wilensky and Charles Lebeaux, *Industrial Society and Social Welfare* (New York: Russell Sage Foundation, 1958).

[5] Alfred J. Kahn, ed., *Issues in American Social Work* (New York: Columbia University Press, 1959), pp. 4, 14.

[6] Herman D. Stein, "Implications of Social Change Theory for Social Work Practice and Education," *Proceedings, 1960* (New York: Council on Social Work Education, 1960).

[7] Raymond E. Murphy and J. E. Vance, Jr., in Jack P. Gibbs, *Urban Research Methods* (Princeton, N. J.: D. Van Nostrand Company, 1961).

land, to the residential environment that exists in the area, to the customs, beliefs, practices, and social organization of the people. The edges of the inner city are marked by changes in typical residential land use. The inner edge is found where permanent residences terminate and the commercial and business facilities of the central business district begin. The outer edge is marked by several changes in the residential environment: housing ceases to be deteriorated or blighted, density of habitation and the proportion of land allocated to industrial use decline, open space increases, and so on. The edges of the zone are not regular and equidistant from the center of the city.

From the appearance and the persistence of inner-city zones in almost all American cities of any size it would seem that this zone serves the metropolis in some ways. There is a discussion of this point in a later section. However, few, if any, ties bind the inner city into an interwoven entity. Rather the inner city would seem to be made up of a number of diverse subareas and neighborhoods. It is really a zone of specialized neighborhoods adjacent to the center city, each with functions relating it to the metropolis but which are not necessary to their mutual existence. Ameliorative action in the inner city probably will be specific to a particular subarea rather than to the total, just as social problem conditions may be indigenous to one inner-city locality and not to another.

EMPIRICAL ASSESSMENT OF SOCIAL CONDITIONS [8]

What conditions existing in the inner city have become defined as social problems? This question can be approached empirically, even though the boundaries of the inner city are not exactly specified. The empirical research about the internal structure of cities has been dominated by three hypotheses.[9]

The gradient hypothesis holds that many phenomena increase or decrease continuously in one direction with increasing distance from the center to the periphery. From the findings of research generated by this

---

[8] This section of the paper was prepared with the help of Mrs. Louise Klein, then Research Associate, Segregation and Urban Renewal Project, University of Washington, School of Social Work.

[9] Harold M. Mayer, "What We Need to Know About the Internal Structure of Cities and Metropolitan Areas," in D. J. Bogue, *Needed Urban and Metropolitan Research* (Oxford, Ohio: Miami University, Scripps Foundation for Research in Population Problems, 1953), p. 14; Henry A. Bullock, "Urban Homicide in Theory and Fact," *Journal of Criminal Law and Criminology*, Vol. 45, No. 5 (January–February, 1955), pp. 565–575; Amos H. Hawley, *Human Ecology: A Theory of Community Structure* (New York: Ronald Press, 1950) ; Homer Hoyt, *The Structure and Growth of Residential Neighborhoods in American Cities* (Washington, D. C.: Federal Housing Administration, 1939) ; James A. Quinn, *Human Ecology* (New York: Prentice-Hall, 1950), pp. 100–110, 115–132.

hypothesis the conditions that occur near the center of the city can be identified. This is the starting point of this analysis.[10]

The second, the sector hypothesis, modifies gradient theory to propose that land uses are distributed in particular sectors of the city, especially along lines of transportation. Within the sector, however, the gradient principle is in operation. The sector hypothesis is conceded to require modifications in the gradient hypothesis but not to negate it. Research testing the sector hypothesis in general underlines an earlier comment that the inner city is not a regular concentric doughnut surrounding the central business district but an irregular mass extending in a star-shaped blob along the lines of transportation, outward from the center. The findings, following the sector hypothesis, do not negate the valid use of gradient data to identify conditions in the inner city.

The third hypothesis that has dominated empirical research about the internal structure of cities has been the multiple nucleus hypothesis, which holds that the city tends to be organized around several centers, each of its own type or function. My definition of the inner city as a zone of specialized neighborhoods adjacent to the center partakes of this theory. A great amount of research has attempted to describe the "natural areas," some using anthropological field study methods in a single city, others refined statistical indices on a broad sample. Insofar as these studies are about subareas located in the inner city, they will contribute information to this analysis.[11]

Two shortcomings of the present mode of analysis should be noted. First, the sources consulted largely deal with the United States and with cities of more than 100,000. The findings may therefore pertain only to a highly industrialized private enterprise economy and to cities that have been subjected to waves of in-migration from Europe and rural areas of the United States. Second, the review tends to minimize the contribution of studies by local agencies that have not received national publication. A primary source of information about the inner city is in the work of welfare councils, planning departments, studies of health and education, or of special problems made by local universities or social agencies. Such studies frequently are action-oriented and are rich in detailed information about the inner city gathered over a period of years. These studies are usually judged by criteria that are appropriate and necessary to intercity comparisons. However, it may well be that valid and reliable procedures for local planning purposes

[10] Sven Erik Astrom, "Kaupunkiekologiset Teoriat Ja Historiallinen Todellisuus" (Urban Ecological Theories and Historical Reality), *Suomal Suomi*, Vol. 24, No. 2 (1956), pp. 77–82.

[11] Wendell Bell, "The Utility of the Shevky Typology for the Design of Urban-Sub-Area Field Studies," *Journal of Social Psychology*, Vol. 47 (February 1958), pp. 71–83.

will not meet these broader criteria. In turn, it may well be that measuring devices which must be quite specifically directed to intercity comparisons, to particular theoretical and methodological purposes of broad study, will lack an adequate cutting edge when applied for local planning purposes. If this is so, the present procedure may be appropriate for analysis of social problem conditions but not for evaluation of ameliorative efforts. In any case it should be noted that there is inadequate coverage here of specific local studies of the inner city.

A third limitation on the paper is always unavoidable. No description of conditions in the inner city can be exhaustive. This paper is focusing on conditions for which information was available with reasonable search and also on those of particular interest to the investigator. The conditions are also those that have high incidence in the inner city as contrasted with other sections of the metropolis, principally the residential sections at the outer periphery and in the suburban ring around the center.

Table I is a listing of these conditions found by those who have pursued the gradient hypothesis. The findings that these phenomena generally distribute on a gradient is helpful as "proof" that the conditions exist in the inner city. Once having said this in tabular form, however, I shall move on to a more extensive discussion of conditions classified under three headings: (1) land use in the inner city, (2) people of the inner city, and (3) social control in the inner city. Conditions in a fourth category, namely social welfare facilities and service, are dealt with in detail in the succeeding section.

TABLE I—CONDITIONS ASSOCIATED WITH THE CORE OF THE CITY

Land use:

- High proportions of multifamily dwellings of multiunit lodging for quasi-transient single persons.
- When cleared and rebuilt (relatively few areas nationally), residential structures, either low-income public housing or "high rise" luxury apartments.
- Increasing intensity of construction in central business district— especially office buildings—intensifying traffic and congestion in surrounding residential area.
- Churches losing strength, tending to become service centers.
- School buildings old, often dilapidated.
- Public parks and playgrounds in relatively low ratio to population.
- "Gray areas" of blight increasing, tending to expand to middle zones.
- Housing available to low-income groups old and substandard (except public housing projects).
- Mixed (built up before zoning ordinances in effect).

Population:
- High density resulting in residential crowding.
- High mobility into, out of, and within the area. "Perennial search for better housing."
- Decentralization to middle and suburban areas.
- Relatively high proportions of adults, males, single men and women, fatherless families, foreign born, nonwhites (especially Negroes), low-income earners, poorly educated persons with low-status occupations, unemployed (especially youth).

Social control:
- Informal social participation high in many groups, low in white-collar rooming house areas.
- Participation in organized community improvement activity very low.
- Economic control by absentee landowners.
- Effective planning by city governments not made or not carried out.
- Relatively high rates of juvenile delinquency, adult crime, organized vice, suicide, physical illness, mental illness (especially schizophrenia), family disorganization.

Land Use

In this section we are concerned primarily with residency and with those other land uses that encroach on and downgrade residential use.

Types of structure

RESIDENTIAL. Multiple-unit housing is the rule in the inner city. One study, for example, found that 24 percent of the residential structures in the inner census tracts were single-family dwellings as against 90 percent in an outer zone. Another found multifamily dwellings "concentrated in dense aggregations" near the hearts of five cities and tending to expand outward along lines of transportation.[12]

In addition to multifamily dwellings, there is the housing that caters to transients and to single men and women. According to Hayner, for example, "the deteriorated area around the central business district is characterized by the cheap lodging house and white-collar rooming house."[13]

---

[12] Calvin F. Schmid, *Social Saga of Two Cities: An Ecological and Statistical Study of Social Trends in Minneapolis and St. Paul* (Minneapolis: The Minneapolis Council of Social Agencies, 1937), pp. 200–202; Harland Bartholomew, *Urban Land Uses* (Cambridge, Mass.: (Harvard University Press, 1932), maps between pp. 22–23, 38–39, 50–51.

[13] Norman S. Hayner, *Hotel Life* (Chapel Hill, N. C.: University of North Carolina Press, 1936).

COMMERCIAL. Declining growth rates and obsolescence in the residential portions of the inner city are not being reflected in the central business district in which vitality continues and intensity of land use is increasing. Although manufacturing and distributing industries tend to leave the downtown areas in favor of more space and lower tax rates in the suburbs, those activities that are oriented toward interorganizational, face-to-face communication (elite decision making, trade in volatile money markets, sale of the unstandardized products, etc.) are gravitating to central locations. Hence commercial land use in the form of office buildings is increasing.[14]

Obsolescence. The existence of blighted "gray" areas between the commercial core and the outlying zones and suburbs has been documented by nearly every writer on the American urban scene. A few references are cited here by way of example only.[15]

Glenn H. Beyer, one of the leading authorities in the field of housing research, defines three concentric belts of which the inmost, containing the oldest housing and worst slums, and the middle belt, containing deteriorating middle-aged housing, together "form much of the basis of the need for urban renewal." [16]

Vernon notes that the slums have a population cycle of their own which follows the earlier exodus of nonslum dwellers. The slums spread to the middle zones rather than to the periphery. Thus the trend toward obsolescence expands. He sees no end to this "gray area" growth unless (1) middle-income families decide to return to the city in great numbers or (2) subsidized governmental intervention such as low-income housing is undertaken on an unprecedented scale.[17] Urban redevelopment has thus far not begun to reverse the trend of increasing blight in the inner city. Catherine Bauer Wurster tells us that

> the over-all rate of progress can hardly equal the rate of obsolescence thus far, and has not even begun to affect the middle-class exodus. Since 1950 about 15,000 acres of slums and blight have been acquired

---

[14] Miles L. Colean, *Renewing Our Cities* (New York: The Twentieth Century Fund, 1953), pp. 20–21; Raymond Vernon, *The Changing Economic Function of the Central City* (New York: Committee for Economic Development, 1959), p. 61; Arthur Dunham, "The Outlook for Community Development," *The Social Welfare Forum*, 1958, pp. 33–42, 48–49; George Sternlieb, "Is Business Abandoning the Big City?" *Harvard Business Review*, Vol. 39, No. 1 (January–February 1961).

[15] Rose Hum Lee, *The City, Urbanism and Urbanization in Major World Regions* (Philadelphia: J. B. Lippincott Company, 1955), pp. 473–486; Catherine Bauer Wurster, "Framework for an Urban Society in Goals for Americans," *The Report of the President's Commission on National Goals* (Englewood Cliffs, N. J.: Prentice-Hall, 1960), pp. 229–230; Colean, *op. cit.*, pp. 3–4, 64–66.

[16] Glenn H. Beyer, *Housing: A Factual Analysis* (New York: Macmillan Company, 1958).

[17] Vernon, *op. cit.*, pp. 42, 61–62.

for redevelopment and public housing, but several hundred thousand acres would be cleared. Perhaps a million and a half substandard houses have been demolished (only a fraction through renewal efforts), but up to 10 million more remain.[18]

The single factor that, far more than any other, is responsible for substandard conditions in the inner city is the lack of standard housing available to low-income groups. Some 60 to 70 percent of the population is simply priced out of today's housing market.[19] Catherine Bauer Wurster tells us further: "[The necessary] rate of construction cannot be achieved if the market for new housing remains limited to the top 30 to 40 percent of the population (less in high density development), with a tiny volume of public housing (2.5 percent of new construction in 1959) at the bottom." [20]

The residential quality of the inner city is impaired not only by structural deterioration but by the mixed nature of land use before the area was built up and controls such as zoning ordinances were put into effect. Obsolescence is further reflected in the sharp drops in land values proceeding outward from the central business district. One author visualizes Chicago land values in terms of a relief map with "the Himalayan Peaks" at the center surrounded by the "deep valleys of the blighted areas" (beyond which the relief terrain rises again).[21] Another finds drops of 80 percent within a quarter of a mile of the highest value in New York and within a half mile in Chicago.[22]

Traffic. Those who could afford it have escaped these blighting influences by moving outward, but these same people who must cross the inner city daily to work and do business in the central business district create a traffic problem that further intensifies misuse of land. Not only is there heavy traffic flow, but land in the inner city is

---

[18] Wurster, *op. cit.*, p. 230.

[19] Each year the National Housing Conference conducts a survey of the costs of housing. The national median price for a three-bedroom home in 1959 was $10,990. This assessment is based on a sample of twenty-five cities. The minimum annual income necessary to purchase the median home was estimated at $6,617. At that time only 29 percent of the nation's families could afford to purchase the median home. Monthly rental for an equivalent three-bedroom apartment in 1959 required $137.50. To afford this rent according to proper household budgeting, the family income had to be $8,250 per year. The full results of the survey are published in the *1959 Yearbook of the National Housing Conference* (Washington D.C.: National Housing Conference, 1959).

[20] Wurster, *op. cit.*, p. 235.

[21] R. D. McKenzie, *The Metropolitan Community* (New York: McGraw-Hill Book Company, 1933), p. 234.

[22] Homer Hoyt, *One Hundred Years of Land Values in Chicago* (Chicago: University of Chicago Libraries [distributors], 1933), pp. 297–298; McKenzie, *op. cit.*, p. 234.

usurped to create parking space unavailable in the central business district. According to the editors of *Fortune,* residents of the few cities in the country in which most downtown travel is by public transportation "may find it hard to appreciate how heavily most other American cities are dominated by the automobile . . . in fifteen of the nation's largest cities, 60 percent or more of all riders entering the downtown business district arrive by automobile." [23] Thus those whose fate it is to live in the inner city occupy land that is hazardous and congested as well as subject to other forms of blight.

Cultural and social welfare. The inner city is not an area of strong churches. Although the downtown church in the city center tends to develop a city-wide character, in the surrounding areas churches tend to die, to follow their escaping members, or, not infrequently, to become service centers to fill the needs of the new, less privileged population. [24] Schools tend to be dilapidated. Conant tells us that "the contrast in money available to the schools in a wealthy suburb and to the schools in a large city jolts one's notions of the meaning of equality of opportunity . . . (a) significant contrast is provided by looking at the school facilities . . . in the suburb there is likely to be a spacious modern school . . . in the slum one finds a crowded, often dilapidated and unattractive school. . ." [25] The inner city typically has a smaller ratio of public parks and playgrounds to population than have outlying districts. [26] On the other hand, private recreational facilities cater to poorer districts much as do stores. For example, one study found a taxi-dance hall located characteristically in or near Chicago's inner city area. [27] Social welfare services and facilities are the subject of the next part of the paper and so are not reviewed here.

Population

In this section there is a brief description of the characteristics of the population, its size and density, mobility and movements.

Size and density. Various studies have found that inner city areas have the highest density of population. For example, in one study all census tracts in the three higher of seven categories of density were found to lie well toward the center of the city. [28] In another, twelve of

---

[23] *The Exploding Metropolis* (Garden City, N. Y.: The Editors of *Fortune,* Doubleday and Company, 1958), p. 37.

[24] Quinn, *op. cit.,* pp. 100–110, 115–132.

[25] James B. Conant, *Slums and Suburbs* (New York: McGraw-Hill Book Company, 1961), p. 72.

[26] Quinn, *op. cit.,* pp. 484–485.

[27] Paul G. Cressey, *The Taxi-Dance Hall* (Chicago: University of Chicago Press, 1932), pp. 224–233.

[28] Howard Whipple Green, *An Analysis of Population on Data by Census Tracts*

thirteen census tracts in the highest of five categories of density were located close to the center.[29]

Heterogeneity of population

1. Within this dense cluster of people is a great diversity: first, there is a high proportion of males. The lodging houses and institutions that serve homeless men, both migratory transients and older down-and-outers, are located here. One study found a heavy proportion of males over twenty years of age, a smaller proportion of women, and few children.[30]

2. It follows from the analyses of age-sex structure that married couples, especially those with children, do not gravitate to the inner city in the same proportions as they do to other sections. Colean notes a corollary observation that "in their recent expansion, suburban areas have attracted numerous families of moderate means, mainly young families with children. . . ." Nevertheless, there are more than enough families of less than moderate means who cannot afford this escape. Among those that are confined to the inner city many are not intact. Usually it is the father who has deserted or the children are illegitimate and the mother is struggling to bring the family up on her own.[31]

3. Percentages of foreign-born whites have tended to be greatest in the inner city.[32] Historically, the inner city has served as the point of departure of immigrants to other parts of the city and elsewhere. This diffusion process sometimes has taken a generation or more. The minority neighborhood is crystallized at the crest of the immigration with the appearance of the foreign-language press and many institutions transplanted from the "Old Country." As the children become Americanized and move away, the minority neighborhood gradually dissolves. Many inner city areas have had a succession of immigrant groups pass through, generation by generation.[33]

4. Negroes from the southeastern United States and Puerto Ricans are the latest newcomers to arrive in the inner city in large numbers. There is no major city in the United States that did not have a growing Negro population in 1960.[34] The percentage of Negroes in each of the

---

with Location Index, Cleveland and Vicinity (Cleveland: Cleveland Health Council, 1927), p. 8.

[29] Quinn, op. cit., p. 434.

[30] McKenzie, op. cit., pp. 180–182; Quinn, op. cit., p. 438.

[31] Ernest R. Mowrer, Family Disorganization (Chicago: University of Chicago Press, 1927), pp. 109–223, and The Family (Chicago: University of Chicago Press, 1932), pp. 187–194; Colean, op. cit., p. 20.

[32] Quinn, op. cit., pp. 438–439.

[33] Paul F. Cressey, The Succession of Cultural Groups, Ph.D. thesis, University of Chicago, 1930; Quinn, op. cit.

[34] Donald O. Cowgill, "Trends in Residential Segregation of Nonwhites in American Cities, 1940–1950," American Sociological Review, Vol. 21, No. 1 (February

central cities in the twelve largest metropolitan areas was New York (14), Los Angeles (12), Chicago (22.9), Philadelphia (26.4), Detroit (28.9), San Francisco (14.3), Boston (9.1), Pittsburgh (16.7), St. Louis (28.6), Washington (53.9), Cleveland (28.6), and Baltimore (34.8). That most nonwhites, especially Negroes, live in the inner city is exemplified in a study that found the Negro population heavily concentrated near the heart of the city, with the percentage dropping from more than 40 to less than 3 within a distance of three miles out.[35] Banfield and Grodzins speak of the "racial schism" between the central, especially inner, cities and the suburbs.[36]

5. The low-income status of residents in the obsolescent areas of cities contrasts with the high incomes of residents in those few areas that have been rebuilt. Besides building for commercial use, the little reconstruction that has taken place in inner city areas has consisted of either low-income public housing or "high rise" luxury apartment dwellings. Thus, in Colean's words, "the central city under present circumstances tends to become a locale of the rich and the poor, with the middle group—particularly families with small children—finding its way to suburbia." Needless to say, although a slum and a "gold coast" may be adjacent to one another, segregation on the basis of income is the rule in residential patterns.[37] The presence of low-income residents in disconcerting numbers in the central city while the bulk of middle- and upper-income groups pay taxes in the suburbs (though earning their living in the city) results in staggering municipal services and financing problems. The blighted inner city is the locale in which low income reaches its nadir.[38]

6. Population characteristics have been combined into composite indices for area analysis which epitomize the diversity found in the

1956), pp. 43–47; Morton Grodzins, "Metropolitan Segregation," *Scientific American*, Vol. 197, No. 4 (April 1957), pp. 33–41; John T. Howard, "Future Metropolitan Growth and Planning," *Annals of the American Academy of Political and Social Science*, Vol. 313 (September 1957), pp. 32–37; Harry Sharp, "Race as a Factor in Metropolitan Growth; 1930–1960." Paper presented in New York City at the 1961 meetings of the Population Association of America. Detroit Area Study, Survey Research Center, University of Michigan, Project 870, May 1960; Philip M. Hauser, "Urban Boom and Crisis in the Sixties," speech prepared for the International Municipal Assembly, the U. S. Conference of Mayors, Chicago, May 1960.

[35] Quinn, *op. cit.*, pp. 438–439.

[36] Edward C. Banfield and Morton Grodzins, *Government and Housing in Metropolitan Areas* (New York: McGraw-Hill Book Company, 1938), p. 24.

[37] Colean, *op. cit.*, pp. 15–16.

[38] Nelson Foote *et al.*, *Housing Choices and Housing Constraints* (New York: McGraw-Hill Book Company, 1960), pp. 122–123; Robert K. Merton and Robert A. Nisbet, *Contemporary Social Problems* (New York: Harcourt, Brace & World, 1961), p. 633; William W. Nash, *Residential Rehabilitation: Private Profits and Public Purposes* (New York: McGraw-Hill Book Company, 1959), p. 235.

city. One of these, known as "urbanization," contrasts areas character-ized by many apartments, families with few children, and families with working wives (high urbanization), with areas characterized by single-family dwellings, many children, and nonworking wives. This index has been found to vary concentrically, which means, of course, that the inner city is highly "urbanized." [39]

Mobility. The diversity of the inner city may be intensified by the high residential mobility rates in the inner city. This mobility is of two sorts. First, the inner city serves as a "port of entry" for im-migrants from other countries or other cities and regions of the United States. Some of these people sooner or later find their way to other parts of the city, some remain. Second, in the words of Foote *et al.*, the search for better housing is a "perennial center-city quest, even among families established in it." They note further that "though the slum-dweller moves whenever he can in search of better housing, he does not move far." [40]

Decentralization. A long-range decentralizing shift in city structure has been apparent for several decades. Cities have been steadily declining in rates of population growth in relation to surrounding metropolitan areas, and inner zones of cities have been declining in relation to outer zones. First to move outward were the higher income classes, motivated by a desire for outdoor space, escape from obsolescence and antisocial activity, and by improved transportation which made working in the city and living out of it possible. More recently, families of more moderate means have joined in the exodus. Trade and industry have followed or grown up to meet suburban needs and this intensifies the trend.

This decline in population growth does not mean that there is a lessening in crowding and congestion in living conditions in the inner city (reported above under Density). In only a few cases has the decline so far been absolute—population still increases but space in-creases only with outward creeping obsolescence. In the second place the inner-city residential areas are constantly being squeezed by pres-

---

[39] Theodore R. Anderson and Janice A. Egeland, "Spatial Aspects of Social Area Analysis," *American Sociological Review,* Vol. 26, No. 3 (June 1961), pp. 392–398; Christen T. Jonassen, "Functional Unities in Eighty-eight Community Systems," *ibid.,* pp. 399–407.

[40] Fern M. Colborn, "Bulletin on Urban Renewal" (New York: National Fed-eration of Settlements and Neighborhood Centers, 1936); Howard Whipple Green, *Movements of Families within the Cleveland Metropolitan District* (Cleveland: Real Property Inventory of Metropolitan Cleveland, 1934; George Henderson, "Twelfth Street: An Analysis of a Changed Neighborhood" (Detroit Urban League, 1961) (Mimeographed); Quinn, *op. cit.;* Thomas Trevor, "San Francisco's Hous-ing Market—Open or Closed?" (San Francisco: Council for Civic Unity, 1960).

sures from the central business district which is growing in size. In some cases the recent influx of nonwhites has counteracted the decline of inner zones, at least temporarily.[41]

It is principally the white population that has participated in the great exodus. The proportion of whites in outlying areas has changed little, whereas nonwhites immigrating from other regions have invaded the vacuum left by whites and brought about enormous changes in the white-nonwhite ratios of the inner areas. Nonwhites are now exhibiting a decentralization pattern of their own but mainly to the middle zones rather than the suburbs.[42]

Although some Negro families are moving into predominantly white residential areas in central city and suburbs, for the most part the practices of discrimination and segregation are effectively containing the Negro and other colored minorities in the inner city.[43] Most Negro families have inadequate regular income to acquire dwellings in other areas, but even with adequate income, the structure of the housing market is such that the Negro is discriminated against by the sellers of housing and their agents, the mortgage and financing industry, and by sections of the public at large. This situation pertains to other minority races as well but not so stringently.

Social Control

The inner city has frequently been characterized as lacking in social controls.[44] A report on recent research in participation and anomie, economic controls, and various indices of social breakdown, such as juvenile delinquency and crime, is presented in this section. Some of the points raised here are elaborated elsewhere in the paper.

[41] Richard W. Redick, "Population Growth and Distribution in Central Cities, 1940–1950," *American Sociological Review*, Vol. 21, No. 1 (February 1956), pp. 39–42; Violet M. Sieder, ed., "The Stake of Social Work in Urban Renewal" (New York School of Social Work, Columbia University, 1957); Colean, *op. cit.*, pp. 17–20; Quinn, *op. cit.*, pp. 346–347.

[42] Sharp, *op. cit.*

[43] Charles Abrams, *Forbidden Neighbors* (New York: Harper & Brothers, 1955); Thomas L. Gillette, "A Study of the Effects of Negro Invasion on Real Estate Values," *American Journal of Economic Sociology*, Vol. 16, No. 2 (January 1957), pp. 151–162; Luigi Laurenti, *Property Values and Race: Studies in Seven Cities* (Berkeley: University of California Press, 1960), pp. 3–64; Albert Mayer, "Can City Planners and Social Planners Get Together?" Paper presented at the Fortieth Conference of NAIRO, Chicago, 1957; Davis McEntire, *Residence and Race: Final and Comparative Report to the Commission on Race and Housing* (Berkeley: University of California Press, 1959), and "Government and Racial Discrimination in Housing," *Journal of Social Issues*, Vol. 13, No. 4 (1957), pp. 60–67; Stuart H. Palmer, "The Role of the Real Estate Agent in the Structuring of Residential Areas." Ph.D. thesis, Yale University, 1955.

[44] James S. Coleman, *Community Conflict* (Glencoe, Ill.: The Free Press, 1957).

Participation and anomie. In considering participation different types must be distinguished. One consists of the informal social life of kinship, friendship, and neighboring groups. A high degree of this kind of participation characterizes parts of the inner city. Thus Foote *et al.* note the "striking finding" that the slum-dweller is not anxious to leave the slum, despite the miserable conditions under which he lives, and they attribute this reluctance in part to the fact that leaving would mean abandoning "a flourishing social life with neighborly assistance to be had in times of stress." An exception to this condition is found in the white-collar rooming-house areas. Roomers in these areas are usually single men and women, without kinship or strong social ties who seldom interact with one another and are inclined to be isolated, anonymous, and mutually distrustful.[45]

A special subtype of this informal participation occurs in the cultural ghetto in which recent immigrants are held together by a common language, common customs, the mutual aid of ingroup members in a new setting, and discrimination from without.[46]

In a second type of participation residents of the inner city remain in the slums as clients of the welfare services. Foote *et al.* note that among the resources that slum-dwellers are reluctant to leave are the city services, such as free public health service, with which they are thoroughly familiar.[47] Banfield enlarges on this fact by noting the extent to which poor people in depressed areas are sometimes "taken care of" with jobs, favors, and protection by the local precinct social system. In this sense the inner city resident participates as the client of the politician.[48]

On the other hand, participation as a client in a free or low-cost service contradicts the American principle of self-reliance and consequently is frequently rejected even when it is available and potentially helpful. In a study of sixty-two tenement-house families few were found to have used nursing and family services, even though substantial proportions knew of their existence. Reasons most frequently given were that they objected to accepting "charity" or having to "depend on somebody else." More had used health services, but many did so only in

---

[45] Harvey W. Zorbaugh, *The Gold Coast and the Slum: A Sociological Study of Chicago's Near North Side* (Chicago: University of Chicago Press, 1929); Foote *et al., op. cit.*

[46] Lee, *op. cit.,* pp. 292–298; Herbert J. Gans, *The Urban Villagers, Group and Class in the Life of Italian Americans* (New York: The Free Press of Glencoe, 1962). See especially Part 2.

[47] Foote *et al., op. cit.*

[48] Edward C. Banfield, "The Political Implications of Metropolitan Growth," *Daedalus,* Vol. 90, No. 1; *Proceedings of the American Academy of Arts and Sciences* (Winter 1961), p. 70; Stephen Fleck, "Recognition and Utilization of the Motivation of Volunteers," *Mental Hygiene,* Vol. 41 (1947), pp. 222–227.

case of extreme need. Besides avoidance of "charity," the subjects tended to feel that the health services were too impersonal and that they did not want family service social workers "interfering" with their lives. It is further pointed out that there are two sides to the coin of the "rentless self-reliance" principle. Potential clients avoid community resources which might help them, but evidence also exists that successful members of society remain bystanders, partly in the belief that in the interests of his self-respect a poor man has a right *not* to be helped. It may be considered that one of the conditions of the inner city is the unconcern and inaction of the bystander outside who does nothing to contribute to the solution of its problem conditions.[49]

In a third type of participation the resident takes part as a leader or member of a formal or informal action-oriented (as distinguished from social-oriented) organization. (The concern here, of course, is with organizations devoted to community and social welfare.) Of this kind of participation there is a greater dearth in the inner city. Studies show that participation of this type is negatively correlated with low income, low education, low-status occupation, low social class, and not having school age children—all conditions characterizing the inner city.[50]

Another institutionalized contributing factor to nonparticipation in voluntary organizations deserves more attention than it has received. This is the prevalence of the service-client type of participation—or at least of the philosophy that it is the suitable source of help for poor people. This relationship by its nature inhibits the development of community-action programs. When a client has received the particular service he applied for, the service-client relation is terminated. Thus no sequence of such relations builds up into an organized program to tackle the larger problems on an ongoing basis. The service agency workers and the client never become peers and co-workers. There is also the reason suggested above that the potential leader is a bystander. According to Bredemeier and Toby, "those members of slum communities with the ability to organize neighborhood improvements do not perceive this as their responsibility. (They are more likely to move out of a blighted area than to try to arrest the blight.)"[51]

For all of these reasons such participation as is characteristic of the

[49] Earl L. Koos, *Families in Trouble* (New York: King's Crown Press, 1946), pp. 79–85.

[50] W. A. Anderson, "Family Social Participation and Social Status Self-Ratings," *American Sociological Review*, Vol. 11 (June 1946), p. 253; Stuart F. Chapin, "Social Participation and Intelligence," *ibid.*, Vol. 4 (April 1939), p. 161; Mirra Komarovsky, "The Voluntary Association of Urban Dwellers," *ibid.*, Vol. 11 (December 1946).

[51] Harry Bredemeier and Jackson Toby, *Social Problems in America* (New York: John Wiley and Sons, 1960), p. 221.

inner city does not serve to make it in any sense an autonomously functioning unit or assembly of such units. Rather, a condition of anomie characterizes the area as a whole and a great many of its residents.

Economic control

TYPE OF OWNERSHIP. As is well known, inner-city residents do not as a rule control the land and housing they occupy. They stand at the mercy of absentee owners who willingly collect rents but are unwilling to improve substandard property in deteriorating surroundings. Various researchers have found areas of least owner occupancy occurring near the hearts of cities.[52]

EXTENT OF PLANNING. In an area characterized by anomie citizen participation in planning for the development or improvement of the area would not be expected. What, however, of general city planners? Banfield points out that in the American political arena "those in authority seldom try to make or impose comprehensive solutions." A mayor, for example, waits for private groups to agree on a project and get their plans accepted by a city council. And what private groups undertake and succeed in this? Certainly not those in the inner city! Banfield asserts that plan making is for Americans an idle exercise because they neither agree on the content of a "public interest" that ought to override private ones nor permit the centralization of authority needed to carry plans into effect.[53]

Breakdown of social control

JUVENILE DELINQUENCY. Various studies of the distribution of juvenile delinquency have found the highest rates (except for automobile theft) in the slum areas around centers of business and industry. Such areas are most often located in the innermost zones. For example, results for nineteen cities show higher rates in the inner zones, and in all but three of these the rates also declined regularly from innermost to outermost zones.[54] Conant considers the widespread and growing unemployment of youth out of school and under age 21 to be an extremely serious factor contributing to delinquency. He refers to this condition as "social dynamite." [55]

---

[52] Quinn, *op. cit.*, pp. 466, 468.

[53] Banfield and Grodzins, *op. cit.*, p. 71.

[54] Clifford R. Shaw and Henry D. McKay, "Social Factors in Juvenile Delinquency," *National Commission on Law Observance and Enforcement, Report on Causes of Crime,* Vol. 2 (Washington, D. C.: U. S. Government Printing Office, 1931) ; Shaw, McKay *et al., Juvenile Delinquency in Urban Areas* (Chicago: University of Chicago Press, 1942) ; Frederic M. Thrasher, *The Gang* (Chicago: University of Chicago Press, 1927).

[55] Conant, *op. cit.*, pp. 33–35.

CRIME. The distribution of adult crime is similar to that of juvenile delinquency, except that adult criminals are somewhat more mobile and in particular may operate in the main business district as well as in the "transition zone" around it. Schmid, for example, defines a "central segment" comprising the main business district and contiguous areas in which he finds a heavy concentration of crime. (These statements do not include white-collar crime which shows a reverse distribution.) [56]

VICE. As might be expected, organized vice is also concentrated in the inner city. Gambling and prostitution which may be found beyond the suburban fringes are prevalent in the inner city as well. Other forms of vice are strictly inner-city phenomena.[57]

SUICIDE. Studies of the distribution of suicide show highest rates in the inner zones of cities. Suicide is reported to reach its highest density in the mobile, anonymous rooming-house type of population.[58]

MENTAL ILLNESS. The evidence from studies of the distribution of mental illness shows marked concentration of all types of psychosis in the inner-city zones. This is particularly true of schizophrenia, which shows a much narrower distribution and a clearer concentric pattern than the manic-depressive disorders.[59]

FAMILY DISORGANIZATION. Family disorganization is common in the inner city. Mowrer, for example, notes, among other things, that desertion, the "poor man's divorce," characterizes low-income areas.[60]

HEALTH. The conditions of poor sanitation, poor heating and ventilation, fire and other hazards that are rife in crowded, dilapidated housing are inimical to the fundamental requirements of a healthful residential environment.[61]

In the next part of the paper we turn to an assessment of a group of social conditions not yet covered—those under the heading of social services and facilities.

[56] Calvin F. Schmid, "Urban Crime Areas; Part II," *American Sociological Review*, Vol. 25, No. 5 (October 1960), p. 655; Quinn, *op. cit.*, pp. 493–494.

[57] Walter C. Reckless, *Vice in Chicago* (Chicago: University of Chicago Press, 1933), pp. 166–167.

[58] Ruth Shonle Cavan, *Suicide* (Chicago: University of Chicago Press, 1929); Ernest R. Mowrer, *Disorganization, Personal and Social* (Philadelphia: J. B. Lippincott Company, 1942), p. 348.

[59] H. Warren Dunham, "Current Status of Ecological Research in Mental Disorders," *Social Forces*, Vol. 25 (March 1947), pp. 321–327; R. E. L. Faris and H. Warren Dunham, *Mental Disorders in Urban Areas: An Ecological Study of Schizophrenia and Other Psychoses* (Chicago: University of Chicago Press, 1939).

[60] Mowrer, *Family Disorganization*, *op. cit.*, pp. 109–123; *The Family*, *op. cit.*, pp. 187–194.

[61] World Health Organization, Expert Committee on the Public Health Aspects of Housing, Technical Report Series No. 225, Geneva, 1961, pp. 17–33.

RECOGNITION OF SOCIAL PROBLEMS BY SOCIAL WELFARE

To what extent, traditionally and currently, has organized social welfare recognized the conditions that exist in the inner city as social problems appropriate to their work? This is the question to which this section of the paper is addressed.

American social work is usually traced back to origins in the Elizabethan Poor Laws in England of the seventeenth century. A brief excursion into the history of social welfare organization will point out that from then on great emphasis has been placed on local responsibility for "problem solving." Social welfare has had great interest for a long time in housing and neighborhood life in the inner city. Two of the most prominent pioneers in social work have pursued these problems— Mary Richmond in describing some of the origins of social casework and Jane Addams in describing some of the origins of group work.[62] Some of their writings are examined briefly, and an account of current social work emphasis is summarized under four headings: (1) crisis programs, (2) local facilities, (3) minority neighborhoods, and (4) community development.[63]

The intention in this chapter is to document the position that the presence of extensive social welfare organization is prima facie evidence of recognition of social problem conditions in the inner city.

When the Elizabethan Poor Laws were first enacted in 1601, the local community was assigned the responsibility of organizing and financing relief and sustenance for the handicapped, the unemployable, and children and to provide work for the able-bodied. At first the local community was empowered with the right to return to their former residences any newcomers who might become public charges at some time in the future. Thus the city could rid itself of costly boarders on public relief. However, these stringent regulations were gradually modified, and newcomers were accepted for public relief after a waiting period, for a tem-

---

[62] Mary E. Richmond, *The Long View* (New York: Russell Sage Foundation, 1930) ; Jane Addams, *Twenty Years at Hull House* (Signet Classic CT 85, 1961).

[63] Harry C. Bredemeier, "The Federal Public Housing Movement: A Case Study of Social Change." Ph.D. thesis, Columbia University, 1955; Frank Bruno, *Trends in Social Welfare* (New York: Columbia University Press, 1948) ; Nathan Cohen, *op. cit.*; Walter A. Friedlander, *Introduction to Social Welfare*, 2d ed. (Englewood Cliffs, N. J.: Prentice-Hall, 1961) ; John B. Hill, "Fifty Years of Social Action on the Housing Front," *Social Service Review*, Vol. 22, No. 2 (June 1948), pp. 160–179; Gisela Konopka, *Eduard C. Lindeman and Social Work Philosophy* (Minneapolis: University of Minnesota Press, 1958) ; Charles Madge, "Survey of Community Facilities and Services in the United Kingdom," *Town and City Planning Bulletin*, Vol. 1, p. 31; Lorene M. Pacey, *Readings in the Development of Settlement Work* (New York: Association Press, 1950).

porary period, or with some other stipulation. In any case, cities gradually began to care for most persons in need, whether they were born there or not. The principles and practices established in Great Britain carried over into colonial America and became one of the foundation stones (or should one say millstones) on which current public practice is based.

The typical device employed by most local communities to comply with the provisions of the Poor Laws was to give "indoor relief" in a public workhouse, where men, women, and children were forced to live and work to pay for their keep. But conditions were so appalling in terms of infant mortality, sickness, brutality, immorality, graft, and squalor that public protest forced their modification and, ultimately, their discontinuance in most localities. After this, "outdoor relief" was provided to those willing and able to work while they remained in their own homes.

The movement to "outdoor relief" served to focus attention on community conditions and offered a challenge to the then current belief that poverty was the personal fault of the poor brought on by their congenital defects or by indolence, gambling, drink, vice, or at least mismanagement. Local charities, both public and private, sent "friendly visitors" into the homes of the relief recipients to help them organize their lives so that they would no longer remain public charges. This excursion probably was more enlightening to the visitor than the visited.

> The visitors found that there were other factors that caused destitution, when they became more intimately acquainted with the conditions of their families. They recognized that unhealthy neighborhood and housing conditions prevented the maintenance of health and morals, that low wages did not allow the purchase of adequate food and clothes even with careful housekeeping and thrift. Jobs were scarce in periods of economic depressions, and it was not the fault of the unemployed worker that he could not find a new position. In times of sickness or unemployment, families became the victims of "loan sharks" who caused them to go into debt for years by charging high interest and heartlessly demanding money. Others lost their meager savings by fraud.
>
> The practical experiences of the visitors thus revealed that the concept of individual fault did not stand the test of honest analysis. They began to ask for measures which would fundamentally change those social conditions, and became advocates of social reform. In order to implement the findings of their members, Charity Organization Societies became active in promoting social legislation for improvement of housing, clearance of slums, and better enforcement of tenement legislation, as well as in measures for prevention and treatment of tuberculosis, widespread among the poverty-stricken

classes. Some societies established employment bureaus, loan societies, workshops, laundries, lumberyards, wayfarers' lodges and shelters, and legal-aid bureaus.[64]

From this brief account it is apparent that for some time public agencies have been concerned with the problems of the inner city and the impoverished residents who came there to look for work and for other reasons. The "friendly visitor" movement is also credited with having profound effects on the development of social casework by private agencies. This process is vividly described by Mary Richmond in her account of the work of Octavia Hill, whom she considers as one of the two persons "pre-eminent [in her] influence upon social casework in America." This brief account brings out necessary interrelationships between social casework, community organization, welfare policy, social action, and research.

> . . . The Hills had arranged to have a gathering in their kitchen of the poorer women of the neighborhood once a week, and help them then in cutting out and making clothes. "One night," Octavia's sister Emily reports, "one of the women fainted; and we found out that she had been up all the previous night washing, while she rocked her baby's cradle with her foot. Next day Octavia went to the woman's home, and found her living in a damp, unhealthy kitchen." Miss Hill applied at many places in search of healthier quarters for this tenant, but at none would they take a family with children. This unhappy incident was fresh in her mind when she paid one of her regular visits to Ruskin to receive his instruction. His father had died not long before, and he began complaining to her of the responsibilities of the fortune that had just been left him. Miss Hill at once suggested the provision of better houses for the poor as a good way of spending one's money, and showed such a practical grasp of the problems involved that Ruskin agreed to finance her plans; adding, however, that, though he did not care for the money, he expected her to realize 5 percent on the investment, because only so could others be induced to follow his example.
>
> Accordingly, in 1864, three houses were purchased in one of the worst courts in Marylebone, and six others were added a little later, with ten more in 1869. Out of this small experiment grew a plan for better housing management which extended to many parts of London, to other cities of the United Kingdom, and to the United States. Before Miss Hill's death in 1912 she had become the recognized authority not only on better housing and open spaces but on the development of volunteer service in social work.
>
> It would have been comparatively easy to have torn down existing houses, to have put up model tenements and filled them with model

---

[64] Stephen Fleck, "Recognition and Utilization of the Motivation of Volunteers," *Mental Hygiene*, Vol. 41, No. 2 (April 1957), pp. 222–227.

tenants, but this was not Miss Hill's way. The inhabitants and their surroundings, she felt, must be improved together, and this must be done gradually. In other words, this was a case work job; for one perfectly good definition of social case work is the development of the character and welfare of the individual through adjustments effected between him (or her) and his social surroundings. Sometimes the surroundings need to be radically changed, sometimes the person needs to be, but more often a change, to be permanent, must be effected in both.

The story of Octavia Hill's attempt to be a good landlord in those early years to tenants who were sullen and hostile at first should be studied in her own graphic account of dark staircases, of banisters burned for firewood, of violent quarrels between the tenants, of doors locked against the rent collector, of sodden despair and neglect. And yet, in a year's time the effects of her steady and resourceful rule became apparent. People were helped by every sort of ingenuity to keep out of debt, to meet their own fundamental obligations, and then, by training here, a chance of better work there, by visits to the country, an invitation, a gift of flowers, the loan of a book, new interests and ambitions came to them, and their true worth became known. They were not *thrust* up and out of their former selves only to drop back again when the helping hand was removed, but the whole process was a *partnership* process, which you will find described in very simple and convincing terms in *Homes of the London Poor* published half a century ago. . . .

In social work it is only the long views that are cheering. Thus, we are still engaged in a running fight with many casualties to assure in New York the better housing to which Octavia Hill devoted a lifetime of service. The battle for tenement house reform begun by the Charity Organization Society in Mrs. Lowell's time still goes on. Gains have been made in many directions, however, that would cheer her heart. Thus, in a census study that we have just made here in Gramercy District, where we are meeting today, the children of school age that are in school made a better showing than did Manhattan as a whole, though Gramercy is a poor district and overwhelmingly a foreign one. Credit for this belongs in part to the fact that there are many social workers in the neighborhood and that they are making a great point of keeping the children in school. Then no longer can children be taken out of school prematurely and put to work, and when they do go to work the working conditions are much better than they were formerly. But there are far too many street accidents. Whereas 33 children were killed outright hereabouts in street accidents during the last year, a recreation pier, taken away from the children during the European War has never been restored to them by the city. We find that it is being used at the present time to store street-cleaning apparatus.[65]

---

[65] Richmond, *op. cit.*, pp. 575–577.

No account of the social welfare interest in the inner city and its problems would be appropriate without reference to the settlement house movement. The step from friendly visiting in deprived areas to the establishment of settlement houses, with the worker living in the area herself, was not a long one. However, it marked a significant change in the rapid growth of cities. Jane Addams wrote of reasons for the establishment of Hull House in 1889 in the following terms: "The Settlement, then, is an experimental effort to aid in the solution of the social and industrial problems which are engendered by the modern conditions of life in a great city." The functions of the settlement house were to "heal neighborhood ills," to act as "the big brother whose mere presence on the playground protects the little ones from bullies." [66]

> Its residents must be emptied of all conceit of opinion and all self-assertion, and ready to arouse and interpret the public opinion of their neighborhood. They must be content to live quietly side by side with their neighbors, until they grow into a sense of relationship and mutual interests. Their neighbors are held apart by differences of race and language which the residents can more easily overcome. They are bound to see the needs of their neighborhood as a whole, to furnish data for legislation, and to use their influence to secure it. In short, residents are pledged to devote themselves to the duties of good citizenship and to the arousing of the social energies which too largely lie dormant in every neighborhood given over to industrialism. They are bound to regard the entire life of their city as organic, to make an effort to unify it, and to protest against its over differentiation.[67]

By the close of the nineteenth century certain gross features were evident in the organization of social welfare in the United States which have relevance to the subject of this analysis: (1) It was established that local communities had the responsibility for providing social welfare services to the needy. (2) Such services for the able-bodied were to be given within the setting of the recipient's own home and family. (3) Economic and social conditions, as expressed in poor housing and inadequate residential areas, were believed to have some effect on the recipient, his needs, and his potential for rehabilitation. (4) It was generally believed proper for social agencies either to work directly with the individual in need or to strive for the amelioration of the social problem conditions per se, or both, such ameliorative efforts encompassing research in the problem conditions or removal of the problem condition by reform measures.

Crisis Programs

The inner city is crisis prone. Most inner cities did not start out with a

---

[66] Addams, *op. cit.*, pp. 98, 144.
[67] *Ibid.*, pp. 99–100.

plan except for their immediate needs. The passing of time changes the uses to which the inner city is put. A careful archeological study probably would reveal a relic mound of uses long forgotten, plus some that still remain, often transformed beyond recognition. In this paper concern is with the residential land uses that characterize the area.

The inner city is not only a relic mound of the past, it is the dumping ground of the present. It is overpopulated by the poor. Many do not live there by choice; they lack the steady income to live elsewhere. Because of inadequate income and the high costs of living, the poor must crowd together, often with many families in a dwelling that once housed one family. This practice is condoned by the city administration when codes for safe and sanitary housing are absent or not enforced. Consequently, large numbers are crammed into the inner city in flimsy, unhealthy firetraps. It has been said that the number of persons living in firetrap areas is exceeded only by the number of rats and vermin. In any case, the people of the inner city are subject to recurrent threats of fire, flood, epidemic, and accident. The high cost of police, fire, health, and other public services in many sections of the inner city has been amply documented. Similarly, there is a demand for public and private welfare services.

Every now and then special recognition is given to the chronic conditions of the inner city: a particularly bad fire, rats biting little babies, a juvenile "crime wave"—the stuff from which newspapers build circulation or on which reform candidates run for mayor.[68] In addition, there are those who are permanently or professionally outraged. Citizen groups and social agencies traditionally conduct studies and make recommendations to "do something."

What has been described are social conditions or sets of events defined as a problem and transmuted into action. The action may take the form of an *ad hoc* protest committee or it may congeal into a program of an existing organization. Once in a while a new organization attains permanency and influence, or dominance, in a field of service. Such a crystallization seems to be a function of many factors: whether the problem conditions are real or "manufactured"; the possibility of success in a program of action; the power, prestige, and stability of the problem definers; the success of the public relations campaign; the potentials for invidious comparison; the extent to which "vested interests" are challenged. Historically, there seems to have been an ebb and flow in the crystallization of problem conditions in the inner city. Organized social welfare has played a prominent part in this history.

---

[68] Shaw and McKay, *op. cit.*

Local Facilities

When crises are recurrent, local facilities may be developed to nullify them. The local problem is transformed by organization. An adequate education at minimal cost, a problem faced by the poor for centuries, has been partly resolved by the establishment of free public schools. Perhaps in prehistoric periods churches were the outgrowth of certain problem conditions. In any case, by the end of the nineteenth century schools and churches had become standard equipment in most sections of the city, including the inner city.

Although the principal function of school and church is not social welfare, they become involved with their programs if only because they are available meeting places. However, some social services are built into many school and church programs. The school social worker visits the families of the children who are having difficulty at school. Adult education programs in the high schools reach out into the community in many ways. Parent-teacher associations work on neighborhood social issues. A similar pattern of activities evolves about the church. People in need of material help and family guidance take their "troubles" to the minister. In turn, the minister may visit his "troubled" parishioners. Church and school become community facilities for youth-serving organizations, such as the Boy Scouts, Campfire Girls, and Girl Scouts. In many areas churches have established neighborhood houses next door and have provided the same range of services as the settlements.

The settlement is a local facility which differs from church and school in that it is oriented primarily to social welfare services rather than to the religious or educational. Furthermore, the site of a settlement house is selected with a view to assisting special segments of the population, usually the underprivileged. Originally the settlement provided permanent living quarters for its staff and leading volunteers and a temporary residence for persons in need. As this function was discontinued, the name of the settlement sometimes changed to "neighborhood house" and "community center," still advertising its primary commitment to the immediate locality.[69]

Church sites are chosen for the convenience of their members and those they wish to serve. Some churches have "missions" in the inner city; others locate there deliberately to help the "downtrodden" and "sinful." Recently some large downtown churches with members scattered all over the city have instituted special programs for the rehabili-

---

[69] Grace L. Coyle, "The Great Tradition and the New Challenge," *Social Service Review*, Vol. 35, No. 1 (March 1961), pp. 6–16; Arthur Hillman, *Neighborhood Centers Today* (New York: National Federation of Settlements and Neighborhood Centers, 1960).

tation of the inner city and to reach out to persons located around the church site.

Traditionally and currently there are close relations between the churches and social welfare. The YMCA and YWCA were established more than a century ago to provide residence and services for people living in the inner city. In many cities there are special branches located in the Negro minority neighborhood. The Young Men's Hebrew Association, of course, is the equivalent for the Jewish community.

Schools ostensibly are located where there is educational need; primary schools, in particular, are generally within walking distance of the homes of the small children in attendance. Insofar as there is an educational need, schools are located in the inner city. This, of course, is oversimplification. The schools in the inner city were built years ago and frequently are inadequate for present purposes. Furthermore, there is very little empty space for new schools and playgrounds. With shifts in population, it is difficult to estimate the demand for facilities. Consequently, there may be too many students per classroom and occasionally too few. The growth of the ghetto in the inner city has led to larger numbers of Negro segregated schools. Parents complain about inadequate schoolrooms, obsolete equipment, prejudiced teachers, "tough" neighborhoods, and many other things. Teachers object to the same conditions and also point to crowded, inadequate home environments that do not carry their share in the education of young minds. School and community are at cross purposes on many issues, and these controversies boil up into the schools, churches, neighborhood houses, and community centers. The local institutional facilities, which have sustained functions in the area, are continually being challenged to take a stand on the crisis programs.

Minority neighborhoods.[70] Social services also have been organized on the basis of special populations concentrated in the inner city. In the initial definition the inner city was described as a zone of specialized neighborhoods, some of sufficient duration and homogeneity to allow the development of their own institutions, including social agencies. Schools, churches, and community centers tend to be tied into city-wide alliances and official administrative structure. They are frequently the "outpost"

---

[70] Leonard Blumberg, *Migration as a Program Area for Urban Social Work: Pilot Study of Recent Negro Migrants into Philadelphia* (Philadelphia: Urban League of Philadelphia, July 1958); David Fogel, "Social Work and Negroes," *Phylon,* Vol. 18, No. 3 (Fall 1957), pp. 277–285; Lester B. Granger, "Negroes," *Social Work Year Book, 1945* (New York: Russell Sage Foundation, 1945), pp. 280–288; Marvin B. Sussman, "The Role of Neighborhood Associations in Private Housing for Racial Minorities," *Journal of Social Issues,* Vol. 13, No. 4 (1957), pp. 31–37; Preston Valien, "Racial Programs in Social Work," *Social Work Year Book, 1951* (New York: American Association of Social Workers, 1951), pp. 412–422.

of the total community located in the inner city. The social agencies serving the minority neighborhood, on the other hand, are often autochthonous. The primary allegiance of these services is to the area from which they draw their membership. Although this characteristic is generally true of agencies serving minorities, it is not unique to them. Many neighborhood and settlement houses (and political precinct organizations) have held the same view. In the case of the minority neighborhood the ties are likely to be more binding.

A minority neighborhood is defined as one in which the preponderant majority of residents have a common life history and continuing tradition, who are subject to discrimination, and who are objects of prejudice.[71] These neighborhoods are usually formed on the basis of race, nationality, religion, or language but may also have the basis of any permanent disvalued ascription.[72]

Settlement houses traditionally have tried to serve the needs of immigrant groups. Jane Addams sought to make Hull House a home for them, a place in which parents' customs might be preserved and appreciated by their children—to act as an insulation against the demoralizing neighborhood environment and to help newcomers to learn about America. Professional workers in the social services organized for the purpose of assisting disadvantaged Negroes frequently perceive their "clients" as the total community because the problems of the Negro are rooted in discriminatory practices in the larger society or because the full utilization of the work and talents of the Negro is in the interest of all. However, insofar as the preponderant majority of the Negro population is confined to an inner city "ghetto," continuing attention will have to be devoted to this locality, and such services can be considered as locality based.

There are other minority neighborhoods exisiting within the inner city which are segregated largely by the choice of their "members" and by permissive policies of the police and city administration: skid rows, "Little Bohemias," and "red-light districts." Some agencies providing specialized social services to these people are located near to them. Skid

---

[71] Edward Suchman, J. P. Deam, and R. M. Williams, *Desegregation: Some Propositions and Research Suggestions* (New York: Anti-Defamation League of B'nai B'rith, 1958), pp. 67–76.

[72] H. M. Blalock, "Economic Discrimination and Negro Increase," *American Sociological Review*, Vol. 21 (October 1956), pp. 584–588; Flora Y. Hatcher, "The Role of Social Work in Urban Renewal," *The Stake of Social Work in Urban Renewal Developments* (New York: Workshop of the New York School of Social Work, June 1957, Violet M. Sieder, Co-ordinator), pp. 29–36; Reginald R. Isaacs, "The Neighborhood Unit as an Instrument for Segregation," *Journal of Housing*, Vol. 5, No. 8 (August 1948), pp. 215–219; Hylan Lewis and Mozell Hill, "Desegregation, Integration, and the Negro Community," *Annals of the American Academy of Political and Social Science*, Vol. 304 (March 1956), pp. 116–123.

rows are served by the Salvation Army, St. Vincent de Paul, rescue missions, and the like. Similarly, VD clinics, homes for unmarried mothers, and other services are frequently located near the areas in which the usual codes of morality are not strictly enforced.

Community Development

With the great proliferation of social agencies and *ad hoc* groups interested in one or another of the social welfare issues, there has been a continuing demand for coordination, planning, and program development. This was one of the objectives of the Association for the Improvement of Conditions of the Poor, which was founded in New York City in 1843. There have been many such coordinating councils ever since. At the present time almost every city of more than 100,000 supports, by private donations, a community welfare council, usually staffed by professional social workers. The typical community welfare council has many functions. It acts as a center for exchange of information among member agencies, supports central fund-raising campaigns to maintain its members not receiving tax funds, and from time to time conducts research on community needs and agency effectiveness. It also promotes new programs of services. If it is not the father of new community programs, it tends to become a parent by adoption. Except for "demonstration projects" now and then, the council does not provide staff for direct services. It would prefer that local or specialized agencies take the lead, each in its own particular field of service. The function of the council is to facilitate such programs and to prevent duplication and overlapping of services.

The abundance of social problem conditions in the inner city has led community welfare councils to direct attention to this zone. There is no end to the types of program that have been sponsored: day care centers, well-baby clinics, home management projects, family counseling, and organized recreation; programs for the youth, the aged, for better human relations and minority understanding, and for the use of polio vaccine; campaigns for more parks, athletic facilities, public housing projects, mental health facilities, and so on.

From time to time area councils have been established in the inner city to facilitate the work. The composition of the local area council is somewhat different from that of the community welfare council. Both are represented by delegates of city-wide organizations and social agencies. However, the local area council tends to become a membership organization, drawing on leaders and residents of the neighborhood, including some whose allegiance is pretty much to the small area rather than to the metropolis.

Small-area coordinating councils, independent of the city organization, may also spring up. In the 1920's citizen groups established coordinating councils in many cities for the single purpose of treating and preventing juvenile delinquency. In the 1930's great attention was paid to councils of the unemployed. This was followed by committees to obtain public housing and to promote community planning. More recently there have been single-purpose coordinating councils in aid of problems of the aged, community mental health facilities, and alcoholism. The single-purpose campaigns tend to take on the characteristics of crisis programs, discussed earlier.

Problem conditions, however, tend to run ahead of ameliorative effort. There are always more requests for service than can be filled. The community welfare council, just as the single-purpose campaign, operates in a state of crisis, always in the face of a backlog of uncompleted projects and committees, not discharged because their work is not yet finished. And every year in the welfare council activities are suspended because all manpower must devote its attention to the achievement of the federated fund drive. To some people the community welfare councils must seem like a sponge without a goal. Of its three major functions, coordination of services is emphasized but seldom achieved—the sponge cannot contain all the substance about it. In the process, community planning and program development seem to have been lost.

During the last two decades, and especially since the passage of urban renewal legislation in 1949 and 1954, growing emphasis has been placed on something called "community development." Community development has been given many meanings.[73] Sociologists see it as a natural *process* inherent in the dynamics of social organization; social workers see it as a deliberate *method* for guiding ameliorative changes. Community development in this paper is defined as a comprehensive *program* of substantive services that are necessary to the "well-being" of the com-

---

[73] Charles E. Hendry, "Implications for Social Work Education in Community Planning, Community Development and Community Organization," in *Community Organization, Community Planning, and Community Development, Some Common and Distinctive Features* (New York: Council on Social Work Education, 1961), pp. 3–18; George A. Hillery, "Definitions of Community: Areas of Agreement," *Rural Sociology*, Vol. 20, No. 2 (June 1955), pp. 111–123; Albert G. Rosenberg, "Community Organization in Urban Renewal: A Case History and Housing Evaluation" (International Workshop on Community Organization Development and Community Organization, Brandeis University, 1960). (Mimeographed); Karl Taeuber, "Residential Segregation by Color in United States Cities, 1940–1950." Ph.D. dissertation, Sociology, Harvard University, 1959; "The Outlook for Community Development," Dunham, *op. cit.*

munity, which is readily acknowledged to be the business of more than its social welfare organization. However, comments are necessarily limited to organized social welfare.

Until recently community welfare councils have not taken an active role in community development programs. To be sure, frequently they have *not* been invited to do so by the sponsors of urban renewal projects, the mayor and his advisory committee, the housing authority, or the planning department. An account of the urban renewal activity of welfare councils is described in a later section.

This brief analysis of the historical development of organized social welfare points to the impact of social conditions on the definition of social problems and on the generation of social services. It is not evidence that a specific set of social conditions per se is established as *the* cause of a specific set of problem behaviors; nor is it a denial of condition-problem relationship. What is being said is that members of society believe in such a relationship. In particular, many social welfare practitioners and theorists have held this belief: one hundred years ago, fifty years ago, and now.

When does a social condition become defined as a social problem? To some extent, this depends on the current theory that acounts for the etiology of the problem. There has been a fluctuation in the popularity of various theories. Cohen, Konopka, and others have pointed to an "inward turn" of social work with an emphasis on the psychogenetic causation of problem behavior during the 1920's.[74] Macdonald puts it pungently: "The facts about social conditions had lost their power to produce action." [75]

A depression and a war in the next two decades brought the conditions of the society again to the fore. However, social planning and reform programs were submerged during the depressive climate of McCarthyism during the 1950's. In retrospect, it might seem that the existing social conditions had a profound effect on the theories of problem causation and amelioration dominant at at given time.[76]

Brevity has required that this history of social welfare developments in the inner city be one-sided. Emphasis has been placed on those events that are commonly thought to be progenitors of the social work specialties. This, of course, fails to tell the story of the vital role of the municipal reform movement, organizational efforts that led to the establishment of the National Housing Association in 1911, and of its activities there-

---

[74] Nathan Cohen, *op. cit.*, pp. 317 ff.

[75] Macdonald, *op. cit.*, p. 11.

[76] Joseph M. Gillman, "Welfare Capitalism in the Capitalistic Crisis," *Science and Society* (Spring 1958), pp. 97–112.

after.[77] Nor is there an adequate account of public health, city planning and intergroup relations activities.[78]

THE SMALL-AREA APPROACH TO CAUSE AND CURE

From the foregoing analysis it becomes evident that some types of social agencies are concerned with problem conditions found in the inner city but do not limit their work to that area. In fact, geographical locality per se may be unimportant in the structuring of services of such agencies. On the other hand, some social agencies concerned with these same social problem conditions limit their activities largely to the inner city. In general, these are agencies to which geographical locality is of major importance in structuring services. In this paper greatest emphasis is placed on locality-based agencies which are in the business of "small-area programs" for the amelioration of social problem conditions. The next step in the analysis, then, is to explore further the components of the small-area approach. This is done first by contrasting the small-area approach with the "clinical approach" in the cause and cure of problems.

Both the small-area approach and the clinical approach have ruled out the theory that social problems are a product of the genes. If such were the case, there would be little need for social work intervention except to relieve the suffering of the damned. The two approaches seek much more than this. In general they believe that man makes his social problems and consequently can unmake them. In effect, this means that both approaches believe in cultural and psychosocial theories of human behavior and its motivation. However, there is a difference in stress. A brief description of the activities of each approach will help to bring out the difference and point to similarities.

The clinical approach tends to form a picture of society and its problems from detailed case studies. At best, the model of society is built from careful empirical observations in the clinical (casework) situation from the sample of clients who come to the therapist asking for help. These observations are usually conducted in the diad of the therapist

---

[77] Ira S. Robbins, "Housing Goals and Achievements in the United States," *American Journal of Economic Sociology*, Vol. 15, No. 3 (April 1956), pp. 198–203; Richard S. Childs, "A Half Century of Municipal Reform," *ibid.*, pp. 321–326; Bredemeier, *op. cit.*

[78] Edward S. Rogers, *Human Ecology and Health: An Introduction for Administrators* (New York: Macmillan Company, 1960); Richard Shryock, *The Development of Modern Medicine* (New York: Alfred A. Knopf, 1947); Frederick J. Adams, "Changing Concepts of Planning," *Amercian Journal of Economic Sociology*, Vol. 15, No. 3 (April 1956), pp. 245–251; William Holford, "Plans and Programs," *Annals of the American Academy of Political and Social Science*, Vol. 314 (November 1956), pp. 94–100; William Shack, "Zoning Boards, Synagogues and Bias," *Commentary*, Vol. 23, No. 5 (May 1957), pp. 430–438.

and client, although there may be home visits or observations in another setting. For example, a group may be specially constructed for therapeutic purposes. The conduct of the therapist is supposed to be guided by the rules of the profession and the social conventions of the culture. In the first instance to preserve the confidential nature of the information given by the client, the rules of the profession generally preclude, or otherwise deter, any doublecheck on the therapist's observations. In compensation, the therapist has information from whatever battery of tests the client is willing to undergo. To be sure, the therapist is not confined to his own observations; he can consult the observations of others made in similar situations. The sum total of this chain of communication is that the therapist tends to rely on explanations of problem behavior that are subject to his manipulation. He looks for the root in distorted perceptions or experiences of the client, usually at some early stage in child socialization or in inappropriate family interpersonal relations. This assessment of the nature and root of social problems may be entirely appropriate to the bulk of persons seeking help from the clinical services.

The worker in the small-area approach (neighborhood worker), on the other hand, tends to form his picture of society and its problems from work with a diverse set of people living in the small area and from the representatives of organizations interested in the area and/or its social problems. At best, the model of society is built from careful empirical observations of ongoing action at a given point in history. A range of procedures is available for observation, from systematic surveys under the guidance of professionally trained researchers to community process records compiled by the worker to casual observations of an observer. Much of the action is subject to doublechecks, but history also unfolds in unexpected places with startling rapidity and in such a broad panorama that it is frequently impossible to translate it into accurate firsthand observations. Unlike the clinical situation, it is difficult to specify the client. Is the client the person experiencing the problem or the community that suffers from it? The roles of the neighborhood worker are often not clear. No one came asking for help. If the neighborhood worker is helping to crystallize a program of action already in incipient stages, then, in fact, he is the one who is asking for help, not the client.

The role relationships in the clinical situation are seldom as ambiguous. These have been studied rather carefully, and there are some fairly well-established theories about role relationship and therapy in the diad.[79] In this two-person situation the worker has few organizational

79 Leonard S. Kogan, ed., *Social Science Theory and Social Work Research* (New York: National Association of Social Workers, 1960).

problems over which to maintain control in the interests of therapy. Furthermore, the client has entered into the clinical relationship with confidence that the therapist has the knowledge necessary to the successful outcome of the treatment.

In the ambiguous community situation the motivation of the worker and his "clients" are to a large extent unknown. Obviously they are cooperating to solve a problem or to establish a program. But why *this* interest? What is to be gained in the long-run distribution of prestige, power, or profits? These questions are always latent in community organization, whether in the small area, city, state, or nation. In addition, the goals of the immediate action are frequently not clear or are misunderstood.

Two organizational conditions that are manifest for the neighborhood worker in the small area are not relevant to the therapist in clinical practice. In the small-area approach the worker must build continuing relationships with his "clients" that endure beyond the action on present problem conditions. Hence the model of interpersonal relationship is to establish friendships and mutually helpful collaboration. For the clinician, friendship with the client may actually impede therapy; affective neutrality is the rule. Although friendships may occur in clinical practice, they are usually clearly separated from the therapeutic situation; it is generally considered unprofessional to "date" the client.

No major organizational superstructure has been formed of therapeutically organized diads. However, citizen organization in the amelioration of social problem conditions in small area or large area has the potential at least for modest redistribution of power, prestige, or profit. It has the potential of cumulative organization.

The broader nature of organizational activity in the small-area approach is seemingly paralleled by a more eclectic approach to theories of causation of social problems. In addition to the clinical theories of distorted perception and inappropriate socialization, based on the one-by-one analysis, there is also frequent reference to the effects on behavior of stressful situations, antisocial climates, intergroup conflict, economic exploitation, and the like. The current situation and organizational dysfunctioning play a larger part in the theory. Some programs of amelioration based on the small-area approach are directed toward mass education and persuasion, legislative effort, and organizational reform. From these gross changes in the social environment it is believed that there will be a direct accrual to the individual.

Even though the program of action may be focused on a small area, some of those who take this approach believe that the problem behavior is broader in scope and thus the reform must be directed toward city, state, or nation. The theory of cause and cure employed by this school seems to be continually directed toward social controls resident in the broader society. Thus there is always the danger of overdiffusion in theory and practice. The removal of one problem condition may generate a new one. Similarly, in the emphasis on the general, specific individual responsibility for self-help may not be sufficiently reinforced.

Other distinctions can and should be made between the clinical and the small-area approaches. To some extent this dichotomy is similar to that between clinical medicine and public health epidemiology. The two are accepted branches of medicine. They live together and contribute to one another. This is the relationship that should be established between the clinical and small-area approaches to welfare organization. To adopt one does not mean the exclusion of the other. It may well be that a social problem resistant to one approach may be amenable to the other. A single social problem has many facets, each of which may require different treatment. The form of treatment should be established by research rather than preconception.

To some extent the two approaches are implicit in the customary classification of the three major social work methods. Casework and group work are neutral terms. They do not point to any particular locality, whereas "community" organization has a specific geographical referent—neighborhood, metropolis, or other area. Traditionally, casework has been characterized as clinical practice, and much of recent group work is cast in a similar framework. The trichotomy seems to be evolving into a dichotomy somewhat along the lines of this paper.

It is impossible within the scope of this paper to set down a complete theory of the small-area approach. However, a few propositions are suggested for further consideration and research:

1. Social services are provided in the open society rather than in an institutional setting.

2. The client to whom the services are directed may be an individual, the public at large, or the population exposed to the social problem condition.

3. Social services may be directed toward the achievement of the "good life" as well as toward the reduction of risk from social problem conditions.

4. Activities are directed toward cumulative social organization which enhances the democratic problem-solving process.

5. Services located in the small area may be planned, organized, and administered by agencies located in the area or elsewhere. However, the means for the effective participation of local residents in policy of action should be worked out.

6. The selection of the small area as the focus of work must *not* be

based solely on the convenience of the worker or on residency laws governing the client.

7. The delineation of a particular small area for social problem-solving purposes must have theoretical relevance in terms of one or more of the following:

(a) The problem is caused by conditions that are concentrated or exist primarily in the area; that is, the element of location is necessary and/or sufficient for the explanation of the etiology of the problem.

(b) All or most of the persons requiring the service, or exposed to the risk, reside in the area.

(c) The type of service or treatment must be provided in the small area to have maximum effectiveness; that is, the element of location is necessary for the treatment of the problem or its prevention.

8. Insofar as possible, the small area should form a "natural" social unit; that is, traditional and political boundaries should be observed whenever possible to facilitate the flow or communication and action through both formal and informal channels.

9. It would seem that the small-area approach would be most effective with those social problems that have a physical locational component and reality in the social environment experienced by the "client" or the exposed population.

It would seem to be fruitful to study in detail the programs that partake of aspects of the small-area approach. "Delinquency area" projects have been organized directly by social workers or in collaboration with them. Public housing and urban renewal projects have often received the blessing of organized social welfare, although it was not until very recently that social work agencies were drawn into this activity in a meaningful way.

There are a number of advantages and disadvantages to the small-area approach. It is essentially a program to keep the normals "normal" by reducing the risk of exposure to social problem conditions. To do this there is a control and gradual (or rapid) elimination of the conditions that cause much of the incidence of the problem behavior. The epidemiological methods used in the small-area approach are also necessary to the localization of persons who need more intensive treatment. It is no substitute for the more intensive clinical treatment once persons have been identified and diagnosed as needing it. In the process of broadscale education some persons who might become problem casualties may perhaps be caught before the event. The potential offender may be identified and worked with. The program of treatment may be more objectively evaluated in the small-area approach simply because the worker can see the effects in everyday work with the individuals treated. On the other hand, the results of mass programs are often ambiguous. Hence there is little to go on in measuring success or failure. Unfortunately, there are no short-cut valid and reliable ways to measure the success or failure of social welfare programs.

Programs organized in a small area may be less costly in personnel travel time. If the neighborhood is to become a therapeutic milieu, it is essential that the agency be recognized and accepted as a friend. The small area should provide more contact and easier communication among those involved. The worker by intimate contact will derive firsthand knowledge of the problems and organizational potentials of the area. The possibility of cumulation in small-area organization has been stressed; there is no social addition of clinical diads. In the small area are the building blocks of social change. However, there are limits to the amount of change that can be effected in conditions more widespread than the small area itself or generated by activities not within local area control. For example, the removal of poverty, race hatred, and economic exploitation is going to require more than changes in one small area. This is not meant to imply that social change in a broader arena may not be sparked by local efforts. The change in society has to start somewhere!

SUBAREAS: DEFINING THE APPROPRIATE UNIT

The inner city is a balloon concept. As one talks about it the balloon is inflated; it can be seen; it is dramatic in its impact; but it is difficult to store. Its round shape leaves a lot of wastage around the corners, of which it has none. Then, too, it is rather fragile for constant use.

What are the advantages of the concept of the inner city? The major use is that it identifies the location of the small area and then definitely ties its section of the city to the other sections. Elsewhere in this paper several functions that the inner city seems to perform for the balance of the city have been discussed. (1) It is the spillover area for the central district. (2) It is the port of entry in the city for impoverished newcomers. (3) It is a back room in which sinful practices can be carried on and civic eyesores can be hidden. In addition, the slum ghettos are profitable to their owners.[80] They are an excellent real estate

---

[80] It is instructive to read materials sent out by the American Committee to Improve Our Neighborhoods. Frequently they are aimed at people in real estate, building, and banking. They indicate the substantial increment in value of the property and in rentals contributed by renovation of the property under urban renewal plans.

In "Blight and the Changing Neighborhood," *Interracial Review*, Vol. 34, No. 3 (March 1961), pp. 72–74, Sister Mary Liguori cites several cases of exorbitant

investment for the absentee landlord. The rate of return annually is two to three times that of real estate located in other sections of the city. Furthermore, tax assessments are low and housing code enforcement is minimal. Corrupt political machines have also been based on rigged support from the inner-city precincts.[81]

The concept of the inner city is justified if only because it illustrates in a neat descriptive package some of the hidden life and the social dysfunctions of the city as a whole. However, having said this, where does one move next, especially for purposes of social welfare planning and organization? If the inner city is a zone of specialized neighborhoods, how can these smaller units be identified? Can they then be combined to form an operational definition of the inner city? This is the problem that this section of the paper considers.

An attempt will be made to characterize four typical subareas considered in government and planning and by social scientists: school district, microdistrict, census tract, and neighborhood. Selected studies of administrators, planners and social scientists will be examined to see what they tell about social problems and their amelioration. What urban subarea concepts have been advanced by each of these groups? What do these concepts contribute to the description and etiology of social problems? How do they help in social welfare planning for the amelioration of the problems?

---

profiteering. A typical case would be as follows: "The owner had paid $25,000 for a six-apartment building in 1952 and then converted the structure into 24 apartments with chicken wire and plasterboard. Rentals 'converted' too, and yielded $1,800 a month instead of the mere $500 which the former owner had collected. These rentals repaid the entire capital investment in little more than a year, i.e., an interest rate of almost 80% per annum. One unpleasantness the landlord met, however, was a building inspection disclosing 98 violations of the City Code which ate into his profits to the sum of $305 for penalties and court costs and reduced his profits to a miserable 72% a year. Fortunately there is a sad end to this tale: the building burned down at ten o'clock in the morning and none of those at home at that hour were hurt on the deteriorated stairs or inadequate fire escapes" (p. 73). This rather bitter recital is documented in more measured terms in other sources.

And, according to Hauser, *op. cit.*, p. 13, housing courts have been called "notoriously ineffective, with procedures and sanctions designed more to safeguard the slumlord and his property than the tenant or the urban commuity at large." The depredations have reached such an extent in larger cities that Mayor Wagner in his Annual Message on the State of the City delivered to the City Council on April 5, 1960, called for more drastic action, including authorization for a city "to take control of a building, collect the rents, and apply them to remedy the violations."

81 Martin Meyerson and E. C. Banfield, *Politics, Planning and the Public Interest: The Case of Public Housing in Chicago* (Glencoe, Ill.: Free Press, 1955); Coleman, *op. cit.*

City and County Government

The city and the county are the basic governmental units that must be taken into consideration in any discussion of urban social problems and their amelioration, whether located in the section called the inner city or any other part.[82] This is because both government units by law are responsible for the provision of certain services and protections and are accountable periodically to the citizenry for how well the job is done. In addition to having its own locally established government, the county is also frequently used as the territorial unit on which state and national organization is based and to which federal and state funds are directed.

Two of the smaller subunits of the inner city, smaller in area and number of residents, are the school district and the political precinct. The paragraphs that follow describe some of the characteristics of such subareas. As the paper proceeds it will become evident that the government subarea—the school district and the political precinct—is quite different in its nature from the subarea created by the social welfare planner or the social scientist. In brief, the governmental subarea can be both a descriptive category and a social action system, to be considered in any evaluation of the inner city as a viable concept in the amelioration of social problems.

It would seem that the governmental subarea, as exemplified by the school district and the political precinct, has at least the following characteristics:

1. It has clearly defined boundaries that can be easily located on a map.

2. It is a social-action system with authority for certain delegated functions.

3. It defines potential channels for membership, office holding, communication, organizational activity, and change in a small geographical area.

4. It has high potential for becoming a reference group for residents in the subarea, since its functions are traditional and thus are fairly well known to residents, even though they may have lived in the subarea only a short time.

5. It is linked to other subareas in a functional relationship and to the entire city.

Before passing on to a discussion of typical subareas of social welfare planning organizations, it would be useful to comment on "neighborhood units" or "microdistricts" established by the planning departments

---

[82] W. S. Foster, "Municipal Public Works and City Planning," *American Journal of Economic Sociology*, Vol. 15, No. 3 (April 1956), pp. 277–284.

of many city governments. The microdistrict is an area comparable in size to the school district which is frequently made the basis for residential planning, whether in the inner city or elsewhere in the metropolis.

First, it should be noted that microdistricts are established with reference to the total system of city zoning. Each section of the city is assigned one or more functions by the planning staff, working with the city government, which are believed to be most compatible with its topography, natural resources, existing underground facilities, location with respect to the city center, and transportation routes. The economic, cultural, and social development of the city, its people, institutions, and physical plant are also taken into consideration.

If the function of the microdistrict is established as primarily residential (or any other function), then short-range and long-range plans are established to eliminate land uses inimical to residency and to maintain such controls and to foster the optimum conditions for pleasant and abundant living. In establishing the boundaries of the microdistrict and its future development, measures are taken to preserve fine architecture, tradition, and history whenever possible; to utilize existing neighborhood social-action systems, whenever possible; and to involve residents of the microdistrict to a degree in the planning process, whenever possible.

Some of the goals of the city planner are frequently ravished by brutal facts of economic life and the expedient bargains that politicians and governments must make in order to get along.

Frequently the main business of city planning offices has been non-residential in character, more concerned with the physical property of the city, with beautification of avenues and parks. However, during the last quarter of a century interest in renewal of the older parts of the city—the central business district and its adjacent fringe, the inner city, has been stimulated by the availability of federal money, first, for housing projects, then for slum clearance, and later for many purposes of urban redevelopment. The master plan for the development of a system of microdistricts has been drawn up in a few planning departments and implemented partially in a handful.

Thus the microdistrict, based on the realization of beautiful and healthy neighborhoods, is still an image of the future in the United States. Yet it is an image than can be realized, for parts of it are being brought to life here and there across the country and in other parts of the world.

Consider whether the subarea, that is, the microdistrict, is similar to other governmental subareas. Quite obviously it is not. Of the five characteristics only the first and fifth are somewhat achieved. The microdistrict can be given sufficiently precise boundaries so that it can be located easily on a map; it is also linked functionally to other sub-areas and to the city through the Master Plan and the functions of the planning office as part of city government. Essentially the microdistrict in the United States lacks legal recognition and authority. It is too new and artificial to have become a reference group, except when it coincides with an older established neighborhood; thus it also lacks the other characteristics of a governmental social action system as well.

The subareas established by the planner—not so much the micro-district as the "region" that incorporates many cities, towns, and counties for a particular planning purpose—were set up because of inadequacies of city-county units. In addition to divided authority existing in the many different political corporations, the city frequently is not of suffi-cient size to allow appropriate physical, economic, and social planning. As these new units—the region and the microunit—demonstrate their utility, they may become the government subunits of the future.

It is likely that the amelioration and solution of social problems is going to be a long-run task for social welfare organization. At the present time the city planning department is one of the technical adjuncts of the city government. It is not asked to deal directly with the ameliora-tion or solution of social problems. In the current division of labor social problems are more likely to be routed to the department of welfare, education, health, recreation, or police rather than to the city planning department. This would seem to be an appropriate assignment. How-ever, it would also seem well to keep in mind the subareas created by planners. By the creation of beautiful and healthy neighborhoods they may be setting the preconditions necessary for permanent solution of social problems.

Social Welfare Planning Council

Social welfare planning councils have taken an essentially pragmatic approach to the delimiting of subareas in which they will work toward the amelioration of social problems. When geographic-political units are made the basis for organization, city-county boundaries most fre-quently are used. Otherwise, a typical procedure has been to spot an area in which the social problem condition flourishes and in which one or more agencies are willing to provide services. The scope of the area and/or the number of clients served is made dependent on the extent of the organizational resources. Hence the size of the subarea is quite arbitrarily set.

Some welfare councils have established area branches which have gained recognition among the residents of the subarea. In general, more effort has been devoted to central cities than suburbs in the work of area councils. Their program of action is usually based on the control of problem behavior rather than its prevention or elimination. They are client-oriented rather than area-centered in focus.

In general, welfare councils have *not* established city-wide systems of subareas that tie together the entire city and county, except perhaps for fund-raising purposes. Even in this case, the basis of organization is more likely to be by category of giver than by subarea.

Many area councils have surveyed the problems of their home communities. These surveys tend to be every now and then rather than periodical. The results are not published in a form in which the information is easily available across the nation. In addition to these sporadic social studies, most councils analyze and use data from the federal census and other sources. Sometimes in this effort subarea clusters of census tracts are created, which in the main follow the design of social scientists.[83]

The Social Scientists

Most information about the city and its subareas is found in studies of the social scientists.[84] Such studies vary widely among the academic disciplines. The economic geographers originally stressed the physical habitat of man but have moved over to city human ecology; the anthropologists visited agrarian communities overseas but now probe into industrialization and urbanization, no matter where its locus may be; political scientists have tended to examine the formal and informal boundaries of power and its social structures, investigating international, state, and local questions; rural sociologists and adult educators traditionally have been concerned with small-town social-action systems. There would seem to be no bounds for the investigations of sociologists. For more than a century they have developed concepts of neighborhoods and communities. They have sliced the city into subareas, sectors, concentric zones, stars, rings, and census tracts. They have attempted to describe and measure "natural areas," suburbs and exurbs, minority communities, slums, and ghettoes.

[83] Genevieve Carter, "Measurement of Need," in Norman Polansky, ed., *Social Work Research* (Chicago: University of Chicago Press, 1960), pp. 201–222; Bernard Farber and John C. Osoinach, "An Index of Socio-Economic Rank of Census Tracts in Urban Areas," *American Sociological Review*, Vol. 24, No. 5 (October 1959), pp. 630–640; Bell, *op. cit.*

[84] Lee F. Johnson, "The Housing Act of 1949 and Your Community," in Nathan Strauss, ed., *Two-thirds of a Nation* (New York: Alfred A. Knopf, 1952), Ch. 11; Hawley, *op. cit.*; Quinn, *op. cit.*; Schmid, *Social Saga of Two Cities, op. cit.*; Anselm Strauss, "The Changing Imagery of American City and Suburb," *Sociology Quarterly*, Vol. 1, No. 1 (January 1960), pp. 15–24; Maurice D. Van Arsdol, Jr., Jr., Santo F. Camilleri, and Calvin F. Schmid, "An Application of the Shevky Social Area Indexes to a Model of Urban Society, *Social Forces*, Vol. 37, No. 1 (October 1958), pp. 26–32.

How useful are the studies of the social scientists for social welfare planning purposes? Do they direct attention to the etiology of social problem conditions found in urban subareas? Are the subareas used by the social scientists functional to programs of action to ameliorate or solve the social problem conditions? To answer these questions, two of the subareas frequently referred to in studies of the social scientists may be examined: the census tract and the neighborhood. Both may be found in the inner city. The "neighborhood" is a concept that has been exploited by sociologists and others for a century or more. It is a synonym for "community," especially when the size of the place has been small or located in rural areas.[85] Cooley more than fifty years ago described the neighborhood as a primary group, the same kind of face-to-face group as the family or play groups of children.[86] Some years later Robert E. Park characterized the neighborhood as the smallest local unit in the social and political organization of the city. He said:

> Proximity and neighborly contact are the basis for the simplest and most elementary form of association with which we have to do in the organization of city life. Local interests and associations breed local sentiment, and, under a system which makes residence the basis for participation in government, the neighborhood becomes the basis of political control. In the social and political organization of the city it is the smallest local unit. The neighborhood exists without formal organization.[87]

One aspect of the lack of formal organization of the neighborhood entity has been difficult to define precisely. There is even a running argument about whether neighborhoods have ceased to exist in the modern metropolis.[88] The elusive character of the neighborhood has led quantitatively oriented social scientists to establish another area unit of about the same size as the neighborhood. This is the census tract. Most large metropolitan areas are now divided into a grid of census tracts, each containing a few city blocks and about 1000 to 10,000 persons. Ideally, the boundaries of the census tract should be set once and for all and no changes allowed in them. In this way it would be possible to enumerate spatially distributed phenomena from year to year with maximum accuracy and to make comparisons over time and among different cities.

---

[85] Floyd N. House, *The Development of Sociology* (New York: McGraw-Hill Book Company, 1936), pp. 136–195.

[86] Charles H. Cooley, *Social Organization* (New York: Charles Scribner & Son, 1909).

[87] Robert E. Park, *The City* (Chicago: University of Chicago Press, 1925), p. 7.

[88] Coleman, *op. cit.*

The census tract scheme for each city typically is created by social scientists and other knowledgeable people. In some instances the tracts are not purely arbitrary, but there has been an attempt to capture the homogeneity of the area and its more significant distinctive natural characteristics in terms of land use, physiography, demographic and socioeconomic features, and even incidence of social disorganization.[89] However, in many cities this has been given up as a hopeless task because people move, land uses change, and buildings deteriorate. Hence the census tracts tend to become more and more a statistical unit and to lose whatever congruence they once may have had with functioning social-action systems or "natural" areas. How do the neighborhood and the census tract compare with governmental subareas on the five criteria mentioned earlier?

The census tract is specifically bounded and can be mapped easily. Census tracts can also be grouped according to specified criteria into urban subareas and zones and can describe the whole city or large parts of it. Many statisticians prefer to work with city blocks rather than census tracts, since this allows greater flexibility. Nevertheless, census tracts are frequently used and are helpful in social welfare planning.

Comment has already been made on the ambiguous boundaries of the neighborhood. Furthermore, the elements in the action system of the neighborhood are usually not written down and enacted in law. In this way it differs quite markedly from governmental units of a similar size, such as the school district. Does this mean that the channels for membership, leadership, organizational activity, and change are less well known and are less effective in the neighborhood than they are in the school district? This is not necessarily so. In fact, these facets of the social-action system may be well established by tradition and practice. Similarly, the functioning of the neighborhood social-action system may be subject to accurate empirical description and prediction, even though its exact boundaries cannot be plotted on a map. The neighborhood differs essentially from the school district in that the former is indigenous to the subarea, whereas the latter may have been superimposed on the subarea. The motivation leading to neighborhood formation grows out of residents in the immediate area, usually as a process of gradual accretion, whereas the school district is part of a plan to provide educational facilities to each of many subareas of the city. From this it is seen that the governmental unit has a functional relationship with other sections of the city. Quite the contrary may be true of the neighborhood. The neighborhood may be parochial and oriented toward its

---

[89] Calvin F. Schmid, "The Theory and Practice of Planning Census Tracts," *Sociology and Social Research,* Vol. 22, No. 3 (January–February 1958), pp. 228–238.

own activities and problems and quite resistant to city-wide matters. Since the school district draws its funds and personnel largely from outside the immediate neighborhood, it must necessarily have a dual orientation—to the city as a whole and to its own immediate district.

One major point should be made about the subareas employed by social scientists. Regardless of the differences that are stressed in the subareas used for conceptual analysis, there is a central focus to the social studies that is quite different from those made by the government administrators and the social welfare planners. The social scientists' interest in the city is largely academic. The criteria they apply to subarea definitions pertain to the theoretic cogency of the concept or to its methodological soundness. On the other hand, the administrators and planners want to know if the subarea is the most effective unit and mode of organization for accomplishing a program objective. This is not intended to mean that social scientists are disinterested in planning effective action toward the amelioration of social problems. To be sure, many of them have this disinterest. There are some, however, whose social studies are manifestoes for change. But even with the most action-oriented of the social scientists there is a strong element of observation and description and testing of methods and theories.

In summary, it would seem that there are essentially three types of urban subareas: statistical, administrative, and natural. The ideal statistical subarea has permanent, well-marked boundaries so that periodic counts and comparisons can be made with complete reliability. It is desirable but not necessary that the statistical unit be congruent with administrative and natural social systems located in the area. The administrative subarea is an incorporated, governmental, or political subdivision. By law it must define its activities; thus the potentials for social action are always inherent in the administrative unit. Because its boundaries are well marked it can also serve as a statistical unit. The natural subarea is the product of organized social life in an area.

Among the factors that shape the social life are the physiographic. The natural subarea can be studied empirically. However, its social boundaries are usually not so clearly defined; it is not fully contained in any statistical or administrative units. The natural subarea is made up of actors, but the instructions for their action are not established, as in the administrative unit. What type of subarea is most useful for the analysis of social problems and their amelioration, for social welfare planning purposes? [90] It has already been indicated that planning and amelioration will of necessity need to flow through governmental ad-

---

[90] Walter Gropius, "Organic Neighborhood Planning," *Housing and Town and City Planning Bulletin,* Vol. 2 (United Nations, 1949), pp. 2–5.

ministrative apparatus. Furthermore, it was suggested that in the future the microdistricts may be setting the preconditions necessary to permanent solution of locality-based social problems; hence they must be taken into consideration. In the long run local administrative units may be formally established to coincide with microdistricts.

The subareas most useful to action and amelioration, however, may not be most appropriate for describing and understanding social problems. Area-based social problems, such as blight and ghetto conditions, do not stop at statistical and political boundaries; frequently they also leap over the natural boundaries established by physical environment. On the other hand, social problems, as defined in this paper, reside in the conditions of social life experienced by certain populations. Hence it would seem that for the understanding of locality-based social problems an investigation should be made of the conditions in the "natural" subareas of the city.

As a "sensitizing variable, the concept of the inner city has much use *when applied to the United States.* The sensitivity of the concept for other nations and cultures is a moot point and must remain so until definitive research is completed. For small area programs an examination must be made, whenever possible, of administrative units that are representative of the "natural area" neighborhood. This will facilitate both description and action.

A CONCEPTUAL MODEL FOR ANALYZING THE HOUSING PROBLEM

One final phase of the analysis remains to be completed. At various places it has been emphasized that a social problem has three aspects: (1) social conditions, (2) adjudged to be "bad," (3) which people feel can be improved or eliminated. The second section described the social conditions that exist in the inner city. The third section pointed to their recognition, historically and currently, by organized social welfare, that is, they have been defined as "social problem conditions" by organized social welfare. The fourth and fifth sections disposed of central questions having to do with amelioration approached on an area basis. In this section of the paper, a particular area-based social problem, "the housing problem," is subjected to more detailed scrutiny.

This section is concerned with the ways in which a particular set of problem conditions is affected when it is singled out for amelioration. The key question conceptually is: when a social problem is approached from the standpoint of amelioration, how does this approach affect the "facts" of the problem? How does it affect the mode of analysis of the problem? It is the thesis of this paper that the mandate for action introduces a new dimension. The social problem must now be considered from the standpoint of directed social change. The definition of the problem becomes the first step in the process. All the ramifications of this position cannot be exhausted, but some of them are explored. What set of conditions would constitute a solution to the housing problem? To answer this, the values implicit in the non-problem state must be considered. A second question is: is a solution to the housing problem possible within the inner city? If so, by what process(es)? To answer these questions a full assessment of the feasibility of alternate courses of action would be required. A full range of alternatives cannot be pursued here. Instead, those utilized by housing, intergroup relations, and "traditional" social work agencies are examined within a conceptual framework based on stages in residential integration: (1) home finding, (2) moving in, (3) getting settled in the new area, and (4) the management of neighborhood crises. This conceptual framework is what is called in this paper a "theory" of residential integration. Of course, only the outline of the theory is broached, but it provides a dynamic setting for the consideration of practice. The social problem conditions are thus placed within a framework of practices necessary for directed social change. These "stages" in the process of neighborhood integration offer different sorts of subsidiary social problems. The stages of "home finding" and "moving in" seem to involve "help" given to individuals in need, whereas the stage of "management of neighborhood crises" seem to be a form of "control over problem conditions." If the whole process of neighborhood integration is planned so that there is a minimum of difficulties in the process, then this might be considered "prevention of social problems." The potential roles of the social worker are examined in each of these stages of residential integration. Some of the roles lie within the "clinical" framework; others involve the roles of program organizer or technical consultant.

The coverage of literature regarding the relationship of social welfare and housing is supplemented by the findings of several small studies conducted by the author and his associates. The author is also indebted to Robert N. White, then a graduate student at the University of Washington School of Social Work, for his review of the literature made in 1960–1961. This is published as a M.S.W. report entitled, "An Analysis of Social Services Provided in Connection with Housing Problems of the Negro Within the Urban Renewal Program."

What Constitutes a "Solution"?

It is not sufficient merely to have a solution for removing the conditions that irk us, such as slums, ghettoes, sprawl, clutter, ugliness. An image of the neighborhood of the future must be created by and for the citizenry through their architects, city planners, engineers, social scientists—and social workers. We must know what we are moving *toward* as well as what we are moving *away* from; the lack of an inspiring image for tomorrow is perhaps equally as serious a deficiency for social workers as the failure to recognize current social problems and to work for their amelioration.

The full "solution" to the housing problem cannot be explicated in this paper. The five points listed below are major considerations it would be well to keep in mind in dealing with this problem. There are many discussions of this subject, including detailed standards for what housing and neighborhood should be. For further information the reader is referred to other sources.[91]

1. The "housing problem" refers both to housing per se and its neighborhood environs, facilities, and services.

2. The neighborhood should be amenable to comfortable, healthy, and pleasant living, both immediately and in the long run. Neighborhoods should be organized to maintain these characteristics with minimum deterioration.

3. Housing should be adequately constructed, properly equipped with household machinery, beautiful to look at, and functional to its residents.

4. Since the image of what constitutes an "ideal" home in an "ideal" neighborhood varies, there should be variety in housing and neighborhoods.[92]

5. To achieve these goals, land use must be controlled by a master plan that can be implemented and enforced. The plan must be sufficiently flexible to allow for technological progress and changes in taste.

Is a "Solution" Possible?

Obviously most inner cities at the present time do not meet the re-

---

[91] American Public Health Association, Committee on the Hygiene of Housing, "Planning the Neighborhood" (Chicago: Public Administration Service, 1948); World Health Organization, *op. cit.*

[92] The emphasis on planning should not be taken to condone a plan simply because it is a plan. The author agrees with Jane Jacobs when she inveighs against planning that creates the "Great Blight of Dullness." This is the planning that isolates primary land uses, in which one commercial use has a monopoly of a large area, in which each section is maximally used for only a few hours of each day, in which homogeneous residential areas have the effect of segregating racial groups and groups at different income levels, and so on. Rather, planning should ensure diversity, flexibility, and optimal land use. *See The Death and Life of Great American Cities* (New York: Random House, 1961).

quirements of "ideal" homes in "ideal" neighborhoods. Comment has already been made elsewhere in the paper about the old, dilapidated, unsafe, and unsanitary housing located in the crowded neighborhoods of the inner city, many of which are seriously deficient in parks, playgrounds, and social services adequate to the needs of the people living there. In addition, there is heavy traffic, smog, and noise. Certain forms of adult recreation, plain and commercialized vice, are inappropriate for family life. Schools frequently are inferior, and the youth environment would not seem to be conducive to normal socialization for many children.

Given this assortment of hazards, what assets remain in the inner city that lead people to live there if other city residential areas are open to them? Recent studies have shown that the city core continues to attract residents, not only to the luxury apartments downtown, but also to other sections of the inner zone.[93] What features of the inner city should be preserved in sound future planning for residential use?

Perhaps the primary reason for living in the inner city is to be near the functions that seem to be economically and efficiently located in the central business district: the offices of government and business, major shopping centers and department stores, cultural and educational facilities. In the long run, if the hazards of the inner city are removed, workers in the downtown facilities may want to live nearby with their families. The downtown district is a great employer. Many people must be there during the working day. Unless they are within walking distance, some form of private or public transportation must be used. Cities everywhere in the United States have experienced a tremendous growth in traffic, in problems of automobile parking, in lengthened travel time from home to work. Living nearby would reduce the transportation difficulties. At the present time, and in the long run, it would seem that the functions of the central business district have sufficient power to attract into residency sections of its work force who would live in the inner city. The proportions of employees desiring to make their homes nearby would, of course, be affected by the attractiveness of the inner zone for this purpose. Another solution to the crowded downtown life would be decentralization of the central business district. However, the desirability and functionality of unicentered or multicentered cities still remain to be demonstrated. Residential areas will be shaped by the number of city centers and by the nature of the functions performed.

The educational and cultural facilities, which frequently are located

---

[93] Chester Rapkin and William G. Grigsby, *Residential Renewal in the Urban Core* (Philadelphia: University of Pennsylvania Press, 1960).

near the core of the city, attract both transient and permanent populations. The age and family status of students will require one form of residential accommodations; the vacationers, visitors, and temporary users of the facilities, another. Cities have already established hotels, apartments, rooming houses, and other types of temporary lodging on the basis of demand. These requirements will undoubtedly continue as long as the city center contains cultural, recreational, and historical facilities. The diversity and excitement of the inner city has been a powerful magnet to the population. Contributing to this are both the facilities—the theaters, galleries, concert halls, museums, shopping centers, historical sites—and the rich variety of "strange" peoples who inhabit the inner city. Not the least of these are the minority neighborhoods. As already noted, the inner city has served as a port of entry for immigrants, some of whom have been formed into "ghettoes" both by external pressures and their own wishes. In a democratic society the minority neighborhood has a right to maintain itself; people sharing the same cultural, national, religious, or racial background should be permitted, even encouraged, to retain their own identities if they so desire. It is the coerced aspect of ghettoization that is repugnant to the democratic ethos. An "open housing" situation should prevail everywhere in the metropolis, with free choice to each family to select the best neighborhood and housing it is able to find and can afford.[94]

The minority often develops its own facilities and business life in a geographic area, which then comes to be identified by the cultural characteristics of its residents. The "Chinatowns," "Little Italies," and the "Harlems" become a part of the cultural and historical tradition of the inner zone. But minority neighborhoods have been shifted and transplanted. In the long run, do they belong in the inner city? Will they impede the growth and development of the "necessary" functions of the central business district which require centrality? Procedures for assigning priorities in land use must be developed and evaluated. Do historical and cultural values supersede the economic values? These are planning decisions of considerable complexity.

Conflicts between individual choice and the social good seem inevitable when there are changes in land use or when new sites are needed. The old homesite acquires added sentimental and monetary value when it must be taken for a road or an urban renewal project. The alternatives usually are neither all white nor all black. Who is to say which is more to be desired, the preservation of historical and traditional values or a new project? Proposals for a change seem to

---

[94] Suchman, *op. cit.*

bring political issues and latent conflicts to the fore. This is frequently the case in interracial areas, in which the existing patterns of segregation seem to be of high importance in the decisions relating to land use.

In summary, it would seem that the assets of the inner city are its proximity to the central business district and the presence of historical and cultural facilities and land uses. These assets are probably of sufficient worth to ensure the continuance of the inner city as a desirable residential area, provided that its negative features can be muted and transformed. The inadequate neighborhoods of the inner city have received attention from organized social welfare, and social work in particular, for well over a century. It would be impossible and undesirable to catalog all the "solutions" to the housing problem that have been tried somewhere at sometime. Some of these efforts will be identified in the context of the three approaches to amelioration, the stage of neighborhood integration, and the most typical roles of the social worker.[95]

Direct Aid to the Person in Need

Home finding. Customarily, people find their own housing without the aid of a social agency.[96] The social agency usually becomes involved only when the home-seeker is a client for some other reason, and problems in "residential adjustment" are raised in the course of the treatment, or when a category of persons has more than usual difficulty in this process.

Public welfare agencies, in particular, have continually been faced with difficulties in home finding experienced by persons receiving public assistance grants, whose level of income may be so low and so unsteady that the usual private housing market is ruled out. Others with chronic house-finding problems who come before social agencies are families with many children, newcomers, old persons with small pensions, and minority households. In all these categories low, unsteady income is a factor. Their need is one reason given for the advent of low-cost public housing.

During the last decade large-scale demolition in urban redevelopment programs has forced the removal of many persons from their dwellings in the inner city. In New York City alone, for instance, in which there have been many clearance projects, almost 80,000 persons were moved during the five-year period between 1954 and 1959. In Philadelphia

---

[95] John G. Vaughan, "Housing in Changing Neighborhoods," Ohio State University Conference on Human Relations, July 1960. (Typescript.)

[96] Eunice Grier and George Grier, "Market Characteristics in Interracial Housing," *Journal of Social Issues,* Vol. 13, No. 4 (1957), pp. 50–59.

66,000 families have been displaced since 1949, more from highway construction and code-enforcement programs than from federally aided urban renewal clearance projects.[97] It is estimated that one fourth of the Philadelphia housing supply will be replaced in the next twenty-five years. This situation pertains in other cities, even if the numbers are not so large.

The most comprehensive study of relocation practices was recently completed by H. W. Reynolds, Jr., of the School of Public Adiministration of the University of Southern California.[98] From an analysis of 47,282 relocated families in forty-one major cities throughout the nation, he found that (1) the primary source for relocatees were newspaper and realtor lists; (2) about one-fifth are eligible for public housing, but less than half this number enters this type of accommodation.[99] (3) about 80 percent were forced to pay higher rents in their new dwellings, although these were located for the most part within a mile of their former residences. Reynolds rated fifteen of the cities studied as superior to the others in their use of planned relocation, which usually included the use of trained social workers to aid in intensive counseling of the displaced persons or in the conduct of information and public relations activities. He reports that only 34 percent of the families in the good-practice cities relocated in non-recommended, usually substandard housing, as contrasted with 85 percent in the poor-practice cities. The relocatees in good-practice cities also paid lower rent increases.

Aid in moving. The traditional emphasis on local responsibility for the welfare of residents has already been discussed, but in many cases this has meant that newcomers in need were given only enough money to get across the county line under the penalty of police action if they failed to do so. This same procedure is continually cropping up. It is not too infrequently that one hears the old proposal that the way to solve the problems of the inner city is to ship the newcomers out. The growing Puerto Rican population in New York City is only the latest of the newcomers to bear the brunt of this charge.

In recent years subsidies have been given to many permanent resi-

---

[97] Dorothy S. Montgomery, "Relocation and Its Impact on Families," *Social Casework*, Vol. 41, No. 8 (October 1960), pp. 402–407.

[98] Harry W. Reynolds, Jr., "Family Relocation Can Succeed in Urban Renewal Work," *The American City* (April 1960), pp. 183 ff.

[99] James G. Banks, Assistant Commissioner for Relocation and Community Organization of the Urban Renewal Administration, reported that as of June 1960 about 50 percent of the persons displaced by urban renewal were eligible for public housing but that only 18.7 percent actually moved into it. These factors were reported in a speech before the National Association of Housing and Redevelopment Officials in Washington, D.C. in October 1961.

dents of the inner city to aid them in their move from one section of the city to another. The granting of subsidies has led to many forms of graft.

The lack of money to cover the cost of moving is not the only difficulty faced in the relocation of families. Housing, no matter how inadequate, is often associated with family life and familiar routines, which may result in a reluctance to move. For the old, the handicapped, and the insecure the move may represent a seemingly insurmountable barrier. For the builder the delays in clearance are costly. However, public opinion and law usually will not allow the summary eviction of tenants. Hence it is frequently seen as both good business and humanitarianism to employ social workers to help with the "hard core" families during the moving process. This may be done in many ways: by educational and public relations programs to win support for the urban renewal program in general, by the organization of citizen committees to interpret the move and aid in its accomplishment, or by direct counseling and guidance of the persons to be moved. The full range in social work methods may be used in this process: casework, group work, and community organization.[100]

Getting Settled in the New Area

The relocation services offered typically seem to be geared to getting the families out of the clearance area. Only recently has there been even the most meager form of follow-up to see how the replanted family is flourishing in its "new environment." These words are placed in quotations because, too often, all that occurs is a shift from one slum to another. Reynolds found that two thirds of *all* relocated families tended to settle within twelve blocks of their former homes. He concluded, "The result was an extension outward of the same problem

---

[100] Drayton S. Bryant, "The Next Twenty Years in Public Housing," *Social Work*, Vol. 4, No. 2 (April 1959), pp. 46–54; Colburn, *op. cit.*; Cooley, *op. cit.*; David H. Keppel, "Public Welfare and Public Housing," *Public Welfare*, Vol. 18, No. 2 (April 1960), pp. 99–102, 124–125; Beatrice McKibbin, "Social Services for Public Housing," *Journal of Housing*, Vol. 17, No. 10 (November 1960), pp. 408–412; Murray E. Ortof, "Public Housing: New Neighbors in Old Communities," *Social Work*, Vol. 4, No. 2 (April 1959), pp. 55–63; Danile J. Ransohoff, "Today's Housing Program, the Community and Social Casework," *Marriage and Family Living*, Vol. 27, No. 2 (May 1955), pp. 156–161; Mel J. Ravitz, "Effects of Urban Renewal on Community Racial Patterns," *Journal of Social Issues*, Vol. 13, No. 4 (1957), pp. 38–49; Florence Ray, "Planning Decentralized Programs," *Social Welfare Forum, 1955* (New York: Columbia University Press), pp. 221–230; Marion O. Robinson, "Community-wide Planning for Family Health and Welfare," *Marriage and Family Living*, Vol. 19, No. 2 (May 1957), pp. 198–203; Violet M. Sieder, "What Is Community Organization Practice in Social Work?" *Social Welfare Forum 1956* (New York: Columbia University Press), pp. 160–174; Sussman, *op. cit.*

conditions that marked the original, blighted areas and caused their decline." [101]

The fact that approximately three-fifths of the persons relocated from urban renewal sites are nonwhites helps to explain this pattern. It is very difficult to find adequate housing for Negro families outside the "ghetto"—or as a matter of fact in the ghetto as well. This is neatly epitomized by a recent incident:

> . . . in San Francisco, according to testimony given before the San Francisco Grand Jury by the Director of the Redevelopment Agency. The Western Addition Project required the removal of 8,000 persons living on the clearance site, eighty percent nonwhite. The report states:
>
> In locating dwelling units for people displaced by the urban renewal program, the Redevelopment Agency ran into race discrimination. At the time Attorney General Mosk ordered the agency to cease accepting discriminatory listings, there were 65 vacancies listed with the agency, only five of which were available to nonwhites. Three housing workers from the agency subsequently turned up 425 rental vacancies, of which only 15 were offered on a nondiscriminatory basis—and only eight of these met the agency's standards.
>
> The critical housing problems of the nonwhite minorities were pointed up by the presence of state legislation forbidding discrimination in housing. But then aggressive work by the redevelopment personnel was able to turn up only a picayune of standard housing, available to the minority. To be sure, the aggressive work was needed on the part of the agency personnel to expand the vacancy listings from sixty-five to 425. There were then eight dwellings units, the agency's contribution to an estimated 6,000 displaced minority persons. [102]

In recent years three sectors of social agencies have provided direct services to families in the process of neighborhood integration: Intergroup relations, public housing, and traditional social services—particularly the neighborhood houses, community welfare councils, Urban Leagues, and the area councils.

It is customary among social workers to believe that the intergroup relations commissions and other minority-based agencies are primarily concerned with mass education, the formulation of human relations social policy, and legislative enactment and enforcement and not with direct service to individuals. But this is only half the story of their work. Such offices frequently receive requests for information that

---

[101] Harry W. Reynolds, Jr., "Relocation Statistics for Philadelphia Show Rehousing Patterns," *Journal of Housing*, Vol. 13, No. 10 (November 1956), pp. 389–402; Colean, *op. cit.*

[102] Montgomery, *op. cit.*

cannot be routinely given. Those who ask for information often are leaders. The executive of the intergroup agency sees this as an opportunity for education and policy making that extends beyond the person who makes the request. In addition, there is much counseling and guidance that goes under the heading of "firefighting," which may involve a visit to a person who objects to a Negro family moving into the neighborhood. Protective efforts may be extended to the Negro "pioneer" who is first of his race to enter a "white" neighborhood.

Some intergroup relations commissions have a fraternal interchange with the local branch of the National Urban League, and people who seem to require long-term counseling are referred to that agency. The Urban League generally is viewed as a "social work" agency, whereas human relations commissions have not yet firmly established their professional identification with organized social work or social welfare associations.[103]

Nor have the intergroup agencies, in general, yet established systematic programs of help for Negro pioneers to facilitate their movement out of the ghetto, although now and then assistance is given. The available studies indicate that these pioneers are fairly resourceful business and professional people with sufficient income to maintain or better the standard of living of the neighborhoods into which they move; they do not seek agency services in finding housing, nor after they have moved in, unless there is a crisis. Social agency personnel are sharply divided in their opinions about the effectiveness of social agency intervention to prepare the neighborhood for the move-in, or to give direct aid to the pioneer except in a crisis.[104]

Elsewhere in the paper it has been noted that low income is the major barrier preventing drastic depopulation of the inner city. The significant decline in rates of growth of the white population in inner cities, plus the absolute decline in numbers of whites in many older

---

[103] The parent organization of the commissions is either the Conference of Commissions Against Discrimination or the National Association of Intergroup Relations Officials. The latter is not a member of the National Conference of Social Welfare which brings together a large number of professional organizations, including the National Association of Social Workers, National Housing Conference, National Association of Housing and Redevelopment Officials, National Urban League, and others concerned with the housing problem. NAIRO has rejected such an affiliation three times in the recent past, according to its chairman, Mr. Routh. The reasons for this are complex and should be studied. Helen E. Amerman and Joyce Barnes, "A Resurvey of Local Public Intergroup Relations Agencies, (New York: National Association of Intergroup Relations Officials, October 1957) ; Blumberg, *op. cit.*; Fogel, *op. cit.*; Granger, *op. cit.*; Valien, *op. cit.*

[104] L. K. Northwood and Ernest A. T. Barth, *Neighborhoods in Transition— The New American Pioneers and Their Neighbors* (Seattle: University of Washington, 1964).

cities of the Northeast, is evidence of a trend that might ultimately lead to a significant reduction in their numbers in these areas. Regardless of the long-range population trends, the mass of people needing the traditional social agency services continues to live in them. The millions of whites and nonwhites who pour into the inner cities each year become tenants of public housing projects and many other residential inner-city areas. They also are the targets of a variety of social services, some of which are described in the paragraphs below.

There is no "welcome wagon" in the slums to greet newcomers getting settled in the area. Although some neighborhood churches visit nearby, the practice is customary only with fundamentalist groups seeking converts; most other churches visit only regular members who are sick or for some other reason.

The workers in most casework agencies receive their clients in their offices. They do not go out into the neighborhood looking for persons with problems in order to offer them help. This does not mean that home visits are neglected, nor does it mean that new clients are never discovered by the initiative of the caseworker. In fact, workers with youth, school social workers, and public health nurses may adopt a more "aggressive" attitude on this question. Similarly, the neighborhood-house workers find that often they must literally take their programs into the homes of residents to win acceptance for them. This is particularly true of urban renewal programs. In many localities "block organization" has been established, in which the initial contacts and subsequent organization resulted from visits initiated by the neighborhood worker. Such programs frequently are credited for the success of conservation-type urban renewal programs. This is a long-run endeavor. Thus the success of the rehabilitation or conservation of housing and neighborhood is believed to depend on the active "reaching out" and participation of social agency personnel with individual residents of the area on a continuing basis.[105]

Similarly, many public housing projects have a trained tenant relations staff, for whom programs of visiting the tenants are a part of the routine to be made by the officer, himself, or by a citizen committee. In such cases the tenant relations officer can act as an effective link between the resident and the local social agencies, able to transmit information that can be of great help in planning and providing services.

[105] Leonard J. Czarniecki, "Detroit—Summary Proceedings of the Working Conference on Citizen Participation in Neighborhood Conservation and Rehabilitation," *Action* (September 12, 1958); William C. Loring, Jr., Frank Sweetser, and Charles F. Ernst, *Community Organization for Citizen Participation in Urban Renewal* (Cambridge, Mass.: Cambridge Press, Housing Association of Metropolitan Boston, 1957); Philadelphia Housing Association, *A Citizen's Guide to Housing and Urban Renewal in Philadelphia* (June 1960).

On the other hand, the tenant relations officer may be too closely associated with the "management" activities of maintenance and custody to serve effectively in this capacity.[106]

Control of Problem Conditions

A fourth stage in neighborhood integration is the management of crises that recur in neighborhood life. Elsewhere in the paper differences were noted between the inner city and other residential neighborhoods. The inner city has potential for recurrent crises for many reasons: frustrating housing conditions, great cultural diversity of the inhabitants, and laxness of police enforcement. In the normal healthy neighborhood the good citizen is one who assimilates the values and ways of life of his peers, always with the provision that he not become too parochial in his outlook. In the inner city the good citizen may be the one who is able to insulate himself and his children from antisocial values and activities.[107]

Social agencies have tried both the carrot and the club methods of social control. Each is now believed to have its legitimate uses. Most social agencies stress information, education, and persuasion as their major work.[108] These agencies could be classified by the number and nature of their audiences, by the results desired from the program of communications, and by the follow-up expended to achieve the results. A communications model for the analysis of social agency structure would seem to be appropriate because so much of agency work is in individual counseling, in committee discussions and conferences, in the preparation of policy and research statements, in the dissemination of literature on an issue to a selected audience, in public statements through the mass media, and in annual reports and newspapers for memberships.

---

[106] Agnes Meyer, "A Civic Leader Speaks Out on the Human Side of the Housing Problem," *Journal of Housing*, Vol. 16, No. 11 (November 1959), pp. 390–400.

[107] The differences in the "morality" of the inner-city neighborhoods and neighborhoods elsewhere is a moot point. The "beatniks" are ready to indict the smugness of the middle classes, especially their indifference to the very real inequalities and exploitation that exist in the inner city. They see an injustice in which the slum dweller is held to blame for the conditions that enrich the middle-class absentee owners of the slums. Similarly, the petty thieves and the grafters, after they are caught, often complain of the thieving and grafting politicians and businessmen who carry on similar practices at a higher level with seeming impunity. These accounts have been proved to be true. Is the morality of the inner city, which may be conducive to "beatnik" escapism and petty criminalism, inferior to the morality of middle classes, which may be conducive to other forms of escapism and criminalism? This is a point frequently made by researchers and writers on crime and juvenile delinquency.

[108] Dennis Clark, "Urban Renewal and Intergroup Relations," *Journal of Intergroup Relations*, Vol. 2, No. 1 (Winter 1960–1961), pp. 68–78.

The rational permissive methods of information, education and persuasion—which are the main line of endeavor of social agencies—can also be supplemented by economic and political measures. In the field of housing political measures include efforts to secure legislation and administrative rulings to control land use (zoning laws), to require healthy, safe, and sanitary housing (housing codes), and to forbid discrimination in housing (open housing acts). Organized social welfare has been active in such legislative campaigns and reform movements for a century.

The drive to overcome opposition and obtain the passage of housing, planning, and discrimination ordinances is extremely difficult, and there would seem to be as many failures in such campaigns as successes.[109] In recent years these campaigns have been greatly facilitated by the urban renewal legislation, which requires an adequate set of city codes as a prerequisite for federal aid; also federal housing aid may be terminated if there is inadequate code enforcement. However, the passage of such laws is never so difficult as the enforcement.

Among the problems in enforcement are the following: [110]

1. Tenants frequently do not know there is a law to protect them, what it provides for, or how to file a complaint. They may not believe anything will be done. They may not want to get "mixed-up" with the "police." They are afraid to complain because their rents may be hiked or they may be forced to move.

2. The number of complaints is so great in ratio to the number of inspectors that routine inspections are few and far between, and the processing of complaints takes a long time. Inspectors are subject to bribery to do nothing about complaints. Because of the shortage of inspectors, the emphasis is placed on ensuring good standards in new housing rather than on correcting deficiencies in the old.

3. Sometimes it is difficult to find the owners of slum housing that requires repair. Rents are collected by an agency and paid into a housing management corporation. Frequently it is cheaper to pay the fines than to make the repairs. The fines become a part of the overhead in the business.

4. When the owner can be found and he seems willing to make the repairs, his position sometimes is that the costs are so great that he would have to raise rents sky-high to recoup them; that it would be cheaper to tear the building down and establish a parking lot—this

---

[109] Guy Greer, "Housing: Let's Not Kid Ourselves," *Survey Graphic*, Vol. 36, No. 9 (September 1947), pp. 469–472; Johnson, *op. cit.*; Vernon, *op. cit.*; Bredemeier, *op. cit.*

[110] Martin Millspaugh and Gurney Breckenfield, *The Human Side of Urban Renewal* (New York: Ives Washburn, 1960).

would further contribute to the housing shortage; that a slum clearance project is planned for the area in which his tenements are located and that the housing will be torn down in three years. Therefore, he cannot be expected to do anything.

5. The repairs are made but not much care is taken of the property by the transient residents. They cannot see the value of taking good care of housing located in an area infested with rats, in which the garbage is not collected regularly, and in which police protection is poor or discriminatory. The failure to provide adequate maintenance by tenant or owner reinforces the statement: these people are too ignorant and filthy to take proper care of the property—they just let it run down because it isn't theirs. Too often, the prediction is fulfilled and the cycle starts again.

Each of these problems has led to forms of social welfare amelioration. The block and area councils, which sometimes are helpful to newcomers in getting settled, often base their organizational campaigns on efforts to improve the physical and social environment.[111] The clean-up and beautification campaigns are also paralleled by activities to inform renters of their "rights" under the housing code; area councils in the inner cities frequently become tenant councils; in the suburbs they are comprised largely of property owners. Inner-city area councils "protest" the lack of services or enforcement in their home neighborhoods and form committees to meet with local government agencies and lobbies to pressure for reform.

The area councils in the "open" neighborhood have their parallel in "tenant councils" formed in some public housing projects. In the past great things were expected by many social welfare personnel of tenant organizations in public housing.[112] The public housing movement believed that the advent of low-cost public housing would, by itself, bring about a renaissance in slum life, that by the act of providing more adequate housing there would be a flowering of democracy, citizen participation in social life, and an end to many problems of the inner city.

This widespread belief is one of the factors that have been responsible for the development of public housing social services.[113] During the war years federal funds helped to establish a variety of programs for "defense" workers and the military. After the war the federal appropriations were cut off and the services withered on the vine. Recently, however, the "citizen participation" requirement of urban renewal legislation has

---

[111] Alva B. Maxey, "The Block Club Movement in Chicago," *Phylon*, Vol. 18, No. 2 (June 1957), pp. 124–131; Henderson, *op. cit.*

[112] Robert M. Fisher, *Twenty Years of Public Housing: Economic Aspects of the Federal Program* (New York: Harper & Brothers, 1959); Hill, *op. cit.*

[113] Bredemeier, *op. cit.*

again aroused interest in such social services.[114] Of course there are other reasons, not the least of which has been the difficulty in coping with vandalism and rowdy conduct in such projects. Straight punitive measures have not been notably successful and have led to renewed efforts to win voluntary cooperation of tenants by the provision of social services.[115] The physical arrangements of the projects and the presence of facilities and meeting rooms make the project a "natural" center for social service programs. With the cooperation of a wide range of community agencies, some projects have established "model apartments" for demonstration purposes to teach home care and decoration. These may be coupled with adult classes and other activities to upgrade housekeeping practices in the project and thus increase pride in living there.[116] Similar demonstrations have been made in conservation-type urban renewal programs of home or apartment remodeling, directed at the owners of housing rather than tenants.

In all of these programs there is a strong element of education, persuasion, and voluntarism. Even when housing code offenders were found guilty in Baltimore, they could be "sentenced" to attend a special "clinic" to help to educate them in the need to correct housing abuses.

There has been no notable success in the control of conditions that create and maintain slums in the United States.[117] In fact, the best informed current estimates are that the production of slums exceeds the production of housing, and this is one reason for the critical housing problem. The solution may require drastic measures for the control of land use and for community development and planning that have long existed in other nations.

The existence of different minority neighborhoods in the inner city has long been a source of friction and conflict, especially when a minority is expanding into a new area.[118] Many social welfare programs have been directed toward the control of tensions in such situations. It is

---

[114] Raymond M. Foley, "Evolution of the U. S. Housing Program," *T & CP Bulletin*, Vol. 3 (United Nations, 1950) pp. 3–11; Murray B. Meld, "Housing and Planning: Today's Social Frontier," *Social Work*, Vol. 2, No. 2 (April 1957), pp. 32–36; Fern M. Colburn, *The Neighborhoods and Urban Renewal* (New York: The National Federation of Settlements, 1963).

[115] Ludwig L. Geismar, "Three Levels of Treatment for the Multi-Problem Family," *Social Casework* (March 1961) (Reprint); Osborne McLain, "Social Work in a Public Housing Project," *Social Casework*, Vol. 41, No. 8 (October 1960), pp. 408–412; Agnes Meyer, "The Problem Family: New Devices Are Being Tested for Prevention and Cure," *Journal of Housing*, Vol. 16, No. 10 (November 1959), pp. 363–366; Colburn, *op. cit.*; McKibben, *op. cit.*

[116] Jonassen, *op. cit.*

[117] Catherine Bauer, "Housing, Planning, and Public Policy," *Marriage and Family Living*, Vol. 17, No. 2 (May 1955), pp. 101–102.

[118] Coleman, *op. cit.*

probably not an accident that the growth of city human relations commissions has paralleled the growth of the Negro minority in urban centers.[119]

The immigrant ghettoes have tended to dissolve over time; the Jewish minority neighborhood has been accepted by others largely as something its members wish to preserve and who have this right in a democracy. However, with the majority of Negroes, the desire is for an end to segregation and the ghetto. Agencies have taken steps to move in this direction.[120] These efforts have taken one or more of the following courses: (1) to help the Negro move out of the ghetto; (2) to encourage whites to remain in neighborhoods undergoing racial transition; (3) to control the racial composition of housing projects and other facilities by administrative regulations and "quotas"; (4) to select the sites for public housing projects and other facilities so that the users will not be of a single race.

These courses of action have had limited effectiveness up to the present time. Only a few affluent and enterprising Negro families have successfully moved into new or stable white residential areas. Perhaps the major effect on the inner-city ghetto of "pioneering" in the outer city is to demonstrate that resistance in the white areas can be overcome.

As we have pointed out in many places in the paper, the area of the Negro minority neighborhood is continually expanding with their influx into the cities. So long as the expansion occurs, it will be difficult to select sites for facilities and projects that will maintain an interracial character unless a substantial proportion of the white families remain. Whether white families will remain will depend to some extent on the continuing attractiveness of the neighborhood for residential life. Recent studies in some cities have shown that when white renters have been replaced by Negro owners the physical qualities of the housing and neighborhood have distinctly improved. Therefore, it need not be the fear of property loss that leads the white family to move from a transition area. The escape needed by both the oldtimer and the newcomer is from prejudice. It is this general line of reasoning that characterizes much of the effort to maintain white residency in transition areas. Human relations commissions and urban leagues have been the social agencies involved in such programs, but many seemingly successful campaigns to maintain interracial areas have been waged by local citizen groups,

---

[119] Robert C. Weaver, "Northern Ways," *Survey Graphic*, Vol. 36, No. 1 (January 1947), pp. 43–47, 123–124.

[120] Frank S. Horne, "The Open City—Threshold to American Maturity," *Phylon*, Vol. 18, No. 2 (June 1957), pp. 133–139; Isaacs, *op. cit.*; Davis, *Residence and Race*, *op. cit.*; Eleanor P. Wolf, "The Invasion Succession Sequence as a Self-Fulfilling Prophecy," *Journal of Social Issues*, Vol. 13, No. 4 (1957), pp. 7–20.

often associated with the church. The approach of such groups is that this is a spiritual or moral issue, rather than a program for professional social services.

A fourth course of action frequently taken by public housing authorities to control the formation of the ghetto has been the institution of an informal quota system in which a fixed ratio of white to Negro is set for each project. It was hoped that this would prevent projects located in interracial areas from becoming all-Negro. Some privately financed luxury apartments and cooperatives in the inner city have attempted to follow the same plan. Some, in fact, from the start have been built as interracial housing with the quota as a publicly stated objective.[121] When "open housing" legislation exists, such quota practices are usually forbidden by law, a source of considerable conflict among intergroup relations workers, some of whom would like to support *both* "open housing" legislation and "quota" practices to prevent areas from remaining all-white or becoming all-Negro.[122]

The difficulties for organized social welfare in the control of conditions that create and maintain ghettoes match the difficulties in the control of conditions that create and maintain the slums.[123] Minority group members are in double jeopardy. They must be able to cope with slum and ghetto conditions. Those agencies that serve the minority must solve both problems to be successful.

Planning Prevention

It is seldom that local social agencies become directly involved in long-range planning for housing and community development. To be sure, from time to time conferences and meetings are devoted to gaining perspective about the trend of the times and the major social problems. However, such conferences are held largely for two purposes: to educate the persons in attendance and to lay down broad social policies to guide the individual agencies in their legislative and social actions. Such conferences, especially when they are convened by an important government official or legislative body, may have an effect on the actions subsequently taken by the government. But this is not a necessary consequence of the meeting. In other words, there is seldom a direct tie between policy making, planning, and organizational implementation in the fields of housing and community development for social welfare.

---

121 Grier, "Market Characteristics in Interracial Housing," *op. cit.*

122 Dan Dodson, "Can Intergroup Quotas Be Denied?" *Journal of Intergroup Relations*, Vol. 1, No. 4 (Autumn 1960), pp. 12–17; L. K. Northwood and Louise Klein, "The Benign Quota: An Unresolved Issue," *Phylon*, 1964. In press.

123 Loring, Sweetser, and Ernst, *op. cit.*

In addition, a recent survey by the author in forty cities indicated that as late as 1960 the policy committees in urban renewal seldom included professional social workers or human relations personnel.[124] The city planner and the executive of the local public housing authority were more likely to be represented on such bodies. However, most top policy makers in urban renewal were recruited largely from business and political circles.[125]   Among the initial findings of this study were these:

1. A great overspecialization has occurred among agencies providing social services for minority housing.   The human relations agencies seldom participate in urban renewal or the broad range of traditional social services in the community and have become narrowly interested in "minority" and "racial" problems and clientele.   The official authorities in housing, planning, and urban renewal are focused on physical and economic rehabilitation of the city rather than on its social needs; in general, they are little concerned and fail to involve the traditional social services of the community; in particular they avoid explicit statements and activities that concern the racial minority in their cities.   The traditional social agencies, with the possible exception of some urban leagues, neighborhood houses, and area councils,

---

[124] Information was sought about the housing problems of low-income groups, with special reference to racial minorities and a description and evaluation of the work of social agencies to implement certain provisions of the urban renewal legislation: housing-code enforcement, citizen participation, and aid to persons displaced by clearance projects.

Interviews were completed with three to fourteen agency executives in each of fifteen target cities: Baltimore, Boston, Buffalo, Chicago, Cincinnati, Cleveland, Detroit, Indianapolis, Kansas City (Mo.), Los Angeles, Newark (N.J.), New York City, Philadelphia, Pittsburgh, and Seattle.   In addition, single interviews were obtained in twenty-five other cities. The collaborators are Daniel Anthony, Herbert Aurbach, Tom Blair, Leonard Blumberg, Butler Jones, Rose Hum Lee, Robert O'Brien, Morton Rubin, Edward Shaffer, and Karl Taeuber.   The following graduate students also helped with this study: William Berleman, Sue Sumioka, Takashi Watanabe, Patricia Weeks.

The findings of this study were consistent with those of Gerda Lewis who studied citizen participation in 91 cities having approved, workable programs as of July 1956. See Gerda Lewis, "Citizens Participation in Renewal Surveyed," *Journal of Housing*, Vol. 16, No. 3 (March 1959), pp. 80–87. *See also* Lawrence K. Northwood, "The Threat and Potential of Urban Renewal—A 'Workable Program' for Better Race Relations," *The Journal of Intergroup Relations*, Vol. 2, No. 2 (Spring 1961), pp. 101–114; L. K. Northwood, "The Institutionalization of Social Services in Urban Renewal," *The Social Service Review*, Vol. 37, No. 1 (March 1963), pp. 64–75.

[125] Lewis Mumford, "The Good Life Must Be the Goal for City Planning," *Journal of Housing*, Vol. 6, No. 1 (January 1949), pp. 7–10; Stephen G. Thompson, "Where Realty Leaders Stand on Urban Renewal," *Architectural Forum*, Vol. 110, No. 4 (April 1959), pp. 109–111, 214; Millspaugh and Breckenfield, *op. cit.*

are concerned only with the clientele they presently serve; they do not reach out to engage in minority housing social services and in general fail to take even moderate leadership in social planning efforts, which might accompany urban renewal. This is especially true of the community welfare "planning" councils.

2. Urban-renewal social services for persons displaced by clearance projects in most cities are organized under the housing authority; services are minimal in character and little special effort is devoted to minority families; the handful of professional social workers employed by these agencies, all in cities of more than one million, with certain exceptions, such as Boston, Baltimore, and Philadelphia, are used in routine and nonprofessional ways. It is only very recently that social workers have been used in this capacity.

Although the participation of organized social welfare and professional social work in planning is relatively limited at the present time, there seem to be many valuable contributions that the social worker might make as a technical advisor in both short and long-term planning. In the short-term functions of the planner he attempts to "mesh" the various activities of the community so that it can continue to operate in a relatively harmonious and prosperous state.[126] The small-area worker's intimate knowledge of the local neighborhood should be helpful in establishing the boundaries of the planning area and in assessing resistance to plans. He will know the social organization of the small area necessary for their implementation, and his association with the people of the neighborhood will provide information in regard to the most advantageous location of facilities for maximum convenience and use. These are examples of the kinds of advice the social worker might be able to provide.[127]

In the long-term functions of the planner it is his duty to initiate and direct plans for what the community is to become. It is at this point that there could and should be linkage between the planning staff and organized social welfare.[128] City planners tend to be in-

---

[126] Eugene V. Schneider and M. Lustig, "What Can Sociology Contribute to Planning?" Paper presented before the American Sociological Association, 1960.

[127] Jack Barsoum, "Opinions and Attitudes of Cambridge, Massachusetts, Residents Toward Urban Renewal." M.S. thesis, School of Public Relations and Communications, Boston University, 1956; Morris Cohen, *Research and Action in Neighborhood Movement.* Paper delivered before the Society for the Study of Social Problems in Chicago, August 1960; Hatcher, *op. cit.*; Loring, Sweetser, and Ernst, *op. cit.*; Mayer, "Can City Planners and Social Planners Get Together," *op. cit.*

[128] Catherine Bauer, "Social Policy and Social Research in Housing," *Journal of Social Issues,* Vol. 7, Nos. 1 and 2 (1951), pp. 1–34; Bauer, "Housing, Planning and Public Policy, *op. cit.*;" Bauer, Redevelopment: A Misfit of the Fifties, *op. cit.*; Arthur Dunham, *op. cit.*; Sharp, *op. cit.*; Gans, *op. cit.*

fluenced greatly by the engineer, architect, and economist. The result is that we have a city laid out to facilitate its functions as a business center. The social welfare specialist might supplement this combination in ways in which the human needs of the people would be given a greater voice.

Among the traditional social agencies at the metropolitan level the community welfare council is most closely associated with social planning.[129] Elsewhere in the paper we have noted three other functions that have been emphasized by such councils: federated fund raising, program development, and coordination of agency services. Most recently, a move has been made toward reorganizing the welfare council to make it more efficient for the purpose of program development. Hopefully, this will not be at the expense of its coordinating and planning functions. In particular, there is need for machinery to bring together the varied organizations and programs that become involved in housing and urban renewal. The public housing authority often stands aloof from other planning efforts and social welfare organization. In many cities several departments of the city government are engaged in urban renewal. In Chicago there are thirteen different agencies managing some urban-renewal projects; in New York City there are five.[130]

In voluntaristic social order it is next to impossible to bring about effective coordination over a long period, especially in terms of control of the budget. Many tax-supported agencies are legally accountable to another board than the welfare council. They can be advised but not controlled. This is also true of the large hospitals and other corporate entities with large budgets. Nevertheless, working relationships can be established for the exchange of information and for cooperation on programs of mutual interest.[131] The traditional social welfare organization frequently has a backlog of knowledge of techniques and channels of communication which are points of leverage in community-housing decisions. In particular, the community welfare council could do effective research on housing needs and programs if it were pointed in this direction.

---

[129] Mel J. Ravitz and Adelaide Dinwoodie, "Detroit Social Workers Mobilize Citizen Aid for Urban Renewal," *Journal of Housing*, Vol. 13, No. 7 (July 1956), pp. 232–234; Gerda Lewis, *op. cit.*; Millspaugh and Breckenfield, *op. cit.*

[130] The research project in which the author and his collaborators is presently engaged is conducting detailed studies of urban-renewal planning in these and other major cities.

[131] Luther Gulick, "Metropolitan Organization," *Annals of the American Academy of Political and Social Science*, Vol. 314 (November 1957), pp. 57–64; Thomas H. Reed, "The City of the Future," *American Journal of Economic Sociology*, Vol. 15, No. 3 (April 1956), pp. 343–351.

Conclusions

It is quite obvious that the residents of the inner city are not going to create ideal housing in ideal neighborhoods by their own efforts alone. The entry by the federal government into housing and urban renewal, together with the acceptance of these programs by great numbers of cities, big and small, is clear evidence that "the housing problem" will not be solved strictly at the city level or by exclusive reliance on private industry.

On the other hand, there is equally clear evidence that ideal housing in ideal neighborhoods cannot be superimposed on residents by a government Leviathan. To begin to be successful requires a partnership of national, metropolitan, and local agencies.

It has been suggested that there are many roles for the social worker, cutting across the three specialties. Included are direct clinical case-work services with individuals and groups at various stages in the neighborhood integration process. Also needed are program-organizational services of community organization and planning to achieve the ideal neighborhood. Organized social welfare can take the lead in promoting adequate social planning or it can fit into the effort as practitioner, administrator, or consultant.

SUMMARY AND CONCLUSIONS

This paper represents a first step in the examination of social problem conditions in the inner cities of the United States. The primary purpose has not been to derive either a specific program of action with respect to dealing with particular social problems or a program of reform of particular social welfare practices, though to be sure there are comments on these subjects. The main objective has been to examine some of the difficulties in the conceptual analysis of a particular set of social problems. This examination has been limited by the time and current knowledge of the author, who has been conditioned by his sociological upbringing and by the fact that research was limited to reading about the United States, with a little of Great Britain thrown in.

The findings are summarized in seven points:

1. The obvious is demonstrated: social problem conditions have existed for more than a century in the inner cities of the United States. The inner city per se is a zone of specialized neighborhoods of widely diverse character. Although luxury apartments and hotels may be located there, most residents live in inferior rented housing; they have low, unstable annual incomes and large proportions are Negro or another minority. The Negro ghetto is expanding.

2. The durability and intransigence of the social problem conditions in the inner city are good evidence that they are woven into the total social fabric of metropolis and society. They are one consequence of relatively uncontrolled urbanization. The inner city endures not only because it is economically profitable to some but also because it serves other sections of the city symbiotically, including certain segments of the population that value the relaxation of social controls enforced elsewhere.

3. Organized social welfare has attempted to ameliorate social problem conditions in the inner city in a wide variety of programs and services directed (a) at helping the "victims"; (b) at controlling antisocial practices; and (c) at removing the conditions. In different eras different problems have been emphasized and/or singled out for treatment.

4. The principle of local responsibility for social welfare services continues. However, more and more help is being given by government and private organizations, organized at the state and national levels. Government aid is taking the form of insurance programs, grants-in-aid, and subsidies for housing and urban renewal, health facilities, and research about particular social problems, such as juvenile delinquency. This is recognition that the locality by itself has insufficient resources to cope successfully with health, housing, and income maintenance problems of its citizenry or to accomplish the removal of the specially resistant problem conditions entrenched in the inner city. The oldest of these national programs has been in existence for scarcely more than twenty-five years.

5. Organized social work has adopted many approaches to meet social problems. The gross features of the clinical and small-area approaches were contrasted. Pending definitive empirical research, it is impossible to state with precision which approach is most appropriate for the amelioration of a specific problem behavior. Logically, clinical methods would seem to be of greatest help in correcting the clients, distorted perceptions of reality and in providing him with reinforcements necessary to handle persistent problem conditions. On the other hand, the small-area approach is prophylactic. It nibbles at the social problems that exist in an area. By the collective action of citizenry, in conjunction with organized social welfare and other agencies which have parallel or complementary objectives, some steps can be taken to control antisocial practices in an area and thus to reduce the risk of exposure. The small-area reforms have a cumulative potential and may be the starting place for broader planned and/or directed social

change. The potential for directed social change in the clinical situation is minimal. The two approaches are seen to be compatible and reinforcing.

6. The inner city and its subareas have been studied by many disciplines and professions. Although certain values are seen in the utility of the concept of the inner city as a descriptive category, none of the literature examined dealt in detail with the concept. Smaller subareas have been used for description and action, four of which were reviewed: school district, microdistrict, census tract, and neighborhood. The optimum small social-action system for social welfare organizational purposes should represent the "natural" neighborhood, most closely circumscribed by a government administrative unit. On the other hand, it is perfectly appropriate to establish arbitrary boundaries in a geographic area for the purpose of a reliable and valid count. Such enumeration districts (census tracts) are usually inappropriate for social action. When boundaries of the enumerative district and the social action system do not coincide, the small area will be dysfunctional for the enumerator and the actionist. It is not necessary that the goals of both be served at the same time. The enumerator must also recognize that any social phenomenon is subject to empirical description and research.

7. When approached from the standpoint of amelioration, the mode of analysis changes from straight description to an examination of the many facets of the social problem which are amenable to directed change. It is necessary to know the "facts" about the problem: but it is also necessary to know what comprises a solution—what is the nonproblem state. This kind of analysis is broached by using as an example "the housing problem" in the inner city. In order to effect changes in "the housing problem," it is necessary to employ the many approaches of social work, including that of the small area.

There is always an agenda of unfinished business. Research which has attempted to establish a cause-effect relationship between a given social condition and a given problem behavior has not been discussed. There are leads to this in the work of Chapin and others on the effects of poor housing on mental health.[132] Shaw and others describing the

---

[132] Stuart F. Chapin, *The Relationship of Housing to Mental Health* (Geneva: World Health Organization Expert Committee on the Public Aspects of Housing, June 1961) ; Robert Merton, ed., "Social Policy and Social Research in Housing," *Journal of Social Issues*, Vol. 7, No. 1 (1951) ; Albert Rose, *Regent Park: A Study in Slum Clearance* (Toronto: University of Toronto Press, 1958) ; Louis Wirth, "Housing as a Field of Sociological Research," *American Sociological Review*, Vol. 12, No. 2 (1947), pp. 137–143.

effects of "delinquency areas" on those who live in them.[133] Nor have we presented a full picture of the social costs of the slums.[134]

It provides a beginning bibliography within a skeleton of a theory for the analysis of social problems and their amelioration in the inner city. Perhaps the next step would be to take a particular social condition and determine how it becomes transformed into a social problem and a program for action. That the identification of a "problem" can be the first step in directed social change has been stressed. Thus problem definition is definitely linked with the chain of events that may lead to changes. The problem still remains a social condition, but it is no longer a part of the anonymous web of life. It is singled out for consideration. Lippitt, Watson, and Westley have digested much of the research about professional workers as "change agents" in the problem-solving process.[135] Although one may disagree with some unfortunate examples of psychological reductionism in the book and its attempt to bring overly large slices of "planned change" into a clinical focus it nevertheless moves in the direction of synthesis of social research in the interests of improving practice. Others are proceeding in the same direction.[136]

In this paper social problems have been dealt with as social conditions scheduled for a change. This is underlined by the frequent telescoping of the terms into "social problem condition," which should not be interpreted to mean that all persons subjected to dysfunctional conditions become "sick." In fact, many persons become rather effectively insulated from the problem condition. The nature of this insulation needs to be studied objectively. In social work, now and again, there is reference to "character-building" agencies. It has been most difficult to identify the elements in "character building." Many social workers have felt rather uneasy about the term because of a general unwillingness to "preach" to clients and because they wanted to allow them full rights of self-determination. Insofar as "character building"

[133] Lowell J. Carr, *Delinquency Control* (New York: Harper & Brothers, 1950); Albert J. Cohen, *Delinquent Boys: The Culture of the Gang* (Glencoe, Ill.: Free Press, 1955); Bernard Lander, *Toward an Understanding of Juvenile Delinquency* (New York: Columbia University Press, 1954); Lloyd Ohlin and R. Cloward, *Delinquency and Opportunity* (Glencoe, Ill.: Free Press, 1960); Clifford R. Shaw, *Delinquency Areas* (Chicago: University of Chicago Press, 1929).

[134] Kogan, *op. cit.*

[135] Ronald J. Lippitt, J. Watson, and B. Westley, *The Dynamics of Planned Change* (New York: Harcourt, Brace and Company, 1958).

[136] Cora Dubois, "The Public Health Worker as an Agent of Socio-cultural Change," *Health Education Monograph Number 5*, 1959; Coleman, *op. cit.*; Hendry, *op. cit.*; Irwin T. Sanders, ed., *Interprofessional Training Goals for Technical Assistance Personnel Abroad* (New York: Council on Social Work Education, 1959); Stein, *op. cit.*

is directed toward enabling resistance to problem conditions, then social work will want to know how "character" is developed so that appropriate professional techniques can be applied toward this end. This points to another necessary line of research.

At many points it has been emphasized that the problems of deterioration in the inner city may be peculiar to America, although it would appear that some other countries share in them.[137] Urban researchers have clearly demonstrated that concentric zonal hypotheses do not pertain in all the great cities of the world but may instead be restricted to some highly industrialized or recently industrialized "Western" nations.[138] Also the inner cities in many old European cities have not the high rates of obsolescence found in the United States. Cross-cultural international research is required for an appropriate statement about the social problem conditions in inner cities. Furthermore, such research may provide suggestions for the sound reorganization of social welfare services in this country.

---

[137] John Barron Mays, "Needs of Old Urban Areas," in Peter Kuenstler, ed., *Community Organization in Great Britain* (New York: Association Press, 1961).

[138] Jack P. Gibbs, *Urban Research Methods* (Princeton, N. J.: D. Van Nostrand Company, 1961) ; Quinn, *op. cit.*

Unmarried Mothers ▶

HELEN HARRIS PERLMAN

THE PROBLEM

A social problem is a complex of behavior and/or circumstances which by its consequences threatens or adversely affects the institutions, mores, standards, and beliefs that are valued—that is to say, emotionally invested—by most members of a society. The existence of the problem is usually recognized when it becomes a clear and present danger to the general welfare. Such danger may lie not simply in the problem itself but also in the problem-solving means which may be a threat to social stability.

The problem complex called "the unmarried mother" in our society presents this double threat: that of the problem's existence and consequences and that of its solution and means of prevention. This paper is an attempt to examine "the unmarried mother" as a social problem, and then particularly as a social work problem, and to identify factors within it and its potential solutions in relation to the goal of "prevention."

Perhaps a first question needs to asked: is the unmarried mother a social problem? If so, why?

It is necessary, first, to state the obvious: unmarried motherhood begins with sex relations "without benefit of clergy" (to use a worn and immediate phrase), proceeds through pregnancy (which cannot be hidden unless the woman hides herself), and culminates with the delivery of an "illegitimate" child. Each of these phases may be seen to represent a threat to American institutions and values and each needs separate attention.

Chastity in women has been a major tenet in American morality. It has been preached and in many places made the object of legislation; its breach has been severely punished, and its necessity has been firmly upheld. The factors that underpin the taboo on illicit sex relations ("illicit" for women, particularly) range from feelings that sex as pleasure is "evil" and "bad" to fears that sexual freedoms threaten the sanctity of marriage, the well-being of the family, and the economic and legal rights of "lawful heirs" to concern about the unhappy social and emotional consequences for the unmarried mother and her out-of-wedlock child, the economic and social costs to the community of a growing "dependent," "immoral" population, and so on, in a chain-reaction cycle.

The girl in high school who is suspected of having sexual relations rouses anxiety in school personnel and parents of other children because she presents a "bad example" and is felt to be a potential source of psychological contagion. The high school girl whose pregnancy is known is expelled or suspended, removed from the sight of her peers; she may return, usually, when she has resumed the proper shape for a high school girl. The unmarried woman who is no longer a minor and who is suspected of having sexual relations may be variously regarded as "immoral," "a tramp," or "a home-breaker," depending on the viewer and the circumstances. But even a permissive viewer, one who believes "it is her own business," tends to anticipate that some hurt will come to her as a result of this "out-of-bounds" relationship—the hurt of unwanted pregnancy, of social censure, or of the loss of self-esteem. In short, actual social strictures combine with undercurrents of feelings that punishment follows on "badness" to support the value of chasity in women.

Yet there is ample evidence that illicit sex relations are fairly widespread.[1] As a threat to moral and religious codes that support virginity in

---

[1] The problems of gathering valid data on the incidence of illicit coition are obvious. Every study made has been subject to criticisms of sampling methods and numbers. Impressions that there is an evident increase in the number of women engaging in illicit coition must be gauged in relation to these facts: the high proportion of females of child-bearing age in today's population, the greatly increased freedom to engage in and to discuss sex openly, and the assumption that books, magazines, movies, plays both reflect and shape what is going on between the sexes.

For a summary of studies of married women who were not virgins at the time of marriage see Winston Ehrmann, *Premarital Dating Behavior* (New York: Henry Holt & Co., 1959) Chapter I. Among the data: Kinsey found that 48 percent of all married women studied had had premarital intercourse, a figure with which several other independent investigators essentially agree; a recent study by Gilbert Youth Research finds that one in every four girls between the ages of 17 and 22 years of age admits to having had sexual intercourse. Terman's findings (Lewis M. Terman *et al.*, *Psychological Factors in Marital Happiness*, New York: McGraw-Hill, 1938) indicate a steady rise in premarital coition.

The January 1963 issue of the *Journal of the National Association of Women Deans and Counselors* is devoted to the sex standards and behavior of college students in the belief that "the proportion of college students engaging in premarital intercourse is increasing. . . ." *See also* Milton I. Levine, M.D., and Maya Pines, "Sex: The Problem Colleges Evade," *Harper's Magazine*, October 1961.

women, marital fidelity, childbirth solely in wedlock, and sanctity of family life, this growing sexual license presents a problem exacerbated by disturbing indications that former stereotypes about the "kinds of girls" who indulge in illicit sexual relations no longer hold. It is further complicated by the generally recognized fact of marked inconsistency between parental, church, and school standard-setting and all the vivid sources of commercial and artistic communication, cheap and crass or precious and aesthetic, which present "illicit" sexual experience as fun, exciting, enhancing, even as the mark of maturity.[2] Thus, because it threatens the peace of mind or the balanced security of stabilizing groups and institutions in the community, illicit coition in itself may be viewed as a social problem.

Out-of-wedlock pregnancy is proof positive of illicit coition. Unless pregnancy is aborted, it cannot be long hidden or denied. It is open evidence that primitive id impulses have conquered individual and social superego injunctions.[3]

The individual and social implications are now cast into bold relief. For the girl or woman there are immediate emotional consequences. She is "caught." However much she may want a baby, consciously or unconsciously, for whatever mature or immature reasons, whatever the defense system she calls up for self-protection, these facts remain: her family, friends, neighbors, and perhaps even her sexual partner see her as "disgraced" or, at the very least, a "fool," a "dupe," "holding the bag." Since people primarily tend to view themselves by their reflections in the eyes of others, she cannot help but feel disgraced and/or demeaned. (Of course, many other complicating emotions and attitudes may accompany these two social and self-judgments.)

During this emotional crisis the pregnant woman must begin to plan for what is, literally and figuratively, a growing problem. What shall she do? She will need from others many kinds of services, to be paid for if she can afford it, to be asked for free if she cannot. Abortion is probably her first thought. No one knows how many pregnancies are aborted

---

[2] Whether in the "trashy" novel or in the novel of high literary quality, there are few to be found today that do not portray sexual relations between a man and woman not married to one another. At times such illicit coition is the protagonist's goal, at times a taken-for-granted part of the life situation, at times the core of conflict. As reflectors of life or as standard-setters for sexual behavior, these novels (as well as plays and movie scripts) differ from those of the past (*Tess of the d'Urbervilles, The Scarlet Letter,* for example) in that sexual transgression is not "punished" by pregnancy, disgrace, or shame.

[3] Interestingly enough, only a generation ago even blessed, legitimate, and desired pregnancies were hidden or disguised, and expectant mothers were supposed to keep evidence of their having had sexual relations with their husbands under "drape and coat" so as not to offend the public eye.

by self-applied drugs and other means, but every corner pharmacist will attest to the frequency with which he gets requests for such nostrums. Abortion by surgery is available only to those who can prove that it is necessary to life and therefore "legal," or those who are willing to pay for it and able to locate that legally and socially condemned physician, the "abortionist." ("Rings" of abortionists now and again are brought to public notice as social problems.)

Failing these means, the unmarried pregnant woman must reach out for medical services before, through, and after delivery; for means of support when she has to leave her job or her family's care; for the shelter and seclusion of a maternity home if she wants to hide her disgrace or shame and protect her family from such censures; for placement of the baby once it is born, through adoption (which will free her) or through placement (which will give her time to make decisions) or for support for herself and the child as a unit.

Thus the unmarried pregnant woman becomes a social problem to the community as well as to herself and her family. Her needs rouse an admixture of emotional responses. At the one pole is the righteous anger that the religious and moral code has manifestly been flouted. At the other is that combination of compassion and the championship of the "weak" or "exploited" that represents the positive side of the Puritan ethic. Our belief in the reformation potential in every sinner, our readiness to give a first-time wrong-doer another chance, and our pervasive concern with physical health all combine to mobilize concern that the pregnancy of even the illicitly pregnant woman should be a healthy one, conducive to the delivery of a healthy baby. The social problem for the community, then, becomes that of inventing and providing the means by which health, often food and shelter, concealment, and "reformation" needs can be met. (Cast into social work language, this might read "how to meet her current physical, economic, and emotional needs and help her to work through the psychosocial conflicts that led to her sexual 'acting out.' ")

Once the pregnant woman gives birth, a most tangible problem is presented to the community: an infant who is to become a person. This infant must be fed, clothed, sheltered, and given the rights and opportunities that society holds as necessary and desirably equal for all citizens. From the moment of his birth he presents problems of general social import. If he is to become a "good citizen," an asset rather than a liability to his society, certain basic provisions must be made for him. The social question: what is to be done with children born out of wedlock?

Perhaps no attitudes about the problems of illicit sex relations and their consequences have undergone more rapid and radical changes

in the last few decades than those about the child himself. Not too long
ago he was considered the "spawn of the devil." State laws required
that he be registered as "illegitimate" and his rights to parental support
and inheritance were denied. He and his mother were legal and social
outcasts—and thus they presented no unduly recognized social problem.

Today, for a complex series of reasons that cannot be traced here,
one major group of babies born out of wedlock is no longer considered
a social problem. Indeed, these white, physically healthy babies are
considered by many to be a social boon, an asset. They are awaited with
impatient eagerness by married couples unable to have children of their
own who want to make a child their heir, their love object, their own.
By whatever defenses or inner fantasies these adoptive parents manage
their individual feelings about the circumstances and sources of a child's
conception, at the point of adoption they actually feel, or have convinced
themselves, that the child inherits no badness, that he is, indeed, innocent of original sin, that he will be what they make him. Because there
are many more married couples wanting to adopt newborn white babies
than there are babies, it may almost be said that they rather than out-of-
wedlock babies are a social problem. (Sometimes social workers in adoption agencies have facetiously suggested setting up social provisions
for "more baby breeding.")

The current answer, then, to what to do with the baby born out of
wedlock is simply this: if he is white and healthy (and if his mother
is willing), give him in adoption; moreover, because prospective adoptive parents outnumber such babies, give him in adoption to people who
have been carefully selected for their ability to love him and to provide
him with economic, social, and emotional security. The "social problem"
becomes one of developing and maintaining the means by which the
needs can be met—in this instance, providing the channels for selection
and matching of wanted babies and wanting parents.

But the nonwhite baby born out of wedlock is another story. He is
not readily adoptable. Typically, the baby born to a nonwhite mother
cannot be "put away" or "given away"; she must usually keep him.[4]
Although within the last few years a number of child welfare agencies
have been working to develop adoptive homes among Negro couples
and also to find adoptive parents for babies of "mixed blood"—Cau-
casian-Negro, Caucasian-Indian, Caucasian-Oriental—there remains the
fact that the numbers of unwanted nonwhite babies are great, the num-

---

[4] ". . . only between 3 and 5 percent of the nonwhite illegitimate children are
adopted," according to the U. S. Bureau of Public Assistance report, *Illegitimacy
and Its Impact on Aid to Dependent Children Program*, (Washington, D.C.: U. S.
Government Printing Office 1960), pp. 35–36. This is in contrast to about 70 percent of white out-of-wedlock babies who are taken in adoption.

bers of prospective adoptive parents small. It is this fact that produces a social problem. The nonwhite out-of-wedlock baby, in union with his unmarried mother, often needs economic, social, and psychological support from the community.

When a Negro unmarried mother gives birth, she has three economic alternatives: she can depend, with her baby, on her family's (or the putative father's) support, she can go to work to support herself and her baby, or she can apply for ADC. In the last two instances she must have someone else care for her baby. If it is not her mother or grandmother, this care must be paid for, and her earnings are rarely enough to buy adequate child care. If she applies for ADC, she and her child become a "burden on the taxpayer." (The recent Newburgh, Louisiana, and Illinois attempts to cut off relief rolls any unmarried mother who had a second child out of wedlock were eruptions of a continuous under-the-surface turmoil in political bodies about the cost to the community of supporting unmarried mothers and their children.)

The state of economic dependency on a regular relief grant is not the unmitigated pleasure that it is sometimes made out to be. The fact is that this money grant to child and mother is a minimal one that meets only marginal food, shelter, and clothing needs. It may be said that this grant is good or better than what this woman had before, and it cannot be argued but that it is a dependable, regular source of support. Nevertheless, it cannot be said that it allows either unwed mother or her growing child opportunity for expansion of their experience, for pushing back the constricting walls that poverty without end imposes, or for looking forward with hope. This subsistence at ground level, coupled with periodic attacks in the public press on "reliefers" or, more recently, on the unmarried mother on ADC in particular, may be expected to have its psychological offshoots, chiefly these: an apathy or resignation, which is the end-product of hopelessness, a lowered sense of self-esteem and worth, the product of being held of small account by others, and a heightened sense of being an outsider to the larger society. Sometimes the outcast manages her feelings by indifference, clowning, self-depreciation. Sometimes she strikes out blindly against those who, to her, represent the "ins."

Whether these attitudes and behaviors do in fact characterize the unmarried mother and child on ADC has not been studied and established. However, social workers will attest to the frequency with which such attitudes and behaviors are found among unwed mothers on ADC, and, moreover, they are psychologically to be expected.

Other social and psychological stresses accompany economic stress. The unmarried mother who keeps her baby finds few avenues of self-expression and pleasure open to her. She is housebound with the care of her baby or she is neglectful of him. She has no husband to whom to express her aggravation and boredom. The baby more often than not causes her to lose a man who might have been a husband someday, if her pregnancy and its consequences had not scared him off, or to lose a man who gave her some sense that she was wanted. So the baby often represents the fruit of her badness or foolishness as well as the betrayal by the man who got her into trouble. Mothering rarely flows warmly and dependably toward the baby thus ruefully or angrily borne.

As the child grows older, whether he is an only child or one of several, he becomes aware, in school, in street play, in movies, or on television, that children are supposed to have fathers, present or respectably dead, that children usually carry their father's name, that his mother silences, laughs off, or yells off the question of who and where his father is. Except under circumstances of warm kinship support or unusual maternal maturity, the out-of-wedlock child develops an ambiguous or impaired sense of his identity. Who he is, what he is, how he "belongs" are questions no one answers for him in ways that build up his self-respect or sense of security.

There are to date very few facts about the growth and development of the children of unwed mothers on ADC—of their personality development, their school and work functioning, their social adaptation, and the like. So it is not known, in fact, whether these children, who drop out of school early or become involved in petty or grave delinquencies, are without future because they have no past in any higher proportion than others of their social class or ethnic group. However, these problems of personal and then social maladjustment are, by today's best knowledge, considered to be closely related to the child's early experience of distrust, of feelings of inferiority, and of being "outcast" and of impoverished nurture.

Meantime, the unwed mother, herself seeking, as every human being does, some sources of satisfaction and affection, hoping that the next man will keep his promise, perhaps will marry her, at least will continue to give her a few extra dollars and some companionship, may find herself sexually involved again, and too often (for the indignant or the socially concerned citizen and for her rueful or annoyed self) pregnant again.

Implied above are possible reasons for recidivism. There are counts of repeated out-of-wedlock pregnancies and childbirth; there are only speculations as to the causes of recidivism.[5] It remains a social prob-

---

[5] Many caseworkers and psychiatrists who have worked with "repeater" unmarried mothers postulate that recidivism is due to the persistence or the re-emergence of

lem of major concern and resentment in communities in which it is paid for by tax funds.

One criterion of the seriousness of a social problem is its size and prevalence. As has been indicated, there are no reliable statistics on the incidence of women's extra- or premarital coition. Nor are there any statistics on illegitimate pregnancies that are not brought to term either by self-induced or illegal abortions.[6]

Only the count of live illegitimate births is available. There is general agreement among all researchers on the subject that this count is probably less than the actual numbers. Underreporting is due to false information given by many women who have been able to make private medical and adoption arrangements, to uncertain reporting in rural areas, especially when delivery is by someone other than a licensed physican, and to the fact that fifteen states no longer record illegitimacy on birth certificates. The latest estimate (National Division of Vital Statistics, Public Health Service, H.E.W.) shows 224,300 illegitimate births in 1960. More detailed figures for 1959 state that "there were about 52 illegitimate births out of every 1000 live births, or a total of about 221,000 illegitimate births in the United States." [7] Roughly, then, six hundred babies are born out of wedlock daily in this country.

The number of illegitimate births—and of unmarried mothers—is on the increase. In the twenty years between 1938–1958 the *"number* of illicit births increased from 87,900 to 208,700; the *illegitimacy ratio,* or estimated number of illicit births per 1000 live births, rose from 38.4 to 49.6; the illegitimacy *rate,* or estimated number of illicit births per 1000 unmarried females of child-bearing ages, increased from 7.0 to 21.0." [8] Interpretations of these figures vary among a number of commentators on them. What is commonly overlooked is that the number of *all* live births in this same twenty-year period has almost doubled and that there has never before been so numerous a population of females of child-bearing age in this country. Whether or not the situation is one to be

---

the same deep-seated needs that led to the first pregnancy. What has been insufficiently queried is the relationship between recidivism and economic-cultural deprivation. Clark Vincent suggests on the basis of his study of Negro and white unmarried mothers that the "association [of recidivism] with socioeconomic status is almost as significant as with race." See *Unmarried Mothers,* (New York: Free Press of Glencoe, 1961), pp. 57–59.

[6] Estimates by Planned Parenthood Association and others agree on the probability that some 750,000 to one million illegal abortions are performed yearly in this country.

[7] U. S. Department of Health, Education, and Welfare, Public Health Service, news release No. 036, July 28, 1961.

[8] Vincent, *op. cit.,* p. 1.

viewed as a crisis, the implacable fact is that the rate of illegitimate births is increasing and that the unmarried mother and her illegitimate child are to be found in increasing numbers in our society.[9]

Is the unmarried mother a social problem? On the basis of the threats she presents to community values and standards and the economic and social dilemmas she and her child arouse, she is. In differing degree and kind of impact on community well-being, depending on her race, economic class, and the stage of her "transgression," she presents the following problems and threats to social balance:

1. She has clearly engaged in illicit sex relations, which threaten long-approved (though increasingly violated) moral values, held to be basic to marriage, marital fidelity, family moral fiber, and social stability.

2. An illegitimate pregnancy is flagrant proof of these sexual transgressions. Particularly as it occurs in minors, in white females, and in middle-class women, it is of concern not only to the woman involved, to her sexual partner, and to her family, but to many socially minded citizens who fear it as a source of moral infection or who anticipate that it may curtail or damage the woman's own future opportunities for marriage, respectability, and social "adjustment."

3. Protective health, economic, and concealment provisions have been developed out of this concern to harbor the pregnant [girl or]woman who is sensitive enough to wish to conceal her "shame." In recent years these services have also taken on the purpose of protecting the well-being of the baby-to-come, valued today for its adoptability. The development and maintenance of such services may, however, become "social problems" in themselves when their money cost begins to be felt as onerous and when need for them outruns supply, as it does today.

4. The birth of a child out of wedlock presents, literally and figuratively, several full-blown problems in the community. For that majority of babies born to nonwhite, economically disadvantaged mothers financial support must be provided for both mother and child. This is an economic drain, and the economic well-being of the taxpayer is threatened. Shaken, too, are long-held American attitudes about self-responsibility, self-control, and self-dependence. (The relation between the rigidity with which these virtues are valued and the unconscious wishes against which they are defense works need not be gone into here.) In an era of population explosion and increasing technological

---

[9] For differences from popular "viewing with alarm" see, for example Vincent, *ibid.*, indexed under "Illegitimacy, increase in," and Elizabeth Herzog, "Unmarried Mothers: Some Questions To Be Answered and Some Answers To Be Questioned," *Child Welfare*, October 1962.

unemployment gratuitous addition to a population problem may be viewed with concern.

5. As for the problem of the unmarried mother herself, if she has, by her own efforts or with help, been able to give away the living symbol of her "sin" or "mistake" and pick up where she left off, she is "solved" as a social problem. (Whether she feels her problem to be solved, no one knows.) If she keeps her child but needs no economic support, she is lost to public view. So, as far as is known, she is no problem. The assumption is that she is paying for her transgressions—and this is a morally satisfying assumption. If, however, she keeps her child and requires economic aids for the support of herself and child, she is not "paying." Indeed, it commonly appears that perhaps she is being paid for sins and, by such payment, even encouraged to further sexual irresponsibility.

6. Finally the baby and growing child himself presents a problem of social concern when he is kept by a socially, economically, and culturally impoverished mother. There is question and concern whether children reared under such complex disadvantaged conditions can grow into "good citizens." Moreover, the provision of necessary physical and mental health services, of long-time economic maintenance, of developmental opportunities in order to counteract the effects of deprivation present formidable money costs. That such resources are at present undeveloped or inadequate in quantity and quality is a further problem of social solutions. Particularly does this concern the citizenry, for there is evidence both of recidivism and of the transmission of undesired standards of economic dependence and "immorality" from one generation to the next.

Thus in this mixture of social values and concerns in regard to morality and money, the sanctity and desirability of good family life, the provision of "reformation," and of open opportunity for the sound development of children into "good citizens," the mother and child out of wedlock present society with problems of widespread concern.

Is this a "social work problem"? All professions, as Whitehead has said, are concerned with making certain that the rights of individuals are safeguarded at the same time as a sense of community and effective social living are maintained. In examining the various aspects of the social problem of unmarried motherhood, it is clear that the services and concerns of a number of professions would be involved. Medicine, the ministry, law, and education are perhaps the professions whose functions and authority place them in a forefront position on the problems that lead to unmarried motherhood. Social work is the profession, that, traditionally, provides the services and develops and mans the resources by which a problem, once it exists and becomes a matter of community concern, is dealt with. Social work most frequently encounters the problem of the unmarried mother in the person of the illegitimately pregnant woman who needs shelter, concealment, economic support through pregnancy and childbirth, medical care, and planning for the disposition of the child once it is born; in the person of the woman who has given birth to her out-of-wedlock child and asks for economic support (although she may also need many other practical and psychological services as well) ; in the person of the woman who, after childbirth, decides to place her child or give it in adoption. In short, the profession of social work most often encounters the problem of the unmarried mother when it has already gone through its incipient stages and is no longer subject to reversal or halt. The professional functions of social work, then, become those of inventing and providing such services and resources by which the problem's consequences may be confined, curtailed, or ameliorated. One comment on another sense in which the unmarried mother is a problem for social work: because social work is charged with the responsibilities of providing for the woman who is clearly a transgressor and for her socially as well as personally unwanted child, and because this is costly, social work is sometimes tarred with the brush of opprobrium, held responsible, somehow, for the undesirable state of affairs.

The foregoing suggests that, particularly in relation to considerations of prevention, social work would do well to state clearly where its functions and those of other more powerful professions begin, leave off, and intertwine. Meantime, the profession of social work considers unmarried motherhood, its causes, and its consequences, as one of its problems to be solved and, ideally, to be prevented.

What, specifically, does social work do about this complex problem? What actions does it take, what means has it invented to curtail its occurrence, to ameliorate or minimize its traumatic effects, to avoid the new cycle of problems it carries in its wake? Since professional actions are based on values and on knowledge derived from practice and theory, a prior question must be asked. What beliefs and theory guide and shape social work's actions?

VALUES, KNOWLEDGE, AND ACTION

What Does Social Work Believe, Know, and Do About the Unmarried Mother?

A profession's value system, like a society's value system, is its mode of organizing its conduct. Judgments based on professional experience relating to what is good or bad, desirable or undesirable, constructive or destructive are basic to decision-making actions and goals. What a profession does and seeks to bring into being or to prevent is heavily determined by the consensus within it of what is or is not desirable. The firmer and clearer these values, the more purposive its professional direction and action. The more ambiguous or uncertain they are, the more likelihood of uncertainty and diffusion in professional planning and performance.

Professional action in relation to any problem depends also on its explanations of the nature of that problem, its causes, its consequences, and the connections between them, and the means that have been developed for problem solving. A theory seeks to outline the rules according to which events occur and the reasons by which they may be understood. Without such explanations all action would be trial and error. With such explanations a profession has guideposts that direct and focus its perception and interpretation of a problem and its consequent action on it. Obviously, if the theoretical framework within which a problem is viewed is inadequate or inappropriate, professional perception, interpretation, and action will be affected in similar ways.

In the examination of the question of what social work believes, knows and does, the problem of unmarried motherhood is viewed in its several stages: illicit coition, illegitimate pregnancy, and actual motherhood of an out-of-wedlock child.

Illicit coition. The problem of illicit coition comes to the social worker's professional attention when it is part of a "problem syndrome" for which a girl is sent for help (or seeks it herself). The usual referral or request for help involves an adolescent or postadolescent young woman whose general behavior (in family or school, usually) gives evidence that she is "headed for trouble," "going with bad company," and "rebellious and unmanageable." Occasionally, with a mature unmarried woman (or divorced or widowed), there is confession of a current extramarital relationship; occasionally an adolescent girl is brought to social work with parental accusations about her sexual misbehavior as the presenting problem.

The usual service sought (and available) when parents, schools, or courts accuse the minor girl of illicit sex relations is that of social casework counseling. The hope is that the social caseworker, by all the means of psychological influence she may wield, will help the accused to "cease and desist" these practices.

Only a rough guess can be ventured as to what social work's value judgments about illicit sex relations would be, rough because social workers are likely to be relativists rather than absolutists and to say "it depends" on many factors—age, person, time, place, who is affected, and so on. Social workers would probably be less likely than many other members of the general population of their class and level of education to call such behavior "immoral." This is because their theory system postulates that all behavior has the purpose of meeting internal needs and that in order to rechannel such needs they must be understood rather than condemned. Added to this are convictions developed and supported by psychoanalytic theory that when sexual maturity is reached sexual expression is "natural," even "healthy," and the further recognition that society makes marriage dependent on many social factors that take precedence over biological and psychological readiness for mating. For the woman past "the age of consent" social workers would probably feel that what she did was "her own business" unless her actions affected the lives of others (her family, her children) in deleterious ways.

Yet, because in their practical experience social workers have known chiefly the women and girls who have been "caught" and have been hurt by illicit sexual experience, they are alert to and concerned about possible unhappy consequences. Because of this there would probably be a consensus among social workers that illicit coition is risky and potentially hurtful, not only in terms of the possibility of unwanted pregnancy but also because of possible social censure and emotional conflict.

How widely social caseworkers have considered the prevalence of pre- and extramarital relations in our society and all the meanings, conscious as well as unconscious, that this behavior holds is not a matter of record. There is considerable evidence in casework writing on the unmarried mother that caseworkers have insufficiently differentiated motivations for sexual relations from those for pregnancy and motherhood. In this failure they have been supported by many writings on this same subject, usually by psychiatrists serving as consultants to social agencies that are dealing with already pregnant women. There tends to be a bunching together of illicit coition, illegitimate pregnancy, and unmarried motherhood as a single psychodynamic phenomenon and little notice is given to the fact that far greater numbers of women and girls engage in illicit coition than become pregnant. (The theories held to explain this several-phased behavior are discussed under Illegitimate Pregnancy.)

The actions taken by social work in relation to the problem of illicit coition are confined to the individual instances presented as problems to a social agency. The service asked is usually that of casework counseling. The caseworker would attempt by interviewing the woman to understand the factors that led to this potentially dangerous or presently conflicting behavior, the factors that operate in its continuance, and the conscious and (possibly) unconscious satisfactions gained from it. In ongoing discussions she would attempt to draw out and point out possible consequences and their implications for the happiness of the woman involved. She would further attempt to reshape or modify the attitudes and behavior of those persons and conditions in the family and other milieus of the young woman toward maximizing their benign and minimizing their noxious effects on her.

The expectation would be that the recognition of implicit dangers, plus the supportive bonds of an emotional relationship with the caseworker and the reduction of social stresses and heightening of social satisfactions, would lessen whatever needs were being sexually expressed, and thus the sexual ties would be loosened or sexual drives diluted. This expectation would be based on the assumption that sexual relations were being used for some purpose other than a love relationship because, as every caseworker knows, social work has no substitute to offer for sexual attachment based on love. Like the church, parents, or teachers, it can inject conflict into such relations, but it cannot offer substitutes for them. Casework treatment would be based further on the knowledge that sexual relations may be motivated by many kinds of need—to have "a steady," to be "liked," to be "popular," to escape from or defy parents, to "prove maturity, or to buy some "fun." It is these secondary kinds of motivation for sexual relations to which social caseworkers address themselves when in individual cases they are confronted by evidence of illicit coition.

The social caseworker, concerned with the many personal and social problems that may ensue from the client's illicit coition, is typically caught in an intransigent conflict about what she does *not* do. For example, she does not give or openly refer a client who is having illicit sex relations to sources of contraceptive information. (There may be exceptions to this generalization, but they *are* the exceptions.) If the worker were free to make such referrals or connections for her client, the possibility of illegitimate, unwanted pregnancy might be all but nipped off, and the long chain of unhappy consequences might never be set in motion. But the use of contraceptives, especially by unmarried women, is a subject of considerable community disagreement accompanied by high feeling. Most social agencies, responsible to their watchful and pluralistic supporters, constrain or even prohibit the referral of unmarried women for contraceptive aids. The alternative goal of abstinence is affirmed.

Therefore, what social work presently does in relation to illicit sexual behavior is to attempt by its methods of psychological influence to deal with its problematic aspects for the particular persons involved.

However, even if the social worker knew what to say and do on the subject (which is to say, even if social workers were not themselves caught up in society's conflicting values and standards), it is doubtful that its voice on the subject of illicit sex relations would be much heeded. Traditionally the authority on "morality" and "moral truth" is the church and the home.[10] The medical profession, in its physical and psychiatric branches, might carry several kinds of authority related to prevention of conception. On the issue of illicit sex relations, social work's voice is the quiet and occasional one of the one-to-one interview.

Illegitimate pregnancy. The problems that the illegitimately pregnant woman brings to social work are of two major kinds: (1) need for material provisions and special arrangements and (2) need for counseling on a whole range of conflict-laden relationships. Material provisions and special arrangements include such things as money to buy maternity clothes or layette, to pay for transporation to prenatal clinics, housing away from the eyes of curious and disapproving familiars, and clinic and hospital-care arrangements. Accompanying these needs for tangible means by which pregnancy may be brought to term with physical and (relative) mental health is a host of intra- and interpersonal problems for which counsel and guidance are needed.

The crisis of illegitimate pregnancy varies in intensity, of course, with the personality of the woman involved, her class, self-concept, social standards, future orientation, and the like. But it always involves the woman's self, self and sexual partner, self and family (particularly parents), and eventually self and baby.

Perhaps this point deserves to be made more explicit: the woman who comes to a social agency is one whose normal sources (family, friends, lover) are unable or unwilling to help her. This is why her pregnancy is a compounded crisis (and this is a complex of circumstances on which some of the theory on which social work operates in relation to this group of clients has been insufficiently considered). There is ample evidence that many pregnancies begun out of wedlock are the basis for "forced" or "pushed" marriages.[11] Many of these marriages may not be successful, but at least the girl has solved her problem of illegitimate pregnancy. There is considerable evidence that many women are aided

---

[10] In a recent discussion on the subject of illegitimacy, a prominent churchman spoke of "the failure of the church to saturate the social structure with the moral truths it holds, thus in some measure contributing to the problem. . . ." The Very Reverend Howard S. Kennedy, D.D., in his discussion of "Illegitimacy—the Community's Concern," at the National Conference on Social Welfare, May 18, 1961.

[11] Among high school girls who marry, between 30 and 50 percent are pregnant. Among all first marriages the estimated percentage is 16 to 20 percent. *See* "Pregnant Brides—Record Linkage Studies," Harold T. Christensen, Ph.D., in *Sex Ways in Fact and Faith*, Evelyn Duvall and Sylvanus Duvall, eds. (New York: Association Press, 1961). A November 1961 news story in the Chicago Sun-Times quotes Dr. Leslie Weatherhead, a British "leading Methodist," as reporting that one British bride in four under the age of 21 is pregnant on marriage and in all marriages one bride in six is pregnant. Among other factors the high incidence of divorce in teenage marriage suggests that many of them were "forced."

by their sexual partners or families to pay for abortion. There are, moreover, large numbers of women whose pregnancies are brought to term under conditions of privacy and concealment paid for and arranged for by their families or their sexual partners.[12] In all such cases the pregnant woman has had evidence of obligation felt toward her, at the least, and of protective concern, at the best. The woman who brings her problem of pregnancy to the social agency has been failed by those she most needs—even if the reason for the sexual partner's or family's failure is actual *inability* to provide for her rather than unwillingness.

Thus, in addition to the material provisions and living arrangements the illegitimately pregnant woman seeks from social work, she also needs protective concern, guidance, counseling, and emotional support toward alleviating some of her distress and conflict so that she can look and plan ahead with relative balance; and there is further need for strengthening the ties with whatever persons in her normal milieu can help her during and past this crisis.

One "need" or solution-means has not been named here. Probably the majority of unmarried pregnant women would like to "get rid" of the fetus. Except for those who would shun this because of religious or other fears, many would want the help by which abortion could take place. How often this is openly asked for is not known. That it is not asked for more often is undoubtedly because of the general knowledge that abortion is illegal and therefore would not be provided or arranged for by a social agency. The fact that the pregnant woman often first applies to the social agency late in her pregnancy has most frequently been interpreted as her attempt to deny her pregnancy to herself as well as to others. But it is quite possible that she has resorted to home remedies for inducing miscarriages or has cast about in the hope of finding the ways and means to medical abortion and that she comes to the social agency only when these efforts have failed. Needless to say, help toward abortion is offered by no social agency.

The attitude that may be said to permeate social work with regard to illegitimate pregnancy is that it is a serious, unfortunate occurrence. The closer the girl or woman is to the social worker in terms of class, education, and future orientation, the greater the likelihood that concern will be felt for the woman herself and for the present and future effect on her of this "mistake." When a considerable class or caste gap exists (as between a lower-class, uneducated Negro woman and a white middle-class social worker), there is probably less empathy with the pregnant woman and more concern with the outlook for the child to

---

[12] *See* Vincent, *op. cit.,* for various data on middle-class, economically "able" unmarried mothers. In one year, for example, 130 physicians reported that they had attended a total of 252 unmarried pregnant women as "private" patients (p. 55).

be born. This may in part account for the fact that there are far fewer shelter and concealment resources for illegitimately pregnant Negro women than for their white counterparts. Another explanation, of course, lies in prevailing ideas about differences in Negro sexual mores.

As the ideas that constitute the theory underlying social work treatment of the illegitimately pregnant woman are examined, it becomes clear that there are two different categories. One is sociological, the other, psychoanalytic. The sociological is applied chiefly to Negro women, the psychoanalytic, to white. (The writer is aware that these are flat statements. They aim to express major positions. It is recognized that many variations and interpretations lie between these poles.)

The explanations for illegitimate pregnancy in Negro girls and women are based largely on their "culture." In this culture, for reasons that began with slavery and carried along over years of economic dependence on plantation life, the Negro woman was seen as the center of the family, a producer of children who could in turn become plantation hands. Whether these children were legitimate or illegitimate was of small concern when marriage was controlled by others than the couple involved, when there was nothing to inherit, when the children belonged to a plantation or farming community more than to the parents.[13]

To this historical explanation of tolerance of illegitimate pregnancy and illegitimate children are added subsequent economic and class explanations. Moving from rural southern to urban northern life, the Negro has found himself economically and socially disadvantaged in many ways unconducive to maintaining a secure marriage and stable family life and to new acculturation. Thus, it is postulated, illegitimate pregnancy is less stigmatized among Negroes than among whites and is even, some believe, accepted as "natural."

The question that is being asked in some places today—and perhaps needs to be asked more loudly and persistently—is whether this historical explanation is not ancient history being substituted for possible different present-day perceptions both of social workers and of the social communities in which Negroes are a large part of the population.[14]

The fact is that the Negro woman predominantly known to social work today is an urban Negro living in the North. She is almost one

[13] *See* E. Franklin Frazier, *The Negro Family in the United States* (Chicago: University of Chicago Press, 1939), pp. 108–124. *See also*, Gunnar Myrdal, *An American Dilemma* (New York: Harper & Brothers, 1944).

[14] *See* particularly Herzog, *op. cit.*, and Hylan Lewis, "Child-Rearing Practices Among Low-Income Families," *Casework Papers, 1961* (New York: Family Service Association of America, 1961), for considerations of relation of standards to economic status. *See also* Elizabeth Herzog and Hylan Lewis, "Priorities in Research about Unmarried Mothers," presented at Eastern Regional Conference, Child Welfare League of America, New York, April 1961. (Mimeographed.)

hundred years removed from plantation slavery, though she may be only very recently removed from what Frazier has called "the naïve and ignorant peasant folk who are newcomers to the city." The evidence of push, surge, and change in the northern Negro community in the Negro's self-concept and future orientation is open to see. There is reason to question—certainly reason to examine—what attitudes toward illegitimate pregnancy actually are in concentrated urban Negro communities. Are they, indeed, as tolerant as social workers have assumed? Is such tolerance, if it exists, associated with a racial or with a lower-class culture? Is it, if it exists, a defensive mask that is assumed in the face of white inquirers and helpers, one of the ways by which the "outs" protect themselves from intervention by the "ins"?

Several recent studies open some chinks in the long-solidified notions about illegitimate pregnancy among Negro women, both that such pregnancy was relatively unstigmatized or that it was actually sought as a way of maintaining dependency. In one study more than six hundred mothers whose youngest child was illegitimate were interviewed on their attitudes about illegitimacy. "All but a few felt great guilt at having illegitimate children . . . these mothers did not accept illegitimacy as a normal way of life. They resented their status and recognized the handicaps." [15] An earlier study of fifty unmarried Negro mothers found that thirty-two of fifty families of unmarried mothers were "overtly bitter and tended to penalize the young women for their mistakes. . . . Many of the unmarried mothers did not want the first child nor subsequent children. They confided in the worker oftentimes their plans to abort. . . . Usually the clients were hesitant in telling the worker about the pregnancies and expressed a desire for a protective situation whereby they might place the baby for adoption." [16]

Psychological tests and casework interviewing reveal a range of possible explanations for pregnancies, including "retaliatory hostility" directed "against a mother figure and the environment at large," "desire to be popular and sophisticated," and "wanting to be loved and to love." These explanations combine factors of relationship to parents, to self, to society, and of self to a love object. Apropos of the last of

---

[15] Greenleigh Associates, *Facts, Fallacies, and Future,* A Study of the Aid to Dependent Children Program of Cook County, Illinois, 1960 (New York: Greenleigh Associates, 1960).

[16] A summary of a study of fifty unmarried Negro mothers in pending or active aid to dependent children cases in the Marion County Department of Public Welfare, Indianapolis, Indiana, 1957, by A'Lelia Josephene Osili and Frieda Alice Parker (mimeographed).

these, the Greenleigh study indicates that "half the mothers had dated the fathers for over a year" and that "in only 10 percent of the cases was the relationship a casual one." [17]

There are many (and variant) statistics on the Negro unmarried mother. However, studies of the physical, social, and psychological aspects of her illicit coition, illegitimate pregnancy, and out-of-wedlock motherhood are notable for their absence, and experience with her by sophisticated caseworkers has, until very recently, been markedly limited.

Prevailing social work theory about the illegitimately pregnant white girl or woman is heavily dependent on psychoanalytic theory; that is, it gives particular attention to the unconscious drives that motivate a girl to become pregnant and to early unresolved parental relationships as causative factors in "acting out" sexual behavior.

In the 1920's and 1930's prevailing explanations of illegitimate pregnancies were of social inadequacy (broken homes or ignorance stemming from inadequate opportunities) and mental inadequacy (feeblemindedness or other inherent weaknesses of cognition and control). In 1941 there was put forward the hypothesis that a cause-effect relationship exists between unresolved oedipal conflicts and unmarried motherhood.[18] In the two decades that have followed a large number of writings by psychiatrists and social workers developed the themes of unconscious and unresolved emotional relationships with parents as the explanation for illegitimate pregnancy and unmarried motherhood.[19] The assumptions made are that pregnancy and its culmination in unwed motherhood is a way of meeting a variety of unconscious (and sometimes just preconscious) needs which include self-punishment for forbidden sex fantasies, punishment of one or both parents, self-assertion as a woman, self-assertion as a "whole" person, gratification of sexual fantasies in conjunction with or in competition with sexualized parent figures, and so on. The most complete exposition

---

[17] Greenleigh Associates, *op. cit.*

[18] J. Kasanin, M.D., and Sieglinde Handschin, "Psychodynamic Factors in Illegitimacy," *American Journal of Orthopsychiatry*, Vol. II (January 1941), pp. 66–84.

[19] Florence Clothier, M.D., "Psychological Implications of Unmarried Parenthood," *American Journal of Orthopsychiatry*, Vol. 13 (July 1943), pp. 531–549; Helene Deutsch, M.D., *Psychology of Women* (New York: Grune & Stratton, 1945), Vol. II, Chapter 10, "Unmarried Mother"; Leontine Young, *Out of Wedlock* (New York: McGraw-Hill, 1954); Margaret Millar, "Casework Service for the Unmarried Mother," *Casework Papers*, 1955 (New York: Family Service Association of America, 1955); Marcel Heiman, M.D., "Out-of-Wedlock Pregnancy in Adolescence," *Casework Papers*, 1960 (New York: Family Service Association of America, 1960); A. Ferdinand Bonan, M.D., "Psychoanalytic Implications in Treating Unmarried Mothers with Narcissistic Character Structure," *Social Casework*, Vol. 44, No. 6 (June 1963).

of these points of view is the 1954 book, *Out of Wedlock*, which sums up the position that "everything points to the purposeful nature of the act." [20]

"The act" referred to is not specified. Whether it is illicit coition, illegitimate pregnancy, or bringing pregnancy to term is not clear. A current article on the subject of unmarried mothers states, "Many girls act out sexually, but these particular girls [the fifty-one in the sample] have done so *to the extent of becoming pregnant.*" (Italics in original.) "Once pregnant, they have not married, they have not aborted spontaneously, and they have not sought therapeutic abortion. . . ." [21] Implied here is that there *is* some differentiation to be found between women who have illicit coition and those who become illegitimately pregnant and carry their pregnancy to completion. Implied also is the pervading theory that illegitimate pregnancy and out-of-wedlock motherhood have their causes in psychodynamic factors and, beyond this, in personality pathology. "The evidence of emotional pathology in unmarried mothers lies in their insistence upon having a baby despite their knowledge of the social attitute and the consequent cost to themselves." [22]

Just as the sociological stereotype of the illegitimately pregnant Negro woman deserves examination for its validity and its implication for social work, so the psychoanalytic explanations that have become stereotyped call for critical analysis. [23] Within the purposes and limits of this paper only some of the questions presented by social work's theory of illegitimate pregnancy can be posed. A few are these:

1. Are the factors that explain illicit coition the same or different from those involved in illegitimate pregnancy and in actual unmarried motherhood? If they are the same, are they only psychological? Chiefly psychological? What factors of physiology, economic means, social opportunity, and social deprivation need to be considered? If it is thought that different factors explain sexual acting out, pregnancy, and out-of-wedlock childbirth, are the differences those of degree or of kind? Obviously, the ideas of cause of each of the several phases involved in this problem of illegitimate pregnancy bear importantly on ideas of treatment, resource development, and prevention.

2. ". . . pregnancy has a psychologic meaning of its own apart from

[20] Young, *op. cit.*, p. 22.

[21] Bonan, *op. cit.*

[22] Young, *op. cit.*

[23] A first move in this direction was made by Rose Bernstein in an article, "Are We Still Stereotyping the Unmarried Mother?" *Social Work*, Vol. 5, No. 3 (July 1960). Several of the points that follow in the above were first made in Mrs. Bernstein's article.

the fact that it is a prelude to motherhood" and ". . . the wish for pregnancy . . . is not always equivalent to the wish for a child. . . ." So says one of the outstanding psychoanalytic interpreters of the psychology of women.[24] This differentiation alone suggests the need for examining some blurred assumptions.

3. Most women who have illicit coition apparently do not become pregnant. What factors account for this difference? The unconscious wish for or rejection of pregnancy may surely be one. But what of the physiological factors, such as the coincidence of ovulation and intercourse? Of relative sterility or fertility in one or the other partner? [25] What of circumstantial factors such as the conditions under which sexual intercourse takes place in relation to contraceptive means? What of interactional factors such as the male partner's cooperation in contraception? (It is of interest to observe that writers on the unmarried mother focus and place "cause" almost exclusively on the drives and behavior of the female partner in what is by definition a two-way transaction.)

4. Among the women whose illicit coition leads to illegitimate pregnancy what factors account for the difference between those who "get rid" of the fetus and those who carry it to birth? The unconscious wish for a baby may be a strong need that drives a woman to carry her baby, with open bravado or shame or elaborate defenses. But are other factors involved? Is it possible that many of the pregnant women who come to social agencies have tried and failed in the effort to end their pregnancy, a fact rarely revealed to the social worker because abortion is known to be illegal, is felt as "sinful," akin to "talking a life"? It is interesting to note that the unmarried pregnant woman who comes to the social agency is usually at least three months pregnant, past the time of her possible hope for spontaneous or for induced abortion. Has she any choice? Unless she has considerable money (the illegal abortionist cannot take the chances he does except for ample reward), unless she has sources of information that can help her to find this usually hidden resource, and unless she is willing to risk the fancied and real dangers involved in this illegal, unsupervised surgery, she has no recourse but to allow her pregnancy to take its natural course.

5. Is it possible that some of the explorations of illegitimate pregnancy in terms of unconscious psychodynamics have been self-perpetuating and

[24] Deutsch, *op. cit.*, pp. 334–335.

[25] Irene Josselyn, M.D., made this point in her book review of *Out of Wedlock* in *Social Casework*, Vol. 35, No. 7 (July 1954), p. 11, and pointed this up earlier in a paper read at the National Conference of Social Work 1953: "What We Know About the Unmarried Mother," National Association on Service to Unmarried Parents. (Mimeographed.)

have resulted in circular thinking? The illegitimately pregnant woman most known to social workers represents a particular group. They are the women who have no close-by sources of support or help. Their sexual partners, their parents, or immediate family either cannot or will not provide or buy the protection and planning they need. In the case of minors the parents are frequently the seekers of help for the girls, but their own resourcelessness, economic or social, becomes a complicating factor in their relationships. Within this group, which lacks means of its own, is a smaller group among whom conflict, emotional disturbance, or emotional inaccessibility is marked. This is the group that social workers have typically presented to psychiatrists for consultation and guidance. This is the group from whom, by and large, the personality and psychodynamics of "the unmarried mother" have been limned.

It may be argued that although the theory of psychodynamics may not hold for *all* illegitimately pregnant women it *has* been developed from the experience of those who come to social work and therefore it is useful for this particular group. Yet, if other explanations are possible, they merit consideration if only to keep perception open.

In support of the theory of unresolved parent-child relationships is the experience that in interviews with the illegitimately pregnant woman about her background there almost always emerges evidence of parent-child difficulties of one sort or another. What needs to be considered is that the very crisis of unwanted pregnancy and the shame, guilt, and fear it arouses may exacerbate anger, fault-finding, and disappointment in the parental-daughter relationship.[26] Underlying this idea is the probability that at moments of crisis in relationships between self and others the account by the one of the other in past as well as present relationships is likely to be heavily colored by current feelings of disappointment and anger. We view our past through the lens of the present. May this not also be true of the unmarried mother who proffers her history as she defends against those she has hurt by her act or those who have hurt her because of it?

A recent study, the first systematic inquiry into the likeness and difference in personalities of unmarried mothers and a matched group of single, never-pregnant girls, was done by Clark Vincent.[27] His general conclusion is, "Unwed motherhood is not the result of any one personality type, intrafamilial relationship or social situation."

The answers to the foregoing questions about the underlying theory

---

[26] This point is similar to that made by Bernstein, *op. cit.*
[27] Vincent, *op. cit.*, pp. 99–123.

of the causes and consequences of illegitimate pregnancy may be presumed to have some relevance for what social work actually does today and then for what it ought to do for the illegitimately pregnant woman.

In its concern for the protection of the illegitimately pregnant woman's physical and emotional well-being, for the protection of both the woman and her family from social disgrace, for the prevention of recidivism, and for the future well-being of the baby, social work has developed a number of material and tangible means accompanied by guidance and counsel. The tangible aids consist of economic support during pregnancy and beyond childbirth, shelter and concealment in "maternity homes" or in agency-purchased boarding care, arrangements for necessary medical and dental prenatal care, and for hospitalization, postpartum shelter until the woman has made other living arrangements, and temporary foster homes and/or permanent adoptive homes for the baby that is to be given up. The guidance and counseling help, given chiefly by social caseworkers, consists of the warm interest and support that women particularly need in this period of discomfort and crisis, of discussions and planning about physical needs, about current and future relationships with family, friends, sexual partner, and especially about decisions regarding the baby to come: is it to be relinquished for adoption or kept by the mother? If it is to be adopted, many emotions—guilt, loss, mixed relief and fear—need to be worked through, along with considerations of the woman's plans for herself when she resumes her single status. If she decides to keep her child, she must also work through, with the caseworker's guidance, what lies ahead when she undertakes to carry the role of unmarried mother.

In the task of providing these several major aids to the illegitimately pregnant woman, a number of kinds of social agencies have been involved—maternity homes, family welfare agencies (public or private), child welfare agencies (public or private), child-adoption services (sometimes part of and sometimes separate from the child welfare agency), and the social service departments of hospitals. Each of these agencies approaches the problem within the framework of its particular function: hospital social work may be most concerned that necessary medical services be used by this pregnant woman; the maternity home is likely to be concerned about the woman's ability to fit into the particular living-in situation that it offers and about her postpartum plans; the adoption service has a clientele of prospective parents impatiently awaiting the delivery of an adoptable child and its view of and services to the illegitimately pregnant woman will be shaped thereby. But every one of these agencies shares, in different degree, some of the same concerns for this woman: her physical and psychological welfare, the physical welfare and life-fate of her baby, that childless couples have access to available babies, and that the "mistake" of illicit coition and/or its unfortunate consequences should not be repeated.

When the illegitimately pregnant woman asks for assistance, the kind of agency that becomes her major source of help depends on a number of factors: the resources actually present in a given community in which the woman happens to apply, the stage of her pregnancy—whether she has a long waiting period ahead of her or whether she is on the verge of delivery, whether she regards her problem as the need for her own present or for her baby's future protection, whether she has already chosen to "get rid of" or "give up" the child or to undertake mother-hood, and how the social worker assesses the problem and its potential outcome. Because of these factors, as well as those involved in the special concerns and functions of special agencies, the unwed pregnant woman may find herself dealing with several social agencies and with several different social workers at the same time or in rapid succession.[28] She may be moved from a family-agency caseworker to a caseworker (or her equivalent) in a maternity home to a caseworker representing an adoption agency. It is probable that most social caseworkers working with the illegitimately pregnant woman are aware of how important a single reliable relationship with one helper would be to a woman in these most crucial and shaking months of her life, important not only in terms of security for the woman but in terms of developing a relationship of emotional depth. At present, the particular dividing lines between and among agencies, although permitting of joint planning and collabora-tion in the interests of their client, rarely permit one worker to carry the woman through from discovery of pregnancy to, say, giving her baby in adoption. Perhaps this is one reason for the problem that follows.

Social agencies, in their concern for the future social and emotional adjustment of the illegitimately pregnant woman and toward prevention of a repeated pregnancy, have often offered postchildbirth or post-adoption counseling. Typically, caseworkers attest, the woman does not follow through; typically she drops out of contact. Probably a number of factors are involved here (to be discussed further on), but the split of relationship among too many "helpers" may be one of them.

The social services by which social work attempts to ameliorate or solve the problems of illegitimate pregnancy have a number of other shortcomings. The most obvious is that they are in short supply. In

---

[28] *See* Mary Lynch Crockett, "Examination of Services to the Unmarried Mother in Relation to Age of Adoption Placement of the Baby," *Casework Papers, 1960,* from the National Conference on Social Welfare, Family Service Association of America, New York. "It is not unusual to find that a mother has had to deal with a family agency, a maternity home, an adoption agency, a hospital social service, a court, and a department of public welfare, all at the same time. . . ."

many communities they do not exist. Where they do exist they often have more demand than they can supply. Outstanding is the deficiency of resources for the illegitimately pregnant nonwhite woman. Coupled with this fact is the minimal use made by the nonwhite woman of the resources that are open to her. Both facts deserve further consideration.

About 60 percent of all illegitimate births are to nonwhite mothers. Yet only about one in 50 nonwhite unwed mothers receives maternity-home care, compared with one in every four white unwed mothers.[29] What this disproportion represents is not known—whether resources are not available to the nonwhite woman who seeks them or whether she does not seek them so frequently. Perhaps, based on other experiences of rejection, she feels that she has no chance of getting them; perhaps she feels insufficiently stigmatized by her illegitimate pregnancy to seek concealment. Perhaps the community's (and social work's) assumption that she does not feel shame has led to obliviousness of the need for maternity shelter for nonwhites; perhaps these attitudes circle in a cause-effect-cause reaction. There are a few facts: among 48 Florence Crittenton maternity homes (each autonomous, although they belong to the national Florence Crittenton Association of America, Inc.) 20 have restrictions against Negroes. In the other 28 homes one in 10 women admitted was a Negro.[30] On the other side, the data from a recent study in New York City on the use of social and health services by illegitimately pregnant women [31] showed that "ninety percent of the white unmarried mothers . . . of all ages were also known to social agencies" ("also" means in addition to their hospital or public aid contacts). "In contrast only 5 percent of the Negro and 10 percent of the Puerto Rican mothers were served by specialized [that is, shelter, adoption, counseling] agencies." [32] Interviewers who asked these women why they had not used social services judged that most of them did not see the relation between their problems and what they conceived social agency functions and services to be.

Even if she is able to apply for and use medical, shelter, and counseling services during her pregnancy, the nonwhite woman can only rarely get adoption for her baby. Estimates are that about 70 percent of the white babies born out of wedlock are taken in adoption, but only about

---

[29] Hannah M. Adams and Ursula M. Gallagher, "Some Facts and Observations About Illegitimacy," *Children*, Vol. 10, No. 2 (March–April 1963).

[30] *Report of Service*, 1960, Florence Crittenton Association of America.

[31] Blanche Bernstein and Mignon Sauber, *Deterrents to Early Prenatal Care and Social Services Among Women Pregnant Out of Wedlock. See also* commentary on this study by Hannah M. Adams, "Two Studies of Unmarried Mothers in New York City," *Children* (September–October, 1961).

[32] Adams, *ibid.*

5 percent of the Negro babies are adopted.[33] Several factors play some part in the lack of adoption resources for the Negro baby. One is the apparent assumption by the nonwhite group that the baby is to be kept by the mother. (Actually many Negro babies born in or out of wedlock are "given away" to blood relatives, friends, or to relatives of friends, sometimes for what is thought of as temporary care, at others for un-legalized "adoption." This suggests not that the Negro woman "wants" her baby, as has often been assumed by whites who impute "love of babies" to dark-skinned women, but that she does not believe that there are organizations in her society that will relieve her of it.) A related factor is the nonexistence until recently of a middle-class Negro popula-tion ready to engage in the negotiations with social work and the law that formal adoption requires. Such a population is only now emerging, and in recognition a number of child welfare and adoption agencies are in the beginning stages of finding suitable adoptive families and develop-ing the Negro community's interest in adoptions through socially con-trolled channels. However, as long as one half the Negro population of this country remains below the poverty line (according to latest Bureau of Labor statistics) the prospects for widespread adoption of out-of-wedlock Negro babies remain constricted.

One further service offered by social agencies to the illegitimately pregnant woman who asks for help requires examination. It is what might be called "preventive counseling," that is, the attempt to get at and deal with those factors that seem to have led to the acts of illicit coition and pregnancy, to extirpate them so that the behavior and its consequences will not be repeated. The prevention of recidivism may be said to be one of the major reasons for the community's support of casework counseling of the illegitimately pregnant woman. However, some hiatus seems to exist between social work's intent and the motiva-tions and interest of its clients. A number of casework writers on work with the illegitimately pregnant woman (who then becomes an unmarried mother) state that it has proved extremely difficult to involve the woman in wanting help with anything other than the tangible aids she requests.[34] Typically, it appears, she is not motivated to pursue the problems that social work theory poses as the cause of her current difficulty. Typically, her interest is focused on needs connected with pregnancy, oncoming delivery, and whether to give her child in adoption or to try some other solution. The caseworker attempting to give "psychological services" in the interest of changing the intensity and direction of the drives assumed to underlie illicit coition and pregnancy toward prevention of further

---

[33] Adams, *ibid.*
[34] *See,* for example, Young, *op. cit.,* pp. 200–202; Millar, *op. cit.*

sexual involvement finds the illegitimately pregnant woman unresponsive.

There are probably a number of reasons for this. Pregnancy is a "waiting period," not only a kind of suspension in time but also in feeling. The psyche is focused on the changes of the body and with the life it contains. For the illegitimately pregnant woman there are numerous daily concerns and decisions which must be talked over with her social worker. Important among them is the anticipation of childbirth itself and then the decision—with all its accompanying ambivalent emotions—about giving up or keeping the baby. What she will be or do afterward may seem remote. It may be supposed that once the child is born and is whisked away into adoption it may seem to the woman that her problem is over, even solved. If her feeling is chiefly of release or if she has come to terms with giving up the baby, she is free to pick up where she left off as an unmarried woman who can resume being a schoolgirl, a working woman, or occupation seeker. She does not see her need for continued casework help, perhaps because she and the caseworker have defined her problem differently—she in terms of a pregnancy crisis, the caseworker in terms of a personality difficulty. One wonders whether, by too close adherence to those theories of causation of illegitimate pregnancy that emphasize past and unconscious forces the caseworker has not created a wide gap in understanding and communication between herself and her client. If the caseworker's focus is on plumbing the "personality problems" that she assumes are basic to the pregnancy and the client's concerns fester in her present and near-future interactions between self and sexual partner, self and baby, self and parents, self and schoolmates, teachers, employers, fellow-workers, and so on, there are few touching points. Perhaps recidivism is as much related to the absence of social and emotional satisfactions in the woman's daily life as to unconscious drives and needs, as much to choices of channels for those drives and needs as to their existence. Casework writing on the subject indicates insufficient attention to recent past, current, and near-future interactional factors. Perhaps this is why the woman carried through the crisis of illegitimate pregnancy and childbirth sees little further purpose for casework counsel.[35] Somehow the social caseworker

---

[35] Note must be taken of more recent attention being given to the "unmarried father," particularly he who is emotionally attached to the woman he has impregnated. *See*, for example, Reuben Pannor, "Casework Service for Unmarried Fathers," *Children*, Vol. 10, No. 2 (March–April 1963). *See also* Mary E. Rall, "Casework with the Minor Unmarried Mother and Her Family," *Social Casework*, Vol. 39, No. 9 (November 1958), in which legal as well as social responsibilities of parents and of caseworkers to parents is touched upon. In a more recent article Dr. Marcel Heiman, *op. cit.*, makes these statements: "Out-of-wedlock pregnancy is an expression of both intrapsychic and interpersonal conflict"; "When a social

has not made clear to her (or is not herself clear) that many factors in the present and near future will combine to determine the woman's feelings, needs, and behavior after her child is born, and that these factors are subjects for ongoing discussion and planning within the casework relationship.

One consideration, it seems to this writer, has particular relevance to prevention and has not yet appeared in the writing of social caseworkers on the treatment of the illegitimately pregnant woman. It is the concept of *crisis* with all its attendant implications for preventive treatment.[36] The fact is that illegitimate pregnancy is a crisis in the life of any woman. By the time she gets to a social caseworker she may have pushed under, by elaborate defenses, her first emotions. But these emotions are not too far off because they attach to the whole series of crises along the way to childbirth—leaving her home (or staying there), entering the shelter, explaining her school or work drop-out, relating to her distressed or disgusted family, thinking about her sexual partner, attending the prenatal clinic, planning for nearby next steps, and so on. These are her points of crisis, which is to say, of emotional precariousness. Crisis theory postulates that "the period of disequilibrium is seen as an important intervention point" and that "to help people in crisis situations may prevent the development of chronic disorders and maladaptive coping patterns.[37] This, it may be said, has been implicit in social casework's relationships with the illegitimately pregnant woman. The suggestion here is to make it *explicit*, to focus casework counseling on the crucial interactions between the woman and others in relation to the pregnancy and parturition period *as well as* (not instead of) on the decision to be made about the baby. As the woman feels concern for *herself* (not alone for the baby she bears) and as, in daily problems that may be more real to her than her coming baby, she finds the

---

worker tries to help a teenager who is pregnant out of wedlock, the focus of attention should be the girl's family rather than the girl herself"; "Any agency that deals with the problem of out-of-wedlock pregnancy should make the family as a unit the focus of casework treatment . . . must function as a family agency." These valuable formulations in Dr. Heiman's article, however, lose their full impact and import when he develops his view of the family almost solely in its *unconscious* participation in creating the girl's pregnancy. Here again lies the recurrent danger of losing the *family-in-crisis* through sole focus on the *family-as-cause*.

[36] In a rapidly developing literature on this concept and its relation to social work treatment, see especially Gerald Caplan, ed., *The Prevention of Mental Disorders in Children: Initial Explorations* (New York: Basic Books, 1961); Lydia Rapoport, "Working with Families in Crisis: An Exploration in Preventive Intervention," *Social Work*, Vol. 7 (July 1962); and, for a succinct summary of crisis theory, Lola Selby, "Social Work and Crisis Theory," *Social Work Papers*, Vol. 10, University of Southern California, 1963.

[37] Selby, *ibid.*

caseworker helpful in meeting them, she may develop some deeper relationship with the caseworker, which is the basic condition for building in "psychological prevention."

Finally, there is the fact, as indicated earlier, that most illegitimately pregnant women never come within social work's sights. Many are able, through family or friends, to buy or find private resources of shelter, concealment, support, and medical care. But most are those women and girls of the lower class, economically and educationally, predominantly nonwhite, probably most alienated by feeling or social circumstance from the dominant culture and community. Conceivably this group most needs the services that organized social work offers (though at present in insufficient quantity). If this woman is already on public assistance and if she is able to inform her caseworker of her condition, she may be referred for prenatal care. There also may be a budget adjustment to allow for a pregnancy diet. If she does not see her caseworker (because of heavy case loads) or if she does but is ashamed to reveal her pregnancy, the quick visit made, usually for check of eligibility purposes, will not necessarily reveal her physical state or mental stress. If she reports to the social service department of the hospital when she seeks prenatal care and is referred to any agency for shelter and counseling but is too afraid or ashamed or too lazy to go, she is not often followed up.

When a woman in this group is known to a social worker as a "client," it is usually to an untrained social worker whose attitude and perception about the behavior in question would tend to be shaped by personal rather than professional understanding. Moreover, even if this social worker were trained, her job functions are likely to be so circumscribed by definition and pressures that exploration and work with the woman on the cause and effect of her illegitimate pregnancy would be all but impossible. So it is that little is actually known, understood, or done by social work about the largest group of illegitimately pregnant women —those who do not make use of social services at all or who request only the economic and medical aids under the aegis of public welfare agencies. Recidivism—or at least the count of repeated out-of-wedlock pregnancy—is highest in this group of women.

In sum, for the social problem of illegitimate pregnancy, social work's theory, priorities, and services may be encapsuled thus:

1. The explanations in social work for the occurrence and incidence of pregnancy out of wedlock are of two sorts—one psychiatric, the other sociological. The first is almost exclusively applied to the white woman who actively seeks social agency help for concealment, shelter, and planning. The second almost exclusively applies to the Negro woman who may seek (and get) this same kind of help or who, in far larger

number, is "known about" but actually not known in the social agency. Even a cursory examination of these explanations raises many questions of their partialness, their validity, and the extent to which they exclude or do not take account of many other associated and causal factors. They are of concern on the premise that they affect social work planning, practice, and outcome.

2. Social caseworkers who specialize in work with the woman pregnant out of wedlock attest to the characteristic difficulty they encounter in counseling this client beyond the specific arrangements and plans for immediate care, medical service, and disposition of the baby. Thus the aim of "prevention" of further difficulty seems unrealized. The question is whether this is an inevitable outcome of the client's definition and experience of her problem or whether prevailing social work theory affects meaningful communication between client and caseworker.

3. The tangible resources and services developed by social work to meet the needs of the illegitimately pregnant woman aim to provide the protection—social, psychological, and physical—that this condition (and its consequences) requires. Many helpful aids have been developed. There is indication that the need for such resources is greater than the supply and further indication that for large numbers of illegitimately pregnant women the social agency is not thought of or used as a helping resource. Moreover, for the nonwhite woman such pregnancy-protection services are less readily provided.

4. There are indications that among the various agencies that deal with one aspect or another of illegitimate pregnancy there is need for more careful planning and coordination. This is not only to prevent the individual woman from being shifted from place to place and person to person at a time when security and stability are basic needs but also to allow agencies to define more clearly their separate and joint functions in coordinating their planning for this growing social problem.

5. Unmet needs are greatest among nonwhite, economically, culturally, and perhaps psychologically impoverished women. Among them recidivism is probably highest. The prospect of "prevention" or even of the dimunition of the problem requires a considerable shift of attention and study to what is now an anonymous mass of women and considerably more understanding of the needs and deficiencies, social and psychological, with which their illegitimate pregnancy is associated.

Unmarried Motherhood

With the birth of her child, the illegitimately pregnant woman moves from fantasies of motherhood (or hopes of stillbirth) into the reality role of mother, unmarried. If she relinquishes motherhood by relinquishing her baby to adoption, she presents no social problem. As has been indicated, in a perverse sort of way she may even be regarded as an "asset" by social workers specializing in adoption and by prospective adoptive parents and their families. She may carry her personal problem with her as she leaves the hospital or maternity shelter, but as a social being she resumes her former status and roles without disturbance to social equilibrium.

The mother who remains ambivalent, unable to choose between giving up or keeping her child, may, during the period of her indecision, be considered something of a social problem. This is because her indecision makes it necessary for the community to provide at least temporary or partial economic support for her and her child, along with placement and protection provisions for the child. Accompanying these aids in "good" social work agencies are casework counseling services to help her work out her conflict.

The social problem presented by this mother is not alone her need for special help from the community. It may involve a conflict in social attitudes—whether she should be "punished" by being made responsible for the care of the child she has brought into the world, whether she might be deterred from further "immorality" by such responsibility, and, increasingly over the last few decades, social concern for the fate of her fatherless and disadvantaged child.

These attitudes, ranging from censure of the mother to concern for the child, are seen in boldest relief in relation to the unmarried mother who, out of choice or because she has no recourse, takes her child to live with her. Within social work today these attitudes are considerably different from what they were several decades ago. They also differ according to race and class. There is indication, too, that attitudes in the general community have undergone change, moving from primary intent to punish the mother to primary intent to protect the child. The unresolved conflict here, however, flares up now and again in the attacks on mothers of illegitimate children on Aid to Dependent Children, the punitive actions proposed or taken against them (in the former, of denial of economic aid), and the counterattack from numerous other sectors of the public deploring deprivation of the "innocent" illegitimate children.

Until the 1940's the writings of social work show the professional concern to have been almost solely with the welfare of the baby of the unmarried mother. It was, however, the *physical well-being of the child* that was most stressed. For example, because medical theory of the twenties held that breast feeding was most conducive to good nourishment of the newborn (interestingly enough, a conviction later held firmly by psychiatrists in relation to emotional nurture!), the unmarried mother, under social work's protection in many places, was held to breast feeding her baby for a number of months.[38] The effect of this on the unmarried mother's emotional attachment to her baby and her inability to take on any role other than mother is readily imagined. Nor is it hard to imagine that some retributive satisfaction was experienced among those who promulgated or carried out these ideas, for not only was the baby's welfare being assured but the unmarried mother was being held "responsible."

Concern about the psychological well-being of the unmarried mother herself began to come through in the forties for two different reasons. One was the apparent increase of unmarried mothers among middle-class women. (The war years with marriage postponements, the rising incidence of illicit coition, or the more frequent use of social agencies— all are possible explanations.) So there arose some wish to protect the "good girl" of "good family" who was considered to have "made a mistake." The second reason was the growing recognition of the un-conscious dynamics of all behavior and the clinical attention given to disturbed (or sometimes insufficiently disturbed) women who were illegitimately pregnant. With the high incidence of emotional disturb-ance and poor parent-child relationships evident (possible reasons for which have been noted earlier), there arose concern of two sorts: (1) the unmarried mother's need for help for herself and (2) the kind of mothering she was equipped to give a child in the light of her (assumed) psychological disturbances and immaturity.

For the good of the unmarried mother herself *and* for the good of the baby, then, the conviction has grown strongly and swiftly that the baby should be given up by the unmarried mother for adoption by pre-sumably mature and capable parents. The social acceptance of the child's "innocence" has spread with amazing rapidity over the last few decades (contrast the present-day view of illegitimate children with the wild, elfin, evil streak in Hester's illegitimate child one hundred years ago). Along with this, and for a number of other reasons, a tremendous "market" for adoptable babies has developed. This perhaps fortifies today's social worker's conviction that adoption—and the earlier the better—is best for the welfare of the baby and of the mother.[39] At

---

[38] The source for these data on prevailing notions about what was "good" for the unmarried mother and her child is the doctoral dissertation of Lilian Ripple, *Social Work Studies of Unmarried Parenthood as Affected by Contemporary Treatment Formulations 1920–1940*, University of Chicago, March 1953.

[39] One recent effort to caution social workers against all-out espousal of one solu-tion of the problem of the unmarried mother is Rose Bernstein's, "Are We Still Stereotyping the Unmarried Mother?" *op. cit.*, in which she proposes: "Actually we do not have enough verified data regarding the long-range outcomes of either plan [relinquishing or keeping the baby] to substantiate one assumption over the other."

present it may be said that the unmarried mother who gives up her baby is no longer a social problem. She is lost from the eyes of social work and is indistinguishable from her peers.

In the minds of politicians, legislators, and many citizens the unmarried mother who is a social problem is the one who actually takes on the role of mother to her baby, who does not or is unable to disguise the child's illegitimacy, and who is unable to support herself and child (or children) without assistance from the community. This rules out the number—no one knows how many—of women whose families "absorb" them and their babies, those who are economically and socially able to carry off this anomalous role, those who fabricate a dead husband and father, and other such arrangements. It "rules in" largely the economically deprived, educationally and vocationally untrained, socially devalued and perhaps inept, nonwhite unmarried mother.

She is a social problem from several vantage points. She "shows" by her child that she has violated social norms. She asks, by applying for financial support now and for years ahead, that those who (to all appearances) have been responsible and moral persons should pay for her mistake (or sin). Because she is expected to care for her child on minimal economic aid, she raises him in poverty, poor housing, under strain, with few opportunities for the enrichment of her own or his experience. When, as occurs in many communities, she is expected both to mother her child and to work, the child is left in makeshift care. Without father or father image, and often shifted from one caretaker to another, it would be predicated by psychodynamic theory that this child would develop with little sense of security, trust, or self-respect, and that he might be prone to continued dependency or to demands and depredations on others. As for this unmarried mother, the problem of her underfulfillment at every level of her living, plus the stresses of motherhood under conditions of poverty, censure, or at best, tolerance, is both a personal one which may lead to further efforts to find love, companionship, and security in sexual relationships and also a social one in its contagious effects.

Prevailing notions among the public of the reasons for the unmarried mother range from the idea that this is in the nature of her culture (Negroes are "oversexed" and illicit coition and illegitimacy matter little in the Negro community) to ideas that having babies out of wedlock is a way to gain more economic aid.

Among social workers, prevailing ideas, already discussed, stem from concepts of cultural "acceptance" of illegitimacy. Concern about the welfare of the illegitimate Negro child has perhaps been diluted by ideas about the natural maternal warmth, "mammy warmth," of Negro women, particularly grandmothers, and about the flexibility of Negro family life, which expands to take in children, whether born in or out of wed-lock. As has been said earlier, it would seem that these cultural-psychological explanations deserve some critical re-examination, partic-ularly in the urban industrialized communities of the north.[40] Why a woman who has not been a good mother should become a good mother when she is a grandmother is not psychologically explainable. How a family "takes in" additional members with any warmth or pleasure when housing is already crowded and mouths-to-be-fed are already too many is not easily answerable. It may do so with relatively greater acquiescence or tolerance than would be found in a middle-class family whose standards of room and individual rights are more firmly defined. But that actual welcome and accompanying warmth should be present is questionable. In brief, the stereotypes that govern popular and social work ideas about the nonwhite unmarried mother call for examination against open and plain evidence available in Aid to Dependent Chil-dren cases.[41]

The evidence that prevailing ideas among social workers about the economically dependent nonwhite, culturally and educationally deprived unmarried mother are not too sharply differentiated from prevailing ideas in the general public is the result of several factors. The unmarried mother in her actual on-going role as mother of an illegitimate and un-planned child is scarcely known to professional social workers. She is known largely to workers carrying the name "social caseworker," charged with many social casework functions in the massive public assistance programs, chiefly AFDC, persons who (with some exceptions) have not had social work education or training in its practice. What a person will perceive, how he will interpret the meaning of what he sees, what he will propose as ways of coping with what he sees depend heavily on the knowledge and understanding he brings to endow his experience with meaning. Except as the observers of the greatest mass of unmarried

---

[40] Among the ADC mothers interviewed in the Greenleigh study, *op. cit.*, the interviewers report "a number of mothers asked for help in explaining to children why they had no father. Mothers of adolescent boys were concerned about their sons growing up in a female world" (p. 17). Both the Greenleigh and Marion County studies (*op. cit.*) reveal that for the majority of mothers of illegitimate chil-dren the relationship with the putative father had not been a casual or passing one. Of 619 families interviewed in the Greenleigh study, 50 percent of the unmarried mothers had "dated" the father for more than a year and an additional 10 percent for three months or more. For the one third of the cases marriage was out of the question because one partner was married—often the woman herself whose husband had deserted.

[41] Some evidence in the Greenleigh study offers opposing answers to my "loaded" questions. The interviewers report that "in over 80 percent of the families (on Aid to Dependent Children) the feeling of the mother for her children was warm and accepting." It is added that "observations were brief."

mothers are equipped with knowledge of the social, economic, cultural, and psychological factors operating in this complex of problems called "unmarried mother," except as they are aware of their own attitudes and feelings which color their perceptions and actions, except as they are equipped by on-the-job training (if full professional education is not possible) to know how to communicate and reach out to people who speak another language and who live in "another country"—except as these conditions would hold, the unmarried mother is seen as part of a blurred, anonymous mass problem, deplored or sympathized with as the case may be, but not professionally understood. (An analogous situation in medicine and in the profession's delayed relation to it might be that of leprosy, to which, for centuries, medicine turned its back, delegating care of lepers chiefly to religious orders, deploring, sympathizing, but failing to take this disease into the arena of the profession's problems to be solved.)

Recently, however, several breakthrough efforts have been launched which signal the beginnings of professional determination to know, to understand, and to plan for the unmarried mother and her child. The Greenleigh staff's interviews "in depth" of more than six hundred mothers whose youngest child was born out of wedlock is one.[42] A current study in New York of unmarried mothers with a first illegitimate child promises not only fuller understanding of the problem but also of the readiness and capacity of these women to use resources.[43]

A second factor which has acted as an obstacle to social work's "knowing" the unmarried mother has been this: this woman has been defined and therefore viewed not in her role as a mother but in the role of "relief client." Thus, even with social caseworkers of knowledge and sensitive understanding, the reference frame within which the unmarried mother on relief is seen and judged is that of her initial and continuing eligibility for relief. With the usual heavy caseloads of the AFDC caseworker and with the recurrent pressures to get as many people off relief as possible, even a professionally trained caseworker might readily constrict her concerns to those that are characteristic of the AFDC social worker: is there a man in evidence in the unwed mother's life? If so, is he the putative father who can be charged with support of the child? Or does he, whoever he is, already make money contributions to the woman? Are there any evidences of other sources of income than AFDC? Can the woman work? If so, should she not be encouraged to go to work and find someone (a daycare center, a relative, a neighbor,

[42] Greenleigh Associates, *op. cit.*

[43] "Unmarried Mothers Who Keep the First Out-of-Wedlock Child," Community Council of Greater New York, New York, a study begun in April 1962.

or an older child) to care for her child while she works? If there are no gross evidences of child neglect, if there are no blatant evidences of other economic resources, this unmarried mother and her child (or children) will not be seen again by the caseworker for months. The concerns are economic concerns.

If, on the other hand, she were defined as a woman who has unwittingly or unwillingly taken on the role of mother and her baby were seen as being born to a single parent who is neither prepared nor able to provide the physical or psychological nurture for a child's adequate growth and development, then a wholly different kind of content would shape the communication between this mother and her caseworker. Is there a man in evidence? What is he to the woman? What is he like to the child—what meaning has he for the child? Can the woman work? Can she find good steady substitute care for the child? Can she manage working and mothering when she returns home at night? Does the mother understand what a child needs by the way of experiences to grow on, not just food and shelter? Does she care? Is she interested in getting help with this? And so on. These concerns, focused on the mother-child roles, would reveal knowledge of the unmarried mother and of her illegitimate child which neither social work nor any other profession has today.

What, then, does social work do about the unmarried mother? As already indicated, for the woman who comes to the various social agencies that deal with all or parts of this problem the major service today is help to relinquish the baby for adoption and to resume her former status. For the woman who cannot make this decision by the time of childbirth temporary foster placements of the baby are often arranged with on-going work with the mother toward resolution of her ambivalence. However, because the baby often remains in a kind of limbo during this process, social workers have become increasingly intent on helping the woman to solve her "to keep or not to keep" dilemma before the baby is born. For the woman who has no choice but to keep her child, or for the woman who by free choice ("free" at least on a conscious level) decides to do so, social work thus far has not to any significant extent established professional services. Many of the "free-choice" women drop out of sight. With their babies absorbed by their families, supported by the mothers themselves, or given away in "grey" or "black market" adoptions, they present no problem to the community.[44]

---

[44] A 1960 report by the Bureau of Public Assistance shows that of an estimated 2.5 million illegitimate children under eighteen years of age about one third had been adopted and about one eighth were on ADC. For more than half of these

It is the woman who keeps her out-of-wedlock baby and applies for public support for whom social work is repeatedly held responsible by the articulate public and for whom it has as yet developed few actual helping means. The reasons for this lag in social work's "doing" are, again, several-fold. Not only have already-mentioned factors of beliefs, perspectives, and lack of knowledge operated here but more important, perhaps, has been the discouragement to professional intervention efforts by the massiveness of the problem, the relative inadequacy of economic means by which to cope with it, and finally, the public attitudes against the rising tide of "reliefers," especially when they are predominantly nonwhite and obviously "immoral." The effect of such attitudes on those who would work with these pariahs is not difficult to see. Salaries are low because the task is not socially valued. Working conditions are rugged because this is inherent in work with poverty, in slums, under tension, against resistances. Despite federal intent local communities do not often provide adequate funds for anything beyond the most marginal support for mother and child. And finally the recurrent outbreaks of public indignation against the unwed mother on relief tend to bracket in her helper, the social caseworker, who is somehow tarred with guilt by association; at the least this social caseworker is accused of being soft-hearted and muddle-headed, at the worst, of aiding and abetting immorality. Professional social workers have many more gratifying, better paying, better status jobs open to them. That they do not (with occasional exceptions) choose to enter or remain in work with the unmarried mother on AFDC is scarcely surprising. Therefore, in practice, social work does very little about the mass of unmarried mothers.

Nevertheless the professional conscience is strong, and two major kinds of "doing" must be taken account of. One is the consistent and often inspired training programs within public assistance agencies, developed at a national level and carried through on a regional and local basis by trained social workers. These programs consist of publications, in-service training courses, scholarships for professional education, and so on, all aimed at enhancing the understanding and at developing the skills of caseworkers in the public assistance. Considerable professional social work talent and vision is poured into these training programs. But overloaded caseworkers, overloaded often by more paper work than client contacts, and the persistence of community denigration and consequent restricted funds often vitiate these basic efforts to build services.

---

children there are no facts. U. S. Department of Health, Education and Welfare. Social Security Administration, Bureau of Public Assistance. *Illegitimacy and its Impact on the Aid to Dependent Children Program*, April 1960.

The second action of social work in regard to the unmarried mother on relief has been in the nature of interpreting and championing her rights and needs to legislators, politicians, and the public at large. Through the National Association of Social Workers at national and at local chapter levels, through *ad hoc* social action committees, through statements to the press, and so on, social workers have called public attention to and testified in defense of the economic, educational, and social needs of public aid recipients and have strongly suggested legislative and policy changes that would provide more adequate social resources and services.[45]

That the unmarried mother would gain from such general benefits is obvious. What is not always so obvious is that as a woman unready for motherhood she is also often unequipped to undertake it. At her child's birth this mother and her child are the most vulnerable, malleable unit in the whole range of public aid recipients. How she can be helped to be a good mother, how her child can be given the opportunities for healthy development is a major challenge for social work. Along with this runs the question how—or whether—this complex of problems can be prevented.

PREVENTION: PROBLEMS AND MEANS

What a profession does or is able to do about the problems within its sphere of concern depends on several factors:

1. The profession's actual knowledge, beliefs, skills, and developed resources for coping with the problem. These have been examined in the preceding pages in relation to social work's place in dealing with the problem phases that culminate in unmarried motherhood.

2. Society's concern with the problem. When the problem is *of* and *in* society, is potentially *everybody's* problem, not just that of an "out-group," money, open interest, and readiness for leadership and change will be mobilized for a profession's use. When there is wide recognition

---

[45] Some recent examples: the publication of *Public Welfare: Time for a Change*, a report by Elizabeth Wickenden and Winifred Bell of the Project on Public Services for Families and Children, New York School of Social Work of Columbia University, November 1961. This report, which includes additional proposals for representatives of social work throughout the country, was submitted to the President and his incoming administration of the Department of Health, Education and Welfare. An Ad Hoc Committee on Public Welfare, consisting chiefly of outstanding social workers, appointed by then Secretary of Health, Education and Welfare Ribicoff, submitted their report in September 1961, which served as one base for 1962 legislation toward the extension and improvement of the public assistance and child welfare programs. See *Hearings Before the Committee on Finance, United States Senate, Eighty-Seventh Congress, Public Assistance Act of 1962*, H.R. 106–6, U. S. Government Printing Office, pp. 71–85.

that a problem threatens general welfare and that professional means exist to combat it, a profession will have strong popular backing. If, on the other hand, the problem seems to belong to the few and those few are of an out-group, the profession may be called on to act, but with marginal interest and support. Thus what social work can do about a given problem area depends on the community's understanding and interpretation of, and feeling of involvement in, the problem.

3. Its power and status in society. Professional opinion is held to be "authoritative" in direct proportion to its actual or ascribed powers. Social work does not yet generally possess the power or authority attributed to it. Thus, even though social work may have considerable knowledge of a given problem area, and even though this may be recognized by influential sectors of society, its voice will be given less heed than that of some more prestigeful professions.

These factors of knowledge, societal concern, and professional power and prestige will be seen to bear on considerations of social work and prevention.

Involved in each of the problem phases that lead to unmarried motherhood are a number of professions and organized powers in addition to social work. Medicine, law, education, and the church are major professions concerned with social and sexual morality, the family, child rearing, and physical and mental health. There would probably be considerable disagreement among and within these professions as to who was to be responsible for what, but all would agree that unmarried motherhood is a problem to be deplored and, if at all possible, prevented. How? The question is threefold:

1. How can the problem be prevented from occurring at all—how can its causes be rooted out? This is "primary prevention."

2. If the problem occurs, how can it be detected early, "nipped in the bud," so that its consequences will be ameliorated or limited? This is "secondary prevention" and "control" through early treatment.

3. If the problem and its consequences are present, what modifying, ameliorative, or restitutive means may be used to lessen the stress and damage it creates, to contain the spread of its influence, and to substitute rehabilitative for destructive sequelae? This is "tertiary prevention" and involves a number of treatment and restorative means.

Accompanying the questions "how" is the pervasive one "who"— whose is the primary professional responsibility?

Primary prevention. Obviously, abstinence from illicit coition is the primary prevention of unmarried motherhood. However, students of the current scene and of the forces at play in today's society are agreed that illicit coition is probably on the increase, as are the permissions and excitations for its occurrence. Churchmen, educators, and parents continue to exhort the young—but all are aware of the gap between what they preach and other potent social and psychological forces that drive toward sexual freedoms.

If illicit coition is widely practiced, conception control is the obvious "primary prevention." Contraceptive advice and devices are the business of medicine. Contraception is also taken as a moral issue by a powerful sector of the church as a sin against nature even in lawful marriage. In relation to this preventive means it is clear that social work stands in subordinate position to medicine and church, able only to testify to the serious consequences in illegitimate pregnancies and unmarried motherhood.

The Planned Parenthood Federation of America is a voluntary organization which, under a medical director, seeks to establish "child spacing" means in hospitals, public health, and industrial health services. It carries on a program of interpretation to the public, clergymen, and to other professional workers. *In*-wedlock child spacing is its intent. Because many mothers of illegitimate children on Aid to Dependent Children are actually married (but deserted), these contraceptive services might, with the blink of an eye, be extended to them. However, religious, legal, and perhaps unorganized public scruples have blocked such referrals.

Within the last year (1962–1963) in Illinois a raging controversy over the offer of referral and payments for contraceptive means to recipients of public assistance has involved churchmen, social workers, laymen, physicians, and a large articulate group of politicians and political aspirants. Newspaper headlines and weeks of feature stories attested to the widespread interest in whether the Illinois Public Aid Commission (within which there was almost an even split of opinion) should pay for the medical examinations and prescriptions involved in contraception for women (married or not) on relief. The complexity of the contraceptive issue in an American community today could be read in the other kinds of issues attached to this one, expressed by representatives of various professions and by laymen: racial, religious, moral, political, and economic. Among social workers themselves there was no unanimity about this proposal, and, although in a final referendum the Chicago Chapter of the National Association of Social Workers voted by a large majority in favor of the right to free access to contraceptive means.

The conflict in the social worker is not unlike that of many laymen. Religious considerations aside, there remains the fact that free public provision of contraceptive aids to any woman or girl who asks for them seems to give social sanction to illicit sexual relations. It would by implication let down the powerful bars of fear and guilt that now are counted on to deter many girls and women from engaging in such relations. Thus, before doctors, the clergy, or social workers could step forward generally to propose or commend this preventive means, a great deal of thinking would need to be done about the social, physical, and psychological effects of "letting down the bars" on sex relations outside marriage. What effects on marriage, family life, and personality development would social sanction of sexual freedom bring? Puritan repression breeds one kind of neurosis. Does permissiveness breed none? Might there be some limits drawn about who, under what conditions, might have free access to contraceptive instructions and means?

The basic deterrents, of course, are presumed to lie in the individual's conscience structure, in the identification of the girl or woman with strong and loving parental models (actual or substitute) who have held firm to expectations of sexual control. These "expectations" in parents and the parental model itself are, of course, strengthened or weakened by forces in current social life, but if sociologists are right the inner-directed parent grows more rare.

When illicit coition is discussed with caseworkers it is because it has already taken place (or is suspected by parents or teachers of having taken place) and is a source of conflict, internal or interpersonal. A "problem" is already present in psychological form. "Prevention" of further sexual acting out would be the goal. Depending on the girl's relationship with the social worker and her identification with her as an ego ideal, the social worker's position may serve as deterrent and guide. However, the number of girls and women so reached by social workers is very small indeed.

A series of questions is presented at this juncture. Should more interpretation be widespread about social casework so that more unmarried girls and women can (conceivably) be counseled and helped to avoid sexual involvement? Are agencies equipped to offer such expanded services? Are there enough skilled and sophisticated caseworkers to proffer these services? Are social agencies and their caseworkers willing and able to establish communication lines with those segments of the population that seem to be most alienated from them by class identification and culture—particularly for discussion of intimate aspects of life? Are social casework and group work the social processes most appropriate for tackling primary prevention of any social problem?

A preventive plan persistently put forward is that of better and more widespread sex education. At times it is presented as one part of a general family-life education program, at others it is specifically focused, particularly for adolescents, on sex. A variety of professional and quasi-professional persons—social workers, psychologists, sociologists, teachers, and the like—are involved under various auspices in leading discussion groups on preparation for "good" family life. "Good family life," when achieved, is assumed to offer built-in deterrents to violations of social standards, including sexual violations. Yet the insistent question here is, again, whether those who voluntarily gather for such group discussions are not already self-selected by their overt interest in having "good families" and whether, in the face of the fact that girls and women of "good families" are in large numbers involved in illicit coition, there is reason to doubt that assumption.

As for sex education, it is never quite clear what this is. It is doubtful in this day of pervasive and uninhibited communication that illicit coition takes place in true ignorance of the relation between it and pregnancy. Someone has suggested that sex education is like knowledge of the mechanism of a car—it does not deter reckless driving, experimentation, or accident proneness.

Again, however, in such educational efforts social work stands in a minor role. It is seen by the public and by other professions as a social *problem-solving* profession. Its experience with the consequences of problematic behavior equips its practitioners and planners with telling testimony of personal and social needs and with some predictive powers. In the main, however, the evidence of the increase and prevalence of sexual freedoms and illicit coition in our society suggests that "primary prevention" must be the function of those persons and professions involved in the *total and ongoing life experience* of the individual and the family group—parents, who in turn must be underpinned and guided by school, church, and medicine, particularly in its "public health" aspects.

Social work may have a vital, though clearly secondary, part to take in such ongoing educational efforts. In school systems school social workers can be "case finders" and referral agents for children called to their attention by alert and concerned teachers. In collaborative work with public health doctors and nurses social workers may find and refer "vulnerable" young women to appropriate social agencies for counseling and guidance. Possibly social work could broaden its influence in those preventive efforts that have as their targets the attitudes, beliefs, and habitual behaviors of people if it were less tightly tied to certain forms of organization.[46] In their present form social agencies are problem-solving organizations. They are so set up and seen by their communities.

---

[46] The evidence that large sectors of the population do not know what social work is for (*see Bernstein and Sauber, op. cit.*) suggests this, and a recent article by Samuel Mencher, "Principles of Social Work Organization," *Social Casework*, Vol. 44, No. 5 (May 1963) develops the idea of the need for social work's greater accessibility.

If social work is to have any significant place in primary prevention, it must devise ways by which it can more flexibly share its experience and skills with professions with priority standing on matters of primary prevention.

Secondary prevention. Once conception has taken place, there is only one radical means to prevent pregnancy's coming to term: induced abortion. This is illegal, except by a qualified physician's judgment that pregnancy and subsequent childbirth are a health hazard. "Health hazard" is usually taken to mean physical health. It is subject to varied interpretations by physicians and hospital medical boards, but to authorize a "therapeutic abortion" they must "show cause" in terms of danger to pregnant women or fetus if pregnancy is carried to term.

There are countries in which under certain conditions abortion is legal and accessible under public health auspices. In Sweden, for example, on the basis of joint social work, medical and psychiatric evaluations, abortion for unmarried women may be recommended and carried out for reasons of physical or mental health. Swedish social work, as an auxiliary to medicine, supplements medical judgment by assessment of the sociopsychological consequences of illegitimate pregnancy for the individual woman. In Japan abortion has been legalized, chiefly to put controls on its population explosion. In the United States, however, despite estimates that about 1 million illegal abortions per year are performed, there remain strong emotional barriers against it.[47]

If illegitimate pregnancy must be carried to term, are there any kinds of "secondary prevention" possible—any kinds of treatment that would ameliorate the stress or change the course and nature of the consequences—that may be expected to obviate repetition?

The purposes of secondary prevention may be said to be those of the kinds of services and methods currently proffered by social work. In the shelter and concealment provisions developed and staffed by social workers the effort is to avoid the social stigmatization of the woman herself and of her family group, which might affect not only her present but her future prospects for life adjustment. In the medical and dental care provisions (actually under the aegis of public health maternity clinics or under private hospital auspices, but their use often occurs through social work referrals) the prevention as well as treatment of physical problems associated with pregnancy and childbirth is assured for the mother-to-be as well as for the child *in utero*. In the case-by-case effort to develop a supporting, meaningful relationship with the illegitimately pregnant woman, to show her acceptance, and to provide under-

---

[47] For a discussion of the problems of abortion *see* Robert E. Hall, M.D., "Thalidomide and Our Abortion Laws," *Columbia University Forum*, Vol. 6, No. 1 (Winter, 1963) and the letters which responded to this article in the Spring, 1963 issue.

standing, social casework seems to establish a basis for identification with a "good" substitute parental model. In the ongoing effort to get at the feelings, thoughts, and desires that brought the woman to her present state, to talk and think about them and their consequences, social casework (and sometimes group work) operates in the hope of preventing repetitions of the same behavior. The development of continuing group discussions, educational programs and of some vocational training opportunities in some maternity homes underpins the hope for a future different from the past. When this is accompanied by casework planning that considers the woman's own needs, motives, and aspirations (rather than planning solely for the baby, as if the woman were simply a "producer"), then the woman's sense of herself as acceptable, respectable, and potentially restorable may be enhanced. These present-day developments in social work may be seen as efforts toward prevention of recidivism, of personality deterioration through social disgrace and self-denigration, and of makeshift future arrangements.

Unfortunately, as already noted, these services reach only a small proportion of illegitimately pregnant women, those who of their own accord or by referral have asked for (and have been judged "eligible" for) these services. A large number—no one knows how large—of illegitimate pregnancies are carried under cover of private medical, shelter, and adoption arrangements. Of greater concern to social work and to the general community, however, is that apparently far greater number of women who need but do not get services aimed at prevention of personality scarring, of undesirable birth and postnatal child-care arrangements, and of a repeated pregnancy. They are not exposed to these "secondary prevention" possibilities because there has been restricted extension to them of social resources (such as maternity homes and adoption possibilities) and also because they do not know that such resources may actually be open to them.

Even if it were possible, by some magic, to multiply the resources of tangible aids and guidance and counsel available during the months of pregnancy, account ought first to be taken of their present deficiencies and of the ways by which they could more surely achieve their preventive goals. The problems present in social work's secondary preventions today have been examined herein at length.

One is inherent in the organization of social services, the other in the helping process itself. In brief recapitulation, it is not always clear whether the social agency's planning for the pregnant woman is more concerned with the welfare of the baby, the mother, or the adoptive parents. Often, the particular focus derives from the function of the social agency into which the pregnant woman happens to fall. If she goes to a child welfare agency the caseworker's major concern (conscious or not) may be for the welfare of the newborn child. If the agency concentrates on adoptions the concern may be that the carefully selected adoptive parents be provided with a baby. If it is a family agency, there may be more concern with the pregnant mother-to-be and the family of which she is part. What is done of a preventive, looking-to-the-future nature depends on whose future is held to be the center of attention.

Moreover, in the course of help from discovery of pregnancy to decisions about self and child, an illegitimately pregnant woman may find herself dealing with a number of different social agencies. Prevention of confusion and conflict for the woman by stabilizing her life situation, prevention of flighty or defensive relationships and impulsive decisions rests on more concerted organization and cooperation among the many social agencies now dealing with one aspect or another of unmarried motherhood.

This situation is made even more complex by the conflict, open or covert as the case may be, between social agencies and private physicians and lawyers as to whose is the adoption prerogative. Prevention of impulsive relinquishment of the child, of consequent guilt and malaise in the mother, of legal uncertainties for natural mother and adoptive parents, of threats to the latter's security as parents, and of placement of a baby without responsible knowledge of its guardians cannot be achieved until delegated representatives of the several professions of social work, medicine, and law work out, at levels of professional policy and ethics, what their joint and separate functions are in relation to the total problem of the illegitimately pregnant woman and her child.

The second obstacle to effective secondary prevention during the period of pregnancy and parturition lies in some of the ways in which caseworkers have dealt with the pregnant woman. As has been suggested, there is need for a re-examination of the premises and consequent practices that possibly limit casework's effectiveness as an agent of prevention.[48]

To meet the needs for widespread coverage and multiple but combined services, one recent plan has been put forth that seems to hold considerable prevention potential. It is proposed by Clark Vincent that there be publicly supported "maternity-adoption centers." [49] They "could be coordinated at the national level by the Children's Bureau . . . licensed and supervised at the state level by a board of representatives from legal, medical, and social work professions. Staffing would be multidisciplinary . . . legal, medical, pastoral, nursing, public health, and social work professions." Their functions would include (by implication

---

[48] For further elaboration of this suggestion *see* Rose Bernstein, "Gaps in Services to Unmarried Mothers," *Children,* Vol. 10, No. 2 (March–April, 1963).

[49] Vincent, *op. cit.*

—Vincent does not specify them) those presently carried by different social agencies in relation to the illegitimately pregnant woman, from application for shelter or support to provisions of medical care, to work with the woman's family and the putative father (as called for), to counseling with the woman herself about her present and future roles, to planning for and carrying out adoptions or for after care of mother and child (when this is the decision). Possibly private or special-fund pilot and demonstration centers would be needed to test out the value of such a program. Such centers, established with public support, might hold a number of values. As Vincent suggests, they would provide integrated services to all races, at all socioeconomic levels, with far wider coverage than is available today. Good prenatal care would be assured. Centering responsibility in one person (in collaboration with a professional team) could be expected to enhance the unmarried mother's sense of security and trust as she works out her conflicts about herself, her sex partner, her family, her child. Furthermore, on a social problem about which there are still so few facts, such centers would offer tremendous research possibilities.

Yet, again, a solution breeds a new problem. If this were to occur, if maternity-adoption centers were to become large, open public institutions, might this, too, imply that society accepts illegitimate pregnancy and unmarried motherhood as so commonplace that it can give its consequences decent and interested support? However this question is answered, it is apparent that the development of such coverage and resources would require multiprofessional collaboration, with perhaps medicine and social work as the chief interpreters and social engineers. The money and manpower necessary to support such organizations suggest that political bodies at all levels of government and their public supporters would need to be convinced that they were buying that much-sought two-pronged goal: immediate altruism and long-run self-interest.

In all of social work's prevention work with the illegitimately pregnant woman there is the aim of preventing unnecessary hurt to the woman herself, harm to the child *inutero,* and, once the child is born, preventing repetition of the behavior that created the problem. Further, prevention of a hampered and unhappy childhood is postulated in the social agency's efforts to place the newborn child in adoption. In the main, however, the unmarried mother keeps her illegitimate child and is lost to the view of social agencies. Of the six hundred (approximately) out-of-wedlock babies born daily in this country, only seventy-five are brought by their mothers for support to the public assistance agency. It is this daily crop of 75 unmarried mothers and their babies that is the concern or scapegoat, as the case may be, of the public, the press, and political bodies.

Tertiary prevention. Tertiary prevention occurs when the problem and its consequences are already plain to be seen and felt. Restitutive means are called for and the substitution of rehabilitation for anticipated deterioration. The woman who is economically dependent and who takes on the role of unmarried mother to her child is in clear and present need of such help. The prevention need is of two sorts: to prevent her recidivism and a whole chain of destructive sequelae which may stem from the child's position as illegitimate, fatherless, and unintended (if not unwanted), a child dependent on public aid, whose birthright is economic, social, and psychological deprivation. This complex problem and its preventions are placed by the community squarely in the responsibility and competence area of social work. The economically dependent unmarried mother and her child (children) are the "clients" of the public program, Aid to Dependent Children (recently changed in name and concept to Aid to Families of Dependent Children), a program under the aegis of social work. As has already been discussed, the quantity and quality of staff, the level and modes of financing the program, and the general grasp and perspective of the problem do not adequately support the charge on social work to do a job of prevention.

The count of "repeaters" among unmarried mothers on public assistance is high. This is perhaps the sharpest bone in the craw of legislators and the general public and the efforts to punish it are understandable. Recurrently, at different places in the country, legislators or taxpaying groups propose that recidivism could be prevented by cutting off relief grants to the unmarried mother and her illegitimate children—or, at least, by refusing to grant aid to any out-of-wedlock progeny after the first "mistake." Social workers have been active—and often effective—in blocking or cutting short such retributive efforts. They have found sympathy—ready or reluctant—in a public that does not like to punish children for the sins of their parents and is not sure that the medicine might not even exacerbate the disease.

If primary preventions are not utilized—or are not made available —conception may occur. If surgical intervention is not legal, pregnancy will take its course. (Coincidentally, the better the prenatal care, which the medical profession urges on women and which gets unquestioned public support, the greater likelihood of the pregnancy being brought to term!) There are particular factors in the life of an AFDC population that may lead to repeated out-of-wedlock children: relationships between men and women who cannot marry because one (or both) is already married to a mate from whom he or she is separated but not divorced; inability to obtain divorce because of its prohibitive costs, its alien legalities, or because the applicant is already known to be involved in an "adultery"; fears of marrying a man whose employment is far more uncertain and wages often less adequate than the relief grant which can be counted on for basic food and shelter needs; and the search in sex for some transcendence of a life situation which is continuously drab, pinching, and hopeless. These are special hazards to sexual abstention in women who are already unmarried mothers on relief. Surrounding them is a climate of sexual exploitations and experimentations in the total community—white and nonwhite, among all classes, and among figures of international prominence, whether merely notorious or actually notable.

It is worth pondering whether social work has too unthinkingly allowed the community to place on it a responsibility of prevention that it not only cannot carry (and is therefore unjustly held culpable for) but that belongs to the whole community with its manifold lay and professional groups. What, for example, are schools providing that may hold particular significance for standard-setting among lower-class groups, what guidance do they offer, what opportunity for emotionally meaningful contact between teachers and children, what content that connects with what the dark-skinned slum child encounters in daily living? What is the church providing in cooperation, for example, with the self-appointed ministers of the ubiquitous storefront church that draws its group of seeking, anxious Negro women who are, or will become, mothers? What does industry, management and labor unions both, offer by way of actual work or hope to men who, with money in pocket and job in hand, might take on legal and economic responsibility for the women they have and the babies they breed? What is being pointed to here is that, although on a case-by-case basis it is possible for a social worker to affect a woman's sexual attitudes and behaviors, the problem of general prevention of recidivism cannot be placed (in a basket, as it were) at social work's door. It is a problem that legitimately belongs on the doorstep of every profession and every power group in the community.

This same conclusion must be reached by anyone who thoughtfully considers the necessities inherent in prevention of the corrosive life-space impoverishment into which the illegitimate nonwhite child is born. At the moment of his birth a chain of thwarting, depriving emotional and social circumstances can be anticipated. Even if he is wanted and loved by the woman who bore him, he is a burden. He is born into poverty of means, of rights, of culture, and of aspiration. To prevent his growing up either as a hollow man, empty of drive, love, and responsibility, or as a man full of repressed hate and occasionally expressed

violence is a task to which every responsible citizen in his profession
or in his group associations must give thought and work. There is only
one meaningful prevention means available. That is *provision*.

In order to prevent hunger, one must provide food. To prevent ignorance, one must provide education. To prevent child-neglect, there must
be the medical care, the day-care facilities, the parent education, and the
recreation possibilities that feed into the mother's own needs for nurture
and knowledge. To prevent laziness and dependency, there must be provision of work opportunity which promises and yields rewards in pay,
steadiness, and status. To prevent pervasive feelings of hostility and
inferiority, of being both "out-cast" and "out-caste," there must be evidence, in actions as well as utterances, that the community perceives
the person (and his counterparts) as one who "belongs," as one who is
expected to take his place as a fully privileged and fully responsible
citizen. To prevent hopelessness and apathy, there must be evidence that
there is a realistic basis for striving and hoping. In brief, tertiary *prevention consists of provision*.

Social work alone cannot make these provisions. True, within the
public assistance programs as they stand, social caseworkers deal with
this or that unmarried mother and her child, trying to budget them adequately, to find community resources by which their education and
medical and recreation needs can be met, and so forth. The intent of the
federal legislation that changed the name and concept of Aid to Dependent Children to Aid to Families of Dependent Children is to enhance
the strengths and potentials of the whole family unit. But two facts
which have been stated many times must be stated again: there are not
enough social workers nor can enough be trained to cope with every
case to the extent of its needs. Moreover, it is conceivable that individual case needs will diminish as resources are open and readily available to this whole group of socially handicapped mothers and children.
In short, rather than concentration on the recruitment and development
of more and more social caseworkers to fill in the gaps and meet the
rehabilitation needs of more and more unmarried mothers and their children, the concept of *prevention as provision* focuses on the development
of social opportunities. In such effort every organization and profession carries responsibility and potential contribution.

In no sense does this suggest an "out" for social work. Rather it suggests that in relation to the prevention of problems of the unmarried
mother and her child social work has heavier responsibilities to shoulder
than it has taken thus far. They are responsibilities of a different nature.

Social workers have been concerned with providing for the unmarried mother and her baby with the idea of prevention always

implicit if not specified. Such provision has been largely by two means: case-by-case money grants, with occasional attention to upsurges of the social, physical, and mental health needs of the mother-child unit, and, at upper echelon levels, persistent and repeated efforts to interpret needs and to shape public policy and attitudes toward greater adequacy of provision for all sectors of the economically disadvantaged population. Both approaches must be continued, but something more must be added.

The mass of unmarried mothers and their children has been the group least liked, least sympathized with, least identified with by the taxpayer, the legislator, and the learned professions. Social workers have perhaps unconsciously shared this general distaste or have wanted, again unconsciously, to keep their skirts clean of what, as a social problem, has an "illegitimate" status. Whatever the reason, social work today has less knowledge and less practice competence with the nonwhite unmarried mother and her child than with any problem group of comparable size and significance. Its first task, then, is to come to know this woman and child. What does she want for herself and her child? How does she perceive herself as a mother, as a sex object with a baby in tow, or as a potential wife or worker? What does she want for herself and her child? What does she possess by way of motivation and capacity to put into getting what she wants? And the growing child— to whom does he feel he belongs? What does he want to be or to do with himself? The questions have no answers today, for if anyone has asked and answered them it has been in single cases, unrecorded. Social workers cannot answer them. Therefore they cannot testify with knowledge and consequent conviction to the necessary aids to prevention.

Once they know more fully and surely, through planned studies and pilot projects that combine practice and research, then social work will be able with some greater confidence to present itself as planner and co-ordinator for the many kinds of provision for which other professions and powers hold authority and responsibility. For example, the problems of legalizing common-law liaisons are squarely the legal profession's concern; the question of contraceptive aids is within medical and religious bounds. The development of up-to-date vocational schools, of continuing adult education, and of sex and mothering education are functions of teachers as well as social workers. The development of social groups for adults, for discussion, socialization, and recreation purposes, ought to be the joint endeavors of churches and schools as well as settlements. The possibilities for maternal guidance in well-baby clinics, for discussion of problems of child rearing and child guidance should involve doctors, psychiatrists, nurses, and nursery school teachers as well as social workers. Labor union officials and employers ought to be engaged in proposing plans for teaching work skills. The possibilities proliferate.

What is necessary is that one professional group, one group of persons committed to the promotion of the common welfare, take leadership as interpreter of needs, mobilizer or inventor of means, and coordinator of efforts. This should be the social-planning, social-administration function of social work. The beginnings of its necessary competence and confidence to take this function lie in its knowledge of the social problem, its causes and its consequences. Then social work needs to take stock of its own prejudices and beliefs which have shaped its usual practices and limited its operational scope. Last, when *prevention* is seen as *provision,* new perspectives will open to social work. For the unmarried mother, as for any other social problem, social work may be seen as the connection, the linking agent, between all the provisions, actual or potential, that an affluent society holds for all the people who stand hopelessly immobilized by need.

The Broken Family ▶

OTTO POLLAK

THE PROBLEM

In our society families considered normal are created by the marriage of the parents, and both parents are expected to share the home with the children until they have grown up. The term "broken family" indicates a disaster in the development of the family and a loss in the membership. In order to be broken, something must have been whole. It would be an inappropriate use of the term to call a family composed of an unmarried mother and her illegitimate child a broken family. The membership thus constituted is not the result of the disappearance or loss of one who formerly shared the home, nor was the family unit formed on the same generational level as is customary in our society. It was formed on a two-generational level and never attained normal membership. It would be more appropriate therefore to call this combination an "uncompleted family." This is not an idle play on words, for there are differences in the psychological experience, in the possible solutions of the problems created, and in the reaction of society to the two types of family. A broken family is characterized by loss, an uncompleted family by lack of attainment. It makes a difference whether one has lost a husband or whether one has been unable to get one. Inadequacy in acquisition is different from inadequacy in maintenance. Marriage as a solution of the problem would be a first experience for the unmarried mother. For the widowed or divorced mother it would be a repeated experience. For the child of an unmarried woman the introduction of a male adult person and of a father figure into the household by marriage of the mother would be a new experience. For the child of a widow or divorcee her second husband would also be a second father figure and thus again a repeated experience.

In the broken family the breakage itself can be the result of death, divorce or separation, and desertion. Here again the loss experiences are likely to vary from subgroup to subgroup apparently along a line of degrees of definiteness. Death is definitive in its ultimate sense. Divorced people have been known to remarry one another. Whether a husband who has deserted his wife will turn up again may remain a threat or hope for a very long time indeed.

Social reactions also are different. A widow or deserted wife can count on sympathy. She is a victim of destiny or man. The divorcee is under a potential of reproach. Why could she not keep her husband in the marriage? Why has she not prevented the suffering of her children resulting from the loss of a father figure in their daily lives? Why does she have to make her friends take sides between her husband and herself? No such problems arise in relation to a widow. Any analysis of the problems of the members of a broken family and of the problems of society in relation to the broken family will have to take these differences into account.

In terms of membership a broken family must consist at a minimum of parent (father or mother) and one child. In terms of origin the child must be a son or daughter of the spouse who has stopped being a member of the household and his parents must have been legally married.

A family unit of this kind represents a social problem that is independent of the economic conditions under which it operates. The institution of the family is universal; it transcends specific cultures and social classes.[1] Social work must be ever on guard against the conceptual tendency of the past to equate "social" with "economic."[2] Having started with the tangibility of giving to the poor, social work has, even three decades after the great depression, not fully managed to free itself from the impact of this equalization.[3]

The misleading term "social work" testifies to this affiliation of the social welfare task with those whose earnings fall into the lower income brackets. The well-known difficulty that social workers experience in setting realistic fees is also an expression of this tradition. Similarly, the frequent reproach that private social welfare agencies cater more and more to middle-class clients—although statistically or empirically hardly verified—testifies to the strength of the grip that this equalization has on social welfare theory. In this paper the position is taken that a broken family represents a social problem independent of the

[1] See Margaret Mead, "What Is Happening to the American Family?" *Journal of Social Casework*, Vol. 28, No. 9 (November 1947), p. 324; George Murdock, *Social Structure* (New York: Macmillan Co., 1949), pp. 1–11.

[2] Harriett M. Bartlett, "Toward Clarification and Improvement of Social Work Practice," *Social Work*, Vol. 3, No. 2 (April 1958), pp. 3–9.

[3] See Otto Pollak, "Image of the Social Worker in the Community and in the Profession," *Social Work*, Vol. 6, No. 2 (April 1961), pp. 106–111.

level of income because it implies a constellation of special discomforts for its members and their associates and occurs with frequency in every stratum of society.[4]

For uncompleted families the situation is different. Here, essentially allied with the gap in membership, are economic hardships, predominantly public assistance cases, child neglect, slum housing, and a variety of consequences of the dominance of the pleasure over the reality principle.[5]

The Effects of Broken Families

In order to determine who suffers from the problem, clarity must be established that in every social problem there are direct and indirect sufferers. In the broken family those who continue to share the household from which one parent figure has disappeared are undoubtedly the immediate sufferers. They have lost a human resource person for need satisfaction and must now do without the gratification that this person provided; they must redistribute the resource role among themselves, thereby adding to the roles they had to perform before the breakage occurred, or find a substitute resource person. At any rate they are faced with new problems to be solved with greater demands resulting from these solutions and with new feelings of inadequacy in case of failure. A feeling of self-worth requires also that one perceive in oneself a resource quality for another. Thus suffering in the broken family is not only based on the fact that those left behind have lost a resource person for meeting their needs but also that they have failed to be and can no longer be a resource person to the one who is lost to the family unit. This occurs in families broken by death as well as by divorce or desertion. Wives suffer not only from the reality of having to manage without the husband, they suffer also from every past failure of performance of their spouse role that they may recall. Children not only lose a father or a mother, they also lose the opportunity to be child to this particular parent.

In divorce cases it is almost inconceivable that the spouse who leaves the household does not also suffer. Ambivalence is pervasive, and even when the divorce was fervently desired, the person who leaves will feel loss of home, loss of daily contact with his children, loss of the status of a spouse and parent who is integrated in the family unit, and

---

[4] *See* Wallace W. Weaver, *Social Problems* (New York: William Sloane Associates, 1951), p. 3; Arnold M. Rose, "Theory for the Study of Social Problems," *Social Problems*, Vol. 4, No. 3 (January 1957), pp. 189–199.

[5] Eleanor M. Snyder, *Public Assistance Recipients in New York State, January-February, 1957* (New York: Interdepartmental Committee on Low Incomes, 1958); Alvin L. Schorr, "Problems in the ADC Program," *Social Work*, Vol. 5, No. 2 (April 1960), pp. 3–15.

ultimately loss of self-esteem. The fight for visiting rights and the behavior of many divorced parents in the exercise of these visiting rights testify to the intensity of suffering on the part of the divorced spouse who has left the home.

The next circle of persons who suffer discomfort from the fact that a family is broken is composed of relatives and friends. They must assist financially or emotionally, they must take sides in divorce cases, and they must ultimately defend themselves against the pull of the vacuum which every broken family presents. They feel increased obligation perhaps beyond their capacities or at least conflict between the claims of the members of the broken family and claims of other people. When a resource has disappeared they feel themselves claimed as substitutes. Some people feel this also as a threat. Married women are said to be afraid that their divorced or widowed friends may have designs on their husbands. The Gay Divorcee or Merry Widow are certainly concepts which testify to the existence of this apprehension.

Ultimately in a service-oriented society the members of the wider community, especially taxpayers and donors to private welfare drives, belong also to those who suffer from the existence of broken and uncompleted families. Public assistance, old age and survivors insurance, family welfare, child placement, all are partly called on to help the broken family, all must be paid for, and even in an affluent society obligations to pay are still considered a discomfort.

By extension of the framework of analysis from the present to the future it should also be considered that any developmental handicap that the children in broken families experience may in turn have its impact on the developmental chances of their children. The suffering caused by the broken family may extend to future generations.

It is interesting to examine those who define a condition of inadequate need satisfaction as a problem. Uncompleted families certainly are much more strongly defined as a social problem by social workers, legislators, administrators of public welfare programs, and members of the wider community than they are so classified by the members of these families themselves. The Newburgh plan and measures in the same vein in Louisiana show the intensity of this problem definition, although many will question the appropriateness of the attempted solutions. The clients themselves, however, come frequently from a tradition of being cared for by a resource outside the family, of having to raise children in matriarchal families, and of having to accommodate themselves to a low standard of living. On the other hand, the broken family is more strongly felt to be a social problem by the members of the family unit, whereas other people are less inclined to do so.

particularly if economic hardship or gross psychopathology are not associated with this condition.

Nature of the Experiences

Kurt Freudenthal has written perhaps the best paper in social work literature on the experiences of mothers and children in broken families.[6] According to him, these experiences can be categorized as a sense of frustration, a sense of failure, a sense of guilt, and an occurrence of strong ambivalence between single parent and child. The sense of frustration is traced to a sense of incompleteness which is felt by the remaining spouse as well as by the children. The home and social life as opposed to occupational and professional life are based on couples. A home in opinion and fact seems to be complete only when there is a father as well as a mother to take care of it, the children, and one another. Married people invite married people. Human beings are interdependent, and when a gap in family membership interferes with the role performance that the family members can expect from one another needs will remain unsatisfied and frustration will result. This, in turn, is likely to lead to aggression, which will make the remaining family relationships more ambivalent than they otherwise would have been.[7] Furthermore, the absence of a father or mother figure in the home will force the remaining family members into the assumption of incompatible roles. Women who are single parents are expected to be fathers and mothers to their children, which quite apart from the psychodynamic difficulties involved doubles the burden. Children who have learned to view a parent as either father or mother will question the ability of the single parent to be both. They are on sound perceptual ground if they do so. The law of good continuation which governs perception will almost force them to order whatever new behavior experimentation the single parent may undertake into their previous frames of reference.[8] On the other hand, adolescent sons will be expected by the absence of their fathers to perform roles that under normal conditions a husband would fill; daughters who stay with a widowed father will be catapulted into housewifely roles that normally their mother would have undertaken. Personality conflicts [9] and

---

[6] "Problems of the One-Parent Family," *Social Work*, Vol. 4, No. 1 (January 1959), pp. 44–48.

[7] John Dollard *et al.*, *Frustration and Aggression* (New Haven: Yale University Press, 1939).

[8] Gustav Ichheiser, "Misunderstandings in Human Relations: A Study in False Social Perception," *American Journal of Sociology (supplement)*, Vol. 55 (September 1949), Part 2, p. 2.

[9] *See* Leonard S. Cottrell, Jr., "The Analysis of Situational Fields in Social Psychology," *American Sociological Review*, Vol. 7, No. 3 (June 1942), p. 377.

revivals of repressed oedipal attachments, with concomitant feelings of guilt, are likely to result.[10] Quite apart from the stimulation of these tendencies in both single parent and child by inappropriate role assumption, the mere absence of a parent of the opposite sex is likely to remove a check on oedipal impulses.

Another consequence of the sense of incompleteness which pervades the membership of the broken family is the motivation to fill the gap created by substitute figures. This may express itself first of all in a wish for remarriage on the part of the single parent, and it has been suggested by Paul C. Glick that there is a selective tendency for widows or divorced women with children to remarry more quickly or not at all than for those with no children.[11] A similar suggestion has been made tentatively by Jessie Bernard.[12] Other forms of establishing completion of the broken family through substitutes is moving in with grandparents or having them move in with the single parent and children. It is interesting to note that both forms of rehabilitating the broken family imply a measure of regression. This is obvious in the case of establishing a household with the parent or parents of the single parent, but it is also true in attempts to find another spouse, which requires dating and which in our society is an adolescent activity and part of our youth culture. Although the presence of children may make a great difference in this courtship pattern,[13] the very fact that an activity customarily associated with an earlier phase has to be renewed has elements of regression which may present problems to the single parent who finds himself motivated to engage in such activity.

The sense of failure noted by Freudenthal seems to affect the single parent as well as the children. It is particularly pronounced in divorce but occurs also in death. A divorced woman is likely to blame herself for having made a wrong selection and, if not that, for having failed in performance of her marital function. Children also are reported as feeling that they have failed to attain sufficient emotional importance in the father's life to prevent him from leaving the family unit. When death occurs, the surviving members of the family feel that they have failed to make life as easy for the departed as would have been necessary to protect his life if not his health. In cases of heart failure there may

---

[10] Otto Pollak, *Integrating Sociological and Psychoanalytic Concepts* (New York: Russell Sage Foundation, 1956), pp. 150–151; Herbert S. Strean, "Treatment of Mothers and Sons in the Absence of the Father," *Social Work*, Vol. 6, No. 3 (July 1961), pp. 29–35; Samuel H. Lerner, M.D., "Effects of Desertion on Family Life," *Social Casework*, Vol. 35, No. 1 (January 1954), pp. 3–8.

[11] Paul C. Glick, "First Marriages and Remarriages," *American Sociological Review*, Vol. 14, No. 6 (December 1949), p. 732.

[12] *Remarriage* (New York: The Dryden Press, 1956), p. 62.

[13] *Ibid.*, p. 150.

even be some basis of reality to such self-accusation. Here we have a borderline between a sense of failure and a sense of guilt.

A feeling of guilt is likely to be less pronounced among single parents who have lost their partners in divorce than in those who have lost them in death, for when death wishes have existed the inclination of many immature persons to equate thought with deed will come into existence and cause emotional havoc. Even in much less dramatic situations instances of conflict, of negative feelings, or of missed opportunities to show kindness will come to plague the survivor. A frantic search for an avenue of redemption will lead single parents to efforts of making up to their children for what they feel has been their failure in being good spouses to the departed. That such overdetermined flights into maternity or paternity are unlikely to produce a healthy growth environment for the children is not surprising. In families broken by divorce emotional confusion is aided and abetted by a sometimes unconscious but frequently quite conscious rivalry with a divorced spouse, who, without the test of daily togetherness, can show his best side when exercising visiting rights or, even better, can be invested in the fantasy life of the children with all parental virtues if the contact is completely broken.[14]

In spite of the wish to make up to the children for the loss of their father, mothers in broken families frequently find it impossible to accept without resentment the double burden of rearing children single-handed and of assuming the role of breadwinner. The children frequently represent reminders of a marriage that failed. Sometimes they represent a realistic obstacle to a remarriage and, even when this is not the case, perhaps an imagined one. Children in turn tend to hold the parent with whom they stay responsible for the divorce and also resent the burdens resulting from increased role demands on their own lives. The negative aspects of ambivalence between single parents and children are likely to be strengthened and to reach overt expression.

An emotional influence specifically identified by Freudenthal is anger. This is probably most clearly felt by the deserted wife, as pointed out by Steigman,[15] but it is likely to exist also in many divorce cases. The extension of anger to other persons of significance [16] in the life sphere of the single parent is bound to have a boomerang effect. It weakens the ability of the single parent to be giving to children, relatives, and friends, and to prospects for remarriage.

Over and beyond these experiences single parents and children in

---

[14] Otto Pollak, "A Family Diagnosis Model," *Social Service Review*, Vol. 34, No. 1 (March 1960), p. 27.

[15] Joseph E. Steigman, "The Deserted Family," *Social Casework*, Vol. 38, No. 4 (April 1957), pp. 167–171.

[16] Lerner, *op. cit.*, p. 6.

a broken family are faced with the problem of overdetermination in dependency and independence. In the economic sphere alone the single-parent family is frequently forced to live on a lower level of income than before the break. In cases of death social security will step in but often with the effect of reducing the flow of money into the household. In divorce cases alimony may be reluctantly paid because of the bitterness attending settlements or court orders. In desertion there will be no financial provision except what is provided by public assistance; in most cases the single parent will also have to assume the role of the provider. The danger of regression will then make itself felt in the economic sphere and will strengthen the pitfalls of moving in with parents or other relatives. For the children, on the other hand, there will be the problem of premature independence. Children in a family with both parents present who might have remained protected from the push and pull of accelerated development will find themselves occupying adult roles which will give them an unrealistic feeling of adequacy and independence.

Finally, single parents may give up normal gratifications of interdependence and lead impoverished lives. For children the opposite danger exists. They may fall into symbiotic relationships with the single parent and thus fail to attain that measure of independence which normal development requires in our society.[17]

A problem area not much discussed in the literature is sexual need fulfillment. Convenience and legality of sexual outlet are often lost. There is a decline in availability of the partner for the sex act and, on the other hand, the temptation of promiscuity. Many dates expect different behavior from a woman who has known marriage than they expect from a girl who has not. The social learning of appropriate courtship behavior which a young woman in the United States gets as part of her social development is unlikely to see the single parent through. There has to be experimentation with new conduct norms, and insecurity in this area frequently remains.

Unlearning and relearning is also necessary in relationship to friends and acquaintances. Social life for adults in the United States is frequently built on the assumption of marriage. To invite a single person requires finding another single person preferably of the opposite sex. The apprehension of encouraging the threat of a Gay Divorcee or a Merry Widow may give a hostess pause. Finally, the widow or divorcee will be faced with the problem of paying her social debts. Entertaining by a person without spouse often presents a problem, financial as well as managerial. Who pours the drinks, who carves, who presides at dinner, who sits with the guests while the hostess is in the kitchen, who sees the

---

[17] Strean, *op. cit.,* pp. 31–32.

children to bed? Sometimes these difficulties are exaggerated in fantasy and result in neglect of the reciprocal demands of social contact. This may result in increased loneliness and in a feeling of being dropped.

On an over-all basis the broken family will present to its membership not only the realistic need of an increase in coping capacity but also a challenge of using the future as a means of contending with the past. A remarriage should work out better than the first marriage, whether it was broken by death or divorce. The new marriage will give the single parent a chance to prove himself a better spouse than he was in the first marriage. Children of broken families will try in their own marriages to prevent a similar turn of events. This produces a new risk of failure. There is fear of repetition of previous mistakes, with potentially immobilizing consequences. The self-image has suffered. It must first of all be repaired or at least protected from the narcissistic wound of repeated failure. Thus the members of the broken family cannot tackle the future in its own terms. They are forced to meet it in terms of the past.

SOCIETY'S VALUES
Social Values Supporting Existence of the Problem

As far as divorce is concerned, an exploration of social norms and values which support the problem is likely to prove suggestive. The pursuit of happiness which so strongly characterizes our culture has led people to think of marriage as a happiness-increasing institution. In the United States more than in any other nation [18] and in Western civilization more than in any other culture romance is regarded as a sound basis for founding a family. Consideration of economic, ethnic, or religious factors is in the eyes of many almost a violation of morality in mate selection. Parental interference in this area is strongly resisted and condemned.[19] In consequence, Americans are likely to marry without concern for differences in their backgrounds and without utilization of the know-how of people who have experienced marriage. They do so in the expectation of attaining a greater degree of happiness than they enjoyed before marriage. That under such auspices the experience should sometimes prove disappointing need not surprise.

Furthermore, Americans do not believe in the acceptance of discomfort. Resignation is not a virtue sanctioned in our culture. When something has proved disappointing, it has to be discarded and replaced. In many cases marriage is considered a terminable proposition and divorce is regarded as a legitimate instrument to be used in the pursuit of

---

[18] Raoul de Roussy de Sales, "Love in America," *Atlantic Monthly*, Vol. 161, No. 5 (May 1938), pp. 545–551.

[19] Mead, *op. cit.*, p. 325.

happiness. Like all problem solutions, however, divorce is also problem creating and thus interferes with the American demand for definitive answers. In such a culture divorce must be frequent and must lead in turn to social and personal demand for remarriage.

In the case of families broken by death or desertion it is harder to find social values that can be considered conducive to creating the problem. Social values, however, which do lead to the continued existence of the problem, can be traced. These values are related to our puritanical heritage which because of a psychological misunderstanding has led to the equalization of success and personal worth.[20] In a sense, divorce, widowhood, and desertion all represent failure in maintaining a successful marriage, and for persons who have puritanical values a feeling of failure turns into a feeling of worthlessness or at least of anxiety about personal worth. If inability to maintain a marriage is a failure, so is living as a single parent in a broken family. Here we encounter a strange convergence of social norms which at first sight appear contradictory but on further inspection seem to be closely related. In an important paper Martha Wolfenstein has drawn attention to the replacement of puritanical values by "fun morality," that is, the feeling that something is wrong with us if we do not get enough fun from life.[21] Single parents begin to worry that something is wrong with them if their lives do not provide them with an adequate amount of thrill, stimulation, and entertainment. The underlying assumption seems to be that life without fun betrays a personality defect. This is only on the surface a change from the old puritanical preoccupation with the question whether one belongs to the elect or to the damned. Freedom from anxiety is in both instances the criterion of personal worth, and the difference lies only in the means of attaining such freedom. Since life for single parents is more difficult on a reality basis than it is for those who have the support of a spouse, they are under the spell of "fun morality" likely to misinterpret the deficit of fun in their lives as a confirmation of their suspicion that personality defects represent the essence of their difficulties.

Perhaps the most important constellation of social values which supports the continuation of the problems of the broken family is provided by those factors in our culture that are conducive to the development of character disorders.[22] Permissiveness in child rearing, anxiety of par-

---

[20] Max Weber, *The Protestant Ethic and the Spirit of Capitalism*, trans. by Talcott Parsons (New York: Scribner's, 1930) ; Otto Pollak, "Cultural Dynamics in Casework," *Social Casework*, Vol. 34, No. 7 (July 1953), pp. 279–284.

[21] Martha Wolfenstein, "The Emergence of Fun Morality," *Journal of Social Issues*, Vol. 7, No. 4 (1951), pp. 15–25.

[22] Otto Pollak, "Social Factors Contributing to Character Disorders," *Child Welfare*, Vol. 37, No. 4 (April 1958), pp. 8–12.

ents about setting limits, relativity of moral codes in a heterogeneous population, fascination with change in values and pattern of behavior, as well as a long historical trend in weakening parental authority provide a fertile ground for the development of individuals who will enter marriage with the expectation of receiving without giving and with an attitude of resentment toward the challenge of misfortune rather than with an attitude of positive response. Such people are likely to become single parents and to smart under the burden of meeting the demands of single parenthood.

Social Values Opposing Existence of the Problem

Glick and Goode have drawn attention to the strong pressure that exists in our society to have single parents remarry and have shown to what high degree single parents respond to the social pressure, which probably coincides with their own wishes.[23] There is also a tendency to believe that one divorce is acceptable but that two divorces betray an unjustifiable amount of interpersonal blundering. This may well lead to greater expression of coping capacity or at least to a greater tolerance for disappointment by the second husband and wife.

The ever widening opportunity for the employment of women in our economic structure increases also the chances of a single parent to meet a prospect for remarriage. The strong tendency to join voluntary organizations for almost any conceivable purpose operates to the same effect. There is also the factual and emotional support that single parents derive from their own organization, the Single Parent Society, which gives its members the assurance and comfort that come from the strength of numbers and the awareness of sharing a fate with many others.

Not to be underrated is the shift of our civilization from a business orientation to a service orientation, from laissez faire to protective or curative intervention and of community acceptance of financial responsibility for services to those who cannot pay for them individually. The increasing concern with mental hygiene at all levels of government, and specifically in the public school system, has also to be listed here as a development that will tend to decrease some of the burdens created by single parenthood.

SOCIAL WORK VALUES

Social Work Values That Help Cope with the Problem

Although parallelism of presentation would suggest that the next step in our discussion should be concerned with social work values support-

---

[23] Glick, *op. cit.*, p. 733; William J. Goode, *After Divorce* (Glencoe, Ill.: The Free Press, 1956), pp. 211, 215, and 276 ff.

ing the existence of the problem, the nature of the social work task seems
to make it desirable to reverse this order. Social work in and by itself
is an expression of social values that oppose the maintenance of a problem. If it contains values that support the existence of the problem, they
must be viewed as flaws or failures to fulfill its mandate but hardly as
factors with the same degree of impact as the forces that counteract the
problems in question. In this respect the model for the papers in this
symposium sacrifices perspective to symmetry.

The social work values that oppose the existence of the problems of
the broken family can be found mainly in the work of private welfare
agencies. Public assistance, which deals particularly with uncompleted
families, is discussed by Professor Helen Harris Perlman.[24] Old-age
and survivors insurance, although in charge of economic support of most
widows and orphans in the United States, is a disbursing operation without case- or group-work services and ready to make referral services
only.[25] Within private social work proper social values applied in com-
bating the problems of the broken family can be stated as opposition to
martryrdom, egotism, and immobilization. On the positive side social
work stands for a widening of perception on the part of the persons com-
posing the broken family in regard to the various facets of the problems
produced by their family situation for themselves and others, for a concern with giving in human relationships as well as with receiving, for
interdependence in place of dependency, and for planning long-term
solutions rather than living from day to day.[26]

Concretely, this would cover the following norms regarding possible
solutions. Plans should encompass the single parent as well as the
children, the parents of the single parent, friends, and prospects of remarriage. For an adult interdependence with persons on his own generational level is better than either interdependence with individuals of
his predecessor generation or with his children. Only on his own level
can ego functioning be preserved or strengthened. Living arrangements
which confine the single parent to contacts with children are id-stimulat-
ing, contacts with aging parents either that or superego-stimulating;

24 *See* Helen Harris Perlman, this volume, pp. 270–320.

25 Neota Larson, "OASI and the Social Services," *Social Work*, Vol. 3, No. 1
(January 1958), pp. 12–17; Ann W. Shyne and Kathryn Rummel, "A Special
Referral Service for OASI Clientele," *Social Casework*, Vol. 42, No. 3 (March 1961),
pp. 111–117.

26 "The Content of Family Social Work," an FSAA Committee Report, *Social
Casework*, Vol. 37, No. 7 (July 1956), pp. 319–326; Gertrude K. Pollak, "Principles
of Positive Parent-Child Relationships in Family Life Education," *Social Casework*,
Vol. 37, No. 3 (March 1956), pp. 131–138; Otto Pollak, "Design of a Model of
Healthy Family Relationships as a Basis for Evaluative Research," *Social Service
Review*, Vol. 31, No. 4 (December 1957), pp. 369–376.

regression in either case is the result. Household arrangements which include grandparents, the single parent, and the children are likely to lead to confusion of authority and may burden the grandparents with responsibilities they feel too old to carry. Role confusions or role inadequacies resulting in "acting out" are likely to occur. At the same time social work recognizes that reality limitations of an economic nature or psychological need may make such arrangements preferable to attempts to maintain a household composed only of a single parent and children. This, however, would be in the nature of a lesser evil rather than a solution of choice.

The need for adult contact would have to find satisfaction also on the social level. Social work values would be directed against self-confinement of the single parent to contact with other single parents. Although there is comfort in the association of people with similar problems, opportunities for catharsis, and a more understanding reception of complaints, misery is not the best company for misery. Here, again, interdependence would be preferable and would make life richer than if it were restricted to peer relationships in the narrowest sense.

With a view toward meeting a prospect for remarriage, social participation would be encouraged by social work values and two major questions would be raised: (1) what would have to be done in terms of self-scrutiny and scrutiny of prospects in order to avoid repetition of marital failure and (2) how would remarriage have to be viewed in the light of opposition on the part of the children.

Social Work Values That Contribute to Continuation of the Problem

As far as the information of the writer goes, there does not exist any social work value that specifically contributes to the existence of the problem of the broken family. By and large, however, social values that oppose an increase in the profession's coping capacity with these problems interfere also with an increase in its coping capacity with other problems within the sphere of its mandate. Among them the following deserve attention. First of all, in casework the emphasis on tertiary prevention,[27] second, a reluctance to take the initiative in offering services,[28] and, third, the frequent noninvolvement of social work in the formation of public

---

[27] *Concepts of Prevention and Control: Their Use in the Social Work Curriculum* (New York: Council of Social Work Education, 1961), p. 4; Lydia Rapaport, "The Concept of Prevention in Social Work," *Social Work*, Vol. 6, No. 1 (January 1961), p. 10.

[28] Alice Overton, "Serving Families Who 'Don't Want Help,'" *Social Casework*, Vol. 34, No. 7 (July 1953), p. 304.

social policy.[29] To these, which have been adequately and challengingly discussed in the literature, the writer would like to add the impact of the bureaucratic organization of social work, which, in ways resembling large business organizations, counteracts rather than encourages creativity, and the failure to use practice observations for posing challenging research questions. One might wonder, for instance, why social workers who incessantly encounter immaturity in personality development as a reason for marital difficulties have not asked for research relating length of engagement to degree of marital difficulties. In this connection it might be useful to ask why caseworkers, although intensely concerned with the etiology of marital conflict, have not used this information for the stimulation of preventive policy rather than confining it more or less to the diagnostic process. Specifically related to the problem of the broken family, it is not so much a single social work value as a hierarchy of values that seems to contribute to the maintenance of discomfort in family living, namely, the assignment of a greater value to personality change than to interactional improvement. Interactional improvement is considered a limited goal, and it is also considered frequently as a sign of professional maturity qua modesty to focus goal setting on interaction rather than on personality.

Actually, interactional change cannot be produced without personality change. What is meant, however, is that improvement in the executive functions of the ego is a lesser achievement than a beneficial change in superego formation or in the defensive functions of the ego. Once this value hierarchy is accepted, interpersonal peace will be a lesser social work achievement than intrapersonal peace. In such a system attention to discomfort resulting from the vagaries of intrapersonal development will take precedence over the hardships arising from a gap in the human resource structure of the family. Having subscribed to this value position, there will also be a temptation to make up for the gap by personality changes in the residual family personnel rather than by drawing on other potential human resources. Social workers would rather be therapists than matchmakers. Only in child placement and in the assignment of volunteers do social workers see themselves as instrumental in bringing about proper combinations of personalities. In the much more decisive function of premarital counseling they have left the field largely to marriage counselors not identified with the profession of social work. In view of the fact that there is tremendous social pressure on single parents to get remarried, the reluctance of social workers to engage their professional knowledge and skill in this area

---

[29] Sanford Solender, "Public Social Policy and Social Work Practice," *Social Work*, Vol. 3, No. 1 (January 1958), pp. 3–11; Charlotte Towle, "Social Work: Cause and Function, 1961," *Social Casework*, Vol. 42, No. 8 (October 1961), p. 394.

of human concern may be considered as contributing to the continued existence of the problems of the broken family.

CURRENT OPERATIONS AND THE IDEAL

Theoretically, the social needs created by the problem of the broken family are prevention, rehabilitation, and alleviation. These have to be seen not only in terms of the individual family members threatened or affected but also of their wider kinship and friends and finally, of those who support the community services on which the members of the broken family can draw. It is interesting to note that the needs of the broken family are hardly ever discussed in these terms by social workers who contribute to the professional literature. Here we stand under the impact of the democratic value system in social work which makes it difficult for social workers to set goals for, or even with, their clients. The only generally accepted exceptions in this respect are remedial changes in the perceptual or emotional makeup of the client personality and the situational corrections attempted by the Big Brother movement. The structure of services currently available reflects this lack of goal conceptualization to a considerable degree.

Prevention of broken marriages, in essence, would have to begin by intervention in the courtship stage. This, however, would involve a challenge of group norms and a tie-up between individual discomfort and the makeup of a specific social institution, which in the climate of intense concern with the psychological dimension is not yet an established pattern of social work responsibility.[30] As far as this writer can perceive from the literature, individual counseling in the family services emphasizes help in marital conflict over premarital counseling and leaves this to the marriage counseling movement which caters more to young persons of middle-class status than to any other population group. In family life education services are offered, which, on a group educational basis, attempt to alert young people to pitfalls in perception and interaction that might threaten an adequate outcome of mate selection.[31] Any attempt to influence legislation, however, with regard to making marriage more difficult does not seem to be traceable in either literature or professional discussion.[32] Still, in view of the decline in age at which people marry in the United States and the concomitant expectation of lack of maturity in the newlyweds, a waiting time between announcement of intent and getting married might be a worthwhile propo-

---

[30] Nathan E. Cohen, "A Changing Profession in a Changing World," *Social Work,* Vol. 1, No. 4 (October 1956), p. 14.

[31] Gertrude K. Pollak, "Family Life Education: Its Focus and Techniques," *Social Casework,* Vol. 34, No. 5 (May 1953), pp. 201–202.

[32] Morris Ploscowe, *Sex and the Law* (New York: Prentice-Hall, 1951), pp. 8, 274.

sition. Family casework undoubtedly would have a wealth of information pro and con to contribute to the discussion of such a change in public policy. The point made is only that no such approach seems ever to have been considered in casework circles. On the level of primary prevention even less is done by casework. Perhaps the greatest enhancement of general well-being in the family would result from a redefinition of masculinity and femininity commensurate with economic and social changes of our time. Social caseworkers encounter this problem in a vast number of cases, but diagnostic discussion in psychiatric consultations and supervisory conferences seems to bend the casework task to helping the client to "accept his own sex" in terms appropriate to conditions which started to become obsolete with the dawn of the industrial revolution.[33]

In the area of rehabilitation it is found similarly that current operations have not fully met the social needs presented by the broken family. The concept of rehabilitation denotes restoration. What needs to be restored in the broken family is the fullness of membership on the parental level. Social pressures on divorcees to remarry clearly reflect public awareness of this need.[34] It is a highly probable assumption that no treatment goal in the case of a broken family has been recorded in any family welfare agency as "remarriage." Equally unconsidered as a challenge to casework effort, except in family life education programs, is premarital counseling for remarriage.

As far as the needs of growing boys for close contact with adult males are concerned, an attempt at rehabilitation is produced by the Big Brother movement, but here again dynamic knowledge has not been utilized fully. Victorian apprehensions apparently have been instrumental in the lack of any consideration of the needs of growing girls who are deprived of the presence of their fathers in that respect. If any emotional protection of a fatherless girl against her indiscriminate reaching out toward male contact is to be provided, a responsible adult male volunteer under professional social work supervision is certainly an instrumentality worthy of consideration.[35] The closest we have come to this solution are big brother-big sister couples, but they may stimulate com-

[33] Otto Pollak, "Interrelationships between Economic Institutions and the Family," *Social Security Bulletin,* Vol. 23, No. 10 (October 1960), pp. 11–12; P. G. Herbst, "Task Differentiation of the Husband and Wife in Family Activities," in Norman W. Bell and Ezra F. Vogel, eds., *The Family* (Glencoe, Ill.: The Free Press, 1960), pp. 339–346; Reuben Hill, "The American Family: Problem or Solution?" *American Journal of Sociology,* Vol. 53, No. 2, (September 1947), p. 130.

[34] William Goode, "Pressures to Remarry: Institutionalized Patterns Affecting the Divorced," in Bell and Vogel, *op. cit.,* pp. 316–326.

[35] Ephraim H. Royle, "The Role of a Social Worker in a Big Brother Agency," *Social Casework,* Vol. 51, No. 3 (March 1960), pp. 139–144.

petitive feelings in a single parent and may be contraindicated on that score.[36]

In the realm of alleviation family casework, at least in principle, seems to do all that is required for members of the broken family. However, in the divorce cases this disregards the father who has left the home and in desertion cases in many instances the deserting spouse.[37] Visiting rights retain the divorced husband in a web of interaction with members of the broken family. Feelings of antagonism to the former spouse, competitiveness with him, or at least an attempt to make up to the children for what they have lost by the breakup of the marriage, may produce damaging results in the children, the single parent, and the spouse who has left the home. Unfortunately, social science has failed to conceptualize the human group composed of the spouse who has left home and the members of the broken family, but it still does present social needs of its own and offers a field for casework services that should not be overlooked. The tendency to make the father the forgotten man crops up in many unexpected places, and this seems to be another example in which a widening of therapeutic perception is clearly indicated.

In summary, problem solution is always problem creation, and the tendency of social work to consider the reopening of a case as a failure of former efforts to help operates also in the area of the broken family. Divorce as well as remarriage presents problems and so do desertion and return. In the last analysis an overriding casework goal must always be the creation and maintenance of coping capacity with problems as they arise. In that sense no improvement in a family situation can be considered final, and the social work task can never be considered as definitely solved.

In the realm of social security an essentially similar situation is found, with a deficit in services only more pronounced than in the private welfare field. In times of ever increasing coverage of people entitled to OASI benefits, widows are likely to make at the social security office their first contact with a resource organization in which secondary prevention could be started. This opportunity, however, is missed on jurisdictional grounds. Only referral services are rendered to individuals who indicate a need for special help, and when community resources are not available referral services are pointless.[38] Even when special opportunities are made available, as in the experimental project undertaken by the Community Service Society of New York in the spring

[36] Bernice Wolf Frechtman, "The Utilization of Volunteers in Sociodynamic Psychotherapy," in Otto Pollak and collaborators, *Social Science and Psychotherapy for Children* (New York: Russell Sage Foundation, 1952), pp. 170–199.

[37] Steigman, *op. cit.*, pp. 168, 170.

[38] Larson, *op. cit.*, pp. 13–15.

of 1958, the practice of referral seems to fall greatly behind any reasonable expectation of need. During the three-month period of the project only 82 referrals were made from an OASI office which handled more than 500 inquiries daily.[39] Obviously this is a problem of communication and education to be solved by OASI and private welfare personnel, which represents perhaps the most significant challenge to the contribution potential of social work in regard to broken families in which the father has died.

Priorities

In order to bridge the gap between the current operations and the ideal, it would seem that social workers in both public and private welfare have three distinct but related tasks. Of first priority undoubtedly is case finding with a particular emphasis on secondary prevention. This implies provision of contacts between social workers and members of broken families at a point where they are likely to suffer from stress, having exhausted their capacity to manage without help. Social security application interviews, the pronouncement of court decisions regarding visiting rights, and the appearance of difficulties in school performance come quickly to mind in this respect. Establishment of liaison between social work and OASI personnel, judges, and teachers is obviously necessary with a view to lightening the burden of these other professions as well as to helping the members of the broken family.

A second priority is the provision of information about the availability of such services in the community. An examination of agency releases about the nature of the services offered is likely to reveal that in many instances no special mention is made of the needs of broken families or of the availability of professional help for premarital counseling. Contact with single-parent organizations would have to be sought and cultivated.

Next in importance is a fresh approach to the problem of volunteers. Case finding and the establishment of new services break down all too frequently when the problems of staffing are encountered. If social work services are ever to approximate the ideal of coverage, a much stronger participation of lay personnel as volunteers under social work supervision will have to be promoted. Here imagination and willingness to abandon the grooves of current service tradition will be necessary to provide a start. In this respect the experience of group work may be useful in an expansion of family life education and the experience of the Big Brother movement in the posting of volunteers as contact persons in OASI offices and court.

---

[39] Shyne and Rummel, *op. cit.*, p. 113.

Finally, social work will have to make available its experience in the etiology and treatment of problems of the broken family to the wider community with a view toward influencing public opinion and, ultimately, legislation. In this respect anxiety about negative reaction on the part of donors and legislators will undoubtedly be encountered. This, however, is largely based on a misconception of public morality. Ours is a society characterized by tremendous readiness to acknowledge guilt for the existence of undesirable conditions and to believe in the remedial power of services. To involve social workers in attempts to stimulate these pre-existing inclinations in the wider community might well be conceived as a demand on professional ethics.

Racial Discrimination ▶

WHITNEY M. YOUNG, JR.

The most crucial social problem facing the nation today is the problem of the Negro in America. And this does not mean "the Negro problem" per se. All of the social problems delineated for study in this NASW project are brought into sharp focus and assume even greater dimensions when they are considered in light of America's most disadvantaged citizen—the Negro.

The problems of crime and delinquency, poverty, dependency, the deterioration of the inner city, the broken family, and unmarried mothers —all of these and others are faced by whites and Negroes alike. But the Negro is in the more exposed position and suffers disproportionately because, in addition to his deprivation, he encounters racial discrimination.

The problem of racial discrimination in America is so complex and cuts across so many areas that it warrants separate treatment in this project.

The Negro in America, in fact, has become the barometer that will predict whether this nation can guarantee the democratic heritage and the good life for the masses of its citizens. The degree to which this dilemma is resolved for the Negro will point the way toward resolving it for all our citizens.

Social welfare in a democracy moves forward on the assumption that the individual is the source of all social value. It exists to serve the needs of the individual, and social institutions must be prepared to change to meet changing needs. Therefore an examination of the challenge to and responsibility of social work in the present racial crisis is relevant to a discussion of its contribution to the solution of social problems.

Definition of the Problem

This treatment of the subject of racial discrimination is approached from the point of view that it is a "social problem" as defined in this project: that racial discrimination is a complex of behavior and circumstances which by its consequences not only threatens but adversely affects those institutions, mores, standards, and beliefs that are the values of our society and which the society holds to be essential to its well-being. Understood in this light, racial discrimination is a threat to democracy. Those who practice it destroy the concept of our democratic heritage and the guarantees of the Constitution and the Bill of Rights; those who suffer from it are denied these guarantees.

The words "racial discrimination" open up a Pandora's box, and out of this box come social and economic forces that have brought our nation today to a critical point in its history. The treatment in this paper, however, is limited to those areas that are most directly concerned with social work and social welfare.

It is necessary at the outset to explain some terminology. When the word "discrimination" is used today, it immediately conjures in the mind a minority group—a group whose homogeneity is based on race, color, creed, or national origin. America's minorities are varied groups, differing from region to region and city to city. They may be Negroes, Jews, Catholics, American Indians, Mexicans, Puerto Ricans, Italians, or Orientals. But the Negro is the nation's largest and, next to the American Indian, its oldest minority group, if the distinction is one based on "race" or color. In this discussion we shall therefore consider racial discrimination in terms of discrimination against the Negro.

When we speak of "race" what do we mean? Scientific classification gives us three major groups—"races" or "stocks" of mankind: *Negroid,* or black; *Mongoloid,* or yellow, and *Caucasoid,* or white.

For general understanding a race may be defined as a group of people who have in common certain physical traits that are inherited. These traits set them apart from other groups who have different combinations of physical traits.

Is the Negro in America a "race"? This question, and the subject of race mixture in the United States, is discussed at length in all of the major treatises and studies dealing with Negroes in American society. American Negroes constitute a highly diverse group, and in view of their greatly mixed quality it is obvious that they are not a race in the biological sense of sharing distinctive common hereditary and physical characteristics. Yet a person of Negroid ancestry, no matter how remote the Negro strain and no matter how little his appearance resembles that of a Negro, is considered a Negro in the United States. The Negro in America, as defined by Maurice R. Davie, "is a race in the sociological sense, that is, a self-conscious group of people who regard themselves as a race and are so regarded by others, whether or not they

actually are a race in the biological sense. Whereas physical or biological characteristics are inborn, sociological race characteristics are
acquired." [1]

The companion of "racial discrimination," although not synonymous
to it, is "racial segregation." Louis Wirth defines segregation as "that
form of isolation in which social distance is based upon physical separation." The Negro in America is segregated—set apart from the
dominant white group. Segregation may be based on custom and
tradition or it may be forced through legal sanctions. In either case
it implies superiority and inferiority, with the segregated group bearing the stigma of inferiority and social ostracism.

What is race prejudice? Among the many descriptions of prejudice
we find those that define it simply as prejudgment or bias for or
against. More complex descriptions involve psychological explanations and theories. In its broadest meaning, prejudice as applied to
individuals is an opinion or feeling, usually unfavorable, conceived
independently of experience or reason.

> Although racial differences are inborn, race prejudice is acquired.
> It is a socially conditioned way of reacting, not an instinctive or
> natural antipathy. It does not manifest itself in infancy but appears
> only after it has been inculcated by adult instruction; it varies in
> intensity in individuals and is modifiable by time, place and cir-
> cumstances. . . . Various factors underlie race prejudice, for example,
> the repulsion of the unlike; economic competition; urges and fears
> for social status; feelings of inferiority, insecurity, and inadequacy
> that may be satisfied by conceit about one's race and group; or hos-
> tility and aggression deflected from its true object, where it is not
> permissible to express it, toward a defenseless scapegoat.[2]

Current discussion of racial discrimination must also consider other
terminology: "civil rights" and "social privilege." The Committee
on Law Reform of the New York Chamber of Commerce in a recent
report points out:

> When this report refers to "social privilege" it uses this phrase in
> contradistinction to civil rights and civil liberties. Civil rights and
> liberties are those rights and liberties guaranteed by the Constitution;
> "social privileges" are privileges which, whether or not protected by
> state or local law, are generally granted to white citizens but not
> always to Negroes and which must be granted to Negroes if they are
> to obtain equal opportunity and mobility on all levels of public life.

---

[1] Maurice R. Davie, *Negroes in American Society* (New York: McGraw-Hill Book
Co., 1949).

[2] Arnold Rose and Caroline Rose, *America Divided: Minority Group Relations
in the United States* (New York: Alfred A. Knopf, 1948).

The words "social" and "society" are used in this report in their broad contemporary sociological sense to refer to the whole complex of relations of man to his fellows.[3]

Oscar Handlin, in a review of the 1963 edition of Gunnar Myrdal's classic study, *An American Dilemma*, provides a succinct transition from this background understanding of terminology to a serious consideration of the social and cultural forces that have placed the Negro in an inferior position in American society. Handlin, in discussing conditions at the time of the Myrdal study, comments:

. . . Myrdal entered upon the active task of writing while the country was engaged in a bitter war against totalitarianism which forced many people to consider seriously the differences between the democratic and fascist ways of life . . . the New Deal had raised to the peak of their influence the progressive aspirations that had swayed Americans since the beginning of the twentieth century. In particular, concern with the welfare of the common man had focused critical attention on the racist ideas of the past. Scientific evidence and social experience had exposed the falsity of the assumption that innate, fixed, biological attributes divided men permanently into superior and inferior races. The significant human differences were now regarded as products of social and cultural forces, susceptible to modification by influences which emanated from the environment.

The Negroes occupied an inferior place in American society because of no inherent inadequacy of their own but because of imperfections in the system about them. Intelligence applied to human affairs could remedy those imperfections, and, in time, improve the status of the colored people, as of other underpriviledged persons.

These assumptions established the basic premises of *An American Dilemma*. The Negro problem was social rather than racial. Slavery had cast the Negro in an inferior role in the productive system; and abolition after the Civil War had helped him but slightly because the forms of Southern agriculture perpetuated his inequality. Complex social discriminations kept him subordinate and closed off access to opportunities open to others. Poverty condemned him to inferior housing, health and schooling; the lack of education confined him to the least desirable jobs; and low status deprived him of political and legal equality. His general degradation, in turn, confirmed his poverty and separated his experience from that of whites who gained in self-esteem, if in no other way, through his debasement.

The Negro problem was thus the product of a vicious cycle. One form of deprivation reinforced another in a chain of effect, the cumulative result of which was to keep the blacks separate and inferior.[4]

---

[3] Committee on Law Reform, New York State Chamber of Commerce, *Racial Tensions in New York State*, 1963, p. 40.

[4] Oscar Handlin, *"The Book That Changed American Life,"* *New York Times Book Review*, April 21, 1963.

It is not possible here to consider at length all of the social phenomena that impinge on the subject. But it is important to select the facts and information that will give us some insight into the problem and to analyze and discuss their effects. This should help to chart some directions and to raise our sights from amelioration of problems to their prevention.

THE FACTS . . . JUST AS THEY ARE

. . . The Negro baby born in America today—regardless of the section or state in which he is born—has about one-half as much chance of completing high school as a white baby born in the same place on the same day; one-third as much chance of completing college; one-third as much chance of becoming a professional man; twice as much chance of becoming unemployed; about one-seventh as much chance of earning $10,000 a year; a life expectancy which is seven years less; and the prospects of earning only half as much.

—JOHN F. KENNEDY

The facts necessary to an understanding of the Negro's position in the American economy are grouped in the following areas: Population Growth and Migration, Education and Training, Employment and Income, Housing, Health and Welfare Services. No attempt has been made to give extensive information, but the data presented point up the gaps between those who "have" and those who "have not."

Population Growth and Migration

The first of the major waves of migration of Negroes out of the South began about 1910. It was a tremendous influx into Northern cities—an unpredicted, leaderless movement, the results of which are evident today.

By 1930 the Negro population of the United States was close to eleven million, or 9.7 percent of the total. In 1950 that population had risen to fifteen million and constituted 10 percent of the total.

> During the past decade the Negro population increased at a faster rate than the white population. By 1960, the Negro population had grown to 18,870,000,[5] a net increase of 25 percent over 1950. During this period the white population increased by only 18 percent.
> The greater rate for the Negro population is attributable primarily to higher Negro birth rates and partly to a lowering of Negro mortality rates.
> The 1960 Census marked the first decennial census when more than half of the nation's Negroes lived outside of the Southeastern States, compared with 56 percent in 1950 and 64 percent in 1940.
> It was also the first decennial census when the state with the largest

---

[5] It is now close to, if not slightly more than twenty million.

number of Negroes was located outside of the South. New York now has the largest Negro population among the states, with close to 1.5 million. Five other states with more than a million Negroes are Texas, Georgia, North Carolina, Louisiana, and Illinois.

New York state also registered the largest Negro population increase during the past decade, with an increase of 500,000. Five other states registered Negro population increases of between one-quarter and one-half million, California, Illinois, Florida, Michigan, and Ohio.

A major population trend during this century, particularly during the past few decades, has been the growth of large metropolitan centers, and the Negro population has been affected by this trend to a greater degree than the total population.

Twenty-one standard metropolitan areas in the U. S., each with a population exceeding one million, now include a third of the total U. S. population. The Negro population now comprises 12 percent of the total population in these areas, compared with 10 percent ten years ago.

On the other hand, the growth of the Negro population in these 21 areas was concentrated in the central cities while many white families moved to the outlying areas or suburbs. The Negro population in the 21 central cities in the last decade increased by nearly 2 million, or 50 percent. At the same time, the white population in these cities actually declined by one million. Consequently, Negroes represented 19 percent of the central city population in 1960, compared with 13 percent ten years before.[6]

One of the factors seldom understood in the Negro's migration from the rural and urban South to the great cities of the North and West is what might be called "personality shock." The pattern of society in the rural areas and in the small towns of the South gave the Negro his "place," both socially and economically, and the system demanded that he stay in that place. His habits of personal and family life, his work patterns, his attitude toward education—all were conditioned by the requirements of that life. He brought that conditioning with him when he migrated to a new and different life in the big Northern city. The adjustment was a traumatic experience, and the problems attendant to it completely overwhelmed him.

C. Horace Hamilton notes in a recent study of the move of the southern Negro to the North:

> . . . except for the world-wide population explosion itself, the movement of Negroes from the southern part of the United States has without a doubt been the greatest and most significant sociological event in our country's recent history. Its repercussions will be felt for a

---

[6] *Economic and Social Status of the Negro in the United States* (New York: National Urban League, 1962).

long time, and the social problems—education, housing, health, inter-racial adjustment—will be most difficult to solve. The great danger is that adjustments needed will be too little and too late.[7]

Education and Training

The lower employment status of Negro workers is traceable in part to differences in educational attainment. These differences, in turn, are the result of deficiencies in the home and community environments and in the schools they attend. Negroes have far less opportunity to acquire a solid education than whites:

▪ Negro youngsters still receive three and one-half years less education than white youngsters. When one considers that their education is often received in inferior slum-type schools with inexperienced teachers, the real difference is probably more like five or six years.

▪ More Negro young people drop out of high school than white, and fewer high school graduates enter college.

▪ Among the country's adult population, twenty-five years and older, 6.2 percent whites and 22.1 percent nonwhites have completed less than 5 years of school.

▪ Nearly 75 percent of the white boys and girls have graduated from high school, but only about 40 percent of the nonwhites have earned diplomas. To put it another way, 25 percent of the whites and 60 per-cent of the nonwhites are school dropouts.

▪ One of every three Negro youths with only an eighth-grade education is unemployed compared with one of six for the high school graduate.

▪ Among nonwhite children aged fourteen to seventeen in the labor force in 1960, one fifth were unemployed, a rate two-thirds higher than for white boys and girls in this age group.

▪ In New York City two large building trades locals with a total mem-bership of about forty-five hundred had no Negro members in 1963.

▪ A survey conducted in 1963 of Federal construction projects in some fifty cities showed that on most of these projects there were no Negroes employed either as journeymen or apprentices in a majority of the skilled trades.

Employment and Income

The employment status of Negro workers has improved considerably during the last two decades, but there are still significant differentials be-tween white and Negro workers. The present employment position of Negroes can be described as follows:

---

[7] C. Horace Hamilton, *The Negro Leaves the South*, 1963 Annual Meeting of the American Association for the Advancement of Science. (Mimeographed.)

1. Negroes are more likely to work in unskilled or semiskilled jobs.
2. When at work, Negroes are employed fewer hours per week.
3. Negro unemployment rates are twice as high as those of whites.

The following facts illustrate these points:

■ More than 75 percent of all Negro workers are found in the three lowest occupational categories—service workers, semiskilled, and unskilled laborers and farm workers, whereas less than 39 percent of all white workers are in these categories.

■ Negro workers make up 11 percent of the civilian labor force, but 22 percent of the unemployed—or to give a more striking figure contrast —among adult men the unemployment rate for Negro workers is 2.5 times greater than that of white workers.

■ Negro married men have the highest rate of unemployment when they are between the ages of twenty and twenty-four—11.2 percent in 1962. In contrast, the unemployment rate for white male breadwinners in this age group was 4.8 percent.

■ Negro breadwinners constituted 9 percent of all family heads in 1960; they held more than one-fourth of all service and unskilled jobs and less than 4 percent of all white-collar jobs.

■ The average income of the Negro family today—$3,233—was little better than half the white family median of $5,835—approximately the same ratio that has prevailed throughout most of the last thirteen years: one half of the Negro families in the United States had $62 a week or less in money income, compared with $112 a week for white families.

■ Nonwhite families headed by persons with some college training had a median income of $5,654, or 77 percent as much as comparable white families.

■ The lifetime earnings of nonwhite elementary school graduates is about 64 percent of the white total.

■ Among college graduates nonwhites have only 47 percent of the white total of lifetime earnings.

■ The average nonwhite with four years of college can expect to earn less over a lifetime than the white who did not go beyond the eighth grade.

NOTE: In discussion of census and other data, much of the available information is classified only for white and nonwhite persons, with no further breakdown of the nonwhite group between Negroes and others. Negroes, however, constitute 92 percent of all nonwhite persons.

Housing

Housing is a major problem facing the Negro citizen. Much of the social disorganization of the family finds its genesis in inadequate housing.

Of many problems, perhaps none is so unjust or arouses so much deep, bitter frustration among Negroes as the search for decent housing.

■ As recently as 1960 one of six nonwhite dwelling units in the United States was dilapidated, compared with one of thirty-two white dwellings.
■ Twenty-nine percent of the nonwhite dwellings were deteriorating, compared with 12 percent of the white dwellings.
■ Nonwhite families receive less housing value for the same price than white families who have access to an open housing market. Even when the Negro can pay an economic rent, he has less chance than a white person of getting decent shelter.
■ In 1961 Negroes occupied 210,000 public housing units, or 47 percent of all public housing units in the United States.

Health and Welfare Services

Gains have been made in recent years in raising the health and welfare status of Negroes, yet the Negro family is still greatly disadvantaged. The breakdown in Negro family life is caused by lack of equal opportunity and by a gamut of destructive influences in urban society. There is so much basic information in this area that it cannot be covered here. Included under health and welfare services come participation in various social security programs (including old age, survivors, and disability insurance, unemployment insurance) public assistance, services to children, and maternal and child health. A few significant figures have been selected:

■ Average benefits to a Negro in old age, survivors, and disability insurance were about three-fourths that of a white beneficiary in 1960.
■ Negroes have less protection than whites under unemployment insurance because a greater proportion of Negroes are employed in occupation groups not covered by unemployment insurance laws.
■ In 1960, 480,000 aged nonwhite persons receiving old-age assistance represented 38 percent of the total nonwhite aged population, three times the recipient rate for white persons aged sixty-five and over.
■ In 1960 more than one of four nonwhite married women with preschool children were at work and not at home.
■ Day-care centers for preschool children are not sufficiently available in many communities.
■ In Chicago licensed facilities for day care for children are so inadequate that they nullify the policy that requires mothers to accept outside work.
■ The nonwhite ADC mother is likely to have more children at a younger age than the white ADC mother, which makes it difficult for the nonwhite mother to find and hold a job.

- There is a significant gap between the mortality rates for white and nonwhite infants, and the gap widened during the 1950's. In 1950 the nonwhite infant mortality rate was 44.5 per one thousand live births, or 66 percent above the white rate. By 1958 the nonwhite rate was 45.7 per one thousand live births, or 92 percent above the white rate.
- The gap between white and nonwhite maternal mortality rates is much wider than the infant mortality gap. In 1958 the nonwhite maternal rate was 10.2 per 10,000 live births, or nearly four times as high as the white rate.

Thus it can be seen that the dimensions of this problem are so great and the needs to be met so diverse that an attack on the influences contributing to this situation will be required if these conditions are to be corrected.

THE NEGRO REVOLUTION

... Those who deny freedom to others deserve it not for themselves, and, under a just God, cannot long retain it.

—Abraham Lincoln

The facts and conditions so far presented bring into sharp focus the wide economic, social, and educational gap that separates the majority of Negro citizens from other Americans. These conditions speak for themselves.

Racial discrimination and segregation, constantly fed by racial prejudice, form a vicious circle surrounding the masses of Negroes in America in all aspects of their living. It is difficult for the Negro to break out of the circle because his limited educational background keeps his job status low. His job status dictates an inadequate income or makes him vulnerable to unemployment. If he is jobless, he is likely to form the hard core of the unemployed and becomes a chronic dependent. His low income predetermines his housing, and he is driven into a crowded slum ghetto. His wife is forced to work and his family life becomes disorganized. The crowded slum ghetto breeds disease, delinquency, and crime. Lacking adequate health and social welfare services, he is overcome by feelings of social rejection. These feelings are transmitted to his children. With no motivation either at home or in the inferior slum schools they attend, the children invariably get caught up in the cycle: poorly schooled, unskilled, and destined to become unemployed, the second generation, inescapably bound to the same life, is labeled "second-class citizens."

These are the problems and grievances to which Negro citizens are addressing themselves in the confrontations with whites in cities and towns across the length and breadth of the land. The Negro citizen can no longer passively accept the reality of his situation. He is determined to change the status quo. He is seeking elementary and fundamental rights. The Negro citizen does not reject democracy. He wants "in." He seeks only to participate in democracy—to share its blessings and to assume the responsibilities that go with that sharing. He is fighting against forces that are undermining the nation and jeopardizing our entire social system.

The average white American does not yet understand this.

Demonstrations, boycotts, sit-ins, and picketing by Negroes have led to retaliation by whites in the form of mass arrests, jailings, beatings, and the use of fire hoses and police dogs. The summer of 1963 marked a significant turning point in the history of Negro-white relations.

The year 1963—the Centennial of the Emancipation Proclamation—ironically turned out to be what is now referred to and what social historians will doubtless describe as the year of "the Negro revolution." August 28, the day of the "March on Washington for Jobs and Freedom," may well become a day of national remembrance.

From this point on there is no turning back for the Negro.

The current demonstrations in the South are mild in comparison to those that are on the verge of taking place in the tinderbox of racial unrest in Northern cities. In these teeming ghettos hundreds of thousands of Negro citizens—struggling beneath the mounting burden of automation, overcrowding, and subtle discrimination—are reaching the breaking point. These unemployed, ill-housed, and disillusioned human beings are seething with the lava of deprivation and denial. Violence and bloodshed can erupt out of this at any moment unless swift and realistic effort is exerted to prevent it.

The "Negro revolution" will continue. This civil rights drive is grass-root and it is universal. In this social ferment Negro citizens of many economic levels—the impoverished, the poor, the middle-class, the educated, the uneducated—all have joined in mass protest against both the form and the substance of inequality.

The civil rights drive is led and directed by what has come to be known as "The Big Five." The Big Five are the five major civil rights organizations: The National Association for the Advancement of Colored People, the Southern Christian Leadership Conference, the Congress of Racial Equality, the Student Non-Violent Coordinating Committee, and the National Urban League. Both whites and Negroes alike consider these to be the "responsible" organizations and their leadership the "responsible Negro leadership" of the present period.

The National Association for the Advancement of Colored People—NAACP—led by Roy Wilkins, was founded in 1909. It is the largest of the civil rights organizations. The NAACP has fought and continues to fight in the courts the battle to win civil rights and respect for the Negro. Its greatest single achievement has been the legal fight against "separate but equal" schools, which culminated in the 1954 Supreme Court decision on school desegregation.

The Southern Christian Leadership Conference—SCLC—led by the Reverend Martin Luther King, Jr., its founder, is a proponent of nonviolent, passive resistance, the technique of Mahatma Ghandi. SCLC came into existence shortly after the successful Montgomery (Ala.) bus boycott directed by Reverend King.

The Congress of Racial Equality—CORE—headed by James Farmer, initiated sit-in demonstrations and Freedom Rides. CORE also seeks its goals through nonviolent demonstration.

The Student Nonviolent Coordinating Committee—SNCC—the youngest of the groups both in its history, founded in 1960, and in its youth leadership, was the outgrowth of a meeting of Southern Negro students in Raleigh (N.C.). James Foreman, its director, leads a campaign of voter registration drives and protests and demonstrations against all forms of segregation in the South.

The fifth organization, the National Urban League, described later in this paper, has shared identity with the other four organizations, although their methods differ from those of the Urban League.

The five civil rights organizations joined together in giving leadership to the 1963 March on Washington. It is this responsible leadership that helped to lend dignity to the August 28 demonstration; and it is this responsible leadership that caused the movement to acquire a vast number of allies among important and influential individuals, institutions, and groups, including thousands of white Americans.

The current social revolution is a challenge to all leadership—both Negro and white. For Negro leadership it has been, and will continue to be, a challenge to provide intelligent and unified direction to a spontaneous movement to gain the rights and respect long denied. For white leadership it represents a challenge to close the economic, social, and educational gap that separates the vast majority of Negro citizens from other Americans. It is a challenge also to white leadership to support the existing responsible Negro organizations and their leadership. Unless such support is given, the heroic activities and peaceful nonviolent demonstrations of the civil rights movement will give way to a fiercer struggle—with its power and direction largely in the hands of the irresponsible.

As President Lyndon B. Johnson pointed out in a Lincoln's Birthday speech in February 1964, discrimination will not be ended by constant promises to those discriminated against, but only by action, "by acts of private citizens, acts of corporations and unions, acts of churches and voluntary groups of all kinds, acts of state and Federal agencies, acts of the President and acts of Congress."

The National Urban League, believing that the nation's leadership must accept this kind of responsibility and that a massive assault on the problem would be required to reverse the widespread social deterioration among Negro families, has proposed a special-effort program of aid to Negro citizens.

During 1963 the Urban League shared identity with other responsible civil rights organizations who are struggling for equality. The League shares their aims but differs in their methods of achieving objectives. The Urban League conceives civil rights and Negro rights as part of human rights. Its method is long-range, and its programs can be conducted only by a professionally structured agency, devoting itself full time to the problem of equal opportunity for Negroes. Founded in 1910, the Urban League is a professional social agency—a community service agency that is nonprofit, nonpartisan, and interracial in its leadership and staff. There are sixty-five local Leagues in cities across the nation, member agencies of United Funds and Community Chests. The Urban League's goal is to eliminate racial segregation and discrimination in American life and to give guidance and help to Negroes so that they may share equally the responsibilities and rewards of citizenship. The Urban League also provides important machinery for effective communication between white and Negro citizens.

A "Domestic Marshall Plan"

The Urban League proposal, known as a "domestic Marshall Plan," was so named because of its similarity to the plan instituted by the United States in the war-torn countries of Europe in the late 1940's. The plan for Europe and the League's proposal are alike in that both are massive aid programs—programs to help those in need get some of the necessities of life and the motivation and assistance to become self-sustaining and to assume the normal responsibilities of citizenship.

The "domestic Marshall Plan" [8] is a ten-point program of special effort which involves the following:

1. Our basic definition of equal opportunity must be broadened and deepened to include recognition of the need for special effort to overcome serious disabilities resulting from historic handicaps.

2. Our society must recognize and put a higher value than it has

---

[8] *A Statement by the Board of Trustees Urging a Crash Program of Special Effort to Close the Gap Between the Conditions of Negro and White Citizens* (New York: National Urban League, June 9, 1963).

ever before placed on the human potential possessed by Negro citizens. And then it must move positively to develop that potential.

3. The best schools and the best teachers are needed to prepare Negro children and other educationally disadvantaged youth to the point at which they will have the desire for excellence in education and will be motivated to achieve and prepare to advance up the economic ladder with full realization of the rewards that will accrue in the process.

4. Token integration and pilot placement in business and industry, labor and government are not enough. A conscious planned effort must be made to place qualified Negroes in entrance jobs in all types of employment and in positions of responsibility, including those in lower and upper management.

5. Affirmative action must be taken to destroy the racial ghetto and open housing opportunities of all types on the basis of need and ability to buy or rent.

6. Public and private agencies in the health and welfare field must offer to the ghettoized segments of the population the best services, staffed by highly competent personnel who understand the reasons for unstable family patterns, the relation between low socioeconomic status and social problems, and what must be done to rehabilitate urban Negro families.

7. Qualified Negroes should be sought and named to all public and private boards and commissions, particularly those that shape policy in the areas of employment, housing, education, and health and welfare services, the areas in which the racial differential is greatest and the need for dramatic change is most urgent. To achieve this objective, strong leadership within the Negro community must be developed. It then will be ready to step into the vanguard of the teamwork effort demanded in resolving the smoldering problems involved in civil rights.

8. Negro citizens themselves, adults as well as young people, must maintain and even accelerate the sense of urgency that characterizes the drive for first-class citizenship. Every opportunity for the acquisition of education and technical skills must be utilized. Every means of strengthening the social and economic fabric of the Negro community must be employed.

9. It is vital that government, philanthropic foundations, and business and industry reassess the extent of their financial support to established organizations committed to obtaining equal opportunity for Negro citizens to share in the fundamental privileges and rights of American democracy. It is imperative that all of these major sources substantially increase their contributions to the preventive programs carried on by responsible Negro leadership organizations.

10. Constructive efforts on the part of Negro citizens must be exerted to carry their full share of the responsibilities for participation in a meaningful way in every phase of community life.

President Johnson, in discussing the unconditional war on poverty, indicated that it is designed to "break the vicious cycle of chronic poverty." The Urban League's "domestic Marshall Plan" is designed to accomplish the same ends. Better schools and better teachers, work-study programs to reduce school drop-outs, expansion of clinic and other health facilities, better housing for families, improvement of slum areas, counseling for troubled families, and employment for family heads—all of these and more—whether under the heading of a "domestic Marshall Plan" or a "war on poverty"—constitute the action on a broad scale that is needed to alleviate the condition of the nation's poor—Negro and white alike.

In a recent interview Michael Harrington, author of *The Other America,* pointed out that the Negro revolution has made an important contribution to the enlightenment of the American people about the serious social conditions in the nation: by drawing attention to the problems of the Negro it has stirred the American public to an awareness that "the poverty of the Negro is part of a widespread poverty that engulfs a large segment of the American people, white as well as Negro; that the whites are also slum dwellers; that joblessness, lack of educational facilities and the effects of automation on unskilled workers affects all elements of the population." [9]

CHALLENGE AND RESPONSIBILITY

He that ignores the lessons of history is doomed to repeat its mistakes.
—GEORGE SANTAYANA

Social work was born in an era of social protest and concern. By identifying themselves with the plight of the sweatshop workers, the children exploited in the cities, the socioeconomic health and educational deprivation of large masses of people, and by playing an active part in social reform, our pioneers in social work earned for themselves society's respect and gratitude. For those who followed in their steps they created a profession that could be entered and pursued with dignity and pride.

But somewhere along the way, between then and now, several things happened. Many people in social work misinterpreted useful psycho-analytical knowledge to make a god of adjustment—"adjust at any cost" became the goal, the major requirement of normalcy. Adjust to injustice, to rejection, to humiliation, to deprivation—but adjust! Somewhat later we in social work became sensitive about our status and

[9] New York: Macmillan Co., 1962.

our roles as "professionals," and this led to an almost fanatical pre-occupation with methodology and technique and a frantic avoidance of things controversial.

We could never project ourselves into aggressive leadership roles for fear of being called presumptuous self-seekers, simply acting out our latent hostilities. Interestingly enough, during this period the literature will show that we reached great oratorical heights in our speeches and papers about social action—when we were talking to one another. Even in the classrooms our students listened to and sometimes participated in spirited discussions of our "role."

Implementation, however, was another matter. For a long while we rationalized and deceived only ourselves by thinking and declaring: "After all, everybody knows where social workers stand and what we think!" Others argued that we could not afford to jeopardize our services to needy people by possibly alienating those who provide the bulk of the money for those services. Some just said flatly that injustice and social problems were only fringe and extracurricular concerns for social workers.

The time for change has overtaken us, and what is important now is the future of social work as a profession and social workers as professionals and human beings.

Elizabeth Wickenden points out that the difficulties in recruiting young people into social work lie in the fact that we have not succeeded in making a clear and valid case for the social role of social work. In speaking on this subject, she says:

> I am personally convinced that "creating a better society" is in fact the essential role of the social worker—whether his immediate task lies in public welfare, a hospital, a family agency, a neighborhood center, a court, or a training school, or any other setting. . . .
>
> The goals of social work are the goals of society itself, embracing at the very minimum the following concepts: personal freedom, personal responsibility, social democracy, social order, and social progress. It is the role of social workers to so bridge the gap between individuals—with their needs and capacities—and the social structure that these goals may be served, not singly or in isolation, but as a mutually sustaining whole. . . .[10]

Circumstance has now provided the social work profession with a magnificent opportunity to prove that its members are worthy carriers of a great heritage. As human beings, we are all mutually dependent. The Negro revolution will be immeasurably aided by the dramatic, aggressive intervention of social workers at all levels. If social work

[10] Elizabeth Wickenden, "Recruiting Young People," *Social Work Education* (October–November 1963).

remains unidentified or just on the fringes of this great social revolution, it will have lost a reason for being and will have missed its greatest opportunity to establish, for all the world to see, its basic belief in the dignity of all mankind and man's ultimate right to realize freely his greatest potential.

Consider the challenge that faces social work in eliminating racial discrimination and in contributing to the solution of social problems.

The challenge to social work and to social work practice is tripartite:

1. To the individual social worker.
2. To the institution or agency—its administrators and governing boards.
3. To the professional associations.

The Individual Social Worker Is Challenged

▪ To resist the temptation to plead for the elimination of racial segregation and discrimination solely on the grounds that it is expensive and provides Communism with the ammunition to win the two thirds of the world's population that happen to be both nonwhite and uncommitted.

Although both are valid arguments, the main concern and persuasion in regard to segregation and discrimination must be made in terms of its contradictions to the democratic promise and its effect on the human personality of both the segregated and the segregator.

▪ To adopt the improvement of intergroup relations as a primary element in achieving the true goals of social work.

In the world of today and even more so in the world of ten years hence, the choice of exclusiveness is foreclosed to all citizens. We are now citizens of the world. Science and technology have made of the world a neighborhood; we must make of it a brotherhood. We have not met the basic goal of social work, the enhancement of social functioning, if we make no efforts with our clients to modify their prejudices. This is a basic function in helping clients to adjust to modern society.

Just as we help clients to express, understand, and, hopefully, work through their hostilities around parents, siblings, spouses, employers, and others, we should also help them to do the same thing around their feelings about race, religion, or national groups. The same justification for assisting clients to a more productive life by enabling them to look more rationally at some of their myths and superstitions around medical care and child rearing would also apply to their stereotyped notions about various ethnic groups. This kind of counseling obviously implies that on his part the worker must develop sound attitudes as well as knowledge of the nature, cause, and results of prejudice.

Aside from this kind of help, given to members of the dominant group who use the services of social work agencies, we also have equal responsibility to assist minority individuals themselves. Since the Negro citizen is not innately superior to other human beings, it follows logically that generations of suppression, exploitation, segregation, and discrimination have left their mark. Individual behavior patterns often indicate hostility, suspicion, aggression, withdrawal, resignation, defeatism, and exaggerated deference. The challenge of practice is first, understand, then, by skillful service, seek to modify attitudes and to suggest appropriate resources that can further alleviate. This is not an easy job. It calls for the best in social workers, for unlike the past, when so many workers felt that their role was to help clients of minority groups to adjust to injustice and to accept a second-class status, this cannot be the case today.

There is no quicker way for social work to violate its basic function and to lose completely the respect of minority groups than to suggest that the future is fixed and they must continue to experience a bleakness of night and despair. Few, if any, members of minority groups now believe this. They know too well the forces of history, world conditions, and the struggle of America to retain the moral leadership of the world. They have observed out of the deep rumbling of discontent in Africa, out of the uprisings in Asia, and by their participation in the legal, nonviolent, but firm protest of the Negro in America that formerly suppressed people have thrown off their shackles and are beginning to walk the earth with dignity, with an opportunity to realize their fullest potential and to participate equally in the destiny of all mankind. The profession of social work is called on to be early allies in this movement toward a new world order. With our clients who are members of minority groups, we are urged to new heights in imagination and creativeness to help develop incentives, provide encouragement and motivation, and stimulate constructive activity for minority members and their families in the absence of still rather obscure rewards.

■ To view the panorama of Negro family life in its historically correct setting.

Many social workers decry the lack of stability and the presence of the matriarchal pattern in the Negro family without recognizing that this is the only ethnic group in world history in which conscious and deliberate effort has been made to weaken and destroy, if possible, this basic institution in our society. Negro families were not only separated forcibly when they were brought to this country but continually throughout slavery as they were sold on the trading blocks. Promiscuous breeding was encouraged as an economic measure. Even after slavery the Negro male was consciously kept at a low-paying level and humiliated daily to prevent him from getting out of place and attempting to effect change. The composition of the Negro family continued to be such that the father, if identified, had no established role, and the Negro male, his manhood weakened, suffered both economically and psychologically.

■ To be motivated by personal concern about the welfare of other human beings and as individuals to identify actively in community programs to improve the employment, housing, and education of Negro citizens.

Ability to identify with the oppressed and to take a stand courageously alongside those who say the time has come to right a wrong will be a measure of the kind of human beings we really are.

Institutions and Agencies, Their Administrators and Governing Boards Are Challenged

■ To reflect the basic concepts in social work in services as well as in administration.

The agency that discriminates on a racial basis in its admission policies is no longer a legitimate social work agency, nor is it staffed by legitimate social workers. In the South such practices are sometimes forced by law, though more often the root cause is tradition perpetuated by apathetic boards and timid professionals.

■ To extend and expand agency services to meet the crucial health and social welfare needs of the urban Negro masses.

This requires a review of program and services to gear them to meet the special needs of urban Negroes. Many of the agencies in the helping professions have done as much to perpetuate segregation and feelings of rejection and indifference as any institution, and more than most, because they have contentedly followed the pattern even though they knew better. Many agencies adopted a posture of "here we are, we can help you only if you ask for our services." There was no reaching out, no recognition by many of these agencies that Negroes would not automatically come to them. Negroes were not aware of their services. Furthermore, seeing nothing but white faces, Negroes were not sure that they would be welcome. To many with southern backgrounds, all institutions are viewed as "white" and therefore not for their use.

■ To include minority-group representation at the policy-making level.

This demands a review of structure to insure that Negro leadership be brought in on this level. The requirement of many national agencies that each local board be representative of its total community has not been taken as seriously as the situation warrants. Lack of such representation perpetuates not only the great social distance between policy maker and client group but also continues the practice that Negroes deeply resent, of doing *for* rather than *with* the Negro citizen.

Some agencies complain that they cannot get reliable contributing Negro board members or a substantial Negro clientele. This reflects limited contact with and knowledge of the Negro community.

A special conscious effort must be made to recruit board members who are truly representative in that they have the respect of the Negro community.

- To make a conscious effort through tangible visible employment practices to demonstrate democratic beliefs.

A major determinant of agency practice is the selection and utilization of staff. Although qualifications, demonstrated competence, and merit should always be the major criteria in selection and promotion of staff, it is still possible within this framework for all agencies to have interracial personnel. This should not be left to chance. Experience has shown us that, unfortunate as it may be with untrained workers and tragic as it is with graduates of social work schools, we cannot assume in either case an absence of racial prejudice, the conviction of the ability to encourage good intergroup relations. Neither can we automatically assume that staff members from minority groups have themselves sufficiently mastered their minority status to operate effectively in this area.

This not only suggests, but makes mandatory, firm administrative conviction and decisions as they relate to selection, orientation, in-service training, and continuing supervisory functions. Hopefully, we have as a profession outgrown the old notion that minorities necessarily work better with minorities or that dominant groups in the society will not accept workers from minority groups. Perhaps it is unjustified optimism, but the writer would like to feel that the large majority of agencies now take the position that the skill and competence of the worker in this regard is far more pertinent than his color. Any agency whose existence, or utilization of its services, is dependent on satisfying the prejudices of its clientele is not too desperately needed in our communities. The exception to the principle expressed in this challenge would be those groups having problems of language or extreme cultural or religious differences.

- To work with organizations committed to securing equal opportunity for all citizens to help in strengthening Negro family life.

The Urban League stands ready to move forward in broadening and widening areas of cooperative effort with agencies in the health and welfare field and to assist in any special effort they may direct toward "closing the gap" for disadvantaged Negro families.

Directives toward this end were encompassed in resolutions coming out of the Delegate Assembly at the 1963 National Conference of the Urban League, relating to family life, education, the aging, adoptions, recreation and leisure time, family services, and health needs and resources.

The Professional Associations Are Challenged

■ To build effective ways for calling what is known of the conditions under which men live to the attention of politicians.

> The most important mission ahead for social work is the application of its professional knowledge to the processes of social change needed to bring lives of freedom and decency within the reach of all our citizens. In the future, the key decisions with respect to the economic and social life of our communities will be made in the public, not the private, sector of the economy. . . . Direct and indirect methods of political action must be sought out and developed with the same energy and devotion that we have given to the shaping of techniques and methods of practice during the past four decades. Only in this way can our profession have a significant impact on community life. If we ignore politics, it will continue to ignore us, and the chances are that our profession will thus lose its great potential as an instrument of a democratic society.[11]

As one expert on the problems of poverty noted recently, "A great national upsurge of public opinion might be necessary to ensure a national effort to obliterate poverty from the American scene." This indeed is a challenge for the professional associations.

■ To translate into action pronouncements, resolutions, and policy statements adopted by delegate bodies.

Many professional associations in the field of social work have passed resolutions, made pronouncements, and enunciated policy at meetings, conferences, and conventions in support of the principle that a democratic society exists for the benefit of its individual members. They have gone on record to support belief in the dignity and worth of every human being and in expressing conviction that a democracy cannot tolerate discrimination directed at any part of its population or arbitrary barriers that isolate groups of individuals from each other.

[11] Alan D. Wade, "Social Work and Political Action," *Social Work*, Vol. 8, No. 4 (October 1963), p. 10.

But in many instances, far too many, these policy statements and resolutions are merely paper documents that have no meaning. It is incumbent on the professional associations—their individual members as a collective group—to seek honestly to make these words come alive through activities of chapters and member associations that will (1) awaken social agencies in the community to the needs of the disadvantaged population in ghettos and encourage them to examine their policies and procedures that are directly or indirectly related to the quantity and quality of service in ghetto communities; (2) support the right of social workers to engage in civil rights activities and to come to the aid of any of its members whose right to participate in nonviolent demonstrations is infringed on by agency boards or executives.

It must be noted here that several professional associations have adopted resolutions and policy statements on the matter of equal opportunity and in support of democratic principles and ideals. Without show of any conscious partiality, and recognizing that many others exist, three are mentioned here: *Policy Statement on Civil Rights* by the Eastern Massachusetts Chapter, NASW; *Resolution on Equal Treatment and Opportunity for All People* by the American Public Welfare Association; *Policy Statement on Equal Opportunity* by the Family Welfare Association of America.

It is the writer's hope that this presentation will encourage social workers everywhere to rethink their own roles as professional workers toward the end that, in the words of Werner Lutz (p. 140), "social work will assume once again the original and traditional responsibility accorded it by society . . . to try to achieve the solution of social problems by removing or altering their causes."

A Social Work Approach ▶

NATHAN E. COHEN

Social work for a period of time dealt primarily with problems of the individual along clinical lines. In dealing with these problems it had attempted also to understand the impact of the social institutions through which the individual functions (family, peer groups, school, church, and the like) on the individual case. In essence, however, it had focused on the individual as the entrepreneur and tried to understand his intrapsychic mechanisms and his relationships with his surrounding environment. This emphasis on the dynamic psychology of the individual has provided much knowledge in the area of interpersonal relations.

In the last several decades social work has begun to feel the impact of the efforts to look at the individual through the telescopic lens of the environment rather than merely to look at the environment through the telescopic lens of the individual. From Marxism and other sociological and anthropological sources we have learned that

> economic forces exert a profound influence on all aspects of human behavior and social organization, that the course of history is shaped powerfully by the way men organize themselves for production, that neither men nor ideas can be studied as abstractions apart from the social environment, and that classes constitute one of the most persistent and influential phenomena of society.[1]

This emphasis led to a study of social conditions as determinants of behavior. As Northwood states:

The reader will note that in some instances the references cited here to articles in this volume cannot be found in the printed version. They were taken from earlier drafts of the papers which were used by the project participants and by the editor in preparing this chapter.

[1] Clinton Rossiter, "Why Marx Failed Here," *Saturday Evening Post* (August 20, 1960).

Social conditions usually refer to a steady state of organization of persons, things, events, and relationships existing in reality. Since these conditions are produced and modified by mankind, they are called *social conditions*. However, in large part, social conditions are independent of any single individual and his perceptions. They are the "given" in which life occurs. This concept of social conditions is akin to Durkheim's "social facts" and Ruth Benedict's "patterns of culture."

Man helps to create social conditions and is also affected by them. A study of man apart from his social conditions can result in an abstraction. On the other hand, a study of environment alone can also lead to a fragmented view of man's behavior. Bridging the two interrelated dimensions was dependent on the development of a dynamic conceptual structure in sociology and anthropology. This has arisen in the last several decades and is providing a better context within which to build a conceptual bridge. As stated by Gordon Allport:

> The individualistic era was principally a time when the methods and concepts of experimental psychology were in the ascendancy and when individual mental operations, interpreted with the aid of statistical method, were held to explain adequately all social behavior. Freudianism with its highly individualistic emphasis was easily assimilated into this line of thought. Two decades ago a reaction set in when both sociologists and anthropologists spoke up vigorously concerning the importance of status, role, caste, and pattern and of the significance of the situation, both immediate and remote, in determining present conduct.[2]

THE PROBLEM

Definition of the Social Problem

A knowledge of the individual and his environment, however, does not define a social problem. This is a relative term whose evaluation may vary with one's value system. Thus the same observable phenomena of social conditions may be viewed differently by those who feel the impact most directly, by those professions organized to deal with the impact of such social conditions on the individual, and by the "decision makers" who have the responsibility of determining the allocation of resources for dealing with the social conditions. Consequently a wide difference in theories to explain the causes and suggest possible solutions may result. Such theories may run the gamut from a concept of the problem as residing in the individual to an emphasis on the cause as re-

---

[2] Gordon W. Allport, "The Genius of Kurt Lewin," *Journal of Social Issues*, Supplementary Series No. 1 (December 1948), pp. 16–17.

siding in the society. Projected solutions therefore vary in terms of their focus on changing and reforming the individual, or the society, or on letting nature take its own course. Within the context of changing the individual or the society the method for achieving this goal may also vary.

The model that was developed and tested in this project places major emphasis on the crucial factor in defining a social problem, namely, the value system. It provides an opportunity to identify the perceptions of different groups in the society in the definition of the problem. It also provides for an examination of the etiology of the problem as inherent in the individual, in the social structure, in existing organizations designed to cope with the problem, and in transitory social phenomena. It takes into account the dual value systems and their implication for both definition and action.

The following distinction was made by the project participants between individual and social problems:

> The term "social problem" as used in this project is limited to those problems that are manifested by family, group, or individual behavior which require intervention by the organized community in order that the community may continue to function. It does not include problems manifested primarily by a state of being, thinking, or feeling.

It was recognized that the question whether specific types of problems are social problems is a complicated issue. For example, at the September 1962 meeting of the project participants in a discussion of marital incompatibility as a social problem, the following was stated:

> There is a conceptual problem in defining marital incompatibility. Is it a social problem or an individual problem experienced by many, yet not a priority social work concern on the basis of values, magnitude, and consequences? It is only in recent history and in a few Western cultures that marital incompatibility has been considered a problem. Our task is to look at the context within which it is defined as a problem.

One view expressed in the group was that any problem engendering unhappiness and capable of being helped by social work is a social problem. In this context marital incompatibility would be a social problem. However, the majority of the group firmly believed that although such a problem might be a social work concern, and defined as a social work problem, it would not necessarily be a social problem.

The several projects varied in the factors emphasized in defining a particular problem as social. For example, Pollak takes the position that broken families represent a social problem independent of their level of income because a constellation of special discomforts for family members and their associates is implied and the phenomenon occurs in every stratum of society. Perlman places emphasis on the inpact of the problem on the mores, standards, and beliefs of the society and on its general welfare. She states:

> A social problem is a complex of behavior and/or circumstances which by its consequences threatens or adversely affects the institutions, mores, standards, and beliefs that are valued—that is to say, emotionally invested—by most members of a society. The existence of the problem is usually recognized when it becomes a clear and present danger to the general welfare. Such danger may lie not simply in the problem itself but also in the problem-solving means which may be a threat to social stability.

Lourie, in analyzing poverty as a social problem, states that "relationships have been observed or assumed between poverty and high morbidity and mortality rates, poor housing, broken families, low education, and high incidence of crime." He further states that "poverty and its effects or constellation of related pathologies have an impact not only on the individuals and families but also on those with whom they come in contact and on society as a whole."

Meier raises the question, "Does the neglect of a child under any and all conditions constitute a 'social problem'?". . . If not, should "the profession limit its attentions to those matters identified as 'social problems' by the community?" She goes on to state:

> The idea of a social problem carries a certain quantitative implication. Only when a certain number of similar situations become troublesome to a community, or endanger the safety and well-being of others, is the phrase "social problem" likely to be applied. But, again, if social work's belief in the value of the individual is to be expressed, its attention cannot be restricted to problems that by their sheer weight of numbers constitute social problems.

Lutz, in discussing marital incompatibility, states:

> The general values of the community determine the structure and functions of marriage, and the particular forms of marital incompatibility most common in the United States are determined, in large measure, by the requirements set on marriage by the culture. . . . If widespread marital incompatibility occurs, then the community is, in some measure, ceasing to function adequately, and intervention by the organized community is necessary.

Northwood, in his paper on the inner city, follows the formulation of Arnold Rose and views a social problem as having three aspects: "(1) social conditions, (2) adjudged to be 'bad,' (3) which people feel can be improved or eliminated." For Northwood social conditions are produced and modified by mankind but, in large part, exist independently of any single individual and his perceptions.

Present in all these definitions in varying degree is the view that a social problem, to be understood in its full context, must be analyzed in terms of the social institutions and value systems within which people function as well as in terms of individual discomforts, frailities, or defects. The question when problems become social is a form of social problem in itself. Since a social problem is related to a value system and since values vary in a pluralistic society such as ours, there may be differences of opinion whether the well-being of a large segment of the society is being undermined or threatened by child neglect, marital incompatibility, broken families, unmarried mothers, or poverty. Problems dealing with the basic needs of food, clothing, and shelter tend to receive consideration if they reach a great magnitude. Problems dealing with self-actualization and self-realization, however, tend to find less community response. The economic consequences of a problem are frequently a key factor in determining the community's perception of responsibility.

Since in the final analysis an operating definition of a social problem involves acceptance of responsibility for the problem by some unit of society, either voluntary or public, those problems around which there is some degree of consensus among the people in need, the professional groups providing the service, and the decision makers in the community will have a greater chance of consideration.

Identification of the problem may be made by the professional group within the context of its goals and values. Acceptance of the problem as a social problem, however, may depend on the power and prestige of the group that accepts responsibility. If the consumer group—that is, the group that is the victim of the problem—is not prestigious or organized with political power, chances are that acceptance of social responsibility by the community may not be easy. Thus problems such as poverty, neglected children, unmarried mothers, marital incompatibility, and broken families may need the aggressive leadership of professional groups to plead their causes.

Etiology of the Problem

Prevention of a problem through rational planning is predicated on knowing the cause of the problem. As pointed out by Lourie, "If rehabilitative action is to be taken when a problem has occurred or to prevent one that may occur, it must be known precisely what is to be prevented." Since the model focuses on prevention, it may be helpful to see whether a fuller analysis of the various problems can lead to a clearer and more meaningful conception of cause.

In his analysis of poverty Lourie states:

> Operating factors are economic, social, and/or personal. Economic factors include economic recessions, technological changes in production processes, variations in increase of productivity within an occupation, market variations, irregular or seasonal demand for labor, and migration of industry from particular communities.
>
> Among social causes for low income are loss of earnings of the head of the family because of death, absence from the family group, or other responsibilities, discrimination in employment because of race, color, sex, religious belief, age, physical handicap, or record of mental illness or imprisonment, and geographic or occupational immobility.
>
> Personal factors contributing to restrictions on employability and earning power encompass physical and mental disabilities. . . .

Meier states:

> It is the business of social work, particularly in the practice of casework, to have the knowledge and skill to understand that there are many causes of inadequate care of children or of injurious behavior toward a child by his parents. These are but a few examples: indifference to a child's needs because the parents are overburdened and their energies are depleted, ignorance of the needs of children, ungovernable impulses symptomatic of the parents' mental illness, and brutality which expresses the neurotic consequences of the parents' own early deprivations.

Lutz divides the causes of marital incompatibility into the following interrelated categories: ". . . causes inherent in culture and social structure; causes inherent in individual personality; situational and transitory causes; and causes inherent in existing institutions designed to cope with the problem." He points out the interrelatedness of these causes:

> There is some overlapping in the assignment of causes to one category or another. Some of this overlapping occurs by design . . . a deliberate attempt is made to play back and forth between cultural values and their institutionalized expression as variables causing marital incompatibility. . . . Finally, it is a cardinal point of emphasis throughout the discussion that sociocultural variables and variables operating within individual personalities exert a continuous influence on one another. . . .

Perlman reviews the various views of unmarried motherhood and points out that "the explanations for illegitimate pregnancy in Negro girls and women are based largely on their 'culture.'" In the case of the white unmarried mother the basis of explanation tends to be psychoanalytic. She states that "just as the sociological stereotype of the illegitimately pregnant Negro woman deserves examination for its

validity and its implications for social work, so the psychoanalytic explanations that have become stereotyped call for critical analysis." In
brief, there are many unanswered questions that need to be examined.

In his discussion of the broken family Pollak points out that "the
breakage itself can be the result of death, divorce or separation, and
desertion." He deals primarily with the consequences of the broken
family, with the nature of the experiences that emerge. Quoting Kurt
Freudenthal, he points out that "these experiences can be categorized as
a sense of frustration, a sense of failure, a sense of guilt, and an occurrence of strong ambivalence between single parent and child. The sense
of frustration is traced to a sense of uncompleteness which is felt by
the remaining spouse as well as by the children."

It is quite evident from the project papers that it is difficult to identify specific causes of the social problems under discussion. For example, poverty can be viewed not only as a social problem but also as
one of the causes of some categories of marital incompatibility, as a
correlate of some categories of the neglected child, and as a consequence
of some of the same personal defects present in several other social
problems. Each problem seems to have many of the same factors, but
perhaps within a different profile. The sharpness of the profile, in
turn, seems to be dependent on some of the factors discussed previously
—values, the subjective or objective nature of the problem, the number
of individuals affected, the prestigiousness of those concerned about the
problem, and so on.

The overlapping of social problems and the multiple causation raises
some question whether the public health prototype of prevention can
be utilized. In public health prevention is not thought of as doing
away with disease in general but with specific diseases as the necessary
knowledge becomes available. In the arena of social problems, in
which the causes are multiple and overlapping, it may not be possible to
eliminate the causes of a particular social problem. This may explain
the more recent trend toward broader programs of social reform and
reconstruction that may provide a foundation for myriad social problems. In the case of specific problems the attainable goal may be better
control and management of the problem rather than prevention in the
cause-and-effect context.

Although at first the difficulty in isolating specific causes for specific
problems may seem negative, it may also represent a positive lead. Attention has been focused so long on individual problems and clusters
of problems reflecting the structural and service arrangements that have
grown up over the years that social workers have not attempted a concerned and coordinated problem-solving effort. Such an effort may call
for a different order of priorities and a different arrangement of co-

operative efforts with other groups than the present pattern. It may also indicate that if prevention is a goal consideration of the political climate and an attendant social philosophy cannot be avoided. Another gain may come from seeking an underlying cause within these overlapping profiles of social problems. One clue is the constant reference to the distortion of values.

VALUES

In discussing values there are two types of question to examine. The first is the diversity in systems of values that affect both perception of the problem and establishment of responsibility for meeting it. The second deals with distortion of values as a key cause of the social problem. Lutz, for example, states that since "many of the major causes of marital incompatibility reside in the basic value-orientations of the society, as expressed by large, complex social systems, proposals for dealing with them must include recommendations for action at the broadest level of social organizations." He goes on to state that "the most significant fact about the current value-orientation of social work, with respect to its potentiality for changing either of the pejorative value-orientations or their derivatives, is that it is itself a distortion of the humanistic value-orientation which it pretends to be."

Lourie states:

Interpretation of insufficiency and determination of a state of poverty must be based on distinctions between legitimate and excessive needs and desires and on appraisal of deviations from a prevailing level of economic well-being. These, in turn, depend on underlying values and norms regarding the purpose of human existence and the historic destiny of a society.

In regard to values, he points out:

The assumed values and norms of social work, like those of other social institutions, are rooted in those of the society of which it is an instrument. Frequently, however, varying emphasis on selected values and norms gives the impression of incongruence. At the present time, although the dominant societal norms and values allow for toleration (or non-recognition) of the phenomenon of poverty, social work stresses values directed toward its amelioration or eradication. Within the field and its organizational framework the difference is less clear-cut.

Pollak views such values as the strong emphasis on the pursuit of happiness and our regarding marriage primarily as a "happiness-increasing institution," along with the American characteristic of not believing in "the acceptance of discomfort" as contributing to the problem of the broken family through divorce. He states further that social values conducive to the continued existence of the problem can be traced. Pollak believes:

> Perhaps the most important constellation of social values which supports the continuation of the problems of the broken family is provided by those factors in our culture that are conducive to the development of character disorders. Permissiveness in child rearing, anxiety of parents about setting limits, relativity of moral codes in a heterogeneous population, fascination with change in values and pattern of behavior, as well as a long historical trend in weakening parental authority provide a fertile ground for the development of individuals who will enter marriage with the expectation of receiving without giving and with an attitude of resentment toward the challenge of misfortune rather than with an attitude of positive response. Such people are likely to become single parents and to smart under the burden of meeting the demands of single parenthood.

Perlman, discussing the value position of social work about illicit sex relations, states that only a rough guess could be ventured because social workers are likely to be relativists rather than absolutists and to say "it depends" on many factors.

> Social workers would probably be less likely than many other members of the general population of their class and level of education to call such behavior "immoral." This is because their theory system postulates that all behavior has the purpose of meeting internal needs and that in order to rechannel such needs they must be understood rather than condemned. . . . For the woman past "the age of consent" social workers would probably feel that what she did was "her own business" unless her actions affected the lives of others (her family, her children) in deleterious ways.
>
> Yet, because in their practical experience social workers have known chiefly the women and girls who have been "caught" and have been hurt by illicit sexual experience, they are alert to . . . possible unhappy consequences. Because of this there would probably be a consensus among social workers that illicit coition is risky and potentially hurtful, not only in terms of the possibility of unwanted pregnancy but also because of possible social censure and emotional conflict.

She states further:

> Even if the social worker knew what to say and do on the subject (which is to say, even if social workers were not themselves caught up in society's conflicting values and standards), it is doubtful that her voice on the subject of illicit sex relations would be much heeded. Traditionally, the authorities on "morality" and "moral truth" are the church and the home. . . . On the issue of illicit sex relations, social work's voice is the quiet and occasional one of the one-to-one interview.

In regard to the value system of a profession in general, Perlman states:

> A profession's value system, like a society's value system, is its mode of organizing its conduct. Judgments based on professional experience relating to what is good or bad, desirable or undesirable, constructive or destructive are basic to decision-making action and goals. What a profession does and seeks to bring into being or to prevent is heavily determined by the consensus within it of what is or is not desirable. The firmer and clearer these values, the more purposive professional direction and action. The more ambigious or uncertain they are, the more likelihood of uncertainty and diffusion in professional planning and performance.

Meier points up the following as some of the similarities and contrasts between the values of social work and those of other forces in the community in relation to the problem of child neglect:

> 1. Many of the values pertaining to adequate care of children or its opposite, child neglect, are shared by many forces in the community, including social work.
>
> 2. The community opposes child neglect in order to ensure its own perpetuity. Social work is likewise concerned with group survival but also places value on the individual.
>
> 3. The community opposes child neglect on the premise that ill-treated children are less likely to become good adult citizens. Social work shares this concern but also holds that the child, as a child, has a need for constructive experiences and a right to be protected against destructive experiences, whether or not they adversely affect his adult behavior.
>
> 4. The community opposes child neglect because the presence of the neglected children may be damaging to well-cared-for children. Thus the neglected child is likely to be "isolated" from other children or pressure is exerted to remove him from the group. In some respects contrary to this, social work values hold that all children need association with their peers.
>
> 5. Equality before the law, regardless of the economic circumstances of parents, is a social work value. Sometimes communities exert pressure against the economically disadvantaged parents, particularly if they are receiving public assistance, holding them accountable in regard to the care of their children in ways in which parents not receiving assistance are not held accountable.
>
> 6. Social work shares with the community the recognition that the "right to self-determination" is not limitless.

Meier discusses the incongruities that might arise between the profession's stated values and its performance. She lists the following possible reasons for such incongruities:

1. The values of social work might be incompatible with those of other forces in the community, which are more powerful and therefore are able to thwart the profession in its desire to help make available to persons those experiences it deems valuable.

2. The values of social work might extend beyond the outside limits of the knowledge and competence of the profession to help create those conditions and bring about the kinds of experiences for individuals that are explicit or implicit within its values.

3. Some social work practitioners may not have the competence to effect the intentions of the profession as a whole, as expressed in its values.

4. The expressed values of social work demonstrate that contradictory values exist within the profession.

5. Professional values pertaining to matters other than the phenomenon of child neglect contraindicate, deflect, or interfere with the pursuit of those activities that would bring about the experiences for children which the values would define as desirable.

6. Social work activities which were developed to intervene in social problems as they existed in an earlier era become institutionalized and resistive to changes that would render them more effective in dealing with changes in the nature of the problem in the current era.

CURRENT OPERATIONS AND OBJECTIVES

Social work has been dealing primarily with individuals who have felt the impact of certain social conditions. This is an essential function in our society but does not lead to primary prevention. Social work knowledge may help locate problems earlier in the cases of some individuals, thus preventing them from become more acute, but primary prevention involves taking into account more than a single dimension such as the individual or social institutions. It necessitates integration of individual, social institutions, and values. Furthermore, the model does not permit use of the treatment tool as a means of diagnosing a social problem. Thus poverty, marital incompatibility, unmarried mothers, broken families, and neglected children, when viewed in their totality, become more than personality problems.

The model helps to formulate the problem within the context that could lead to primary prevention. It attempts to view the total gestalt before isolating specific aspects for special handling. It includes concern on the one hand for the adjustment and development of the individual toward more satisfying human relations and, on the other, for improving the social institutions within which the individual functions. The model emphasizes not only the individual and the social institutions through which he functions but also the relationship between these two dimensions. The bridging concept is the value system. Better family life, improved schools, better housing, more protected economic conditions, more understanding courts, better understanding between the various racial and religious groups, and adequate medical care will help the individual in his adjustment and development. On the other hand, the achievement of these desirable conditions depends on the use the individual can make of existing institutions, the resources he can mobilize for change both personally and in cooperation with other people, and the clarity of the goals he espouses.

It is one thing, however, to be able to diagnose a social problem and another to make ways of dealing with it operational. It is understandable why an applied field like social work has found the one-dimensional answer easier to utilize in dealing with social disorganization. If the cause is fragmented as primarily inherent in the individual, the pattern and methodology for solution can be built accordingly. To change an individual is an accepted function in our society. To change a social condition tends to lead one into the arena of "causes" and away from the more scientific approach. In a sense, however, by ignoring the importance of social institutions as determinants of behavior one has to some degree already identified with a cause, namely, the justification of the status quo. Does not this approach imply that the society is "a given" and that our function is to deal with the changing individual rather than with a changing society or with both?

The crucial issue is again one of values, centering around the question of changing goals. As pointed out by Northwood, in dealing with social problems, "we must know what we are moving toward as well as what we are moving away from; the lack of an inspiring image for tomorrow perhaps is equally as serious a deficiency for social workers as the failure to recognize current social problems, and to work for their amelioration." In dealing with the individual the social worker's issue has been avoided by making him the entrepreneur. Even within this limited approach, however, the concept of self-determination has had its difficulties. To be self-determining, a person must have alternatives from which to choose. If alternatives do not exist, whose responsibility is it to loosen up the social situation so that they might be provided? Furthermore, self-determination is a concept derived from philosophical idealism. The philosophical idealists emphasized that man had a right to do what he chose to do, provided that what he chose to do was right. The growing interdependence of society, however, raises a serious question whether it is possible to avoid greater clarity of goals, to be clear only about what one is against and not about what one is for.

In a democracy the emphasis is on process, with the belief that in the open market of varying ideas and interests the proper goals and programs will emerge. Theoretically, this is excellent, provided the market is a free one and that all groups have access to the opportunity of exchange. Unfortunately, the groups that are feeling the impact of "bad" social conditions frequently lack the strength or the voice to be heard. Such groups as the victims of poverty, neglected children, unemployed youth, migrants, the uneducated, the victims of discrimination, and the aging cannot compete easily in the market of ideas and vested interests. In fact, at times in its history social work has attempted to speak for such groups, to serve as their voice.

As social work has moved more toward application of the scientific, it has shown less interest in social problems, the solution of which seems to reside in a sort of "no man's land." Social problems have been regarded as the province of those who have more in their hearts than in their heads, as belonging to the "do-gooders." In recent years, however, what has been regarded as the "cause" area in the past has found more scientific exploration. Research has been utilized to determine some of the characteristics of social conditions and to evaluate programs that have been developed to change these conditions. One of the areas under study is power and authority and their roles in relation to change.

As indicated earlier, a social problem involves change toward something different. Little has been available in the area of change theory. Even as dynamic a theory as the psychoanalytic has dealt more with defense mechanisms than with ways of coping with stress and change. Sociology and anthropology also have dealt more with how a culture is transmitted than with how it is changed. Part of the trouble is that we are dealing with large segments of the population, and, because it is difficult in advance to know whether the consequence of a recommended program will be satisfactory, the investment of resources and the risks are great. Furthermore, as in medicine a drug may have serious side effects, there are also inherent in any proposed action potential effects in other social conditions that may not be clear until the new proposals are introduced. In brief, social change involves a judgment on *what should be,* which is always more difficult to cope with than the question of *what is* and how it can be maintained.

In some respects the question of dealing with social problems is no longer a matter of choice. We are living in a rapidly changing society that is creating the need for new approaches. We are involved in a scientific revolution that has both the ingredients of destruction and the potential resources of building a "brave new world." It is a difficult period in that we have not fully learned how to cope with the myriad social, economic, and political problems that emerged from the industrial revolution, let alone the problems that are developing from a scientific revolution that demands, as pointed out by Barbara Ward, a redrawing of the social and political map of humanity.

The problem of change is not new, for the processes of change are part of our social system. The uniqueness of today's situation is not change, but the velocity of change. We are no longer being permitted the luxury of crisis planning or sociocultural drift. Change within this scientific revolution has become geometric rather than arithmetic and demands direct planning.

Proposals for Action

Are the recommended proposals for action growing out of analysis within the framework of the model different from our present approach? If so, can they be implemented?

Meier makes these statements:

> . . . on the bases of knowledge of the needs of children and of social work values, it would be expected that major efforts would be directed toward safeguarding family life by economic and social measures and strengthening and supplementing parental capacities when such assistance was needed to ensure adequate protection and care of children. Yet placement of children away from their own families remains a predominant method for intervening in instances of child neglect.
>
> This contradiction suggests that not all professional realities would be accounted for within a claim that social work's knowledge, skills, and values always operate as a coordinated and integrated force in the profession's activities in behalf of individuals and families, in its structuring of services, and in its attempt to influence the social values of the community.

Lourie points out that "numerous programs aim to forestall the emergency or to counteract the effects of [the problem]; some are embryonic; most require development or modification if they are to contribute effectively to solution of the problem. . . ." He emphasizes the point that "social work does not, should not, and cannot assume sole or even primary responsibility for the elimination of poverty. It must not abrogate the responsibility it has."

Lutz outlines a broad-gauge program. He suggests the development of programs to achieve the following objectives:

1. Alter the distorted value orientation of social work
2. Increase the social responsibility of the economic system
3. Bring government close to the people it serves
4. Humanize the operations of bureaucracies

5. Alleviate the pressures on individuals and families to engage in ceaseless strivings for upward mobility
6. Make opportunities for desirable upward mobility available to individuals and families who need them
7. Destroy the discriminatory value-orientation and the social arrangements that proceed from it
8. Provide services for marriages in which incompatibility exists
9. Influence social work education to adjust to the new value position

Pollak states:

> Theoretically, the social needs created by the problem of the broken family are prevention, rehabilitation, and alleviation. . . . Prevention of broken marriages in essence would have to begin by intervention in the courtship stage. This, however, would involve a challenge of group norms and a tie-up between individual discomfort and the makeup of a specific social institution which in the climate of intense concern with the psychological dimension is not yet an established pattern of social work responsibility. . . .
>
> In the area of rehabilitation it is found similarly that current operations have not fully met the social needs presented by the broken family. . . . What needs to be restored in the broken family is the fullness of membership on the parental level. . . . It is a highly probable assumption that no treatment goal in the case of a broken family has been recorded in any family welfare agency as "remarriage." Equally unconsidered as a challenge to casework effort, except in family life education programs, is premarital counseling for remarriage. . . .
>
> In the realm of alleviation family casework, at least in principle, seems to do all that is required for members of the broken family. However, in the divorced cases this disregards the father who has left the home and in desertion cases in many instances the deserting spouse.

Perlman discusses recommendations within the context of preventing the problem from occurring at all, early detection of the occurrence of the problem, and, if it and its sequences are present, what modifying, ameliorative, or restitutive means may be used to lessen its stress and damage, contain the spread of its influence, and substitute rehabilitative for destructive sequelae. Using the public health prototype of prevention, she discusses primary prevention, conception control, and sex education and the legal, religious, and personality factors involved. After reviewing the numerous problems, she raises the question of major function and responsibility, viewing medicine, education, and the church as major operators. In the area of secondary prevention she regards abortion as a policy province for medicine and the church rather than for social work. On the question of amelioration of the stress she cites as necessary

> . . . prevention of the many possible deleterious aftereffects of illegitimate pregnancy and out-of-wedlock motherhood, prevention of exploitation of unmarried pregnant women or of prospective adoptive parents, and more adequate coverage of the needs, protection of the baby's welfare, require more coordinated planning about the organization and administration of the social services that deal with these problems, in single or several aspects; and, beyond this, understandings, agreements, and coordinations among the several professions at present most involved in this problem.

At the tertiary level Perlman examines the problem of the unmarried woman who, by choice or otherwise, has taken her child to live with her but is unable to maintain economic self-dependence. She points out that this problem is viewed as the province of social work, but that social work has given it little attention. The problem is usually defined in economic terms rather than as a problem of mother and child welfare. Perlman's recommendation is for viewing the problem within the latter perspective and recognizing the need for specially developed programs of supportive services for unmarried mothers who keep their babies.

The proposals for action reveal that prevention in the primary sense involves economic, social, and political factors and raises the question of the scope and responsibility of social work. In the areas of secondary and tertiary prevention the question of scope also emerges, but to a lesser degree. Additional questions in these two areas deal with use of new knowledge, better coordination and planning, and a more definitive view of public policy.

Scope and Responsibility of Social Work

Social work has had difficulty in defining its boundaries. In recent years the trend has been toward limiting boundaries in order to define professional development more clearly. The model in its very structure forces a broader look. All authors recognize the importance of the more total formulation but vary in their definitiveness in outlining the specific area of the problem that belongs to social work, the knowledge needed about the total problem in order to define the specific area and to determine priorities of effort, and the patterns of cooperation with other disciplines and fields needed to achieve the goals of prevention.

Lutz calls for limitless boundaries:

> It is desirable that the profession of social work assume once again the original and traditional responsibility accorded it by society. This is the responsibility to try to achieve the solution of social problems

by removing or altering their causes, whatever their nature, whether cultural, political, economic, or social values and organization or intrapersonal values, emotions, and ideas.

Lourie, as pointed out earlier, sees social work as having an important role in the elimination of poverty but not as having primary responsibility. He believes that social work must be conversant with the total problem to carry out its own area of responsibility and through social action affect public policy bearing on the problem. He states:

> In recognizing social action as part of its function and in establishing goals for social policy social work admits that it must go beyond mitigation of present social handicaps and its own efforts in rehabilitation and prevention to participate in drives toward better adaptation of all social policies and institutions to changing needs and aspirations. This recognition must be more extensively and intensively implemented.

Meier follows somewhat the same pattern as Lourie:

> There are reasons to believe that gains in professional knowledge and skills as well as patterns for the realignment of social welfare services now being worked out on a national level for public welfare services will help bring about more effective intervention in those situations in which there is the potential threat of child neglect.

Pollak stays more within the boundaries of social work's "core function." He touches on wider boundaries: "Finally social work will have to make available its experience in the etiology and treatment of problems of the broken family to the wider community with a view toward influencing public opinion and, ultimately, legislation."

Perlman also places primary emphasis on the alleviative function of social work and stays within more limited boundaries:

> Social work, with some rethinking and experimentation, can reshape its processes and organizations of service to more practical, more cogent, more pointed, and more efficient meeting of the already present problem. In social work's ounce of cure lies a pound of prevention. But the problem of basic prevention of this growing social problem—the woman pregnant and then birth-giving out-of-wedlock—remains an unsolved problem of the whole society.

All the authors point up the need for a re-examination of social work's approach even within the more limited boundaries. Pollak identifies the following factors as barriers to social work's coping capacity with social problems: (1) the casework emphasis on tertiary prevention,

(2) a reluctance to take the initiative in offering services, and (3) the frequent noninvolvement of social work in the formation of public social policy.

Meier, referring to the fact that among neglectful parents there may be a considerable number with defects in ego development, raises the question whether the professional social worker is adequately trained to handle problems categorized as character disorders:

> Knowledge concerning neurotic difficulties learned from psychoanalysis has become well integrated into casework knowledge and has been translated into casework skill in helping those individuals who are guilt-ridden and conflicted, who have low self-esteem, and whose psychological defenses against impulses and affects interfere with their functioning. On the other hand, psychoanalytic contributions to ego psychology which illumine the nature of character disorders are less well integrated into professional knowledge and less well translated into skills.

She also points out:

> Perhaps in less direct ways, as well, some of the traditional emphases of casework serve the client poorly in cases of child neglect—whether or not the parent has a character disorder. Appreciation of the great influence of the past on the client's attitudes and feelings, and the emphasis on the client-worker relationship per se as a therapeutic experience, may sometimes blind the caseworker to current reality pressures which in themselves, regardless of the client's past, produce tension, conflict, and a sense of personal disorganization. Underestimating the degree of distress that current pressures may cause leads to a comparable underestimation of the amount of help that practical services—day care, homemaker service, and the educational help of the public health nurse and the home economist—could provide.

Lutz states that contemporary ego psychology has contributed much to the understanding of all aspects of human behavior and interaction, but finds that

> much work remains to be done, both empirically and theoretically. On the empirical side not enough is known about how people see themselves as a result of their biological characteristics, their particular form of life experience, and the various cultural, political, economic, and social milieu in which they live. Not enough is known about how their varying perceptions of themselves influence their actions. On the theoretical side the concept of self or identity cannot be fitted neatly into the structure of personality as this is set forth in psychoanalytic theory.

Lourie points out: "Social work (as well as other social institutions) has failed to devise social inventions to keep pace with (change)." Along with mechanical obstacles, heterogeneity of emphases, and personnel limitations, he states: "The stress on individualism in social work is not always attuned to the broad approach required in solving a social problem. Emphasis on art and trained skill can de-emphasize the need for new scientific methodology." He feels that "new evaluations are urgently needed to determine what changes in structure, policies, and practices within the field will best promote attainment of social work goals."

Pollak refers to the difficulties social workers have in setting goals for or even with their clients. He states that "the structure of services currently available reflects this lack of goal conceptualization to a considerable degree."

Meier, after identifying such circumstances as economic inadequacy, health problems of parents, mobility of families, and broken families that are potentially threatening to the welfare of children, points out the need for more "aggressive" case finding:

> One practical implication is that organizations, institutions, and agencies dealing with problems of physical and mental health, housing and population trends need to develop greater awareness that the specific problem with which they are confronted may have its impact on family life and the care of children. Greater coordination of services is called for. Possibly, too, a neighborhood approach is needed with social service stations as numerous and as readily accessible as branch post offices and public schools. . . .

Lutz states:

> The review of available social work services also shows that the voluntary family agency provides a casework and group work service which can deal with any aspect of marital incompatibility which it can reach. The major problem is how to reach married people who are psychologically or socially inaccessible or who do not "see" the agency as a resource for help with their marital problems. The answer, of course, is a service that can reach into all neighborhoods, all social classes, and all racial and ethnic groups, a service that can be "seen" because it is nearby and because it is performed by a profession known to be concerned about marital incompatibility and about injustices which give rise to it.

Public Policy

The arena of public policy is seen to be important in the elimination of the social problems under discussion. It might be helpful to point up any suggestions that might have emerged for social work's role in this area.

Pollak, as stated earlier, refers to social work's noninvolvement in the formation of public social policy. He points out, for example, that "in view of the decline in age at which people marry in the United States and the concomitant expectation of lack of maturity in the newlyweds, a waiting time between announcement of intent and getting married might be a worth-while proposition." He believes that casework "would have a wealth of information pro and con to contribute to the discussion of such a change in public policy," but that "no such approach seems ever to have been considered in casework circles. . . . Any attempt to influence legislation, however, with regard to making marriage more difficult does not seem to be traceable in either literature or professional discussion."

Meier discusses the importance of economic security as a safeguard for family life and asks why the family allowance system "does not seem to have stimulated the interest of social workers in the United States to any marked degree." In exploring the possible causes she states:

> A variety of causes may be postulated for this lack of interest on the part of the profession. Admittedly, professional education does not and could not be expected to equip social workers to devise and set into operation a national family allowance system. For this, the knowledge and skills of economists, political scientists and other governmental experts are required. Nevertheless, the social worker could be expected to recognize the values for family life that other countries have found in such systems and could be expected to speak out for the values that a similar system might have in this country. This requires that the professional strength in values be matched by strength in facts—information about the economic and geographical location of children, about population trends, about family income in relation to family size, about the limitations in current income tax provisions that are intended to benefit taxpayers responsible for dependents, about variable per capita income among the states. It may be that social work educators do not provide sufficient stimulation to help students make connections between (1) "social problems" as taught in undergraduate study or within the context of social work education and (2) the values they are expected to incorporate within their professional behavior.

Perlman, in discussing the need for expanded casework services, shelter facilities, and adoption openings, states that "private voluntary auspices could not hope to meet such expanded services. Tax support would inevitably be involved. Public concern—if not compassion—would have to precede such tax-supported measures."

Lourie points out:

> Social work and social welfare are too often misinterpreted. Social welfare composes all welfare and health activities depending all or in part on community financing (national, state, local; tax and contribu-

tion). It is a vast "humanitarian" industry made up of many administrative units which employ many professions and occupations. There are various "products" and a variety of degrees of interdependence among the units. The profession of social work (graduates of schools of social work) does not now occupy a large segment of the social welfare working force. It is questionable whether it ever will. The profession needs to grapple with this issue to determine whether a different set of relationships and roles must be developed.

Turning more specifically to the public policy issue, he states:

Public policy is made ultimately by various levels of public authority who are responsible to the taxpaying public. Like all citizens, social workers have a right to express themselves, but no profession can make the public policy. This is not always clear in some professional circles.

An impression has been created that social work theorists are attempting to deal with public policy in terms of protecting professional interests. Although social workers can feel safe in claiming that this is not their motive, it is always a danger in any profession. The struggle between representatives of the public interest (including social workers and the social work profession) and the medical profession is a prime example. The social work profession must develop crystallike clarity between the public and the professional interest.

Lutz deplores social work's retreat to techniques primarily for dealing with individuals. He states:

It is no accident that social work has tended to give only lip service to its responsibility to participate in political and social action. Moreover, the failure of community work or social policy formulation and administration to develop theory and practice comparable in sophistication and effectiveness to those of casework and group work has not occurred because caseworkers and group workers are more intelligent or better educated. The failure is there because in the fairly recent past social work with social problems at the various levels of government and community organization has been vitiated by the discrepancy between the real nature of the variables at work and the social work estimation of what those variables are. The results have been velleity and a form of normlessness among social workers. The sharp self-image and public-image of social work in the early twentieth century has become blurred. Then the leaders of social work assessed the values, motives and goals of their opponents and stood up to them courageously. Today, social work, as a consequence of its unrealistic interpretation of its basic value-orientation, questions its own goals, pursues theoretical fads, wastes its energy in endless critical self-examinations, and always, finally, retreats to the pursuit of more knowledge of individual situations.

LOOKING AHEAD

The application of the model to problems that have traditionally been regarded as the province of social work sharpens the question of social work's scope and goals. Social work can remain clinically oriented and do an adequate job in a relatively limited area. If interest is in prevention, however, new horizons are necessary.

It was found in testing the model that social problems cannot be defined merely in quantitative terms. There is, as well, a qualitative range that depends on the value system utilized. In this connection there is need for research on social problems as perceived by the consumer, the profession providing the program and the services, and the decision makers. There is also need for more knowledge of how to close the gap between these varied perceptions and how to engage the interests of those who have the authority and prestige essential to bringing to bear the resources for dealing with social problems. The challenge is not the expansion of present programs that may still not realize the ideal but rather the identification of barriers to closing the gap and the development of theory and methods to achieve it. As stated earlier, there is a need for a more sophisticated theory of social change.

Social work has tended to consider primarily the voluntary sector as its theoretical approach has been developed. Resources for meeting social problems, especially those with quantitative dimensions, are more and more in the public sector. The methods of tapping the public sector, however, are different from those of voluntary structures. For example, what is the equivalent of the lay board in the public sector? Is it the advisory committees, the county commissioners, or the paid staff? Is it the political party? Furthermore, the public programs have a vertical as well as a horizontal dimension, with the resources frequently coming from state and federal as well as local levels.

There is also the necessity for establishing priorities in social problems. Are some more pressing than others? If these are not dealt with, are efforts at other levels effective? It is not enough for us to say that we are dealing with the economic, physiological, and self-actualizing needs of people. Are these requirements independent of one another, or do they work within a hierarchical pattern in which the emergence of one depends on the gratification of another? Furthermore, do they divide themselves into a social classification of "higher" and "lower"? Maslow and others have projected a pattern for needs that implies such a structural and organized relationship. He states:

> Thus, if physiological, safety, love, esteem, and self-actualizing needs are, in that order, prepotent, i.e., demand prior gratification, then it can be meaningful to say that physiological needs are more powerful and more basic than the love needs, but that the love needs are

"higher" than the physiological needs because, e.g., they are a later phyletic and ontogenetic development, they require more preconditions; they are more sensitive, they require better conditions of life, etc.[3]

From this model the applied fields, such as social work, can move with greater assurance in determining priorities in dealing with individual and social problems, for derived from this model are the following basic assumptions:

1. Ordinarily, these "higher," more approved, and more socially useful needs can appear and be gratified only when the basic needs of food, clothing, shelter, and the like are first fulfilled.

2. This patterning of needs makes obsolete many of the old theories that presented different motives only as mutually exclusive or as set in strict opposition—e.g., love or hunger, security or freedom.

3. It supports a social theory that human nature can be improved by a better environment, that man becomes more loving if his fears are removed, more self-and-other-respecting if his love needs are satisfied, and more capable of actualizing his best potentialities if allowed to respect himself.[4] This type of conceptual approach for tackling the problem of human motivation is more in line with the model that has been projected.

As stated earlier, analysis of the etiology of the social problems explored within the framework of the model reveals many common factors of an economic, social, and psychological nature. Each author refers to these factors with varying emphasis. It is almost as if they are saying that the answers to these problems will not be found until the formula for a "healthy" society is discovered. This moves our considerations in the direction of "grand" theories and raises the question whether it is possible to find a middle ground. If we begin with the premise that the exploration of a social problem involves the responsibility for doing something about it, if the cause can be established, then we are faced with an interesting dilemma. If changes in our social institutions are not part of our consideration and if conditions of our social institutions are identified as causes of social problems, should we refer to such situations as social problems? Or should we refer to them as by-products of social institutions that are to be taken as givens and accept the fact that first aid rather than prevention is the order of the day? The answer is a difficult one in that the etiology for each of the problems under study was not sufficiently definitive to warrant our saying

---

[3] A. H. Maslow, "Social Theory of Motivation," in Maurice J. Shore, ed., *Twentieth Century Mental Hygiene* (New York: Social Science Publishers, 1950), p. 355.
[4] *Ibid.*, pp. 355–356.

that cause and effect have been established. There is, however, evidence that economic, social, and psychological ingredients are present and that attention to one without the others will not suffice in fully tackling the problems. The model helps to emphasize the important fact that "in any given situation there is a mixture of internal and external reality factors . . . and that for practical purposes we must recognize that in some situations the external environmental factors dominate so completely as to minimize the role of internal factors, and vice versa. Theoretically, however, neither one nor the other can be completely excluded." [5]

It is quite evident that the mechanistic will-o'-the-wisp of simple cause and effect can lead to fallacies in dealing with social problems. This means that programs to eliminate the causes or results of specific problems may be meaningless or too limited. The evidence would favor that middle ground which demands broad programs of social reconstruction as against specific programs for specific social problems. Thus economic and physical planning cannot be separated from social and psychological planning.

The achievement of such a goal is complicated by the fact that each profession and field has been so busy in recent years in proving its uniqueness that it has avoided exploring similarities and areas of common concern. It may be helpful to bear in mind that social work is not alone in its concern for people. Social work shares with other related professions and fields an interest in promoting human welfare. As we come to recognize the multidimensional nature of the social problems with which we deal, there should be a corresponding growing interest in cooperative endeavors. To accomplish such a goal, social work along with other professions will have to free itself of the view that what is good for the profession is good for people. Focus must be on the social problem, for too frequently a beginning made with a concern for people shifts quickly to a concern for the agency and the profession.

Better communication between fields and professions will also involve a willingness to examine problems at new conceptual levels. As indicated by the different authors, there has not always been flexibility within social work in absorbing new concepts into its body of knowledge. Unless we take the stand that there are better ways of doing what we are now doing, we lose our objectivity in evaluating what we are doing and become defenders of a cult rather than scientists.

Even if social work education can develop greater flexibility in absorbing new knowledge, there still remains the problem of change in the agencies through which this knowledge is translated into programs and

[5] E. Pumpian-Mindlin, "The Position of Psychoanalysis in Relation to the Biological and Social Sciences," in *Psychoanalysis as Science* (Stanford, Calif.: Stanford University Press, 1952), p. 133.

services. Many programs have become institutionalized and are almost an end in themselves. All the authors refer to the need for change in agency programs and in community planning if social problems are to be dealt with more effectively. For example, there is a growing need in communities for an evaluation of existing programs and services and for a determination of priorities in community planning. Most efforts to date have failed because of their mechanistic approach and their emphasis on evaluating existing services. Many of these services and programs emerged to answer needs of an earlier period and do not necessarily provide the answer today.

The model, as the material reveals, would have real use in helping communities obtain a fresh look at social problems. Essentially, it could help to focus on the gaps between the ideal and what now exists and to identify the barriers to closing the gap. Identification of the barriers would provide a more realistic basis for planning than the assumption that the necessary services now exist and that the only question is expansion or contraction of the same. Furthermore, it would help to sharpen the important questions centering around goals and values.

The question of goals and values is a crucial one. In all the papers under discussion the recommended programs of action draw no line between voluntary and public programs to achieve a solution to the particular social problem. Yet many communities lack the recognition that a community can no longer regard itself as part voluntary and part public. Unless a community can plan in terms of total resources it cannot truly plan. There is, however, still the tendency to refer to the voluntary efforts as "we" and to the public efforts as "they"—this in spite of the fact that in most of the social problems under discussion the population concerned is being dealt with, in the main, by the public sector. Several of the authors point up the problem of the lack of trained personnel in these agencies.

One of the most significant observations emerging from the various papers is the role of distorted values in the "casual" structure of social problems. It asks the question where social work stands on the teaching of values in our society. As pointed out in Perlman's paper, social workers are more likely to be relativist than absolutist and are likely to believe that because all behavior is purposive any form of behavior must be understood rather than condemned. Is this another example of fragmentation in our thinking? Are we again taking the knowledge derived from our treatment instrument for people who have deviated in their behavior and using it to formulate an educational philosophy?

There is no question that a large part of social work has been dealing with clinical problems, with the individual who is involved in deviant behavior. Such efforts are essential in our society and represent an important contribution. The knowledge developed through this experience adds to the general pool of knowledge for those who have the responsibility to treat and cure. However, has this absorption with the deviant tended to encourage a one-sided conception of human motivation and learning and, for some, to equate a theory of adjustment and remediation with a social philosophy? True, Freud contributed magnificently to the objective and scientific approach to human motivation by pointing out to man that he should be skeptical and seek the truth about his own thoughts, feelings, and acts in the same way that he sought the truth about the world around him. On the other hand, the tendency on the part of some clinicians to see unconscious forces as the only or predominant factors in all situations has contributed to a dichotomy in a field like social work. Social work's concern with social reform, with a changing society as well as a changing individual, is predicated on belief in the potentialities of man to control his destiny through intellect and reason—in other words, the belief that man can be master of his own fate and that collectively he can build a better world. Psychoanalytic theory represents an important contribution to our understanding of human behavior, but, like most theories, it does not furnish a total answer. "The influence of external reality upon the rational activities of the individual lies in other disciplines than psychoanalysis." [6]

The more recent interest in ego psychology and in the behavioral sciences should be encouraged. In broadening our horizons, the challenge is the integration of knowledge as against substitution. We have an easy tendency in seeking new knowledge to "throw out the baby with the bath."

If the building of values belongs primarily to other disciplines, such as the home, the church, and the school, what is our contribution? We work with these institutions but chiefly around their problems with deviants. If primary prevention is our goal and we see the value area as basic, it will be necessary to avoid integration of our area of knowledge as the total answer. The information we have is valuable, but it is only a piece of a whole that should be integrated with concepts from several disciplines to provide a base for child and parent education in the area of values.

As analysis of the material proceeds, the question of the scope of social work keeps rearing its head. The application of the model provides a look at a social problem in its fullness. It also makes evident that the solution lies in more than one discipline. Furthermore, it is obvious

---

[6] Pumpian-Mindlin, *op. cit.*, pp. 133–134.

that the total cannot be divided in such a way that each piece fits neatly into the boundaries of a particular discipline. Man does not so order his problems that they will meet the one-dimensional comforts or the fragmented efforts of any given profession. It will be helpful if social work keeps in mind that other disciplines are facing the same problem of scope.

The problem should be viewed in its broader perspective. Before the era of highly specialized efforts the philosopher was the hub of all knowledge and was able to view the whole as well as the pieces. As knowledge became more differentiated, we tended to lose the ability to see the parts in relation to the whole. There was no longer the equivalent of the philosopher to ask the broad and meaningful questions that pertained to the nature of man, the nature of society, and the relationship of the two. As society has become more interdependent and the need for dealing with larger parts of problems more obvious, efforts are being made to integrate our more specialized knowledge into larger pieces. These efforts have run into the barriers of conceptual differences and the institutionalization of practices around fragmented approaches.

The team structure has been one mechanism for trying to meet the problem. In many cases, however, the particular discipline that calls the team together still formulates the questions within the confines of its own boundaries. There is still the tendency to work from structure back to needs rather than have disciplines jointly follow the formula that function grows out of needs, policy out of function, and structure out of policy. This demands a joint willingness of disciplines to take a fresh look at social problems utilizing a model similar to the one under study.

In both the community and in the universities what McGeorge Bundy refers to as "the iron hand of little men," that is, department heads, executives of institutions, and the like, is restricting the pursuit of knowledge across "disciplinary" and "institutional" lines. The structures developed around specialized knowledge have become ends in themselves, and the great contribution they have made in an earlier period is being dissipated by their inability to see the need for change.

In brief, the problem of scope is not the province of any one field or discipline. In a rapidly changing society there is need for new alignments based on a review of the social problems, the ideal objectives and the ways of achieving them, rather than on a review by each field of its own structure and program. Social work can place its energies behind such efforts or become concerned with squatters' rights and uniqueness rather than with the problems of people and new patterns for dealing with them.

SPECIFIC RECOMMENDATIONS

1. The model has an excellent potential for stocktaking. It should be utilized not only in the educational setting but also by communities in looking at their local problems. One possibility is to ask chapters of the National Association of Social Workers to test it out in relation to social problems in their particular area. It would also be helpful if a group of executives could be brought together to explore its application in agency settings with both staff and boards.

2. The material should be reviewed by representatives of various disciplines to test out attitudes toward the issues raised about the scope of a field. An Arden House type of conference would represent a good beginning.

3. The material should be reviewed by the Council on Social Work Education for educational implications. Even if realignments are arrived at through meetings with other disciplines, social work may better prepare its professionals through some such formulation as:

> Basic to the question of how to overcome the dichotomy of duality of responsibilities to individual and society is the pattern of social work education. There is no question of the need to train social workers who will be able to speak with knowledge and understanding of the wider social issues involved and with authority of possible courses of action for society as a whole. There is need also for a larger group of social welfare leaders who will have the necessary knowledge, attitude, and skills to administer large social welfare programs, evaluate existing policies, and help in the creation of new policies and programs. Our profession should be taking the lead in studying the causes of social problems and in establishing priorities within the field of social welfare. The training for such leadership has been foreign to social work curricula of the last several decades; however, recent trends in social work education provide a more consistent and productive basis for fulfilling this program. The emphasis on a common core as a base for all social workers has forced a re-examination of what the caseworker, group worker, and community organizer must know and be able to do to accomplish the functions of social work. The recent curriculum study under the direction of Werner W. Boehm reflects the impact of the social sciences and stresses the interdependence of knowledge of the individual, the social institutions through which he functions, and values and goals. It identifies three major functions of social work, namely, restoration, provision of resources, and prevention of social dysfunction.[7] In the development of leaders for public policy our greatest contribution will be in an

[7] Werner W. Boehm, *Objectives of the Social Work Curriculum of the Future*, Vol. 1 (New York: Council on Social Work Education, 1959).

educational plan that will integrate human factors with economic, political, and social factors and will place a special emphasis on the importance of process in achieving change.

Even if our social institutions are functioning adequately, there will still be a segment in the community who, because of personal and internal factors, will not be able to make sufficient use of them. These people will need a high level of individualized services. In the training of practitioners for this area of work it is important that they understand that "a relationship moves in two directions . . ." and that "the social worker is not only the agent of society vis-à-vis the individual, he is likewise the spokesman of the individual vis-à-vis society." [8] Knowledge obtained by working with the individual and his family can provide an informed basis for research and for legislative and political action.

In brief, individualized services are not a substitute for public policy or vice versa. Each is an integral part of a total approach to social problems and should feed each other. Furthermore, not all social workers will have a high level of skill in all areas. All social workers, however, should have a common core of knowledge that includes dynamics of the individual, the group, and the community, social philosophy, and existing public policy. The pattern for the "treatment" practitioner is quite clear, especially with the modifications taking place through the impact of the social sciences. The public policy professional should build onto this core the knowledge and skills needed to evaluate existing public policy and create new policies. The cluster of courses will perhaps include, among others, community planning, social administration, research, the financing of social welfare, comparative social security systems, and courses from the related behavioral sciences, such as political science, sociology, and anthropology.

What this should yield is a group of professionals trained to study, diagnose, and recommend plans of action for larger social problems, in the same way that practitioners are trained to handle individual, family, and group problems. Both will be essential as part of a team —which would include other disciplines—to help analyze problem areas and to determine the pattern of approach necessary for sound intervention. This might include public policy, group programs, and/or individual services. The problem area might yield to several possibilities, and diagnosis such as in medicine could follow a process of elimination. For example, they would attempt to provide the recommendations for such questions as: Will the problem yield to a public policy approach or to a strengthening of group programs or to individual services? Does it need all three or a combination of two? What should be the order of priority?

---

[8] Elizabeth Wickenden, "New Emphasis on the Social Worker's Second Job: A Better Society." Speech delivered at the School of Social Work, University of Michigan, Ann Arbor, April 22, 1960.

4. As already indicated, the approach to social problems is dependent on the stand we take in relation to other fields. An Arden House conference with other helping professions, such as public health, education, law, nursing, medicine, and public administration, has been recommended. Added to this group would be representatives from the societies of the behavioral sciences, such as economics, political science, sociology, psychology, and anthropology.

There is room, however, for another alignment, one that is more lay-oriented and concerned with broad social goals. As indicated by the material, there is need for joining hands with those groups in the society that are similarly concerned with maintaining and furthering human values. The logical mechanism for this approach would be the National Conference on Social Welfare. It might well review its function and structure in the light of the total approach as developed through the model. Perhaps the time has come for one mechanism in social work that can supply a forum for predominantly lay groups interested in common objectives.

5. The material lends itself to teaching purposes. There is need for social problems material within a formulation that helps the student develop an approach to problem solving. The material might be developed in a form that would make it useful for undergraduate as well as graduate teaching.

11M—P&K
4M—8/66